编写指导委员会

总主编：段　峰　王　欣
编　委：石　坚　叶　英　王　安　方小莉　张　平
　　　　邱　鑫　史　维　佘　淼　敖　敏　刘　佳

丛书总主编：段 峰 王 欣

博文高等学校英语专业系列教材

美国短篇小说导读

A Reader's Guide to American Short Stories

主　编◎王　安
副主编◎周家辉　方小莉　查日新　陈　杰

四川大学出版社
SICHUAN UNIVERSITY PRESS

项目策划：张　晶　刘　畅　敬铃凌
责任编辑：张　晶
责任校对：于　俊
封面设计：阿　林
责任印制：王　炜

图书在版编目（CIP）数据

美国短篇小说导读 / 王安主编． — 成都：四川大学出版社，2021.12
博文高等学校英语专业系列教材 / 段峰，王欣总主编
ISBN 978-7-5690-5181-0

Ⅰ．①美… Ⅱ．①王… Ⅲ．①英语－阅读教学－高等学校－教材②短篇小说－小说评论－美国 Ⅳ．①H319.4：I

中国版本图书馆CIP数据核字（2021）第238225号

书　名	美国短篇小说导读
	Meiguo Duanpian Xiaoshuo Daodu
主　编	王　安
出　版	四川大学出版社
地　址	成都市一环路南一段24号（610065）
发　行	四川大学出版社
书　号	ISBN 978-7-5690-5181-0
印前制作	跨　克
印　刷	成都市新都华兴印务有限公司
成品尺寸	170 mm×240 mm
插　页	2
印　张	24.25
字　数	520千字
版　次	2022年1月第1版
印　次	2022年1月第1次印刷
定　价	88.00元

版权所有　◆　侵权必究

◆ 读者邮购本书，请与本社发行科联系。
　电话：(028)85408408/(028)85401670/(028)86408023　邮政编码：610065
◆ 本社图书如有印装质量问题，请寄回出版社调换。
◆ 网址：http://press.scu.edu.cn

四川大学出版社
微信公众号

总　序

新时代的国际形势和国家需求对我国外国语言文学专业和学科建设提出了新挑战，也提供了发展的新契机。

习近平总书记在给北京外国语大学老教授的回信中指出，努力培养更多有家国情怀、有全球视野、有专业本领的复合型人才，在推动中国更好走向世界、世界更好了解中国上作出新的贡献。这是党和国家对高校外语教育工作者的殷切希望，也是时代赋予我们的重要责任。围绕新时期新要求、新文科新思考，外语人才培养需要进行全方位的改革，教材建设是其中极其重要的一环。因为教材是教育教学的基本依据和重要载体，关乎解决"培养什么人、怎样培养人、为谁培养人"这一根本问题，关乎立德树人目标的根本实现。

基于这样的目的，我们组织专家和一线教师编写了这套多语种的外语专业教材，教材覆盖面广，既有传统的语言技能训练、外国语言学和外国文学，也有医学口译等跨学科的主题，反映了外语学科在新文科概念的导引下所开展的尝试。我们希望以此为开端，逐渐增加教材种类，扩大教材的涉及面，为新型外语人才的培养打下坚实的基础。

总的说来，博文系列教材以"博雅通识，优化创新"为主要目的，具有以下特色。

1. 博雅教育注重培养具有扎实语言能力、深厚人文素养、宽广学术视野、强烈批判精神的高素质外语人才，对外国语言研究、外国文学研究、翻译研究、国别与区域研究、比较文学与跨文化研究有浓厚兴趣，具有一定研究潜能的高素质学术型外语人才。博文系列教材选用了中西方经典文学篇章，以人文素质教育为外语教学的根本,发掘外语语言文化的专业内涵,体现了外语教育强本固基的办学要求。

2. 博文系列教材创建GIDE课程体系,以"引领"(Guiding)、"浸润"(Immersion)、"深化"(Deepening)、"拓展"(Exploration)四个层次为课程目标,分阶段、分层次地将外国语言文学专业培养目标融入教材建设。引领学生形成专业意识,浸润中西方文化文明精髓,深化专业知识和人文素质,拓展思辨能力和跨文化交流能力,形成专业和学科建设的有机衔接,对培养高素质外语类人才和复合型外语人才,具有重要的作用。

3. 课程思政是新时代背景下,稳步推进思想政治教育改革以形成大思政育人体系的一个重要方向。四川大学外国语学院以全课程育人大格局为理念,提升德育实效性,将育人目标贯穿于课程教育的全过程,不断升级人才培养方案,将课程思政的概念和实施,整体、科学、有序地融合进育人机制和教材建设。博文系列教材坚守中国视角、中国立场,在具备国际前沿视野的同时,将社会主义核心价值观融入教材编写,以培养精通专业领域知识,一心为公,拥有家国情怀和国际视野,具备良好的语言运用能力和深厚的人文素养的高端外语人才。

4. 教材紧扣新时代国家对高校外语人才培养的要求,参照教育部新国标,坚持课程思政建设,在上述总体思想的指导下,结合四川大学外国语学院开设的专业课程,从知识传授、技能培养、能力提升等不同层面,进行系列化设计。偏重语言技能训练的教材遵循语言地道、例证典型、解析精当的原则,同时注重选材的权威性和实效性;偏重能力提升的教材精选外国语言学、翻译学、文学与文化研究的经典原文,既传授专业基础知识,又致力培养学生的文本赏析和思辨能力。各教材均在符合学科、专业与相应课程需求的前提下,设计和安排教材的主要内容、知识体系、习题设置与考核要求等,体现了各自的鲜明特色。

四川大学外语学科源自四川大学前身1896年创办的四川中西学堂的英语和法语科目,历史悠久,传统厚重。巴金、吴虞、朱光潜、吕叔湘、钟作猷、周

总　序

煦良、卞之琳、罗念生、顾绶昌、吴宓等著名学者和文化名人曾在本学科任教或就读，为本学科的发展打下了坚实的基础。博文系列教材由四川大学外国语学院教学专家与一线教师共同编写，请国内知名外语类专家担任顾问，编写团队既具有一线教学经验，熟悉学生需求，又具备宽广的国际视野和历史传承。当然，本系列教材编写内容难免存在不足之处，编写团队恳切希望广大教师和学生提出宝贵意见。

博文系列教材编写组

前　言

今天，在消费主义、流行文化、大众传媒、计算机与网络技术等因素的影响下，文学阅读也面临各种挑战。随着数码摄影、电影电视、电脑动画、图像识别、虚拟现实、移动互联网、人工智能等日益成为人们生活中不可或缺的一部分，一个以形象为中心的追求感官愉悦的视觉文化正在形成，审美开始被日常生活侵蚀，有深度的理性沉思让位于快餐式的阅读，国民阅读量下降，人们沉迷于网络游戏与短视频。正如阿莱斯·艾尔雅维茨在《图像时代》中指出的那样，词语趋于钝化，直观与肤浅取代了抽象与深度，"文学迅速地游移至后台，而中心舞台则被视觉文化的靓丽辉光所普照"[1]。尽管面临挑战，文学经典的魅力却永不过时，它是人类最优秀思想的结晶，是天马行空的想象对现实的超越，是连接历史、现在与未来的纽带，是人们在孤独、苦闷、彷徨时的精神慰藉，是拒绝平庸、肤浅、愚昧，实现完善人格的途径，是人类提升道德水平、砥砺意志、升华灵魂的本质性存在。本书紧扣时代特征，引导学习者进行深度阅读，让他们体悟文学中的语言之美、思想之美，以及道德与情感关怀，帮助他们在沉浸式阅读中提升自己的文学素养和思辨能力。同时，本书坚持正确的政治方向，自觉融入课程思政要素，有意识地引导学生批判性地看待美国和西方社会存在的诸如暴力、谋杀、疏离、家庭不睦、性别与种族歧视等问题，在潜移默化中培养他们明辨是非的能力，增强他们的民族自豪感。

此外，由于技术的进步与时代的发展，文学创作与文学赏析也在与时俱进，读者的审美旨趣正在发生变化，审美能力也在不断提升。在我国，随着学

---

[1] 〔斯洛文尼亚〕阿莱斯·艾尔雅维茨著，《图像时代》，胡菊兰、张云鹏译，长春：吉林人民出版社，2003年，第34页。

生英语水平的持续提高和高校英语教学改革的深入推进，社会对大学生的英语水平也提出了更高的要求。本书主要面向高校英语专业本科学生，这一群体面临的主要问题并非语言障碍，而是在阅读中发现问题、分析问题、解决问题的能力不足，文学理论素养有待提高。现有的同类型教材已有一些可供选择，不过这些教材大多参照克林斯·布鲁克斯（Cleanth Brooks）和罗伯特·潘·沃伦（Robert Penn Warren）在《理解小说》（Understanding Fiction）中从情节、人物、主题、技巧等板块进行分析的编排体例。这种编排体例虽然内容比较集中，但难以对每篇短篇小说展开详细的解读，而且分板块统筹和涵盖小说作品的处理方法在实际的课堂教学中也难以操作：一次完成一个板块的话，内容太多；一次完成一篇短篇小说的话，内容又太少，因此，这类教材更适合作为学术专著或自学教材供学生阅读、参考。从方便课堂使用的角度考虑，编者遵循传统文学教材的编排方式，大体上以时间为序，精心选择了美国自浪漫主义时期至当代著名作家的代表性短篇小说16篇，可满足大多数学校一学期教学任务的需求。在选文时，编者既考虑了时代的发展与延续性，能在一定程度上体现美国小说发展的历史脉络，较为全面地呈现美国短篇小说两个多世纪以来所取得的成就，也充分考虑了作家的背景（性属、族裔、阶级等）、文本的长度、内容的差异、语言风格与主题的多样性、小说的难度等因素（如将实验色彩浓厚的《柏林导游》放到最后），还有意识地选择了国内其他同类教材没有收录的经典作品。这些作品分别是坡的《泄密的心》（"The Tell-Tale Heart"，Edgar Allan Poe）、霍桑的《教长的黑面纱》（"The Minister's Black Veil"，Nathaniel Hawthorne）、吐温的《卡拉韦拉斯县驰名的跳蛙》（"The Notorious Jumping Frog of Calaveras County"，Mark Twain）、伦敦的《生火》（"To Build a Fire"，Jack London）、海明威的《白象似的群山》（"Hills Like White Elephants"，Earnest Hemingway）、菲茨杰拉德的《冰宫》（"The Ice Palace"，F. Scott Fitzgerald）、福克纳的《献给爱米莉的玫瑰》（"A Rose for Emily"，William Faulkner）、奈特的《即将成人》（"The Man Who Was Almost a Man"，Richard Wright）、波特的《偷窃》（"Theft"，Katherine Anne Porter）、契弗的《巨型收音机》（"The Enormous Radio"，John Cheever）、卡弗的《这么多水，离家这么近》（"So Much Water So Close to

前言

Home", Raymond Carver)、欧茨的《何去何从》("Where Are You Going, Where Have You Been", Joyce Carol Oates)、奥兹克的《披巾》("The Shawl", Cynthia Ozick)、厄普代克的《天堂制造》("Made in Heaven", John Updike)、莫里森的《宣叙》("Recitatif", Toni Morrison)、纳博科夫的《柏林导游》("A Guide to Berlin", Vladimir Nabokov)。建议教学计划为一学期,进度为每周学习一篇小说。每篇小说后附有6 000至12 000字左右的中文导读,从作家与作品介绍、故事情节、人物、结构、技巧等小说分析的常见要素几个方面,对作品进行了详细的剖析。每篇导读后附有推荐书目,可作为学生的拓展阅读材料;另外还附有五道思考题和一道讨论题,可供学生预习和复习,以帮助他们加深对文本的理解,方便师生组织课堂讨论。

参与本书编写的教师均为四川大学外国语学院长期从事美国文学教学与研究的专家、学者,他们是王安、周家辉、方小莉、查日新和陈杰。具体分工如下:王安除负责全书的统稿、结构安排、文字录入、格式调整等外,还撰写了编者序和《泄密的心》《冰宫》《偷窃》《何去何从》《披巾》《柏林导游》六篇小说的导读,周家辉撰写了《教长的黑面纱》《生火》《巨型收音机》《这么多水,离家这么近》四篇小说的导读,方小莉撰写了《白象似的群山》《即将成人》《宣叙》三篇小说的导读,查日新撰写了《卡拉韦拉斯县驰名的跳蛙》《天堂制造》两篇小说的导读,陈杰撰写了《献给爱米莉的玫瑰》的导读。本教材收录的部分篇目,在四川大学外国语学院英文系开设的相关课程以及中国大学慕课网上的在线课程"美国短篇小说选读"中已多次试用,效果良好。

本教材不仅可以帮助学生系统了解美国小说,特别是短篇小说的发展脉络、代表作家及作品、基本理论常识等知识,还突出对文学作品的深度诠释,通过导读引导学生深入作品本身,培养他们的阅读兴趣,提高他们的阅读能力,从而使其学会从学理层面批判性地解读文学作品,增进对美国文学和文化的了解,提升自己的文学鉴赏水平、写作水平和人文素养。本书可作为高校英语专业本科生相关课程的选用教材,也可作为非英语专业文学方向的研究生和非文学爱好者的补充阅读或拓展学习资料。

本书所选16篇短篇小说出自以下英文短篇小说选集和文学作品选集:

1. "The Tell-Tale Heart", by Edgar Allan Poe, from *The Portable Edgar Allan Poe*,

edited by Gerald Kennedy, London: Penguin Books, 2006, pp. 187-191.

2. "The Minister's Black Veil", by Nathaniel Hawthorne, from *50 Great Short Stories*, edited by Milton Crane, New York: Bantam Classics, 2005, pp. 486-500.

3. "The Notorious Jumping Frog of Calaveras Count", by Mark Twain, from *The Complete Short Stories of Mark Twain*, edited by Charles Neider, New York: Bantam Classics, 2005, pp. 1-7.

4. "To Build a Fire", by Jack London, from *The Penguin Book of American Short Stories*, edited by James Cochrane, Beijing: Foreign Languages Press, 1969, pp. 265-281.

5. "Hills Like White Elephants", by Earnest Hemingway, from *Men Without Women*. edited by Earnest Hemingway, London: Penguin Books, 1955, pp. 35-38.

6. "The Ice Palace", by F. Scott Fitzgerald, from *Flappers and Philosophers*, edited by F. Scott Fitzgerald, New York, London, Toronto, Sydney: Pocket Books, 1920, pp. 41-73.

7. "A Rose for Emily", by William Faulkner, from *Selected Short Stories of William Faulkner*, by William Faulkner, New York: The Modern Library, 1930, pp. 49-61.

8. "The Man Who Was Almost a Man", by Richard Wright, from *Fiction 100: An Anthology of Short Stories*, edited by James H. Pickering, New York: MacMillan Publishing Co., Inc., 1974, pp. 1021-1027.

9. "Theft", by Katherine Anne Porter, from *The Best American Short Stories of the Century*, edited by John Updike & Katrina Kenison, Boston & New York: Houghton Mifflin Company, 1999, pp. 105-110.

10. "The Enormous Radio", by John Cheever, from *The Stories of John Cheever*, New York: Vintage International, 2000, pp. 33-41.

11. "So Much Water So Close to Home", by Raymond Carver, from *Raymond Carver: Collected Stories*, by Raymond Carver, New York: Literary Classics of the United States, Inc., 2009, pp. 273-279.

12. "Where Are You Going, Where Have You Been", by Joyce Carol Oates, from

前言

The Best American Short Stories of the Century, edited by John Updike & Katrina Kenison, Boston & New York: Houghton Mifflin Company, 1999, pp. 450-465.

13. "The Shawl", by Cynthia Ozick, from *The Best American Short Stories of the Century*, edited by John Updike & Katrina Kenison, Boston & New York: Houghton Mifflin Company, 1999, pp. 576-580.

14. "Made in Heaven", by John Updike, from *New American Short Stories: The Writers Select Their Own Favorites*, edited by Gloria Norris, New York: New American Library, 1986. pp. 11-25.

15. "Recitatif", by Toni Morrison, from *The Norton Anthology of American Literature: Literature Since 1945*, 7th edition, Vol. E, edited by Jerome Klinkowitz & Patricia B. Wallace, New York & London: W. W. Norton & Company, 2007, pp. 2685-2698.

16. "A Guide to Berlin", by Vladimir Nabokov, from *The Stories of Vladimir Nabokov*, edited by Dmitri Nabokov, New York: Vintage Books, 1997, pp. 155-160.

众所周知，美国文学大致经历了殖民地时期与独立战争时期（约1607—18世纪末，主要受清教主义思想、启蒙主义、美国独立革命的影响，代表人物有爱德华兹、富兰克林、克里夫古尔、弗瑞诺等）、浪漫主义时期（1800—1865，有早期浪漫主义、新英格兰超验主义、黑色浪漫主义等，代表作家有欧文、库珀、爱默生、梭罗、霍桑、坡、梅尔维尔、惠特曼、朗费罗、狄金森等，是美国文学的黄金时代）、现实主义时期（1865—1918，有现实主义、自然主义和乡土文学等，代表作家有豪威尔斯、吐温、詹姆斯、德莱塞、伦敦等）、现代主义时期（1918—1945，有意象主义、迷惘的一代、南方文艺复兴、哈莱姆文艺复兴、美国戏剧复兴等，代表作家有凯瑟、安德森、弗罗斯特、桑德堡、庞德、威廉斯、奥尼尔、艾略特、菲茨杰拉德、海明威、福克纳、赖特、休斯、斯坦贝克等，是美国文学上的另一个黄金时代）、当代文学（1945年至今，有"垮掉的一代"、"黑色幽默"、后现代、南方文学、妇女文学、犹太文学、黑人文学、其他族裔文学等，代表作家有威廉斯、米勒、贝娄、艾里森、莫里森、金斯堡、海勒等）。从美国文学所取得的辉煌成就来看，小说在其中占据至关重要的地位。

尤其是现当代小说，多元性是其最引人瞩目的特征，表现在小说的流派、创作思想和方法的异彩纷呈上，其内容涉及阶级、性别、族裔等命题。不仅如此，在飞速发展的后工业社会，我们还见证了或正在见证美国文学的电子传媒化过程。许多高科技的艺术形式正在替代传统的文学形式，而这一趋势在进入新世纪之后更加凸显。美国小说正在进入一个创作视角更加多样、视域更加广泛、内容更加丰富，也更加令人期待的新时期。[1]可以预见的趋势是，通俗文化对小说创作产生的影响将日益增大，以环境保护为题材的生态文学会有较快的发展，越来越多的少数族裔小说已经或者正在进入主流文学（犹太小说和黑人小说已经进入主流）并将占有更重要的地位。在20世纪，曾多次有人发出悲叹："小说死了。"这样的断言已被当代小说（包括美国小说）发展的现实撞得粉碎。小说将作为一种富有活力的体裁继续存在，优秀的作品会不断涌现，受到万千读者的喜爱。

一直以来，美国短篇小说在美国文坛占据重要地位。王佐良先生在《美国短篇小说选》的《编者序》中指出："大致说来，从十九世纪到现在的欧美文坛上，短篇小说写得出色的主要是三个国家：以莫泊桑传统著称的法国，以契诃夫传统为特色的俄国，然后就是美国，而以美国为最有活力。"[2]他引述英国作家毛姆的话说："没有一个欧洲国家象（像）美国那样殷勤地培养短篇小说，也没有任何别的地方象（像）美国那样专心致志地钻研短篇小说的写作方法、技巧和发展可能性。……不止一次，美国短篇小说深刻地影响了别的国家短篇小说的写作实践。"[3]美国短篇小说之所以佳作迭出、影响深远，在王佐良先生看来，"这里有一些物质的原因，例如在美国，登载短篇小说的杂志多，读者多，奖金多，选本多；一般性的杂志如《大西洋月刊》、《纽约人》都以精选短篇小说出名，就连上层知识分子读的季刊如《西旺尼评论》、《党人评论》也登短篇小说。也有历史的、环境的原因，如在美国资本主义发展过程中，大批白人涌向西部去淘金，去拓荒，就在旅途上营火旁或小镇酒店里的互相闲扯中，产生了所谓边境故事，其中既有幽默，又有夸张和恶作剧……不论

---

[1] 参见金莉，《20世纪末期（1980—2000）的美国小说：回顾与展望》，《外国文学研究》，2012年第4期，第97页。
[2] 王佐良，《编者序》，《美国短篇小说选（上册）》，北京：中国青年出版社，1980年，第2页。
[3] 同上。

前　言

　　是什么原因，至今美国写短篇小说的作家特别多，除了许多以写长篇小说出名的大作家也常写短篇小说之外，还有一批专门擅长写短篇小说的作家，包括好几个女作家，如凯瑟琳·安·波特，薇拉·凯瑟，尤多拉·韦尔蒂——不知怎的，她们虽也各自写了几部长篇，却总不如她们的短篇精彩"[1]。另一个众所周知的重要因素是，美国自诞生之日起就是一个多元化的移民国家，早期的美国文学虽然深受英国和欧洲文学传统的影响，但随着时代的发展，广袤富饶的北美大陆、建国之父与宪政思想、追求独立与梦想的美国新人、不同于旧大陆的新社会、西进运动与拓荒精神、欣欣向荣的资本主义经济、移民潮和城市化、独立战争与内战、奴隶制与南方种植园、东西差距和南北冲突、清教主义和驱巫运动等，成为美国文学取之不竭的灵感来源。

　　美国短篇小说的先驱者包括华盛顿·欧文、埃德加·爱伦·坡、纳撒尼尔·霍桑等人。"美国文学之父"欧文的传世名作《瑞普·凡·温克尔》（"Rip Van Winkle"）和《睡谷传说》（"The Legend of Sleepy Hollow"）描写了美国本土的风物与传奇。文学天才爱伦·坡在哥特小说、侦探小说和科幻小说等方面作出了开拓性的贡献，他的精美文字、对人物心理的细腻挖掘、令世人惊愕的另类主题等，对当时的欧洲文学和后世的小说创作产生了巨大的影响。霍桑的小说聚焦宗教主题，他念念不忘人的"原罪"，用厚重的充满象征和寓言的文字，揭示人的堕落，反思现代科技的负面作用。上述作家的短篇小说在写作技巧和语言风格上颇有英国文学的风范，用词考究、句式复杂，显得正式而富有书卷气，追求的是技巧上的卓越。强调华丽文笔的写作风格，在亨利·詹姆斯、威廉·福克纳、F.斯科特·菲茨杰拉德、凯瑟琳·安·波特、弗拉基米尔·纳博科夫等大师笔下得到了进一步发扬光大。

　　美国短篇小说里，还有以马克·吐温和欧内斯特·海明威等为代表的另一种口语风格。马克·吐温独具慧眼，用贴近生活的妇孺皆知的口语和俚语，针砭时弊，剖析人性，描摹地域风情，冷眼笑对社会阴暗面，书写了与众不同的美国式幽默。因此，王佐良先生对马克·吐温评价极高，海明威曾说"全部美国文学来自一本马克·吐温的叫作《哈克贝利·费恩历险记》的书"，如果海明威所言

---

[1] 王佐良，《编者序》，《美国短篇小说选（上册）》，北京：中国青年出版社，1980年，第2页。

非虚的话，"美国形式的短篇小说来自马克·吐温的《跳蛙》"。[1]马克·吐温开创了美国本土口语写作的传统，海明威则将其发展至一个新的高度。海明威的小说创作与他传奇的人生经历密不可分，他从新闻报道中发现了一种简练客观的行文风格，往往采用置身事外的摄像机镜头式的视角、大量的人物对话、简练至极的人物与情节设置等方法，书写战争带来的创伤与迷惘，不向命运低头的硬汉形象和斗牛、狩猎等惊险运动，以删繁就简的无声胜有声、四两拨千斤的独特方式，实践其创作的"冰山原则"，成为后来以雷蒙·卡弗为代表的"极简主义"的先驱，其《白象似的群山》和《杀手》便是此方面的杰作。

作为发现海明威天才的伯乐之一的菲茨杰拉德也是美国现代小说大师和重要的短篇小说家，他以一种在其内又出其外的独特双重视角，书写身兼亲历者与旁观者的青年一代的恋爱、婚姻、运动、娱乐、消费文化、职业选择、战争经历、地域冲突、美国梦的破灭等主题，成为"喧腾的20年代"与"爵士时代"的代言人，本书所选的《冰宫》是其170多篇短篇中的"八部名篇"之一。

在美国现代小说家中，人们公认影响最大、成就最高的当属福克纳，他的作品虽大多以虚构的"约克纳帕塔法"县为背景，却全方位地反映了人类社会的普遍经验。他以华丽而凝重的语言，书写逝去的南方传统、农业经济与现代社会的冲突、家族历史、时间与记忆、战争的创伤、畸恋与谋杀、神话与宗教等主题。他在小说创作技巧上的成就同样令人惊叹，他将意识流、内心独白与自由联想等心理分析手法运用到极致，大量采用多声部、多视角等技法，刻意打破时间序列，广泛运用象征、典故和神话，强调作家的超脱等，是美国南方文学及现代主义鼎盛时期的最杰出代表，成为后来众多作家竞相模仿的典范。福克纳也是短篇小说大师，他的许多短篇作品与其长篇一样，早已成为世界文学经典，如《干旱的九月》（"Dry September"）、《熊》（"Bear"）、《烧牲口棚》（"Barn Burning"）、《献给爱米莉的玫瑰》。笔者认为，《献给爱米莉的玫瑰》代表了美国现代主义时期短篇小说创作的最高水平。

自从华盛顿·欧文、爱伦·坡和霍桑开美国短篇小说之先河以来，舍伍德·安德森、海明威、菲茨杰拉德、福克纳等大师将其发扬光大、推向高峰，到

---

[1] 王佐良，《编者序》，《美国短篇小说选（上册）》，北京：中国青年出版社，1980年，第3页。

前 言

了20世纪八九十年代，美国短篇小说出现了空前的繁荣复兴，优秀的作品屡见不鲜。美国短篇小说的繁荣显示其在美国文坛不言而喻的重要性。[1]对美国短篇小说的繁荣作出了突出贡献的除了上述代表美国白人新教徒传统的作家外，还有其他女性作家和少数族裔作家，没有他们的作品，美国文学的多元性将大打折扣。作为美国当代最具影响力的作家，托尼·莫里森一直深受读者和批评家的喜爱，她在继承前辈黑人文学的基础上，将女性主义文学和黑人文学发展到一个新的高度，本书所选的《宣叙》是目前已知的莫里森唯一的短篇小说，有助于读者初步了解莫里森的作品特色。同样身为黑人作家的理查德·奈特曾是"抗议文学"的代表人物，他本人因此颇受争议。尽管如此，他的《即将成人》也不失为一部精品，可以帮助读者了解一位黑人男孩命运不公的遭遇和成长历程。与女性主义文学和黑人文学同样取得了显赫成就的还有犹太文学，辛西娅·奥兹克的《披巾》便是书写犹太大屠杀悲惨经历的杰作。此外，波特的《偷窃》、欧茨的《何去何从》、契弗的《巨型收音机》、卡弗的《这么多水，离家这么近》、厄普代克的《天堂制造》等小说从经济危机、家庭关系、暴力犯罪、信任缺失、社会变迁等诸多侧面反映了美国社会存在的问题。纳博科夫的《柏林导游》则是这位杰出文体大师早年最具代表性的短篇小说之一，其后来小说中令人眼花缭乱的创作技巧在这篇小说中已初见端倪，读者可以借此大致了解后现代主义的一些写作风格。

美国短篇小说的将来如何？王佐良先生指出："显然，会出现各式各样的新风格、新流派、'新浪潮'的变化，但是也许有两样东西是不变的：一是美国文学对于美国现实的注视、发掘、剖析、批判以至抗议，这个强大的传统会继续下去；二是美国文学至今不衰的活力，会使美国短篇小说依然生气勃勃。无论在主题的选择和发掘上，或是技巧的发扬和试验上，美国短篇小说作家会继续作出他们的努力和贡献。"[2]在此基础上，笔者想补充两点：其一，美国文学的多元化书写依然是不可动摇的主流趋势，女性文学、族裔文学、少数群体文学在其中仍将扮演至关重要的作用；其二，由于消费主义、流行文化、网络和人工智能等的不断渗透，文学的创作与阅读都正在经历"有人欢喜有人忧"的变化，喜的人不

---

1 王中强，《翻译文本的选取：论美国短篇小说的翻译》，《名作欣赏》，2013年第8期，第114页。
2 王佐良，《编者序》，《美国短篇小说选（上册）》，北京：中国青年出版社，1980年，第5页。

断发现文学创作的新领域，网络小说、影视文学等开始进入文学殿堂，忧的人则担心文学将走向穷途末路，被"快餐文化"和声像制品所取代。不过，正如前文所指出的，人们对具有深度的精神生活的追求永远不会消失，这就注定了小说的发展将依然生机勃勃，未来可期。

下面来谈谈如何欣赏短篇小说。在分析一篇小说时，人们通常会从情节、人物、主题、场景、语言、技巧等方面来展开，这些概念看似简单，实则非常复杂，迄今都未有定论。

首先来看看情节（plot）。小说是建立在生活的基础上的，但生活不等于小说，要成为小说，必须对生活进行截取、加工与提炼，这就是情节。显然，正如热奈特（Gérard Genette）、普林斯（Gerald Prince）、里蒙-凯南（Shlomith Rimmon-Kenan）、费伦（James Phelan）、申丹、赵毅衡等学者指出的那样，情节是叙事学中最基本、最重要，也是最复杂的概念。在情节的发展上，一个重要的贡献是什克洛夫斯基（Viktor Shklovsky）对故事与情节的区分。故事可以理解为事物按自然顺序发生发展的过程，是情节的素材，而情节则是对故事的取舍与加工。今天广为人知的情节概念来自亚里士多德（Aristotle）。在《诗学》中，他花了大量篇幅论述情节。他指出在构成希腊悲剧的六要素中最基本的是情节，所谓情节，即事件的安排，是构成故事的骨架，包括开端、发展与结尾，其中隐含的是故事发展的时间序列。亚里士多德强调行为与事件，认为情节第一，人物第二。情节可以根据事物变化的类型（顺境、逆境）与人物类型（好人、坏人、中间人）之间的变换关系加以归纳和组合，其中优秀的情节应是单线的，表现有缺点或犯了某种错误的好人由顺达之境转入败逆之境，第二等的情节则包容了两条发展线索，到头来好人和坏人分别受到赏惩。[1]在亚里士多德时间序列的情节观基础上，E. M. 福斯特强调因果关系，指出情节是构成故事时间序列关系的诸事件之间的因果联系，因此，"国王死了，然后王后也死了"是故事，而"国王死了，然后王后因悲伤而死"则是情节。在经典叙事学中，对情节概念作出重大贡献的还有普洛普（Vladimir Propp）的《民间故事形态学》，他从100个俄国民间故事中，抽象出人物的31种功能和

---

[1] 亚里士多德讨论悲剧六要素见《诗学》第6章，讨论情节的部分为第7～18章，其中对优秀和第二等情节的讨论见第13章。

前 言

7种角色，形成了现代叙事学的基本框架。诺斯诺普·弗莱（Northrop Frye）的《批评的剖析》是西方第一部系统、科学的文学批评专著。弗莱将故事结构分为春、夏、秋、冬四种，称之为"原型"。春对应喜剧，如《第十二夜》；夏对应乌托邦幻想，如《神曲》中的天堂；秋对应悲剧，如《哈姆雷特》《奥赛罗》和《李尔王》；冬对应反乌托邦，如《一九八四》和《美丽新世界》。此外，还有热奈特的《叙事话语》，他试图借鉴英语动词语法中的时态、语态、语气等概念，建构一套叙事语法体系，其中的时距、时序、时频、聚焦等概念已成为叙事学中的基本常识。时序（order）是指故事与叙述之间时间的对应关系，故事时间与讲述时间一致是顺序，反之就有倒叙、插叙和预序。时距（distance）是指故事与讲述之间长度的对比，常见的情况是故事很长，讲述很长。如果故事很长，讲述时间很短，就是省略或概述；反之就是停顿与详述。时频（frequency）是指故事发生次数与讲述次数之间的对比，通常是故事发生一次，讲述一次；也有发生N次讲述一次，或者故事发生一次，讲述了N次的情况，后者多见于侦探小说以及现代主义小说中的多声部、多视角叙述。上面这些对情节的讨论属于经典叙事学的范畴。后经典叙事学的情节观，更多地将重心转移到读者的解读以及作者—文本—人物—读者之间的交流上，即强调情节是读者阅读过程中建构起来的一个个故事。这样看来，情节不再是一个静态的概念，而是一个不断情节化的过程，不是plot，而是plotting。最后，需要在此强调两点：其一，故事与情节的区分已是共识；其二，虽然在今天看来，亚里士多德和福斯特等人的情节观似乎过于简单了，但他们在情节概念上的贡献是显而易见的，因为不管生活，或者故事本身如何支离破碎、混乱不堪，人们总会本能地在自己的意识中赋予其某种秩序或因果关系：有人从天上的云朵中看出了群山，有人则看到了绵羊，还有人看到的则是某张人脸、某辆汽车。由此看来，追求时间顺序与因果关系，不正是人们在阅读中的一种情节化的本能吗？

在小说分析中第二个经常提及的概念是人物（character）。首先应当清楚的是，所谓人物，并不局限于人类世界。在小说虚构世界里，具有人类属性的动物、植物、昆虫、飞禽走兽，甚至普通事物，都属于人物的范畴。其次，在西方叙事学中，大体上可总结出两种人物观，一种叫功能型人物观，一种叫心理型人物观。前者视人物为构成故事的某些功能，人物从属于情节，如亚里士多德、普洛普以及结构主义叙事学家罗兰·巴尔特（Roland Barthes）、格雷马斯（Algirdas Julien Greimas）等人提出的观点。这些人把人物看作构成故事情节的某个结构要素、语法成分、符码甚至矩阵，强调人物的结构功能，忽视了人物的真实性，正是在这个意义上，有人才发出了"人物已死"的感慨。后者认为人物是独立于情节的个性化主体，有自己的思想、情感与性格，与我们生活中见到的人类似，比如现实主义作家笔下栩栩如生的人物。有意思的是，近些年来，还有不少叙事学家将注意力转向小说世界里人物本身的心理分析。从心理型人物观的角度，福斯特区分了圆形人物与扁平人物。所谓扁平人物，是指按照一个简单而固定的意念或特性被创造出来，可以用一个句子表达的人物。他们有两个审美特征：一是个性单一，趋向类型化，容易辨认；二是在故事发展中，没有发展变化或变化很少，如灰姑娘、堂吉诃德、李逵。圆形人物是全方位、多侧面、多维度的人物，其性格是发展变化的，不能"一言以蔽之地去概括"，是宛如真人般复杂多面的人物。福斯特认为，小说中不仅需要有扁平人物，也要有圆形人物；在审美效果方面，扁平人物不如圆形人物，但在某些情况下，扁平人物可以取得更好的喜剧效果。当然，福斯特的分类也有缺陷，如过于简单化，分类标准不统一等，但他为人们分析人物提供了一套实用的工具。不过，需要指出的是，扁平人物与圆形人物之间并没有泾渭分明的界限，他们之间是可以转化的。另外，在情节与人物之间，应该认识到，二者同样重要，人物不能脱离于情节，情节也不能独立于人物之外。

小说分析中第三个常见的概念是主题（theme）。主题是指小说要传达的主要思想，通常可以揭示人生的某些意义或道德启示，它往往是由读者从故事中隐含而非直接表明的信息中提炼出来的故事的总体思想。主题不同于题材（subject）和话题（topic），如马克·吐温的《哈克贝利·费恩历险记》中，题材是"哈克贝利·费恩与黑奴吉姆的逃亡"，话题是"种族主义与奴隶制度"，而主题之一是"奴隶制从根本上扭曲了剥削者与被剥削者阶层"。主题是在情节的发展、人物的关系和作者的态度等因素的共同作用下形成的，同一个故事可以有多个主题，不同的故事可以表现类似的主题，也有些作家由于其独特的人生经历、社会背景、思想信仰，而在其诸多作品中表现出相似的主题关切。值得注意的是，20世纪以来，随着科学技术的迅猛发展、两次世界大战和经济危机带来的

前　言

巨大创伤，语言学转向对俄苏形式主义和英美新批评的影响，以及达尔文、斯宾塞、萨特、尼采、马克思、弗洛伊德等思想家对人与自然、人与社会、人与人、人与自身之间疏离关系的探讨，小说也从现实主义对人的道德主题的关切，逐渐转向对小说技巧与文本自身的关注，刻意颠覆的时间序列，意象与场景的并置，意识流、自由联想与内心独白的广泛运用，大量的典故与文字游戏等，成为小说常见的技巧，这些技巧在《献给爱米莉的玫瑰》《偷窃》《披巾》等小说中都有体现。正是由于现代主义以来的文学对文本技巧的潜力几乎挖掘殆尽，20世纪60年代以来才不断有人提出"文学枯竭论""文学已死"的观点。不过，所谓过犹不及、矫枉过正，小说的形式创新并未走向末路，人们对小说主题的关切也越来越受到重视，美国短篇小说的发展依然方兴未艾，前途依然一片光明，我们不妨拭目以待。

我们曾通过电子邮件联系本书选文的国外出版公司未果，故如有版权持有者知晓本书出版，请与我们联系，我们将根据实际情况奉上报酬并致以谢意。

感谢四川大学外国语学院对本教材的资助，感谢四川大学外国语学院2018级学生张丽娜同学耐心细致的校对工作。本书中的作品引文，如无特殊说明，均为编者自译。书中如有错讹疏漏之处，敬请读者谅解。

推荐阅读：

1. Brooks, Cleanth & Robert Penn Warren, eds. *Understanding Fiction,* 3rd edition. Englewood Cliffs, New Jersey: Prentice-Hall, Inc., 1979.

2. Genette, Gérard. *Narrative Discourse: An Essay in Method*. Translated by Jane E. Lewin, Foreword by Jonathan Culler. Ithaca, New York: Cornell University Press, 1980.

3. 程锡麟、王晓路：《当代美国小说理论》，北京：外语教学与研究出版社，2001年。

4. 李宜燮、常耀信：《美国文学选读（上册）》，天津：南开大学出版社，2011年。

5. 李宜燮、常耀信：《美国文学选读（下册）》，天津：南开大学出版社，2010年。

6. 刘海平、王守仁：《新编美国文学史》（1-4卷），上海：上海外语教育出版社，2000—2002年。

7. 申丹、韩加明、王丽亚：《英美小说叙事理论研究》，北京：北京大学出版社，2013年。

8. 申丹、王丽亚：《西方叙事学：经典与后经典》，北京：北京大学出版社，2010年。

9. 王佐良：《美国短篇小说选（上、下册）》，北京：中国青年出版社，1980年。

10. 亚里士多德：《诗学》，陈中梅译注，北京：商务印书馆，1996年。

11. 赵毅衡：《广义叙述学》，成都：四川大学出版社，2013年。

目 录

1. THE TELL-TALE HEART .... *By Edgar Allan Poe, 1843*   1
2. THE MINISTER'S BLACK VEIL (A PARABLE)
.... *By Nathaniel Hawthorne, 1837*   16
3. THE NOTORIOUS JUMPING FROG OF CALAVERAS COUNTY
.... *By Mark Twain, 1865*   40
4. TO BUILD A FIRE .... *By Jack London, 1908*   57
5. HILLS LIKE WHITE ELEPHANTS .... *By Ernest Hemingway, 1927*   84
6. THE ICE PALACE .... *By F. Scott Fitzgerald, 1920*   99
7. A ROSE FOR EMILY .... *By William Faulkner, 1930*   139
8. THE MAN WHO WAS ALMOST A MAN .... *By Richard Wright, 1940*   161
9. THEFT .... *By Katherine Anne Porter, 1930*   184
10. THE ENORMOUS RADIO .... *By John Cheever, 1947*   199
11. SO MUCH WATER SO CLOSE TO HOME ... *By Raymond Carver, 1981*   220
12. WHERE ARE YOU GOING, WHERE HAVE YOU BEEN
.... *By Joyce Carol Oates, 1966*   237
13. THE SHAWL .... *By Cynthia Ozick, 1980*   267
14. MADE IN HEAVEN .... *By John Updike, 1985*   283
15. RECITATIF .... *By Toni Morrison, 1983*   310
16. A GUIDE TO BERLIN .... *By Vladimir Nabokov, 1925*   341

参考文献... 361

1. THE TELL-TALE HEART

By Edgar Allan Poe, 1843

True!—nervous—very, very dreadfully nervous I had been and am; but why *will* you say that I am mad? The disease had sharpened my senses—not destroyed—not dulled them. Above all was the sense of hearing acute. I heard all things in the heaven and in the earth. I heard many things in hell. How, then, am I mad? Hearken! and observe how healthily—how calmly I can tell you the whole story.

It is impossible to say how first the idea entered my brain; but once conceived, it haunted me day and night. Object there was none. Passion there was none. I loved the old man. He had never wronged me. He had never given me insult. For his gold I had no desire. I think it was his eye! yes, it was this! One of his eyes resembled that of a vulture—a pale blue eye, with a film over it. Whenever it fell upon me, my blood ran cold; and so by degrees—very gradually—I made up my mind to take the life of the old man, and thus rid myself of the eye forever.

Now this is the point. You fancy me mad. Madmen know nothing. But you should have seen *me*. You should have seen how wisely I proceeded—with what caution—with what foresight—with what dissimulation I went to work! I was never kinder to the old man than during the whole week before I killed him. And every night, about midnight, I turned the latch of his door and opened it—oh so gently! And then, when I had made an opening sufficient for my head,

I put in a dark lantern, all closed, closed, so that no light shone out, and then I thrust in my head. Oh, you would have laughed to see how cunningly I thrust it in! I moved it slowly—very, very slowly, so that I might not disturb the old man's sleep. It took me an hour to place my whole head within the opening so far that I could see him as he lay upon his bed. Ha! —would a madman have been so wise as this? And then, when my head was well in the room, I undid the lantern cautiously—oh, so cautiously—cautiously (for the hinges creaked) —I undid it just so much that a single thin ray fell upon the vulture eye. And this I did for seven long nights—every night just at midnight—but I found the eye always closed; and so it was impossible to do the work; for it was not the old man who vexed me, but his Evil Eye. And every morning, when the day broke, I went boldly into the chamber, and spoke courageously to him, calling him by name in a hearty tone, and inquiring how he had passed the night. So you see he would have been a very profound old man, indeed, to suspect that every night, just at twelve, I looked in upon him while he slept.

Upon the eighth night I was more than usually cautious in opening the door. A watch's minute hand moves more quickly than did mine. Never before that night had I *felt* the extent of my own powers—of my sagacity. I could scarcely contain my feelings of triumph. To think that there I was, opening the door, little by little, and he not even to dream of my secret deeds or thoughts. I fairly chuckled at the idea; and perhaps he heard me; for he moved on the bed suddenly, as if startled. Now you may think that I drew back—but no. His room was as black as pitch with the thick darkness, (for the shutters were close fastened, through fear of robbers), and so I knew that he could not see the opening of the door, and I kept pushing it on steadily, steadily.

I had my head in, and was about to open the lantern, when my thumb slipped upon the tin fastening, and the old man sprang up in bed, crying out— "Who's there?"

I kept quite still and said nothing. For a whole hour I did not move a

1. THE TELL-TALE HEART

muscle, and in the meantime I did not hear him lie down. He was still sitting up in the bed listening; —just as I have done, night after night, hearkening to the death watches in the wall.

Presently I heard a slight groan, and I knew it was the groan of mortal terror. It was not a groan of pain or of grief—oh, no! —it was the low stifled sound that arises from the bottom of the soul when overcharged with awe. I knew the sound well. Many a night, just at midnight, when all the world slept, it has welled up from my own bosom, deepening, with its dreadful echo, the terrors that distracted me. I say I knew it well. I knew what the old man felt, and pitied him, although I chuckled at heart. I knew that he had been lying awake ever since the first slight noise, when he had turned in the bed. His fears had been ever since growing upon him. He had been trying to fancy them causeless, but could not. He had been saying to himself—"It is nothing but the wind in the chimney—it is only a mouse crossing the floor," or "it is merely a cricket which has made a single chirp." Yes, he has been trying to comfort himself with these suppositions: but he had found all in vain. *All in vain*; because Death, in approaching him had stalked with his black shadow before him, and enveloped the victim. And it was the mournful influence of the unperceived shadow that caused him to feel—although he neither saw nor heard—to *feel* the presence of my head within the room.

When I had waited a long time, very patiently, without hearing him lie down, I resolved to open a little—a very, very little crevice in the lantern. So I opened it—you cannot imagine how stealthily, stealthily—until, at length a simple dim ray, like the thread of the spider, shot from out the crevice and fell upon the vulture eye.

It was open—wide, wide open—and I grew furious as I gazed upon it. I saw it with perfect distinctness—all a dull blue, with a hideous veil over it that chilled the very marrow in my bones; but I could see nothing else of the old man's face or person: for I had directed the ray as if by instinct, precisely upon the damned spot.

And now have I not told you that what you mistake for madness is but over acuteness of the sense? —now, I say, there came to my ears a low, dull, quick sound, such as a watch makes when enveloped in cotton. I knew *that* sound well, too. It was the beating of the old man's heart. It increased my fury, as the beating of a drum stimulates the soldier into courage.

But even yet I refrained and kept still. I scarcely breathed. I held the lantern motionless. I tried how steadily I could maintain the ray upon the eye. Meantime the hellish tattoo of the heart increased. It grew quicker and quicker, and louder and louder every instant. The old man's terror *must* have been extreme! It grew louder, I say, louder every moment! —do you mark me well? I have told you that I am nervous: so I am. And now at the dead hour of the night, amid the dreadful silence of that old house, so strange a noise as this excited me to uncontrollable terror. Yet, for some minutes longer I refrained and stood still. But the beating grew louder, louder! I thought the heart must burst. And now a new anxiety seized me—the sound would be heard by a neighbour! The old man's hour had come! With a loud yell, I threw open the lantern and leaped into the room. He shrieked once—once only. In an instant I dragged him to the floor, and pulled the heavy bed over him. I then smiled gaily, to find the deed so far done. But, for many minutes, the heart beat on with a muffled sound. This, however, did not vex me; it would not be heard through the wall. At length it ceased. The old man was dead. I removed the bed and examined the corpse. Yes, he was stone, stone dead. I placed my hand upon the heart and held it there many minutes. There was no pulsation. He was stone dead. His eye would trouble me no more.

If still you think me mad, you will think so no longer when I describe the wise precautions I took for the concealment of the body. The night waned, and I worked hastily, but in silence. First of all I dismembered the corpse. I cut off the head and the arms and the legs.

1. THE TELL-TALE HEART

I then took up three planks from the flooring of the chamber, and deposited all between the scantlings. I then replaced the boards so cleverly, so cunningly, that no human eye—not even *his*—could have detected any thing wrong. There was nothing to wash out—no stain of any kind—no blood-spot whatever. I had been too wary for that. A tub had caught all—ha! ha!

When I had made an end of these labors, it was four o'clock—still dark as midnight. As the bell sounded the hour, there came a knocking at the street door. I went down to open it with a light heart, —for what had I *now* to fear? There entered three men, who introduced themselves, with perfect suavity, as officers of the police. A shriek had been heard by a neighbour during the night; suspicion of foul play had been aroused; information had been lodged at the police office, and they (the officers) had been deputed to search the premises.

I smiled, —for *what* had I to fear? I bade the gentlemen welcome. The shriek, I said, was my own in a dream. The old man, I mentioned, was absent in the country. I took my visitors all over the house. I bade them search—search *well*. I led them, at length, to *his* chamber. I showed them his treasures, secure, undisturbed. In the enthusiasm of my confidence, I brought chairs into the room, and desired them *here* to rest from their fatigues, while I myself, in the wild audacity of my perfect triumph, placed my own seat upon the very spot beneath which reposed the corpse of the victim.

The officers were satisfied. My *manner* had convinced them. I was singularly at ease. They sat, and while I answered cheerily, they chatted of familiar things. But, ere long, I felt myself getting pale and wished them gone. My head ached, and I fancied a ringing in my ears: but still they sat and still chatted. The ringing became more distinct:—it continued and became more distinct: I talked more freely to get rid of the feeling: but it continued and gained definiteness—until, at length, I found that the noise was *not* within my ears.

No doubt I now grew *very* pale; —but I talked more fluently, and with a heightened voice. Yet the sound increased—and what could I do? It was *a low, dull, quick sound—much such a sound as a watch makes when enveloped in cotton*. I gasped for breath—and yet the officers heard it not. I talked more quickly—more vehemently; but the noise steadily increased. I arose and argued about trifles, in a high key and with violent gesticulations; but the noise steadily increased. Why *would* they not be gone? I paced the floor to and fro with heavy strides, as if excited to fury by the observations of the men—but the noise steadily increased. Oh God! what *could* I do? I foamed—I raved—I swore! I swung the chair upon which I had been sitting, and grated it upon the boards, but the noise arose over all and continually increased. It grew louder—louder—*louder*! And still the men chatted pleasantly, and smiled. Was it possible they heard not? Almighty God!—no, no! They heard!—they suspected!—they *knew*!—they were making a mockery of my horror!—this I thought, and this I think. But anything was better than this agony! Anything was more tolerable than this derision! I could bear those hypocritical smiles no longer! I felt that I must scream or die!—and now—again!—hark! louder! louder! louder! *louder!* —

"Villains!" I shrieked, "dissemble no more! I admit the deed!—tear up the planks!—here, here!—it is the beating of his hideous heart!"

作品赏析

一、作家及作品介绍

埃得加·爱伦·坡（Edgar Allan Poe，1809—1849）是19世纪美国的天才诗人、短篇小说家、文学评论家，也是一位极具原创精神的唯美主义和黑色浪漫主义作家，在世界文学史上占有举足轻重的地位。他幼年时父母双亡，后来被收养，与养父的关系也不好；26岁时与13岁的表妹弗吉尼亚·克莱姆结婚，10年后弗吉尼亚去世，对他打击很大；一生经历坎坷，作为职业作家他生活潦倒，在世时嗜酒如命，作品不被人欣赏，被人发现离奇地死于巴尔的摩街头。在这里简单回顾他的人生，是为了帮助我们理解他的创作风格与主题。我们称他是一位极具

1. THE TELL-TALE HEART

原创精神的天才作家,不仅是因为其奇特的想象、诡异的主题和精心雕琢的凄美的文字,更因其对美国和世界文学所作出的巨大贡献。虽然在美国他曾饱受非议,然而在大西洋彼岸的欧洲,坡的声誉却一直很高。他在小说、诗歌、短篇小说、文学评论的诸多领域都取得了卓越的成就。首先,作为短篇小说大师,他在短暂的一生中,创作了70多部小说,是今天我们熟知的众多小说体裁的先驱和创始人。

(1)坡是哥特小说大师,今天的恐怖小说与影视作品深受其影响。在这些小说中,地点往往是古堡、深渊、暗室,时间往往在日暮或午夜时分,人物饱受孤独、精神反常与死亡威胁的折磨,读来令人毛骨悚然、不寒而栗。其中,《厄舍府的倒塌》("The Fall of the House of Usher")、《一桶白葡萄酒》("The Cask of Amontillado")、《黑猫》("The Black Cat")、《泄密的心》、《红死魔的面具》("The Masque of the Red Death")、《陷坑与钟摆》("The Pit and the Pendulum")等是深受读者喜爱的精品。他的哥特小说打破了严肃与通俗文学的界限,对美国文学,尤其是南方哥特传统产生了巨大影响,伊迪丝·沃顿(Edith Wharton)、威廉·福克纳、尤多拉·韦尔蒂(Eudora Welty)、弗兰纳里·奥康纳(Flannery O'Conner)、哈特·克兰(Hart Crane)、纳博科夫、托尼·莫里森以及其他诸多作家甚至导演希区柯克(Alfred Hitchcock)的作品都有爱伦·坡式的哥特风格。

(2)坡是推理与侦探小说的鼻祖,《失窃的信》("The Purloined Letter")、《瓶中手稿》("Ms. Found in a Bottle")、《莫格街谋杀案》("The Murders in the Rue Morgue")、《金甲虫》("The Gold Bug")等小说情节生动、推理缜密,对后世如柯南·道尔(Conan Doyle)的侦探小说影响很大,他塑造了小说世界里的第一位神探形象奥古斯特·杜宾(Auguste Dupin),可谓夏洛克·福尔摩斯的先驱。

(3)坡还是科幻小说的先驱之一,其作品与儒勒·凡尔纳(Jules Gabriel Verne)、玛丽·雪莱(Mary Shelley)的作品等一道构成西方科幻小说的源头。此外,他的《威廉·威尔逊》("William Wilson")早在斯蒂文森的《化身博士》(*Dr. Jekyll and Mr. Hyde*)之前就已经触及双面人格(doppelganger)的主题,《人群中的人》("A Man of the Crowd")早于波德莱尔(Charles Pierre

Baudelaire）探讨了群氓心态，而王尔德（Oscar Wilde）则受坡的《椭圆画像》（"The Oval Portrait"）的影响写出了传世名作《道林·格雷的画像》（*The Picture of Dorian Gray*）。

其次，坡的诗歌形式精美，用词考究，形象生动，极富音乐性，实现了形式与内容的完美统一，对西方的诗歌特别是现代派诗歌的发展产生了深远的影响。从这个意义上讲，笔者认为坡远远超越了他的时代，可以说是现代诗歌的远祖。法国象征主义诗人波德莱尔、马拉美（Stéphane Mallarmé）、瓦莱里（Paul Valery）等将坡视为至圣。《乌鸦》（"The Raven"）、《安娜贝尔·李》（"Annabel Lee"）、《致海伦》（"To Helen"）等可谓字字珠玑，早已成为世界名诗中的瑰宝。就诗歌的主题、韵律、节奏和遣词造句而言，《乌鸦》算得上美国韵律诗中最好的一首。这里不妨顺便提及坡对纳博科夫的《洛丽塔》（*Lolita*）的影响。《洛丽塔》在美国现代图书馆20世纪100部最伟大的英语小说榜单中高居第4位，今天人们熟悉的"萝莉"一词即来自这部小说。小说讲述了一位欧洲大叔畸恋未成年继女的故事，这一情节显然取材于爱伦·坡的人生，小说中对爱伦·坡及其作品的影射可谓无处不在，如主要人物亨伯特称自己是坡—坡先生，他的初恋叫安娜贝尔·蕾（Annabel Leigh），他反复说"从前在一个海滨的国度"，显然令人想到了爱伦·坡的名诗《安娜贝尔·李》（"Annabel Lee"），他重复的这句话正是该诗每节的首行诗句。

最后，爱伦·坡是美国文学史上第一位重量级文学理论家，他在小说与诗歌理论方面贡献突出，他提出小说要表现"真理"、诗歌要写"美"的唯美主义原则，这些理论集中体现在《诗歌原理》（"The Poetic Principle"）、《创作哲学》（"The Philosophy of Composition"）等著作中。他是第一位自觉地把短篇小说作为一种独立文学体裁的作家，并系统地提出了强调有机统一的"整体效果论"的理论；他强调诗歌应表现美，而最美的是令人心碎的美丽的爱人之死，这正是《乌鸦》表现的主题；他进行大量病态的心理描写，试图以非理性的方式来揭示人类意识中的阴暗面，表现现代人的精神困顿和人性危机，是西方最早进行全面心理描写的作家。[1] 这些独树一帜，有时甚至惊世骇俗的理论与实践，恰好

---

[1] 李宜燮、常耀信主编，《美国文学选读（上册）》，天津：南开大学出版社，2011年，第149页。

可以说明坡的独创精神以及他对美国文学开拓性的贡献。

关于《泄密的心》，批评界普遍认为，这部哥特小说开创了现代心理小说的先河，对后世的意识流小说产生了深远的影响。小说创作于1843年，讲述了一个在精神病态中的杀人犯案发被抓后交代自己犯罪过程与心理活动的故事。一位在精神病态中的青年，因为同屋的老头长着一只酷似鹰眼的眼睛而对他产生了一种莫名的仇恨，这种仇恨不断发酵，最终让他动了杀心。在处心积虑的安排之后，在一个漆黑、沉寂的午夜，青年杀害了老人，然后将尸体肢解，藏在了木地板下。一位邻居听到动静报了警，面对上门盘问的三名警察，青年表现得镇定自若，甚至邀请警察进屋。尸体就藏在他的椅子地板下，他还能与警察若无其事地聊天。就在他自以为高明可以蒙混过关的时候，却仿佛听到地板下老人越来越清晰的心跳声，最后他濒于心理崩溃，主动坦白了自己的罪行。

二、人物与主题

小说主要人物有两位：青年叙述者与鹰眼老人，前者是疯狂的杀人犯，后者是受害人。故事从"我"冷静理智的叙述开始，氛围逐渐紧张，以叙述不断加速近乎失控结束，揭示了坡小说中最常见的死亡、疯癫等主题。

故事是从人物叙述者的第一人称视角讲述的，可以把它看作一个罪犯事发后的供述和内心独白。由于是受限视角，读者对叙述者的了解只能通过其叙述，而对于他的性别、年龄、职业、性格等无从知晓，不过这样做也有好处，就是可以使人更深入地了解人物的内心。故事一开始，叙述者"我"就告诉读者，他虽然疯癫，却并未丧失理智。一方面他质疑读者不应把他当作疯子，另一方面又承认因为自己有病反而使感觉尤其是听觉变得更加敏锐。这种前后矛盾的开场白本身就具有泄密的效果，既呼应了小说的标题，又为故事的发展和结局做了极好的铺垫："我"的前言不搭后语显然暴露了自己的弱点，让读者对"我"的身份生疑，因为从生活常识来看，往往只有疯子才会反复"此地无银三百两"地宣称自己不是疯子，因此"我"自相矛盾的辩护反而让人更有理由怀疑"我"是不是精神错乱了；同时，读者还会下意识地对"我"所说的话是否真实可靠产生怀疑，因此做好了准备要去探究"我"到底是什么样的人，到底藏有什么样的秘密。接下来，叙述者交代他和一位老人住在一起，他很爱老人，他和老人之间也没有矛盾,但却无法忍受他那只浅蓝的、蒙着一层薄膜的秃鹰式的眼睛,于是他周密计划,要杀死老人。从作案动机来看,仅仅因为老人有一只让自己受不了的眼睛就制定缜密的计划要杀害他,这显然不是正常人的思维,只能再次佐证"我"是真的疯子。这样一个神经过敏、听觉尤其敏锐的自以为高明的疯子,无缘无故制定计划杀人,种种表现倒非常符合出现了幻听的偏执狂或者精神分裂患者的症状。在头七个晚上,他提着灯笼夜探老人,可总是因老人睡着了鹰眼紧闭而无从下手。终于在第八个夜晚,他等到老人睁开眼睛,于是杀人分尸,埋尸于地板下。叙述者一方面竭力渲染自己的高明与理智,另一方面他的讲述却越来越颠覆了自己的这一人设,直到最后因实在受不了地板下传来的老人的心跳声而主动招供。不过,从他越来越狂躁的行为举止与语无伦次的叙述中,可以看出他的精神已经处于崩溃的边缘,压垮他的最后一根稻草其实不是老人的心跳,而是他自己的幻听——正是他掩饰不住的剧烈心跳出卖了自己。

对于故事中的老人,读者所知更少,只能从叙述者带有偏见的只言片语中略知一二。我们猜测,老人应该挺有钱,因为"我"一上来就说,"我"并不贪图他的金银财宝。他有浅蓝的、覆着一层薄膜的、鹰一般的眼睛,是否可以认为他是一位白人老人,甚至有可能患有角膜炎?另外,故事明确告诉读者的是,老人很信任"我",因为他的房间从不上锁,在"我"闯入他房间的头七个夜晚里,他都睡得很沉。虽然作者并未交代"我"与老人的关系,但从上述事实可以推测,或许"我"是老人的照料者,"我们"之间是主仆的关系,至少这一可能性不能排除。如果是这样,甚至"我"还有可能是一位黑人青年。虽然作者没有给出明确的答案,但正是这些未知信息,给这一恐怖的故事增添了一分神秘色彩,从而更加激发了读者的好奇心。

除了死亡与逐渐失去理智的疯癫,读者还可以从小说中读出孤独、异化与人格分裂的主题。不管是青年还是老人,他们都是孤独的。"我"和老人虽然同住一个屋檐下,但自始至终没有言语交流,这反映了两个孤独的人之间关系的异化。"我"决意要杀死他,只是由于他有一只鹰一般的眼睛。老人的鹰眼实际上是一种隐喻表达,英文中的I(我)与eye(眼睛)同音,因此,老人的眼睛或许就是叙述者自己。一方面我们不难发现叙述者的讲述中充满精神病人的呓语,是典型的不可靠叙述,这样看来,老人到底是谁还真可以打上问号;另一方面,

1. THE TELL-TALE HEART

I与eye的谐音影射的是"我"分裂的双重人格,或者说"眼睛"是"我"的镜像[1],这与《厄舍府的倒塌》中两兄妹可能是镜像类似,是异化与人格分裂的表现。有学者从心理分析的角度指出,"鹰眼"象征警觉、监督与惩罚,是人格结构的超我部分,而作为自我的叙述者出于对鹰眼的恐惧将"鹰眼"摧毁。但"鹰眼"只是超我的一种投射,这种投射被摧毁后还会以其他的形式体现出来,那就是后来的永不停息的泄密的心。其实并不是老人不死的心脏,而是"我"忐忑不安的超我的良心对自我以及最终对本我实施的惩罚。[2]换言之,"我"在杀死了老人,摆脱了那只邪恶眼睛的同时,也杀死了邪恶的自我。因为杀死了老人,另一半善良的自我感到心虚而招认了罪状,走向了象征意义上的自我毁灭。不管这一解读是否显得牵强附会,一个不争的事实是,《泄密的心》早已成为心理分析中一个经典的范本。

那么,坡为什么对死亡与疯癫之类的主题如此关注呢?这就不得不回到前文说过的他的人生经历与死亡美学。他小说中的这些主题与风格堪称迥异于时代的文学奇葩,他着意描写人的内心世界,探究迄今依然为世人所忽略的人的病态的精神状况,有评论家说他致力用丰富的想象描绘现实和梦幻、晦暗与光明之间的交汇地带,从而扩展、加大了文学表现的广度和深度,对西方现代文学的发展作出了杰出的贡献。[3]因此,他被称为黑色浪漫主义的代表,以他在名诗《乌鸦》中所展示的摄人心魄的美丽爱人之死的凄美,以及在《厄舍府的倒塌》中呈现的从理智到疯癫的完美心理变化过程为典型。在坡的作品中,死亡和恐惧、理智和疯狂、美丽和崇高奇特地结合在一起,给读者一种极致的另类审美享受。这正是埃德蒙·伯克(Edmund Burke)所推崇的由恐怖而产生的文学的崇高美。正如有学者指出的那样,坡拒绝被粗俗花哨的浪漫主义洪流吞噬,坚持走自己的路,为了美的事业甘当一名叛逆者,结果发现了美国前所未

---

1 李慧明,《爱伦·坡人性主题创作的问题意识探讨》,《学术论坛》,2006年第5期,第153页。
2 袁平、李爱庆,《〈泄密之心〉到底泄了什么密》,《学周刊》,2011年第5期,第191页。
3 李宜燮、常耀信主编,《美国文学选读(上册)》,天津:南开大学出版社,第147页。

知的一种高雅的浪漫主义。[1]

三、结构与技巧

《泄密的心》是反映爱伦·坡心理描写和"统一效果"原则的恐怖美学的经典力作,故事采用第一人称的内心独白和心理描写,以眼睛和心为核心意象,通过主人公内心的变化来推动整个故事的发展,引导读者跟随主人公的犯罪过程和思想变化,切身感受其内心的恐惧,从而挖掘人性中的丑恶、阴暗,以及病态的心理。

朱振武指出:"'效果'(effect)是其中最重要的关键词,总是占据着坡的审美思考的中心位置";"在其精心建造的'效果'理论中,产生搅动读者心灵效应的是其创作主旨,而这种效果的实现和增强则是借助了新与奇的结合、和谐的统一和理性的掌控等美学手段。"[2]

为了达到这一统一的效果,故事的篇幅不宜太长,以能一口气读完为佳。在他的哥特小说和诗歌创作中通常要收到的效果是恐怖。首先,在小说的篇幅安排上,《泄密的心》非常符合一口气读完的要求,故事逻辑缜密,结构紧凑,全文2000余词,共144句,从青年自述理智、陡起杀意,到夜探老人、杀人分尸、藏尸地板,再到从容应对警察上门,最后精神崩溃主动招供,情节凝练,环环相扣。短小精干的文字,保证读者能一口气读完,在他们脑海中留下深刻的整体印象。其次,坡不遗余力地渲染恐怖的氛围。在时间和地点的设置上,正如我们在《乌鸦》《厄舍府的倒塌》《红死魔的面具》等小说中看到的一样,故事发生在让读者胆战心惊的夜里的午夜时分一座古老的有着木质地板的矮楼里。午夜一直被视为黑暗、神秘与恐怖的源泉,常与死亡相伴。不论是作者笔下的黑猫还是黑漆漆的厄舍古屋,都因黑色的弥漫而显得诡异神秘。在《泄密的心》中,"我"提着一盏黑乎乎的灯,悄悄地溜进老人那间伸手不见五指的房间,小心翼翼地将被遮得严严实实的灯掀开一条缝,露出一丝诡异的光亮,照在老人的眼睛上,以试探他是否苏醒,鹰眼是否睁开。这午夜时分有人心怀杀机近距离地偷窥的情

---

[1] 转引自李慧明,《爱伦·坡人性主题创作的问题意识探讨》,《学术论坛》,2006年第5期,第154页。

[2] 朱振武,《爱伦·坡的效果美学论略》,《外国文学评论》,2007年第3期,第128页。

1. THE TELL-TALE HEART

景，想想都让人不寒而栗。杀死老人的那一晚，"我"一如既往去窥视，这时老人突然坐起，仿佛是感受到了房间里"我"的存在。在一片漆黑里，两人虽彼此对视，却无法看清对方，内心的恐惧在死一般的沉寂中弥漫、膨胀。黑色构成了小说场景的基本色调，极力渲染了故事的阴沉、诡秘、冷酷和残忍，不仅与死亡直接相关，还隐喻了青年变态的阴暗心理。黑暗中老人令人心悸的鹰眼、轻微的呻吟、两人在漆黑中的相视无言，都在读者脑海中留下了令人恐惧的印象，完美地服务于作家对整体效果的预设。

此外，在技巧上，这篇小说最令人称道的地方是作者采用了第一人称的限知视角，以青年自述的不可靠叙述方式完整再现了他在作案前后的心理变化过程，逼真传神地刻画了"我"病态扭曲的犯罪心理。读者无法预测小说中叙述者"我"的下一步行动，在好奇心的驱使下跟随"我"的叙述，真切地体验了"我"在行凶前、行凶时以及行凶后的内心活动。故事将读者带入真实的环境，令人身临其境。例如，在时间的安排上，一开始叙述者还交代"一个小时""几分钟"，后来这种物理时间就淡出了，取而代之的是人物内心的活动，读者从外部世界被引入人物内心，从而沉浸在故事世界中，与人物达成了共谋。一开始，故事的发展还显得有条不紊，随着"我"心理扭曲程度的加深，叙述也似乎开始失去控制，这不仅表现在作者对两个核心意象鹰眼和心跳的处理，而且也表现在"我"不断加速的失控的讲述上。"我"的杀人起意于老人那只浅蓝的鹰眼，从常理上讲这个理由显然是莫名其妙的。不过，对于心理变态、精神分裂又自命不凡的"我"来讲，这种来自他人的似乎无处不在的窥视，很可能使"我"感到了自己阴暗的心理被人看穿的威胁，而这也成为"我"偏执地想要消灭眼睛却又同时强调"我"对老人并无恶意甚至还爱他的原因。在杀害老人之前，"我"听到他的心跳声像是"裹在棉花里的手表发出的声音"，这声音越来越大，让"我"难以忍受，于是利索地杀死了老人并确保他的心不再跳动。可是，老人死后，"我"依然听到了逐渐增强的心跳声音，那声音"特别像是裹在棉花里的手表发出的声音"。作者两次强调了那种声音就像是裹在棉花里的手表发出的声音，似乎在暗示着读者其实心跳声自始至终都是源于"我"。因为在极其安静的环境下，人只可能听到自己的心跳声。这无疑显示出"我"已经有严重的幻听，精神已经极度扭曲了。为了突出这一精神逐渐失控的过程，作者在句法层面上使用了大量直接、有力、简练的简单句，用以强调变化和动态效果，如第一段共10句话，其中8句为简单句。而在故事快结尾时，作者更是大量使用短促的呼号和重复。作者在小说中罕见地使用了大量的破折号和感叹号，光是破折号就出现了68处。这些符号的大量使用，具有独特的修辞效果。从形式上看，破折号插入密度很大，破坏了正常的语流，使整个文本趋于碎片化，这是叙述者变态心理的真实写照。最后一段的6句全是感叹句，生动展示了杀人者内心的躁狂和情绪的激变，展现了坡高超的叙事技巧。

Suggested Readings

1. Fisher, Benjamin Franklin, IV, ed. *Poe and His Times: The Artist and His Milieu*. Baltimore: Edgar Allan Poe Society, 1990.

2. Fisher, Benjamin Franklin, IV. *The Cambridge Introduction to Edgar Allan Poe*. Cambridge: Cambridge University Press, 2008.

3. Frank, Frederick S. & Anthony Magistrale. *The Poe Encyclopedia*. Westport, CT: Greenwood Press, 1997.

4. Hayes, Kevin J. *Edgar Allan Poe*. London: Reaktion Books, 2009.

5. Hayes, Kevin J., ed. *The Cambrdge Companion to Edgar Allan Poe*. Cambridge: Cambridge University Press, 2004.

6. Kennedy, J. Gerald, ed. *A Historical Guide to Edgar Allan Poe*. New York: Oxford University Press, 2000.

7. Levin, Harry. *The Power of Blackness: Hawthorne, Poe, Melville*. New York: Knopf, 1958.

8. Poe, Edgar Allan. *Edgar Allan Poe: Poetry and Tales*. Ed. Patrick F. Quinn. New York: Library of America, 1984.

9. Poe, Edgar Allan. *Complete Works of Edgar Allan Poe*. Ed. James A. Harrison. 17 Vols. New York: Thomas Y. Crowell, 1902.

10. Poe, Edgar Allan. *The Portable Edgar Allan Poe*. Ed. Gerald Kennedy. London: Penguin Books, 2006.

11. Walker, I. M., ed. *Edgar Allan Poe: The Critical Heritage*. New York:

1. THE TELL-TALE HEART

Routledge & Kegan Paul, 1986.

12. 帕蒂克·F. 奎恩编：《爱伦·坡集：诗歌与故事》，曹明伦译，北京：生活·读书·新知三联书店，1995年。

Questions for Reflection

1. From whose point of view is the story narrated? Why does the author take such a perspective?

2. What details in the story suggest that the narrator "I" is unreliable?

3. Who is the old man in the story? What motivates the narrator to kill him?

4. Although the narrator "I" has planned very cautiously, his criminal act is far from being what he asserts to be perfect. What in your view has given him away?

5. How do you understand the fact that the police officers only chat with the narrator without inquiring into the loud sound?

Question for Discussion

In what ways is the story exemplary in manifesting Edgar Allan Poe's aesthetics views?

（王安　撰写）

2. THE MINISTER'S BLACK VEIL (A PARABLE)[1]

By Nathaniel Hawthorne, 1837

The Sexton stood in the porch of Milford meeting-house, pulling busily at the bell-rope. The old people of the village came stooping along the street. Children, with bright faces, tripped merrily beside their parents, or mimicked a graver gait, in the conscious dignity of their Sunday clothes. Spruce bachelors looked sidelong at the pretty maidens, and fancied that the Sabbath sunshine made them prettier than on week days. When the throng had mostly streamed into the porch, the sexton began to toll the bell, keeping his eye on the Reverend Mr. Hooper's door. The first glimpse of the clergyman's figure was the signal for the bell to cease its summons.

"But what has good Parson Hooper got upon his face?" cried the sexton in astonishment.

All within hearing immediately turned about, and beheld the semblance of Mr. Hooper, pacing slowly his meditative way towards the meeting-house. With one accord they started, expressing more wonder than if some strange minister

---

[1] Another clergyman in New England, Mr. Joseph Moody, of York, Maine, who died about eighty years since, made himself remarkable by the same eccentricity that is here related of the Reverend Mr. Hooper. In his case, however, the symbol had a different import. In early life he had accidentally killed a beloved friend; and from that day till the hour of his own death, he hid his face from men.

were coming to dust the cushions of Mr. Hooper's pulpit.

"Are you sure it is our parson?" inquired Goodman Gray of the sexton.

"Of a certainty it is good Mr. Hooper," replied the sexton. "He was to have exchanged pulpits with Parson Shute, of Westbury; but Parson Shute sent to excuse himself yesterday, being to preach a funeral sermon."

The cause of so much amazement may appear sufficiently slight. Mr. Hooper, a gentlemanly person, of about thirty, though still a bachelor, was dressed with due clerical neatness, as if a careful wife had starched his band, and brushed the weekly dust from his Sunday's garb. There was but one thing remarkable in his appearance. Swathed about his forehead, and hanging down over his face, so low as to be shaken by his breath, Mr. Hooper had on a black veil. On a nearer view it seemed to consist of two folds of crape, which entirely concealed his features, except the mouth and chin, but probably did not intercept his sight, further than to give a darkened aspect to all living and inanimate things. With this gloomy shade before him, good Mr. Hooper walked onward, at a slow and quiet pace, stooping somewhat, and looking on the ground, as is customary with abstracted men, yet nodding kindly to those of his parishioners who still waited on the meeting-house steps. But so wonder-struck were they that his greeting hardly met with a return.

"I can't really feel as if good Mr. Hooper's face was behind that piece of crape," said the sexton.

"I don't like it," muttered an old woman, as she hobbled into the meeting-house. "He has changed himself into something awful, only by hiding his face."

"Our parson has gone mad!" cried Goodman Gray, following him across the threshold.

A rumor of some unaccountable phenomenon had preceded Mr. Hooper into the meeting-house, and set all the congregation astir. Few could refrain from twisting their heads towards the door; many stood upright, and turned directly about; while several little boys clambered upon the seats, and came down again with a terrible racket. There was a general bustle, a rustling of the women's gowns and shuffling of the men's feet, greatly at variance with that hushed repose which should attend the entrance of the minister. But Mr. Hooper appeared not to notice the perturbation of his people. He entered with an almost noiseless step, bent his head mildly to the pews on each side, and bowed as he passed his oldest parishioner, a white-haired great-grandsire, who occupied an arm-chair in the centre of the aisle. It was strange to observe how slowly this venerable man became conscious of something singular in the appearance of his pastor. He seemed not fully to partake of the prevailing wonder, till Mr. Hooper had ascended the stairs, and showed himself in the pulpit, face to face with his congregation, except for the black veil. That mysterious emblem was never once withdrawn. It shook with his measured breath, as he gave out the psalm; it threw its obscurity between him and the holy page, as he read the Scriptures; and while he prayed, the veil lay heavily on his uplifted countenance. Did he seek to hide it from the dread Being whom he was addressing?

Such was the effect of this simple piece of crape, that more than one woman of delicate nerves was forced to leave the meeting-house. Yet perhaps the pale-faced congregation was almost as fearful a sight to the minister, as his black veil to them.

Mr. Hooper had the reputation of a good preacher, but not an energetic one: he strove to win his people heavenward by mild, persuasive influences, rather than to drive them thither by the thunders of the Word. The sermon which he now delivered was marked by the same characteristics of style and manner as the general series of his pulpit oratory. But there was something, either in the sentiment of the discourse itself, or in the imagination of the auditors, which made it greatly the most powerful effort that they had ever heard from their pastor's lips. It was tinged, rather more darkly than usual, with the gentle gloom of Mr. Hooper's temperament. The subject had reference to

2. THE MINISTER'S BLACK VEIL (A PARABLE)

secret sin, and those sad mysteries which we hide from our nearest and dearest, and would fain conceal from our own consciousness, even forgetting that the Omniscient can detect them. A subtle power was breathed into his words. Each member of the congregation, the most innocent girl, and the man of hardened breast, felt as if the preacher had crept upon them, behind his awful veil, and discovered their hoarded iniquity of deed or thought. Many spread their clasped hands on their bosoms. There was nothing terrible in what Mr. Hooper said, at least, no violence; and yet, with every tremor of his melancholy voice, the hearers quaked. An unsought pathos came hand in hand with awe. So sensible were the audience of some unwonted attribute in their minister, that they longed for a breath of wind to blow aside the veil, almost believing that a stranger's visage would be discovered, though the form, gesture, and voice were those of Mr. Hooper.

At the close of the services, the people hurried out with indecorous confusion, eager to communicate their pent-up amazement, and conscious of lighter spirits the moment they lost sight of the black veil. Some gathered in little circles, huddled closely together, with their mouths all whispering in the centre; some went homeward alone, wrapt in silent meditation; some talked loudly, and profaned the Sabbath day with ostentatious laughter. A few shook their sagacious heads, intimating that they could penetrate the mystery; while one or two affirmed that there was no mystery at all, but only that Mr. Hooper's eyes were so weakened by the midnight lamp, as to require a shade. After a brief interval, forth came good Mr. Hooper also, in the rear of his flock. Turning his veiled face from one group to another, he paid due reverence to the hoary heads, saluted the middle aged with kind dignity as their friend and spiritual guide, greeted the young with mingled authority and love, and laid his hands on the little children's heads to bless them. Such was always his custom on the Sabbath day. Strange and bewildered looks repaid him for his courtesy. None, as on former occasions, aspired to the honor of walking by their pastor's side. Old Squire Saunders, doubtless by an accidental lapse of memory, neglected to invite Mr. Hooper to his table, where the good clergyman had been wont to bless the food, almost every Sunday since his settlement. He returned, therefore, to the parsonage, and, at the moment of closing the door, was observed to look back upon the people, all of whom had their eyes fixed upon the minister. A sad smile gleamed faintly from beneath the black veil, and flickered about his mouth, glimmering as he disappeared.

"How strange," said a lady, "that a simple black veil, such as any woman might wear on her bonnet, should become such a terrible thing on Mr. Hooper's face!"

"Something must surely be amiss with Mr. Hooper's intellects," observed her husband, the physician of the village. "But the strangest part of the affair is the effect of this vagary, even on a sober-minded man like myself. The black veil, though it covers only our pastor's face, throws its influence over his whole person, and makes him ghostlike from head to foot. Do you not feel it so?"

"Truly do I," replied the lady; "and I would not be alone with him for the world. I wonder he is not afraid to be alone with himself!"

"Men sometimes are so," said her husband.

The afternoon service was attended with similar circumstances. At its conclusion, the bell tolled for the funeral of a young lady. The relatives and friends were assembled in the house, and the more distant acquaintances stood about the door, speaking of the good qualities of the deceased, when their talk was interrupted by the appearance of Mr. Hooper, still covered with his black veil. It was now an appropriate emblem. The clergyman stepped into the room where the corpse was laid, and bent over the coffin, to take a last farewell of his deceased parishioner. As he stooped, the veil hung straight down from his forehead, so that, if her eyelids had not been closed forever, the dead maiden might have seen his face. Could Mr. Hooper be fearful of her glance, that he so hastily caught back the black veil? A person who watched the interview between

2. THE MINISTER'S BLACK VEIL (A PARABLE)

the dead and living, scrupled not to affirm, that, at the instant when the clergyman's features were disclosed, the corpse had slightly shuddered, rustling the shroud and muslin cap, though the countenance retained the composure of death. A superstitious old woman was the only witness of this prodigy. From the coffin Mr. Hooper passed into the chamber of the mourners, and thence to the head of the staircase, to make the funeral prayer. It was a tender and heart-dissolving prayer, full of sorrow, yet so imbued with celestial hopes, that the music of a heavenly harp, swept by the fingers of the dead, seemed faintly to be heard among the saddest accents of the minister. The people trembled, though they but darkly understood him, when he prayed that they, and himself, and all of mortal race, might be ready, as he trusted this young maiden had been, for the dreadful hour that should snatch the veil from their faces. The bearers went heavily forth, and the mourners followed, saddening all the street, with the dead before them, and Mr. Hooper in his black veil behind.

"Why do you look back?" said one in the procession to his partner.

"I had a fancy," replied she, "that the minister and the maiden's spirit were walking hand in hand."

"And so had I, at the same moment," said the other.

That night, the handsomest couple in Milford village were to be joined in wedlock. Though reckoned a melancholy man, Mr. Hooper had a placid cheerfulness for such occasions, which often excited a sympathetic smile where livelier merriment would have been thrown away. There was no quality of his disposition which made him more beloved than this. The company at the wedding awaited his arrival with impatience, trusting that the strange awe, which had gathered over him throughout the day, would now be dispelled. But such was not the result. When Mr. Hooper came, the first thing that their eyes rested on was the same horrible black veil, which had added deeper gloom to the funeral, and could portend nothing but evil to the wedding. Such was its immediate effect on the guests that a cloud seemed to have rolled duskily from beneath the black crape, and dimmed the light of the candles. The bridal pair stood up before the minister. But the bride's cold fingers quivered in the tremulous hand of the bridegroom, and her deathlike paleness caused a whisper that the maiden who had been buried a few hours before was come from her grave to be married. If ever another wedding were so dismal, it was that famous one where they tolled the wedding knell. After performing the ceremony, Mr. Hooper raised a glass of wine to his lips, wishing happiness to the new-married couple in a strain of mild pleasantry that ought to have brightened the features of the guests, like a cheerful gleam from the hearth. At that instant, catching a glimpse of his figure in the looking-glass, the black veil involved his own spirit in the horror with which it overwhelmed all others. His frame shuddered, his lips grew white, he spilt the untasted wine upon the carpet, and rushed forth into the darkness. For the Earth, too, had on her Black Veil.

The next day, the whole village of Milford talked of little else than Parson Hooper's black veil. That, and the mystery concealed behind it, supplied a topic for discussion between acquaintances meeting in the street, and good women gossiping at their open windows. It was the first item of news that the tavern-keeper told to his guests. The children babbled of it on their way to school. One imitative little imp covered his face with an old black handkerchief, thereby so affrighting his playmates that the panic seized himself, and he well-nigh lost his wits by his own waggery.

It was remarkable that of all the busybodies and impertinent people in the parish, not one ventured to put the plain question to Mr. Hooper, wherefore he did this thing. Hitherto, whenever there appeared the slightest call for such interference, he had never lacked advisers, nor shown himself adverse to be guided by their judgment. If he erred at all, it was by so painful a degree of self-distrust, that even the mildest censure would lead him to consider an indifferent action as a crime. Yet, though so well acquainted with this amiable weakness, no individual among his parishioners chose to make the black veil a subject of friendly remonstrance. There was a feeling of dread, neither plainly confessed nor carefully concealed, which caused each to shift the responsibility upon another, till at length it was found expedient to send a deputation of the church, in order to deal with Mr. Hooper about the mystery, before it should grow into a scandal. Never did an embassy so ill discharge its duties. The minister received them with friendly courtesy, but became silent, after they were seated, leaving to his visitors the whole burden of introducing their important business. The topic, it might be supposed, was obvious enough. There was the black veil swathed round Mr. Hooper's forehead, and concealing every feature above his placid mouth, on which, at times, they could perceive the glimmering of a melancholy smile. But that piece of crape, to their imagination, seemed to hang down before his heart, the symbol of a fearful secret between him and them. Were the veil but cast aside, they might speak freely of it, but not till then. Thus they sat a considerable time, speechless, confused, and shrinking uneasily from Mr. Hooper's eye, which they felt to be fixed upon them with an invisible glance. Finally, the deputies returned abashed to their constituents, pronouncing the matter too weighty to be handled, except by a council of the churches, if, indeed, it might not require a general synod.

But there was one person in the village unappalled by the awe with which the black veil had impressed all beside herself. When the deputies returned without an explanation, or even venturing to demand one, she, with the calm energy of her character, determined to chase away the strange cloud that appeared to be settling round Mr. Hooper, every moment more darkly than before. As his plighted wife, it should be her privilege to know what the black veil concealed. At the minister's first visit, therefore, she entered upon the subject with a direct simplicity, which made the task easier both for him and her. After he had seated himself, she fixed her eyes steadfastly upon the veil, but could discern nothing of the dreadful gloom that had so overawed the multitude: it was but a double fold of crape, hanging down from his forehead to his mouth, and slightly stirring with his breath.

"No," said she aloud, and smiling, "there is nothing terrible in this piece of crape, except that it hides a face which I am always glad to look upon. Come, good sir, let the sun shine from behind the cloud. First lay aside your black veil: then tell me why you put it on."

Mr. Hooper's smile glimmered faintly.

"There is an hour to come," said he, "when all of us shall cast aside our veils. Take it not amiss, beloved friend, if I wear this piece of crape till then."

"Your words are a mystery, too," returned the young lady. "Take away the veil from them, at least."

"Elizabeth, I will," said he, "so far as my vow may suffer me. Know, then, this veil is a type and a symbol, and I am bound to wear it ever, both in light and darkness, in solitude and before the gaze of multitudes, and as with strangers, so with my familiar friends. No mortal eye will see it withdrawn. This dismal shade must separate me from the world: even you, Elizabeth, can never come behind it!"

"What grievous affliction hath befallen you," she earnestly inquired, "that you should thus darken your eyes forever?"

"If it be a sign of mourning," replied Mr. Hooper, "I, perhaps, like most other mortals, have sorrows dark enough to be typified by a black veil."

"But what if the world will not believe that it is the type of an innocent sorrow?" urged Elizabeth. "Beloved and respected as you are, there may be whispers that you hide your face under the consciousness of secret sin. For the sake of your holy office, do away this scandal!"

The color rose into her cheeks as she intimated the nature of the rumors that were already abroad in the village. But Mr. Hooper's mildness did not forsake him. He even smiled again—that same sad smile, which always appeared like a faint glimmering of light, proceeding from the obscurity beneath the veil.

"If I hide my face for sorrow, there is cause enough," he merely replied; "and if I cover it for secret sin, what mortal might not do the same?"

And with this gentle, but unconquerable obstinacy did he resist all her entreaties. At length Elizabeth sat silent. For a few moments she appeared lost in thought, considering, probably, what new methods might be tried to withdraw her lover from so dark a fantasy, which, if it had no other meaning, was perhaps a symptom of mental disease. Though of a firmer character than his own, the tears rolled down her cheeks. But, in an instant, as it were, a new feeling took the place of sorrow: her eyes were fixed insensibly on the black veil, when, like a sudden twilight in the air, its terrors fell around her. She arose, and stood trembling before him.

"And do you feel it then, at last?" said he mournfully.

She made no reply, but covered her eyes with her hand, and turned to leave the room. He rushed forward and caught her arm.

"Have patience with me, Elizabeth!" cried he, passionately. "Do not desert me, though this veil must be between us here on earth. Be mine, and hereafter there shall be no veil over my face, no darkness between our souls! It is but a mortal veil—it is not for eternity! O! you know not how lonely I am, and how frightened, to be alone behind my black veil. Do not leave me in this miserable obscurity forever!"

"Lift the veil but once, and look me in the face," said she.

"Never! It cannot be!" replied Mr. Hooper.

"Then farewell!" said Elizabeth.

She withdrew her arm from his grasp, and slowly departed, pausing at the door, to give one long shuddering gaze, that seemed almost to penetrate the mystery of the black veil. But, even amid his grief, Mr. Hooper smiled to think that only a material emblem had separated him from happiness, though the horrors, which it shadowed forth, must be drawn darkly between the fondest of lovers.

From that time no attempts were made to remove Mr. Hooper's black veil, or, by a direct appeal, to discover the secret which it was supposed to hide. By persons who claimed a superiority to popular prejudice, it was reckoned merely an eccentric whim, such as often mingles with the sober actions of men otherwise rational, and tinges them all with its own semblance of insanity. But with the multitude, good Mr. Hooper was irreparably a bugbear. He could not walk the street with any peace of mind, so conscious was he that the gentle and timid would turn aside to avoid him, and that others would make it a point of hardihood to throw themselves in his way. The impertinence of the latter class compelled him to give up his customary walk at sunset to the burial ground; for when he leaned pensively over the gate, there would always be faces behind the gravestones, peeping at this black veil. A fable went the rounds that the stare of the dead people drove him thence. It grieved him, to the very depth of his kind heart, to observe how the children fled from his approach, breaking up their merriest sports, while his melancholy figure was yet afar off. Their instinctive dread caused him to feel more strongly than aught else, that a preternatural horror was interwoven with the threads of the black crape. In truth, his own antipathy to the veil was known to be so great, that he never willingly passed before a mirror, nor stooped to drink at a still fountain, lest, in its peaceful bosom, he should be affrighted by himself. This was what gave plausibility to the whispers, that Mr. Hooper's conscience tortured him for some great crime too horrible to be entirely concealed, or otherwise than so obscurely intimated. Thus, from beneath the black veil, there rolled a cloud into the sunshine, an ambiguity of sin or sorrow, which enveloped the poor minister, so that love or sympathy could never reach him. It was said that ghost and fiend consorted with him there. With self-shudderings and outward terrors, he walked continually in its shadow, groping darkly within his own soul, or gazing through a medium that saddened the whole world. Even the lawless wind, it was believed, respected his dreadful secret, and never blew aside the veil. But still good Mr. Hooper sadly smiled at the pale visages of the worldly throng as he passed by.

Among all its bad influences, the black veil had the one desirable effect, of making its wearer a very efficient clergyman. By the aid of his mysterious emblem—for there was no other apparent cause—he became a man of awful power, over souls that were in agony for sin. His converts always regarded him with a dread peculiar to themselves, affirming, though but figuratively, that, before he brought them to celestial light, they had been with him behind the black veil. Its gloom, indeed, enabled him to sympathize with all dark affections. Dying sinners cried aloud for Mr. Hooper, and would not yield their breath till he appeared; though ever, as he stooped to whisper consolation, they shuddered at the veiled face so near their own. Such were the terrors of the black veil, even when Death had bared his visage! Strangers came long distances to attend service at his church, with the mere idle purpose of gazing at his figure, because it was forbidden them to behold his face. But many were made to quake ere they departed! Once, during Governor Belcher's administration, Mr. Hooper was appointed to preach the election sermon. Covered with his black veil, he stood before the chief magistrate, the council, and the representatives, and wrought so deep an impression that the legislative measures of that year were characterized by all the gloom and piety of our earliest ancestral sway.

In this manner Mr. Hooper spent a long life, irreproachable in outward act, yet shrouded in dismal suspicions; kind and loving, though unloved, and dimly feared; a man apart from men, shunned in their health and joy, but ever summoned to their aid in mortal anguish. As years wore on, shedding their snows above his sable veil, he acquired a name throughout the New England churches, and they called him Father Hooper. Nearly all his parishioners, who were of mature age when he was settled, had been borne away by many a funeral: he had one congregation in the church, and a more crowded one in the churchyard; and having wrought so late into the evening, and done his work so well, it was now good Father Hooper's turn to rest.

Several persons were visible by the shaded candlelight, in the death chamber of the old clergyman. Natural connections he had none. But there was the decorously grave, though unmoved physician, seeking only to mitigate the last pangs of the patient whom he could not save. There were the deacons, and other eminently pious members of his church. There, also, was the Reverend Mr. Clark, of Westbury, a young and zealous divine, who had ridden in haste to pray by the bedside of the expiring minister. There was the nurse, no hired hand-maiden of death, but one whose calm affection had endured thus long in secrecy, in solitude, amid the chill of age, and would not perish, even at the dying hour. Who, but Elizabeth! And there lay the hoary head of good Father Hooper upon the death pillow, with the black veil still swathed about his brow, and reaching down over his face, so that each more difficult gasp of his faint breath caused it to stir. All through life that piece of crape had hung between him and the world; it had separated him from cheerful brotherhood and woman's love, and kept him in that saddest of all prisons, his own heart; and still it lay upon his face, as if to deepen the gloom of his darksome chamber, and shade him from the sunshine of eternity.

For some time previous, his mind had been confused, wavering doubtfully between the past and the present, and hovering forward, as it were, at intervals, into the indistinctness of the world to come. There had been feverish turns, which tossed him from side to side, and wore away what little strength he had. But in his most convulsive struggles, and in the wildest vagaries of his intellect, when no other thought retained its sober influence, he still showed an awful solicitude lest the black veil should slip aside. Even if his bewildered soul could have forgotten, there was a faithful woman at his pillow, who, with averted eyes, would have covered that aged face, which she had last beheld in the comeliness of manhood. At length the death-stricken old man lay quietly in the torpor of mental and bodily exhaustion, with an imperceptible pulse, and breath that

2. THE MINISTER'S BLACK VEIL (A PARABLE)

grew fainter and fainter, except when a long, deep, and irregular inspiration seemed to prelude the flight of his spirit.

The minister of Westbury approached the bedside.

"Venerable Father Hooper," said he, "the moment of your release is at hand. Are you ready for the lifting of the veil that shuts in time from eternity?"

Father Hooper at first replied merely by a feeble motion of his head; then, apprehensive, perhaps, that his meaning might be doubtful, he exerted himself to speak.

"Yea," said he, in faint accents, "my soul hath a patient weariness until that veil be lifted."

"And is it fitting," resumed the Reverend Mr. Clark, "that a man so given to prayer, of such a blameless example, holy in deed and thought, so far as mortal judgment may pronounce; is it fitting that a father in the church should leave a shadow on his memory, that may seem to blacken a life so pure? I pray you, my venerable brother, let not this thing be! Suffer us to be gladdened by your triumphant aspect as you go to your reward. Before the veil of eternity be lifted, let me cast aside this black veil from your face!"

And thus speaking, the Reverend Mr. Clark bent forward to reveal the mystery of so many years. But, exerting a sudden energy, that made all the beholders stand aghast, Father Hooper snatched both his hands from beneath the bedclothes, and pressed them strongly on the black veil, resolute to struggle, if the minister of Westbury would contend with a dying man.

"Never!" cried the veiled clergyman. "On earth, never!"

"Dark old man!" exclaimed the affrighted minister, "with what horrible crime upon your soul are you now passing to the judgment?"

Father Hooper's breath heaved; it rattled in his throat but, with a mighty effort, grasping forward with his hands, he caught hold of life, and held it back till he should speak. He even raised himself in bed; and there he sat, shivering with the arms of death around him, while the black veil hung down, awful, at that last moment, in the gathered terrors of a lifetime. And yet the faint, sad smile, so often there, now seemed to glimmer from its obscurity, and linger on Father Hooper's lips.

"Why do you tremble at me alone?" cried he, turning his veiled face round the circle of pale spectators. "Tremble also at each other! Have men avoided me, and women shown no pity, and children screamed and fled, only for my black veil? What, but the mystery which it obscurely typifies, has made this piece of crape so awful? When the friend shows his inmost heart to his friend; the lover to his best beloved; when man does not vainly shrink from the eye of his Creator, loathsomely treasuring up the secret of his sin; then deem me a monster; for the symbol beneath which I have lived, and die! I look around me, and, lo! on every visage a Black Veil!"

While his auditors shrank from one another, in mutual affright, Father Hooper fell back upon his pillow, a veiled corpse, with a faint smile lingering on the lips. Still veiled, they laid him in his coffin, and a veiled corpse they bore him to the grave. The grass of many years has sprung up and withered on that grave, the burial stone is moss-grown, and good Mr. Hooper's face is dust; but awful is still the thought that it mouldered beneath the Black Veil!

作品赏析

一、作者和情节

为了更好地理解美国作家霍桑的《教长的黑面纱》这部短篇小说，我们先来了解一下作品的历史背景。在17世纪早期，尤其是1620年到1630年的这10年里，数量庞大的清教徒从英国移民北美洲。1620年从英国驶往美洲的"五月花号"即是这一移民浪潮的标志。清教主义的宗教思想长期统治美国东北地区，渗透到其社会的各个方面。清教主义强调伦理道德和精神生活，给教众的日常生活订立了严格的规矩。

本篇小说的作者纳撒尼尔·霍桑（Nathaniel Hawthorne，1804—1864）是美

2. THE MINISTER'S BLACK VEIL (A PARABLE)

国早期著名的小说家，他对美国文学的发展作出了巨大贡献。

他1804年出生于马萨诸塞州的塞勒姆镇（Salem）的一个清教世家。他的高祖父威廉·霍桑从英国移民美洲，曾担任马萨诸塞殖民地的法官、行政长官等职务。威廉的儿子，约翰·霍桑，即作者的曾祖父，曾担任殖民地法官，不但主持了塞勒姆女巫案的审判，而且从未对其行为表示过后悔。作者的父亲纳撒尼尔·霍桑爵士是一名船长，在作者4岁时病死海外。从此，他家家道中落。大学毕业后不久，作者将自己的姓氏从Hathorne改为Hawthorne，大概就是为了将自己与那些地位显赫但却残忍的先辈们区分开来。

1825年大学毕业后，霍桑回到家乡蛰伏十余年，于1836年去往波士顿。他先后从事过杂志编辑、海关计量管理员等工作。在这个时期，他开始努力创作，积极投稿，逐渐走上文学之路。《教长的黑面纱》正是这个时期的作品之一。

霍桑于1842年娶妻索菲亚·皮博迪（Sophia Peabody）。夫妻二人非常恩爱，育有3个子女。

1850年，他发表了《红字》（*The Scarlet Letter*），取得巨大成功。该书是美国历史上第一部大规模发行的作品。

1853年，他的朋友富兰克林·皮尔斯（Franklin Pierce）当选美国总统后，任命他为美国驻英国利物浦领事。

1864年5月19日，他在旅行途中于睡眠中长逝。

霍桑深受清教主义的影响，尤其受到加尔文教派关于"原罪"和"灵魂堕落"理论的影响，政治和道德观念严谨保守。他信奉清教主义的基本信条，但也在作品中对这一教派的狂热和狭隘进行了揭露和批判。他的作品讨论的话题多是宗教原罪、道德堕落以及社会和人性的阴暗面。他特别偏爱探讨罪恶和赎罪的话题，倡导正视自我的罪孽，诚心忏悔，修行向善，从而涤荡罪恶，实现自我救赎。因此，这些作品往往寓意深刻，甚至晦涩难懂；同时，笔调凝重，气氛阴郁哀伤。不过，阴暗中却透出一丝光明。因为作者在揭露社会和人性的阴暗、感叹人类的堕落的同时，往往也对那些善良的人物表现出深深的同情。霍桑的作品采用浪漫主义的表现形式，语言典雅，构思精巧，想象丰富。霍桑是心理小说的开创者，擅长心理描写。另外，他的象征主义手法，为作品平添许多神秘和朦胧气氛。

霍桑的著名长篇小说包括《红字》、《七个尖角阁的房子》（*A House of the Seven Gables*）、《福谷传奇》（*The Blithedale Romance*）和《大理石雕像》（*The Marble Faun*）；他的短篇小说数量众多，有不少名篇佳作，比如《年轻的小伙子布朗》（"Young Goodman Brown"）、《拉普齐尼博士的女儿》（"Dr. Rappacini's Daughter"）以及本书讨论的《教长的黑面纱》。

《教长的黑面纱》的故事情节并不复杂。一个星期天的早上，新英格兰地区米福尔德镇教堂的司事一边敲钟一边等教长出来。胡珀教长出来的时候，戴着一副黑面纱。他的这一装扮让司事和在场的教民们都倍感惊讶。更为惊讶的是，教长神情镇定，戴着面纱主持了上午的唱诗和礼拜活动。教民们感到既畏惧又压抑，心中充满疑惑，很不喜欢教长的面纱。

下午，教长仍然戴着面纱主持了教堂的礼拜活动，接着主持了一个年轻姑娘的葬礼。在送葬的过程，送葬队伍的许多人都回头打量他，眼里充满恐惧。

晚上，教长主持了一对新人的婚礼，还是戴着他的黑面纱。这给婚礼平添几分阴郁。甚至有人揣测说，新娘被那位刚刚去世的年轻姑娘的鬼魂附了身。主持完毕后，他手里端着一杯葡萄酒，无意间看到了镜子中的自己，大惊失色。他浑身颤抖，双唇发白，还没来得及品尝的葡萄酒被泼洒在地毯上。他匆匆离去，走进无边的黑夜里。他自己也害怕自己戴着面纱的样子，竭力避免照镜子，甚至不愿意从平静的泉水池中取水喝，以免看见自己的倒影。

教长温和谦逊，从谏如流。过去，村里的教友们也乐于指出他的任何疏漏和过错。但是，这次，虽然很多人内心不满，而且村里从来不缺爱管闲事的人，却没有一个人当面表示反对。最后，只得由教会派出一个代表团去劝说教长。但寒暄之后，面对教长的沉默，代表团成员还是难以启齿，最终不了了之。

当教长来看望他的未婚妻伊丽莎白时，伊丽莎白恳求他摘掉面纱，但无济于事。于是，伊丽莎白离他而去。

从此，胡珀教长就一直戴着黑面纱生活。多数人，尤其是小孩，畏惧、躲避他，但也有一些人为了证明自己勇敢去挑衅他。比如，当他默默凝视坟地的时候，一双双眼睛就会从墓碑后面冒出来，无所畏惧地瞪着他。这两种态度都给他带来麻烦和苦恼。

不过，黑面纱倒是极大地促进了他的工作。现在，教长与那些犯错的教友之

2. THE MINISTER'S BLACK VEIL (A PARABLE)

间似乎存在某种默契，产生了共鸣，而且这些教友对他怀有莫名的敬畏。甚至，死神降临时，垂死挣扎的他们，见到教长之后才闭上眼睛。

教长声名远播，而且长寿。但是，现在的他卧床不起，气若游丝。他的妻子以及一众教会人员为他送终。年轻的克拉克牧师准备揭开教长的面纱，但弥留之际的教长突然发力，抓住克拉克牧师的手阻止他。教长居然还坐了起来，发表了一通临终演讲才咽气。

二、人物与主题

胡珀教长是这篇小说中唯一的主要人物，次要人物有教长的未婚妻、教堂司事、克拉克牧师、乡绅桑德斯、当地的医生等。

30岁的胡珀先生是米福尔德镇的教长。他温文尔雅，谦逊慈爱，与辖区教民的关系非常融洽，并深受爱戴。人们以能够接近他为荣，而邀请他回家一起进餐的荣耀则被老乡绅桑德斯所垄断。

但自从他戴上黑面纱之后，绝大多数教民对他心存疑惧，日益疏远。与此同时，那些已经开始内疚忏悔的教友，则对他有莫名的亲切感。

教长的黑面纱，外加他高尚的人品，让他名扬新英格兰地区，人称"胡珀神父"。

除了教长外，比较值得关注的人物是他的未婚妻伊丽莎白和年轻的克拉克牧师。从伊丽莎白与教长的对白来判断，她是一个善解人意、体贴贤惠的女子。同时，她坚决果断，下定决心后便毅然离开了偏执的教长。不过，她对教长的感情从来没有改变。在教长病倒之后，她回到他身边来照料他。至于克拉克牧师，则是一名"年轻、狂热的信徒"，与没有戴上面纱的胡珀教长类似。

这部短篇小说的寓意相当隐晦，对其主题的解读五花八门。但比较可取的解读是，跟霍桑的其他许多作品一样，这部小说主要探讨人类的罪责和人性的阴暗，表达了霍桑关于信仰和道德的一贯主张：人类带有原罪，普遍道德堕落；信徒应该反省自己的过错和罪孽，忏悔并赎罪，以获得灵魂的救赎。

显然，胡珀教长的黑面纱跟他隐秘的罪孽有关。教长戴上面纱的当天对教众发表了关于隐秘罪恶的布道演讲。"这次演讲同样浸染着教长温和的阴郁气质，但比平时的演讲阴沉许多。演讲的题材是隐秘的罪恶，以及那些被我们隐藏起来的悲伤的秘密。我们对最亲近的人隐瞒这些秘密，对自己的良知隐瞒这些秘密，甚至忘记了无所不知的上帝能够洞察这些秘密这一事实。"而胡珀教长临终的评论，则更加清楚地表明了这点。他看着围绕在病榻周围的众人，质问道："男人躲避我……难道仅仅是因为这副黑色的面纱？……等人们不再徒劳地躲避上帝的注视，不再可憎地竭力隐藏他们罪恶秘密的时候，再来指责我……"人们躲避的不是面纱，而是他们隐藏在心灵深处的罪恶。

教长的罪孽应该与那名当天下葬的年轻姑娘无关。作品压根儿没有交代女子的死因，也没有迹象表明教长对异性怀有贪婪之心。并且，从教民对他的态度来看，也不可能是这种罪孽。

教长到底犯下了何种罪孽，读者恐怕很难从这部晦涩的作品中找到确切答案。这种晦涩和朦胧，在教长和未婚妻伊丽莎白的对话中表现得非常突出。教长对伊丽莎白说："会有一个时刻，我们所有人都会卸掉自己的面纱。"伊丽莎白表示不太明白教长的话，并恳请他至少对这句话给出一个清楚的解释。于是教长解释道："伊丽莎白，在我的誓言允许的范围内，我愿意解释清楚。"但是，他只说自己佩戴的面纱是一个标志，却不提这个标志代表的含义。而且，前句话里的"誓言"一词，导致教长的话反而变得更加晦涩。

作者对教长的罪孽的含糊，正是对世人罪孽的昭显。教长对伊丽莎白说："如果我是因为隐秘的罪孽而遮住我的脸，那么，又有哪个世人不会这么做呢？"他死前感叹道："我环视四周，瞧瞧，但见每个人脸上都戴着一具黑色面纱！"在那位姑娘的葬礼上，教长对教民们说，希望他们，也包括他自己，以及世上所有的人们，都能够为揭开他们脸上面纱的恐怖时刻做好准备。在场的教民们似乎隐约领会了他的意思，并且为之颤抖。教长的意思是，甚至那位最近逝去的姑娘也不例外，生前也是戴着一副面纱。作者甚至旁白道："因为大地也同样戴着她的黑面纱。"凡此种种，都反映了作者的观点：世人普遍堕落，身负罪孽。

结合霍桑的时代和家世，我们可以这样理解罪孽，它包含宗教的和世俗的罪孽。宗教的罪孽包括原罪，也包括对神灵的亵渎和对信仰的敷衍。世俗的罪孽，则是指世俗道德定义的过错或罪行。

大家都跟教长一样有罪，但对待自己罪孽的态度却各不相同。正如胡珀教长指出的那样，多数人通常不是真心忏悔改正，而是竭力隐瞒；对亲近的人隐瞒，对自己隐瞒，甚至还想瞒过上帝。成年教民害怕教长，可能是因为教长是一面镜子，会照出他们的堕落和邪恶。教长的黑面纱，会让他们重新记起自己几乎已经忘记的那些罪孽。

而胡珀教长则采取了迥然不同的态度。虽然他没有将自己的罪孽告之天下，但是，他至少能对自己的良心、对上帝坦诚交代，并切实忏悔和赎罪。作品中提到，虽然人们因害怕他的黑面纱而疏远他，但是，他终生清白向善，晚年美名远播。

那些承认自己的罪孽并强烈期望向教长忏悔的教民们的态度，则介于上述两种态度之间。他们不能像教长那样虔诚赎罪，但是至少不再对自己、对上帝隐瞒自己的罪孽。因此，他们理解和同情教长，同时也非常敬畏他的勇气和决心。

也许，作者正是想警醒自欺欺人的芸芸教众，希望他们早日醒悟，采取教长那样的态度，勇于观照自己的灵魂，坦然承认自己的罪孽，诚心受戒，净化心灵，寻求救赎。

三、结构与技巧

一如霍桑的其他许多作品，《教长的黑面纱》讨论宗教、道德和人性的话题。在结构和布局方面，作品颇为传统。故事从一个星期天的礼拜开始，依照时间顺序展开，以主人公的死亡结束。在写作技巧和风格方面，这部小说的语言风格、叙事方式、语调氛围、人物塑造、象征手法等，都值得关注。

第一，作品的语言风格非常典雅精致。文章用词十分丰富和准确，句子结构正式、复杂。霍桑这种语言风格，既体现出那个时代英国文风的影响，也反映了作者良好的家庭和教育背景。

第二，作品的叙事方式独具一格。小说采用不受限制的第三人称叙事角度，依时间线展开。小说叙事简约，并没有详细铺陈和描写。比如，伊丽莎白出场的时候，除了"作为教长的未婚妻"这个定语，没有任何铺陈。再如，对教长在风波之后的数十年生涯，作者也只是做了最为简约的概述。这种简约风格，符合作品的寓言性质，同时增强了作品的可读性和趣味性。

第三，小说的语调沉重，带有几许同情和伤感，营造出阴郁的氛围。在演讲的时候，教民们"随着教长的声音的颤动而发抖"。教民们"觉得教长戴着黑面纱偷偷地从后面靠近他们"，害怕教长发现他们"深深隐藏的罪行和邪念"。教长的黑面纱还给镇里金童玉女的婚礼"平添几分阴沉"，而且"罩上一层凶兆"。此外，"阴郁""恐惧""罪恶"等词，被大量反复使用。甚至教长对自己灵魂的追问以及他对那些忏悔罪孽的教民付出的慈爱都被描写为"阴郁的"。这种遣词造句，读来既沉重又伤感，让整个故事笼罩在阴郁的氛围中。同时，作品在字里行间也流露出对教长的同情。"乌云从黑面纱后面滚滚而来，遮天蔽日，像罪孽又像悲伤，将教长层层包围，从此他再也不能感受到任何怜爱和同情。"面纱导致他被"笼罩在凄凉的怀疑中"，而且"将他关押在最最悲伤的监狱里"。即使面对这种悲伤无奈的局面，教长也始终面带"一丝忧伤的微笑"，善待所有教民。可能正是因为如此，文中多处称呼他为"善良的胡珀教长"，并且通过克拉克牧师的口，说他"有着圣洁的思想和行为，是完美无瑕的榜样"。

第四，作品在塑造人物手段方面也颇具特色：作者极少对人物的性格特点进行直接评判，而是通过描写语言和行为来塑造人物形象，且侧面描写尤其突出。教长使用的优雅语言，展现了教长良好的文化修养；而他临终前的评论，则表现出他的真诚和深刻。他招呼教民们的情景，让他的温柔和礼貌跃然纸上；他在病榻上固守面纱的挣扎，则展现了他内心的坚定和执着。更加独特的是，作品广泛凭借教民们对教长的态度和评论来揭示他的性格特点。教长佩戴黑面纱之前人们对他的敬重，揭示出他虔诚慈爱的胸怀；伊丽莎白起初对黑面纱的轻松态度，揭示出教长相对正直清白的人品；克拉克牧师对教长的总结性评价，则揭示出他自从佩戴黑面纱之后的赎罪努力和对真和善的苦苦追求。

第五，象征是这篇小说最重要的艺术手法。整部作品围绕着教长的黑面纱这一象征展开，但黑面纱的寓意却令人捉摸不定。总的来说，大致存在三层寓意。

其一，黑面纱象征着罪恶。在清教文化里，黑色一般具有悲伤、死亡、罪恶等含义。作者在文末的注释里提到，新英格兰的另一名神职人员意外杀死一位朋友，从此终生佩戴黑色的面纱。一个人犯下罪行后，即使能够瞒过世人，也难以忍受灵魂和上天的注视，所以其良心往往备受煎熬。或许，戴上黑面纱，可以在一定程度上阻隔这种注视，从而减少一些心灵的煎熬。可能跟那名神职人员一样，教长也因感到有罪而佩戴黑面纱。从这个意义上讲，正如爱伦·坡当年解读的那样，黑面纱喻指罪恶。

不过，在上述的注释里，作者同时指出，二者佩戴面纱的原因不尽相同。而且，教长戴上黑色面纱当天，对教众做了关于隐秘的罪孽和邪念的布道演讲。故此，让教长内心布满阴影的罪过，应该是那场演讲讨论的宗教原罪以及抽象意义上的道德堕落，而非若干具体的罪行。那么，教长的黑面纱所象征的，就不只是他个人的罪恶，而是所有世人的罪恶。

其二，黑面纱象征着认罪和忏悔的态度。教长戴上黑面纱，借此向世人和上帝坦承自己的罪恶和堕落，表达自己的忏悔态度。同时，教长的面纱让教民们意识到自己的罪恶，并催促他们认罪、忏悔。

另外，虽然那些教民畏惧教长有形的面纱，但实际上，他们也各自戴着一副无形的面纱。佩戴有形的面纱，是为了向世人、自己和上帝坦白和忏悔自己的罪孽；佩戴无形的面纱，则是为了欺瞒世人，欺骗自己的良知，阻挡上帝的审视。

教长这种忏悔的态度，难免让人联想到作者霍桑的家世及其对作者的影响。后世认为他权倾一时的祖先曾经罪孽深重。到作者父亲这辈时，昔日的名门望族已然没落。也许，作者内心充满忏悔；也许，可以将这部小说看作作者的黑面纱。

其三，黑面纱象征着赎罪的决心。教长戴上黑面纱之后，虽然承受着孤独和误解，但他终其一生苦心劝喻教众，希望他们迷途知返，涤清自己内心的罪恶。照理说，教长算是功德圆满，死后不会愧对上帝，可以卸下面纱了。可是，人们在埋葬他的时候，却没有将他的黑面纱揭下，而是让他戴着面纱下葬。这个结局的寓意可能是：那些教民仍然不愿直面真实的自我，不愿忏悔和自我救赎。于是，教长毕生的努力竟然付诸东流。此刻，我们仿佛能够听到作者的叹息：人类的救赎，仍然任重道远，遥不可期！

Suggested Readings

1. Aronson, Marc. *Witch-Hunt: Mysteries of the Salem Witch Trials*. New York: Atheneum Books for Young Readers, 2005.
2. Bremer, Francis J. *First Founders: American Puritans and Puritanism in an Atlantic World*. Durham, NH: University of New Hampshire Press, 2012.

3. Colacurcio, Michael J. *The Province of Piety: Moral History in Hawthorne's Early Tales*. Cambridge, MA: Harvard University Press, 1984.

4. Crews, Frederick. *The Sins of the Fathers: Hawthorne's Psychological Themes*. New York: Oxford University Press, 1966.

5. Crowley, J. Donald, ed. *Nathaniel Hawthorne: The Critical Heritage*. London: Routledge, 1997.

6. Hawthorne, Nathaniel. *The House of the Seven Gables*. University Park, PA: Pennsylvania State University Press, 2008.

7. Hawthorne, Nathaniel. *The Scarlet Letter*. Beijing: Foreign Languages Press, 2008.

8. Hutner, Gordon. *Secrets and Sympathy: Forms of Disclosure in Hawthorne's Novels*. Athens, GA: University of Georgia Press, 1988.

9. Le Beau, Bryan F. *The Story of the Salem Witch Trials*. Upper Saddle River, NJ: Prentice-Hall, 1998.

10. Miller, Perry. *The New England Mind: The Seventeenth Century*. Cambridge, MA: Harvard University Press, 1939.

11. Moore, Margaret B. *The Salem World of Nathaniel Hawthorne*. Columbia, MO: University of Missouri Press, 1998.

12. Newman, Lea Bertani Vozar. *A Reader's Guide to the Short Stories of Nathaniel Hawthorne*. Boston: G. K. Hall, 1979.

13. Person, Leland S. *The Cambridge Companion to Nathaniel Hawthorne*. Cambridge, UK: Cambridge University Press, 2007.

14. Turner, Arlin. *Nathaniel Hawthorne: A Biography*. New York: Oxford University Press, 1980.

15. Von Frank, Albert J., ed. *Critical Essays on Hawthorne's Short Stories*. Boston: G. K. Hall, 1991.

16. Wineapple, Brenda. *Hawthone: A Life*. New York: Knopf, 2003.

17. 纳撒尼尔·霍桑：《霍桑短篇小说精选（英汉对照）》，青闰、丹冰译注，北京：外文出版社，2012年。

2. THE MINISTER'S BLACK VEIL (A PARABLE)

Questions for Reflection

1. What has possibly motivated Parson Hooper to wear a black veil?

2. How did Parson Hooper get along with his parishioners before he puts on the black veil? How do the parishioners respond to his black veil? Why do many parishioners fear and shun the minister?

3. Some readers may speculate that the minister might have had a dubious relationship with the newly deceased girl. What do you think of the two characters' relationship?

4. During the conversation between the minister and Elizabeth, his plighted wife, does her response to the black veil go through any change?

5. After his death, people buried Father Hooper without taking off his black veil. What do you think is the symbolic meaning of this?

Question for Discussion

Father Hooper repeatedly mentions that people are actually all wearing a black veil. What do you think he means?

（周家辉　撰写）

3. THE NOTORIOUS JUMPING FROG OF CALAVERAS COUNTY

By Mark Twain, 1865

In compliance with the request of a friend of mine, who wrote me from the East, I called on good-natured, garrulous old Simon Wheeler, and inquired after my friend's friend, Leonidas W. Smiley, as requested to do, and I hereunto append the result. I have a lurking suspicion that *Leonidas W.* Smiley is a myth; and that my friend never knew such a personage; and that he only conjectured that if I asked old Wheeler about him, it would remind him of his infamous *Jim Smiley*, and he would go to work and bore me to death with some exasperating reminiscence of him as long and as tedious as it should be useless to me. If that was the design, it succeeded.

I found Simon Wheeler dozing comfortably by the barroom stove of the dilapidated tavern in the decayed mining camp of Angel's, and I noticed that he was fat and bald-headed, and had an expression of winning gentleness and simplicity upon his tranquil countenance. He roused up, and gave me good day. I told him a friend had commissioned me to make some inquiries about a cherished companion of his boyhood named *Leonidas W.* Smiley—Rev. *Leonidas W.* Smiley, a young minister of the Gospel, who he had heard was at one time a resident of Angel's Camp. I added that if Mr. Wheeler could tell me anything about this Rev. Leonidas W. Smiley, I would feel under many

3. THE NOTORIOUS JUMPING FROG OF CALAVERAS COUNTY

obligations to him.

Simon Wheeler backed me into a corner and blockaded me there with his chair, and then sat down and reeled off the monotonous narrative which follows this paragraph. He never smiled, he never frowned, he never changed his voice from the gentle-flowing key to which he tuned his initial sentence, he never betrayed the slightest suspicion of enthusiasm; but all through the interminable narrative there ran a vein of impressive earnestness and sincerity, which showed me plainly that, so far from his imagining that there was anything ridiculous or funny about his story, he regarded it as a really important matter, and admired its two heroes as men of transcendent genius in *finesse*. I let him go on in his own way, and never interrupted him once.

"Rev. Leonidas W. H'm, Reverend Le—well, there was a feller here once by the name of *Jim* Smiley, in the winter of '49—or may be it was the spring of '50—I don't recollect exactly, somehow, though what makes me think it was one or the other is because I remember the big flume warn't finished when he first came to the camp; but any way, he was the curiousest man about always betting on anything that turned up you ever see, if he could get anybody to bet on the other side; and if he couldn't he'd change sides. Any way that suited the other man would suit *him*—any way just so's he got a bet, *he* was satisfied. But still he was lucky, uncommon lucky; he most always come out winner. He was always ready and laying for a chance; there couldn't be no solit'ry thing mentioned but that feller'd offer to bet on it, and take any side you please, as I was just telling you. If there was a horse-race, you'd find him flush or you'd find him busted at the end of it; if there was a dog-fight, he'd bet on it; if there was a cat-fight, he'd bet on it; if there was a chicken-fight, he'd bet on it; why, if there was two birds setting on a fence, he would bet you which one would fly first; or if there was a camp-meeting, he would be there reg'lar to bet on Parson Walker, which he judged to be the best exhorter about here, and so he was, too, and a good man. If he even see a straddle-bug start to go anywheres, he would bet you how long it would take him to get to—to wherever he *was* going to, and if you took him up, he would foller that straddle-bug to Mexico but what he would find out where he was bound for and how long he was on the road. Lots of the boys here has seen that Smiley, and can tell you about him. Why, it never made no difference to *him*—he'd bet on *any* thing—the dangest feller. Parson Walker's wife laid very sick once, for a good while, and it seemed as if they warn't going to save her; but one morning he come in, and Smiley up and asked him how she was, and he said she was considerable better—thank the Lord for his inf'nit' mercy—and coming on so smart that with the blessing of Prov'dence she'd get well yet; and Smiley, before he thought, says, 'Well, I'll risk two-and-a-half she don't anyway.'"

"Thish-yer Smiley had a mare—the boys called her the fifteen-minute nag, but that was only in fun, you know, because, of course, she was faster than that—and he used to win money on that horse, for all she was so slow and always had the asthma, or the distemper, or the consumption, or something of that kind. They used to give her two or three hundred yards' start, and then pass her under way; but always at the fag end of the race she'd get excited and desperate like, and come cavorting and straddling up, and scattering her legs around limber, sometimes in the air, and sometimes out to one side amongst the fences, and kicking up m-o-r-e dust and raising m-o-r-e racket with her coughing and sneezing and blowing her nose—and always fetch up at the stand just about a neck ahead, as near as you could cipher it down.

"And he had a little small bull-pup, that to look at him you'd think he warn't worth a cent but to set around and look ornery and lay for a chance to steal something. But as soon as money was up on him he was a different dog; his under-jaw'd begin to stick out like the fo'castle of a steamboat, and his teeth would uncover and shine like the furnaces. And a dog might tackle him and bully-rag him, and bite him, and throw him over his shoulder two or three times, and Andrew Jackson—which was the name of the pup—Andrew Jackson

3. THE NOTORIOUS JUMPING FROG OF CALAVERAS COUNTY

would never let on but what *he* was satisfied, and hadn't expected nothing else—and the bets being doubled and doubled on the other side all the time, till the money was all up; and then all of a sudden he would grab that other dog jest by the j'int of his hind leg and freeze to it—not chaw, you understand, but only just grip and hang on till they throwed up the sponge, if it was a year. Smiley always come out winner on that pup, till he harnessed a dog once that didn't have no hind legs, because they'd been sawed off in a circular saw, and when the thing had gone along far enough, and the money was all up, and he come to make a snatch for his pet holt, he see in a minute how he'd been imposed on, and how the other dog had him in the door, so to speak, and he 'peared surprised, and then he looked sorter discouraged-like, and didn't try no more to win the fight, and so he got shucked out bad. He gave Smiley a look, as much as to say his heart was broke, and it was *his* fault, for putting up a dog that hadn't no hind legs for him to take holt of, which was his main dependence in a fight, and then he limped off a piece and laid down and died. It was a good pup, was that Andrew Jackson, and would have made a name for hisself if he'd lived, for the stuff was in him and he had genius—I know it, because he hadn't no opportunities to speak of, and it don't stand to reason that a dog could make such a fight as he could under them circumstances if he hadn't no talent. It always makes me feel sorry when I think of that last fight of his'n, and the way it turned out.

"Well, thish-yer Smiley had rat-tarriers, and chicken cocks, and tomcats and all them kind of things, till you couldn't rest, and you couldn't fetch nothing for him to bet on but he'd match you. He ketched a frog one day, and took him home, and said he cal'lated to educate him; and so he never done nothing for three months but set in his back yard and learn that frog to jump. And you bet you he *did* learn him, too. He'd give him a little punch behind, and the next minute you'd see that frog whirling in the air like a doughnut—see him turn one summerset, or may be a couple, if he got a good start, and come down flat-footed and all right, like a cat. He got him up so in the matter of ketching flies, and kep' him in practice so constant, that he'd nail a fly every time as fur as he could see him. Smiley said all a frog wanted was education, and he could do 'most anything—and I believe him. Why, I've seen him set Dan'l Webster down here on this floor—Dan'l Webster was the name of the frog—and sing out, "Flies, Dan'l, flies!" and quicker'n you could wink he'd spring straight up and snake a fly off'n the counter there, and flop down on the floor ag'in as solid as a gob of mud, and fall to scratching the side of his head with his hind foot as indifferent as if he hadn't no idea he'd been doin' any more'n any frog might do. You never see a frog so modest and straightfor'ard as he was, for all he was so gifted. And when it come to fair and square jumping on a dead level, he could get over more ground at one straddle than any animal of his breed you ever see. Jumping on a dead level was his strong suit, you understand; and when it come to that, Smiley would ante up money on him as long as he had a red. Smiley was monstrous proud of his frog, and well he might be, for fellers that had traveled and been everywheres, all said he laid over any frog that ever *they* see.

"Well, Smiley kep' the beast in a little lattice box, and he used to fetch him down-town sometimes and lay for a bet. One day a feller—a stranger in the camp, he was—come acrost him with his box, and says:

" 'What might it be that you've got in the box?'

"And Smiley says, sorter indifferent-like, 'It might be a parrot, or it might be a canary, maybe, but it ain't—it's only just a frog.'

"And the feller took it, and looked at it careful, and turned it round this way and that, and says, 'H'm—so 'tis. Well, what's *he* good for?'

" 'Well,' Smiley says, easy and careless, 'he's good enough for *one* thing, I should judge—he can outjump any frog in Calaveras county.'

"The feller took the box again, and took another long, particular look, and give it back to Smiley, and says, very deliberate, 'Well,' he says, 'I don't see no p'ints about that frog that's any better'n any other frog.'

3. THE NOTORIOUS JUMPING FROG OF CALAVERAS COUNTY

" 'Maybe you don't,' Smiley says. 'Maybe you understand frogs and maybe you don't understand 'em; maybe you've had experience, and maybe you ain't only a amature, as it were. Anyways, I've got *my* opinion and I'll risk forty dollars that he can outjump any frog in Calaveras County.'

"And the feller studied a minute, and then says, kinder sad like, 'Well, I'm only a stranger here, and I ain't got no frog; but if I had a frog, I'd bet you.'

"And then Smiley says, 'That's all right—that's all right—if you'll hold my box a minute, I'll go and get you a frog.' And so the feller took the box, and put up his forty dollars along with Smiley's, and set down to wait.

"So he set there a good while thinking and thinking to his-self, and then he got the frog out and prized his mouth open and took a teaspoon and filled him full of quail-shot—filled him pretty near up to his chin—and set him on the floor. Smiley he went to the swamp and slopped around in the mud for a long time, and finally he ketched a frog, and fetched him in, and give him to this feller, and says:

" 'Now, if you're ready, set him alongside of Dan'l, with his fore paws just even with Dan'l's, and I'll give the word.' Then he says, 'One—two—three—*git!*' and him and the feller touched up the frogs from behind, and the new frog hopped off lively, but Dan'l give a heave, and hysted up his shoulders—so—like a Frenchman, but it warn't no use—he couldn't budge; he was planted as solid as a church, and he couldn't no more stir than if he was anchored out. Smiley was a good deal surprised, and he was disgusted too, but he didn't have no idea what the matter was, of course.

"The feller took the money and started away; and when he was going out at the door, he sorter jerked his thumb over his shoulder—so—at Dan'l, and says again, very deliberate, 'Well,' he says, 'I don't see no p'ints about that frog that's any better'n any other frog.'

"Smiley he stood scratching his head and looking down at Dan'l a long time, and at last says, 'I do wonder what in the nation that frog throw'd off for—I wonder if there ain't something the matter with him—he 'pears to look mighty baggy, somehow.' And he ketched Dan'l by the nap of the neck, and hefted him, and says, 'Why blame my cats if he don't weigh five pound!' and turned him upside down and he belched out a double handful of shot. And then he see how it was, and he was the maddest man—he set the frog down and took out after the feller, but he never ketched him. And—"

[Here Simon Wheeler heard his name called from the front yard, and got up to see what was wanted.] And turning to me as he moved away, he said: "Just set where you are, stranger, and rest easy—I ain't going to be gone a second."

But, by your leave, I did not think that a continuation of the history of the enterprising vagabond *Jim* Smiley would be likely to afford me much information concerning the Rev. *Leonidas W.* Smiley, and so I started away.

At the door I met the sociable Wheeler returning, and he buttonholed me and recommenced:

"Well, thish-yer Smiley had a yaller one-eyed cow that didn't have no tail, only just a short stump like a bannanner, and—"

However, lacking both time and inclination, I did not wait to hear about the afflicted cow, but took my leave.

作品赏析

一、马克·吐温与文学创作

马克·吐温，本名叫塞缪尔·朗霍恩·克莱门斯（Samuel Longhorne Celmens，1835—1910），于1835年11月30日出生于密苏里州。"马克·吐温"原本是密西西比河上的一个航行术语，表示水深两寻（mark two），相当于12英尺，船只可以安全通过。马克·吐温早年在密西西比河上做过领航员，或许是这段经历太过难忘，这句水手口中的"行话"后来成了他的笔名。

马克·吐温家境贫寒，12岁时父亲不幸去世，早早便体味到人生的艰辛，一如他后来的半自传体小说的书名表达的那样，是"艰苦岁月"。面对生活的窘

3. THE NOTORIOUS JUMPING FROG OF CALAVERAS COUNTY

迫和压力,他做过印刷学徒、报童、排字工、水手、记者,也卷入了当时席卷美国的淘金热。这些经历使他接触到美国社会的三教九流,熟知社会底层人群的生活,也为他后来的文学创作积累了丰富、鲜活的素材。这也可能是马克·吐温的作品"接地气"的原因之一。

自1865年以短篇小说《卡拉韦拉斯县驰名的跳蛙》在美国文坛崭露头角后,马克·吐温一发不可收拾,发表了大量的短篇小说和长篇小说。其中较著名的作品有《艰苦岁月》(Roughing It)、《镀金时代》(The Gilded Age)、《汤姆·索亚历险记》(The Adventures of Tom Sawyer)、《哈克贝利·费恩历险记》(The Adventures of Huckleberry Finn)、《百万英镑》("The £1,000,000 Bank Note")、《傻瓜威尔逊的悲剧》(The Tragedy of Pudd'nhead Wilson)、《竞选州长》("Running for Governor")、《败坏哈德莱堡的人》("The Man That Corrupted Hadleyburg")等。

马克·吐温的小说在美国文学史上独树一帜,他擅长用口语写作,形成了土语、俚语文体风格,描绘出栩栩如生的众生画像,深深地影响了后世一些文学大家,如安德森、福克纳、海明威等人。马克·吐温从民间故事、方言土语、中西部幽默中汲取营养加以整合提炼,使之成为他运用自如的文学创作的利器。尤其值得一提的是,他把原本粗俗的插科打诨式的幽默打造成极具特色的、标志性的"马克·吐温式"幽默。

讽刺和幽默是马克·吐温作品的一大特点,但他的讽刺和幽默绝不会让人一笑而过,相反却让人深思,甚至让人沉痛,因为他的作品具有深刻的批判性,直指人性、社会的阴暗、虚伪、邪恶、贪婪、暴力等方面。因此,马克·吐温成为19世纪美国现实主义文学的代表人物。

马克·吐温的成就卓著,后人也不吝对他的赞扬,尤其是对于"年轻的"美国文学而言,马克·吐温俨然成了一位可以比肩世界级文豪的巨匠。

马克·吐温在小说《在亚瑟王宫廷里的来自康涅狄格州的杨基佬》(A Connecticut Yankee in King Arthur's Court)中生造了一个词"New Deal"。这个词后来被罗斯福总统看中,用来给他应对美国大萧条的政策命名,翻译为"新政"。他的小说《镀金时代》的标题后来成为一个社会学术语。

马克·吐温的作品时常涉及金钱和财富的主题。在他的短篇小说《百万英镑》《败坏哈德莱堡的人》中，金钱像一块试金石能测试出人性的善与恶、诚实与虚伪。对金钱的贪欲并不分社会阶层，但"体面人"的贪婪则更具复杂性。因为是"体面人"，他们要掩饰自己的贪婪，而同时，因为贪婪，他们又顾不了"体面"，因此"体面人"的贪婪嘴脸最能暴露出人性之丑恶。在人类的社会文化语境下，金钱和财富永远不可能是中性的物质存在，马克·吐温赋予金钱和财富以腐蚀和败坏人性本真的特质。也就是说，金钱对人施加诱惑，使人为之迷狂，背离人的本性，在追逐金钱的过程中不择手段，但是追逐者往往因贪欲造成的悲剧而毁灭。金钱作用于人性中的弱点，先诱惑之，使其失去对自我的把持，受欲望驱使，然后再毁灭之。于是，人间悲剧不停歇地循环上演。正所谓闹哄哄你方唱罢我登场。

除此以外马克·吐温的作品也秉承了西方文学传统的若干要素，其中一点就是对边缘人物、小人物的关注。马克·吐温来自社会底层，这个群体是他最熟悉、倾注笔墨和感情最多的群体。在西方文学作品中，聚焦边缘人物不是单个、孤立的现象，而是存在于几乎所有的文学形式当中，在童话、传奇、民间故事、戏剧、诗歌、小说中都有大量这样的例子。

马克·吐温笔下最成功的边缘人物莫过于脍炙人口的几位儿童形象，如汤姆·索亚和哈克贝利·费恩。他们具有安徒生童话《皇帝的新衣》中那个小男孩的特质：诚实，作为成人世界的局外人，不必参与成人世界的利益交换，也因此能心口如一地保持人性的纯真状态。因此，他们没有违心地苟活，他们是自由的。而马克·吐温笔下的成人世界则被贪婪、邪恶、暴力所左右，结果是放弃诚实选择虚伪，放弃自我而成为金钱、贪欲的奴隶。哈克贝利·费恩的故事从儿童的视角对成人世界的虚伪、残忍做了"流水账"式的记录。而这些记录对于读者、研究者来说既有文学价值，也有社会历史意义。正如历史上一些经典文学作品一样，它不仅仅是杰出的文学文本，同时也是具有丰富内涵的历史文化文本。

特别强调一下，《哈克贝利·费恩历险记》这部小说是最能代表马克·吐温文学创作价值的作品，它的意义超出了单个文学作品的范围，对美国文学影响重大。海明威对这部小说推崇备至，他本人也深受吐温口语体风格的影响。

主流社会的"体面人"总是把"拯救"哈克贝利·费恩视为己任。对哈克实施拯救的理由是他完全违背了社会认可的好孩子的道德行为范式。他抽烟，说谎，逃学，嘲讽宗教信仰。因此，像道格拉斯太太、华生小姐、撒切尔法官等社会体面人物都自认为责无旁贷，应承担起"拯救"哈克的责任。

哈克终于受不了社会对他的全方位"改造"逃走了，跟一个叫吉姆的黑奴一起乘木筏沿密西西比河顺流而下。哈克的世界与他要逃离的世界是两个不同的社会空间——一个是主流的成人世界，另一个是哈克与吉姆的边缘世界。小说通过描述主流社会意图对哈克实施改造和哈克的抵抗，从哈克的边缘视角对主流社会的虚伪、自欺和暴力进行了批判。

文学文本描述的具有纯真美德的边缘人物，如按社会道德规范来评价，多为被主流社会所不齿的悖逆之徒。不仅如此，主流社会（成人世界、上层社会等）还对这些边缘人物进行定义，将其列为需要"拯救"的对象（"拯救"的形式可以是教育、规训或是法律惩罚）。在西方文学作品中，被定义为"堕落者、迷途者"而需要接受"拯救"或"惩罚"的人物形象不在少数，如托马斯·哈代《德伯家的苔丝》(*Tess of the D'Urbervilles*) 中的苔丝、霍桑《红字》(*The Scarlet Letter*) 中的海丝特·白兰。在上述个例中，所谓主流社会以其道德规范制定者的身份裁定哈克之类的人物是道德行为上的堕落者，找出他们的种种"缺陷"，以此作为他们必须接受"拯救"或"惩罚"的理由，同时赋予自己以正当性，让"被拯救者"处于无力反抗的状态。

在马克·吐温设计的边缘视角的反照下，种植园主、虔诚教徒、法官、警长、地方头面人物、势力强大的家族失去了道德的光环，暴露出内里的残忍与不道德：社会正义被枉法、仇杀和私刑所破坏。

马克·吐温在多部作品中都有这样的"翻转"情节——那些被道貌岸然者谴责的"堕落者"实际上拥有一颗"善良的心"，而自诩为"道德"的人却"良知缺损"。这样的逆转不是靠情节安排上的出乎意料或是巧合，而是让分别属于不同社会空间的人各自选择、行动，充分表现，最后真相才浮出水面。

二、故事情节和人物

实际上在马克·吐温的小说《卡拉韦拉斯县驰名的跳蛙》发表之前，加州地区已有"跳蛙"故事流传，而且不止一个版本，有文字版的，也有口头版的。但马克·吐温笔下的"跳蛙"与其他的"跳蛙"很不一样，其独特的叙事、人物刻画、表现手法、语言风格使得这篇小说成为短篇小说中的经典之作，在文学价值上远远超越了那些消遣性的搞笑作品。

这篇小说实际上讲了一个故事中的故事。第一人称叙述者"我"收到一个朋友的信函，受托去找西蒙·惠勒，再去打听一个名叫利奥尼达斯·斯迈利的人，而实际上这个人应该是吉姆·斯迈利。"我"在西部矿区安吉尔小镇的一家客栈的酒吧间找到了西蒙·惠勒，告诉他"我"要打听一个人。西蒙·惠勒是一个唠唠叨叨的家伙，见到"我"居然用椅子把"我"堵在墙角，向"我"讲起一个古怪的人，一个离奇的故事。

1850年左右，一个叫吉姆·斯迈利的人来到了矿区。这个人嗜赌如命，随便什么东西都可以赌一把，随便拉个人都可以赌一盘。猫打架、狗打架都可以成为他打赌的对象，赌马，赌树上的鸟哪一只先飞走。他无所不赌，但运气却好到无法形容，几乎从没有赌输过，堪称当地的"赌王"。为了赌博，他养了好多动物，有狗、猫、公鸡等，五花八门。

最让吉姆·斯迈利得意的是他的那只"驰名"的青蛙。斯迈利从野外捉了一只青蛙，专门训练了三个月。结果，这只青蛙学会了跳跃、翻筋斗。他经常拿它和人赌钱，结果是每次都赢，成了屡战屡胜的"冠军蛙"。而且，它也有一个响当当的名字，叫丹尼尔·韦伯斯特，与一位著名的政客同名。吉姆·斯迈利用这只青蛙赢了许多钱。但最后一次他失败了。那一天，他遇到了一个陌生人，邀请对方用青蛙打赌，而外乡人没有青蛙。趁吉姆·斯迈利到泥塘找青蛙的时机，外乡人给那只驰名的跳蛙灌了一肚子打鹌鹑用的铁砂。比赛的结果毫无悬念，那只新青蛙赢了。一只没有经过训练的青蛙战胜了他的"冠军蛙"，他输掉了一大笔赌金——40美元。当吉姆·斯迈利最后发现外乡人的欺诈诡计时，那位来自东部的外乡人早已没有了踪影。

主要人物吉姆·斯迈利生活在西部小镇。他痴迷赌博到了走火入魔的程度，随便一个什么东西都能成为他赌博的事由。即便是在赌博心强的西部人当中，他也被看作一个"最古怪的人"。此外，他的形象、言谈、举止都属于"粗人"那一类。粗则粗也，但他在赌博中从没有玩过欺骗的手段，靠的都是他的直觉、运气、能力和付出。比如，他会花大力气去训练他的那匹病恹恹的赛马、那条被人看不起的小狗、那只从野外捉来的青蛙。

3. THE NOTORIOUS JUMPING FROG OF CALAVERAS COUNTY

外乡人来自美国东部。他在小说展开到一半时才出场。而且，从小说中看不出他对赌博有什么擅长。他只是被动地卷入了赌博。但是他却靠着自己的诡计赢了比赛。有理由相信，这不是他第一次使用诡计坑害别人，为自己谋利。

西蒙·惠勒，作为当地的消息灵通人士，遇到"我"这个主动送上门的听众来打听一个人，他自然是求之不得。热情过头让这个人物带有些许的滑稽或喜剧色彩。

在阅读这篇小说时，还有若干非人类的角色也值得关注。这些角色包括小说中羸弱的牡马、小猎狗和那只著名的跳蛙。

按照小说的描述，这匹马疾病缠身，得了好几种病，最要命的是得过肺病，其最大的特点是速度慢。但这匹马常常在赌马的比赛中获胜。在比赛中，它会突然迸发出异乎寻常的力量，跑出异乎寻常的速度，原本的病体变得轻盈、灵活、迅速，总是以领先一个头颈的优势惊险获胜。马克·吐温的这种角色刻画似乎赋予了这匹驽马某种"意志力"来配合主人的一次次赌博。所以，吉姆·斯迈利这个赌徒不简单。经他训练、调教过的动物都获得了某种超越自身状况的力量和智慧。

那条小猎狗有一个响当当的名字——"安德鲁·杰克逊"，与美国第七任总统同名。它其貌不扬，但一上赌场就精神倍增，瞬间变为气势汹汹的斗犬。而且，它还会把握时机，等到赌注全押上时，就使出咬后腿弯的绝招，咬住就不松口，一招制敌。可是，有一次，它失败了。另一条狗是一只残疾狗，被圆锯锯掉了后腿。这一下，叫安德鲁·杰克逊的狗傻眼了。它没办法用上自己的绝招。这一战让它颜面扫地，于困惑中因伤心过度而死。这也从侧面折射出社会现实的复杂和险恶。

最厉害的角色当然是那只青蛙。青蛙捕获自野外。它有天赋，学习能力很强，身手敏捷，很快学会了腾转跳跃，翻出的筋斗像油炸面饼圈，落地平稳如猫，成了当地驰名的跳蛙。按马克·吐温的安排，跳蛙还拥有一个著名政治家的名字——"丹尼尔·韦伯斯特"。所以，这只青蛙应该是具有这位政客的一些特质，可以称作"蛙中豪杰"。可是，它最后还是败给了人的诡计，在社会现实中落入他人不择手段设置的陷阱。

小说叙述者"我"也是人物之一。比较之下，"我"与西蒙·惠勒和吉姆·斯迈利的不同之处在于：他们属于西部，他们的言谈举止是西部的，最重要的是他们的气质是西部的，而"我"始终是个外乡人，完成朋友托付的任务之后的第一个念头就是逃离这里。

三、写作技巧和主题

在马克·吐温的小说中，民间幽默故事的痕迹很重。可以说，美国中西部不仅是地理意义上的区域，也是特定的文化意义上的区域。"淘金热"曾在19世纪席卷加州。在淘金客中流传着许多民间故事，其讲述方式夸张（说大话），表现出典型的西部幽默特征。但在马克·吐温之前，这类西部幽默故事也就停留在粗俗笑话的层面上，没有什么深刻的主题，并不包含思考和批判。一个西部幽默故事的惯常模式是这样的：一天，一个猎人外出打猎。突然，在他右前方出现一只熊，左前方出现一只驯鹿。两只动物向他冲了过来。慌乱中，猎人扣响了扳机。射出去的子弹击中了前方的岩石，子弹头蹦成两半飞了出去，一半打死了驯鹿，一半打死了熊。子弹溅起的岩石碎片击中了附近一棵树上松鼠。猎枪的后坐力很大，把猎人震得脚下一滑，跌进了身后的河里。等他从河里爬起来，他发现衣服口袋里都装满了鱼。听者、读者哈哈一笑，但不会有后续的思考。

低俗的笑话是当时美国中西部文化生态的一部分。马克·吐温耳闻目睹了不少。不过，马克·吐温清楚地意识到中西部幽默粗俗浅薄的缺陷，他结合自己的创作实践，在借鉴的同时，深刻思考，去除空洞无聊的搞笑，使之成为文学创作的有效手段和人性剖析、社会批判的利器。

马克·吐温曾有许多广为人知的名言，比如"幽默是一种拯救的力量"。马克·吐温对人性、对社会看得深，看得透，因此他陷入深深的忧虑。如其所言，"人类是唯一会脸红的动物，或是唯一该脸红的动物"。幽默既是一种表现手法，也是一种自嘲和自我解脱的手段。面对生活中的难解之惑，马克·吐温诉诸幽默。

此外，马克·吐温在这篇小说中多处使用比喻的修辞手法。如跳蛙在半空中翻筋斗，"像个油炸面饼圈"，落地稳得"像一只猫"，扭动肩膀"像一个法国佬"，等等。

再则，第一人称"我"的讲述与西蒙·惠勒的讲述交织在一起。西蒙·惠勒讲述的是吉姆·斯迈利的故事。"我"聆听讲述、观察讲述者、复述讲述的过

3. THE NOTORIOUS JUMPING FROG OF CALAVERAS COUNTY

程又是对西蒙·惠勒形象和性格特征勾画的过程。所以，《卡拉韦拉斯县驰名的跳蛙》这个短篇构筑了一个嵌套型的结构，讲述了一个故事里的故事。西蒙·惠勒——一个没有受过什么教育的故事的讲述者，与"我"这个受过教育的叙述者构成了反差。这一点可以从两人讲述时所用的语言看出来。"我"的语言规范，合乎语法，而西蒙·惠勒的语言则完全是口语化的，语法错误很多，透露出他的教育状况和社会地位。此外，通过马克·吐温的描述，读者可以看到，西蒙·惠勒年事已高，秃头，肥胖，性情善良、随和，其最大的特点是唠叨，兜不住话。这样的人物描述，一般来讲是把他放在一个旁观者的位置，他起的作用是去储存和传播听闻到的事情，而不是事件的主导者、参与者。

马克·吐温还设计了一个悬念：朋友托"我"去打听的人叫利奥尼达斯·斯迈利，但西蒙·惠勒讲的故事自始至终是围绕吉姆·斯迈利展开的。利奥尼达斯·斯迈利在故事中没有出现过。这让"我"非常困惑，不得不去猜测：可能是吉姆·斯迈利的名声不好，让朋友羞于提起，因此他杜撰出另外一个叫利奥尼达斯·斯迈利的人，而实际上两个斯迈利是同一个人。但猜测终究不能解开悬念。直到小说结束，"我"听到的都是吉姆·斯迈利的事儿，而没有关于利奥尼达斯·斯迈利的只言片语。至此，悬念仍在，但故事是完整的。不管故事发生在谁身上，叫什么斯迈利并不重要。这样一个西部的故事可能发生在其他地方、其他人物身上，其个别特征也具有相当的普遍性。

这个故事的主题内涵是丰富的。表面上看，小说讲的是一个赌徒嗜赌如命，挖空心思找机会，或用马克·吐温的话，找"茬儿"去赌博的故事。"驰名的跳蛙"造就了美国文学中的经典。一般来讲，成为经典的作品往往具有丰富深刻的意涵，很难说只有单一的、权威的解读。文本是不变的，但是对文本的解释却是多样化的、新意迭出的。自1865年小说发表以来，这篇小说在研究视野中也有不同的解读。

以社会文化视角为切入点，小说的主题可能涉及美国东西部文化价值信念的差异和冲突。[1] 首先，两位主要人物之一的吉姆·斯迈利生活在西部小镇，在气

---

[1] Sydney J. Krause, "The Art and Satire of Twain's 'jumping Frog' Story", *American Short Fiction: Readings and Criticism*, eds. James K. Bowen, Richard Van Der Beets, New York: The Bobbs-Merill Company, Inc.1970, pp. 105-106.

质和行事方式上属于典型的西部人——有些粗陋，有些单纯（或缺心眼）。陌生人来自美国东部。东西部两相比较，东部城市、工业、商业发达，西部则是旷野千里的边疆地区；东部人世故城府，西部人淳朴拙直；东部实用主义盛行，西部尊崇诚实和坚韧。所以，吉姆·斯迈利和外乡人分别代表了他们背后的美国西部和东部，以及两者之间的价值冲突。应该注意到："驰名的跳蛙"之所以败给了新青蛙，不是这只跳蛙不行，而是被东部来的外乡人给塞了一肚子的铁砂，甚至超过了它的体重。吉姆·斯迈利这个西部小镇的"赌王"，输给了外乡人的欺诈伎俩，从某种意义上讲也是西部的诚实输给了东部的虚伪的算计。

一如马克·吐温的其他作品，这篇小说也带有社会批判的意义。马克·吐温的小说始终不乏对人性弱点的揭露和挞伐。而且，马克·吐温经常把人性的弱点与财富、金钱联系在一起来考察。在《卡拉韦拉斯县驰名的跳蛙》这篇小说里，吉姆·斯迈利和外乡人都表现出对金钱的贪欲。最后，外乡人用欺骗的手段把钱赢走了。不难看出，马克·吐温想告诉人们金钱对人的诱惑和腐蚀。马克·吐温更想揭露的是：众人皆为利往，但谁能胜出呢？现实可能是不择手段的人胜出。但马克·吐温对丑恶现象始终不遗余力地加以揭露、批判，表现出了一个来自社会底层的作家的良知。

小说也暗讽了当时美国社会的投机风气。以吉姆·斯迈利为例，如果把他放在19世纪美国西部的背景下来考察。我们可以看到他对赌博的狂热，其实也折射了当时美国社会涌动的投机风潮。"淘金热"就是投机大潮的集中表现。投机本身也带有赌博的性质，过度投机在本质上与赌博更接近。吉姆·斯迈利所在的矿区小镇就是由这些怀揣发财梦的淘金客（投机者）建立起来的。那些淘金客也是某种意义上的"赌徒"，只不过吉姆·斯迈利更加走火入魔罢了。无论是投机式的赌博，还是赌博式的投机，其关键点都是一个"赌"，结果"馅饼"和"陷阱"模糊不清。所以，把这个故事关联到美国投机风潮的背景下来理解，就不难看出这不仅是一个西部赌徒的故事，更是一个美国的故事。而且，故事中的西部因素也造就了独特的美国文学特质。

Suggested Readings

1. Anderson, Frederick & Kenneth M. Sanderson, eds. *Mark Twain: The Critical Heritage*. New York: Barnes and Nobel, 1971.
2. Bloom, Harold, ed. *Mark Twain*. New York: Chelsea House Publishers, 2006.
3. Bowen, James K. & Richard Van Der Beets, eds. *American Short Fiction: Readings and Criticism*. New York: The Bobbs-Merill Company, Inc.1970.
4. Bradley, Sculley, Richmond C. Beatty & E. Hudson Long, eds. *The American Tradition in Literature*. New York: Grosset & Dunlap, Inc., 1967.
5. Brooks, Van Wyck. *The Ordeal of Mark Twain*. New York: Dutton, 1920.
6. Cox, James M. *Mark Twain: The Fate of Humor*. Princeton, NJ: Princeton University Press, 1966.
7. Emerson, Everett. *Mark Twain: A Literary Life*. Philadelphia: University of Pennsylvania Press, 2000.
8. Kirk, Connie Ann. *Mark Twain: A Biography*. Westport, CT: Greenwood, 2004.
9. Rasmussen, R. Kent. *Mark Twain A to Z*. New York: Oxford University Press, 1995.
10. Robinson, Forrest G. *The Cambridge Companion to Mark Twain*. New York: Cambridge University Press, 1995.
11. Smith, Henry Nash. *Mark Twain: A Collection of Critical Essays*. Englewood, NJ: Prentice-Hall, 1963.
12. Twain, Mark. *The Adventures of Huckleberry Finn*. New York: Bantam Classics, 1981.
13. Twain, Mark. *The Adventures of Tom Sawyer*. New York: Bantam Classics, 1981.
14. Twain, Mark. *The Complete Short Stories of Mark Twain*. Ed. Charles Neider. New York: Bantam Classics, 2005.
15. 米歇尔·福柯：《人文科学》，马海良译，载《后现代性的哲学话语：从福柯到赛义德》，汪民安、陈永国、马海良主编，杭州：浙江人民出版社，2001。
16. 爱德华·W. 赛义德：《赛义德自选集》，谢少波、韩刚等译，北京：中国社会科学出版社，1999。

17. 马克·吐温：《哈克贝利·费恩历险记》，张友松、张振先译，北京：中国戏剧出版社，2005年。

18. 马克·吐温：《马克·吐温短篇小说选》，董衡巽等译，北京：中央编译出版社，2010年。

Questions for Reflection

1. What is Mark Twain's main contribution to American literature?

2. How do you understand the humor and satire used by Mark Twain in his short story "The Notorious Jumping Frog of Calaveras County"?

3. If we say that Mark Twain's works contain certain historical significance, how do you understand this statement?

4. Regarding the American society of Twain's time, what can be demonstrated by Gold Rush?

5. List some of Mark Twain's works that deal with the themes of money, wealth and human nature. How does Mark Twain treat these themes?

Questions for Discussion

How do you understand Mark Twain's humor? What is the influence of Twain's humor on American literature?

（查日新　撰写）

4. TO BUILD A FIRE

By Jack London, 1908

Day had broken cold and gray, exceedingly cold and gray, when the man turned aside from the main Yukon trail and climbed the high earth-bank, where a dim and little-travelled trail led eastward through the fat spruce timberland. It was a steep bank, and he paused for breath at the top, excusing the act to himself by looking at his watch. It was nine o'clock. There was no sun nor hint of sun, though there was not a cloud in the sky. It was a clear day, and yet there seemed an intangible pall over the face of things, a subtle gloom that made the day dark, and that was due to the absence of sun. This fact did not worry the man. He was used to the lack of sun. It had been days since he had seen the sun, and he knew that a few more days must pass before that cheerful orb, due south, would just peep above the sky-line and dip immediately from view.

The man flung a look back along the way he had come. The Yukon lay a mile wide and hidden under three feet of ice. On top of this ice were as many feet of snow. It was all pure white, rolling in gentle undulations where the ice-jams of the freeze-up had formed. North and south, as far as his eye could see, it was unbroken white, save for a dark hair-line that curved and twisted from around the spruce-covered island to the south, and that curved and twisted away into the north, where it disappeared behind another spruce-covered island. This dark hair-line was the trail—the main trail—that led south five hundred miles to the Chilcoot Pass, Dyea, and salt water; and that led north seventy miles to Dawson, and still on to the north a thousand miles to Nulato, and finally to St. Michael on Bering Sea, a thousand miles and half a thousand more.

But all this—the mysterious, far-reaching hair-line trail, the absence of sun from the sky, the tremendous cold, and the strangeness and weirdness of it all—made no impression on the man. It was not because he was long used to it. He was a new-comer in the land, a *chechaquo*, and this was his first winter. The trouble with him was that he was without imagination. He was quick and alert in the things of life, but only in the things, and not in the significances. Fifty degrees below zero meant eighty-odd degrees of frost. Such fact impressed him as being cold and uncomfortable, and that was all. It did not lead him to meditate upon his frailty as a creature of temperature, and upon man's frailty in general, able only to live within certain narrow limits of heat and cold; and from there on it did not lead him to the conjectural field of immortality and man's place in the universe. Fifty degrees below zero stood for a bite of frost that hurt and that must be guarded against by the use of mittens, ear-flaps, warm moccasins, and thick socks. Fifty degrees below zero was to him just precisely fifty degrees below zero. That there should be anything more to it than that was a thought that never entered his head.

As he turned to go on, he spat speculatively. There was a sharp, explosive crackle that startled him. He spat again. And again, in the air, before it could fall to the snow, the spittle crackled. He knew that at fifty below spittle crackled on the snow, but this spittle had crackled in the air. Undoubtedly it was colder than fifty below—how much colder he did not know. But the temperature did not matter. He was bound for the old claim on the left fork of Henderson Creek, where the boys were already. They had come over across the divide from the Indian Creek country, while he had come the roundabout way to take a look at the possibilities of getting out logs in the spring from the islands in the Yukon.

4. TO BUILD A FIRE

He would be in to camp by six o'clock; a bit after dark, it was true, but the boys would be there, a fire would be going, and a hot supper would be ready. As for lunch, he pressed his hand against the protruding bundle under his jacket. It was also under his shirt, wrapped up in a handkerchief and lying against the naked skin. It was the only way to keep the biscuits from freezing. He smiled agreeably to himself as he thought of those biscuits, each cut open and sopped in bacon grease, and each enclosing a generous slice of fried bacon.

He plunged in among the big spruce trees. The trail was faint. A foot of snow had fallen since the last sled had passed over, and he was glad he was without a sled, travelling light. In fact, he carried nothing but the lunch wrapped in the handkerchief. He was surprised, however, at the cold. It certainly was cold, he concluded, as he rubbed his numbed nose and cheek-bones with his mittened hand. He was a warm-whiskered man, but the hair on his face did not protect the high cheek-bones and the eager nose that thrust itself aggressively into the frosty air.

At the man's heels trotted a dog, a big native husky, the proper wolf-dog, grey-coated and without any visible or temperamental difference from its brother, the wild wolf. The animal was depressed by the tremendous cold. It knew that it was no time for traveling. Its instinct told it a truer tale than was told to the man by the man's judgment. In reality, it was not merely colder than fifty below zero; it was colder than sixty below, than seventy below. It was seventy-five below zero. Since the freezingpoint is thirty-two above zero, it meant that one hundred and seven degrees of frost obtained. The dog did not know anything about thermometers. Possibly in its brain there was no sharp consciousness of a condition of very cold such as was in the man's brain. But the brute had its instinct. It experienced a vague but menacing apprehension that subdued it and made it slink along at the man's heels, and that made it question eagerly every unwonted movement of the man as if expecting him to go into camp or to seek shelter somewhere and build a fire. The dog had learned fire, and it wanted fire, or else to burrow under the snow and cuddle its warmth away from the air.

The frozen moisture of its breathing had settled on its fur in a fine powder of frost, and especially were its jowls, muzzle, and eyelashes whitened by its crystalled breath. The man's red beard and mustache were likewise frosted, but more solidly, the deposit taking the form of ice and increasing with every warm, moist breath he exhaled. Also, the man was chewing tobacco, and the muzzle of ice held his lips so rigidly that he was unable to clear his chin when he expelled the juice. The result was that a crystal beard of the colour and solidity of amber was increasing its length on his chin. If he fell down it would shatter itself, like glass, into brittle fragments. But he did not mind the appendage. It was the penalty all tobacco-chewers paid in that country, and he had been out before in two cold snaps. They had not been so cold as this, he knew, but by the spirit thermometer at Sixty Mile he knew they had been registered at fifty below and at fifty-five.

He held on through the level stretch of woods for several miles, crossed a wide flat of nigger-heads, and dropped down a bank to the frozen bed of a small stream. This was Henderson Creek, and he knew he was ten miles from the forks. He looked at his watch. It was ten o'clock. He was making four miles an hour, and he calculated that he would arrive at the forks at half-past twelve. He decided to celebrate that event by eating his lunch there.

The dog dropped in again at his heels, with a tail drooping discouragement, as the man swung along the creek-bed. The furrow of the old sled-trail was plainly visible, but a dozen inches of snow covered the marks of the last runners. In a month no man had come up or down that silent creek. The man held steadily on. He was not much given to thinking, and just then particularly he had nothing to think about save that he would eat lunch at the forks and that at six o'clock he would be in camp with the boys. There was nobody to talk to; and, had there been, speech would have been impossible because of the ice-

4. TO BUILD A FIRE

muzzle on his mouth. So he continued monotonously to chew tobacco and to increase the length of his amber beard.

Once in a while the thought reiterated itself that it was very cold and that he had never experienced such cold. As he walked along he rubbed his cheek-bones and nose with the back of his mittened hand. He did this automatically, now and again changing hands. But rub as he would, the instant he stopped his cheek-bones went numb, and the following instant the end of his nose went numb. He was sure to frost his cheeks; he knew that, and experienced a pang of regret that he had not devised a nose-strap of the sort Bud wore in cold snaps. Such a strap passed across the cheeks, as well, and saved them. But it didn't matter much, after all. What were frosted cheeks? A bit painful, that was all; they were never serious.

Empty as the man's mind was of thoughts, he was keenly observant, and he noticed the changes in the creek, the curves and bends and timber-jams, and always he sharply noted where he placed his feet. Once, coming around a bend, he shied abruptly, like a startled horse, curved away from the place where he had been walking, and retreated several paces back along the trail. The creek he knew was frozen clear to the bottom—no creek could contain water in that arctic winter—but he knew also that there were springs that bubbled out from the hillsides and ran along under the snow and on top the ice of the creek. He knew that the coldest snaps never froze these springs, and he knew likewise their danger. They were traps. They hid pools of water under the snow that might be three inches deep, or three feet. Sometimes a skin of ice half an inch thick covered them, and in turn was covered by the snow. Sometimes there were alternate layers of water and ice-skin, so that when one broke through he kept on breaking through for a while, sometimes wetting himself to the waist.

That was why he had shied in such panic. He had felt the give under his feet and heard the crackle of a snow-hidden ice-skin. And to get his feet wet in such a temperature meant trouble and danger. At the very least it meant delay, for he would be forced to stop and build a fire, and under its protection to bare his feet while he dried his socks and moccasins. He stood and studied the creek-bed and its banks, and decided that the flow of water came from the right. He reflected a while, rubbing his nose and cheeks, then skirted to the left, stepping gingerly and testing the footing for each step. Once clear of the danger, he took a fresh chew of tobacco and swung along at his four-mile gait.

In the course of the next two hours he came upon several similar traps. Usually the snow above the hidden pools had a sunken, candied appearance that advertised the danger. Once again, however, he had a close call; and once, suspecting danger, he compelled the dog to go on in front. The dog did not want to go. It hung back until the man shoved it forward, and then it went quickly across the white, unbroken surface. Suddenly it broke through, floundered to one side, and got away to firmer footing. It had wet its forefeet and legs, and almost immediately the water that clung to it turned to ice. It made quick efforts to lick the ice off its legs, then dropped down in the snow and began to bite out the ice that had formed between the toes. This was a matter of instinct. To permit the ice to remain would mean sore feet. It did not know this, it merely obeyed the mysterious prompting that arose from the deep crypts of its being. But the man knew, having achieved a judgment on the subject, and he removed the mitten from his right hand and helped tear out the ice-particles. He did not expose his fingers more than a minute, and was astonished at the swift numbness that smote them. It certainly was cold. He pulled on the mitten hastily, and beat the hand savagely across his chest.

At twelve o'clock the day was at its brightest. Yet the sun was too far south on its winter journey to clear the horizon. The bulge of the earth intervened between it and Henderson Creek, where the man walked under a clear sky at noon and cast no shadow. At half-past twelve, to the minute, he arrived at the forks of the creek. He was pleased at the speed he had made. If he kept it up, he would certainly be with the boys by six. He unbuttoned his jacket and

4. TO BUILD A FIRE

shirt and drew forth his lunch. The action consumed no more than a quarter of a minute, yet in that brief moment the numbness laid hold of the exposed fingers. He did not put the mitten on, but, instead, struck the fingers a dozen sharp smashes against his leg. Then he sat down on a snow-covered log to eat. The sting that followed upon the striking of his fingers against his leg ceased so quickly that he was startled, he had had no chance to take a bite of biscuit. He struck the fingers repeatedly and returned them to the mitten, baring the other hand for the purpose of eating. He tried to take a mouthful, but the ice-muzzle prevented. He had forgotten to build a fire and thaw out. He chuckled at his foolishness, and as he chuckled he noted the numbness creeping into the exposed fingers. Also, he noted that the stinging which had first come to his toes when he sat down was already passing away. He wondered whether the toes were warm or numbed. He moved them inside the moccasins and decided that they were numbed.

He pulled the mitten on hurriedly and stood up. He was a bit frightened. He stamped up and down until the stinging returned into the feet. It certainly was cold, was his thought. That man from Sulphur Creek had spoken the truth when telling how cold it sometimes got in the country. And he had laughed at him at the time! That showed one must not be too sure of things. There was no mistake about it, it *was* cold. He strode up and down, stamping his feet and threshing his arms, until reassured by the returning warmth. Then he got out matches and proceeded to make a fire. From the undergrowth, where high water of the previous spring had lodged a supply of seasoned twigs, he got his firewood. Working carefully from a small beginning, he soon had a roaring fire, over which he thawed the ice from his face and in the protection of which he ate his biscuits. For the moment the cold of space was outwitted. The dog took satisfaction in the fire, stretching out close enough for warmth and far enough away to escape being singed.

When the man had finished, he filled his pipe and took his comfortable time over a smoke. Then he pulled on his mittens, settled the earflaps of his cap firmly about his ears, and took the creek trail up the left fork. The dog was disappointed and yearned back toward the fire. This man did not know cold. Possibly all the generations of his ancestry had been ignorant of cold, of real cold, of cold one hundred and seven degrees below freezing point. But the dog knew; all its ancestry knew, and it had inherited the knowledge. And it knew that it was not good to walk abroad in such fearful cold. It was the time to lie snug in a hole in the snow and wait for a curtain of cloud to be drawn across the face of outer space whence this cold came. On the other hand, there was no keen intimacy between the dog and the man. The one was the toil-slave of the other, and the only caresses it had ever received were the caresses of the whiplash and of harsh and menacing throat-sounds that threatened the whiplash. So the dog made no effort to communicate its apprehension to the man. It was not concerned in the welfare of the man; it was for its own sake that it yearned back toward the fire. But the man whistled, and spoke to it with the sound of whiplashes, and the dog swung in at the man's heels and followed after.

The man took a chew of tobacco and proceeded to start a new amber beard. Also, his moist breath quickly powdered with white his mustache, eyebrows, and lashes. There did not seem to be so many springs on the left fork of the Henderson, and for half an hour the man saw no signs of any. And then it happened. At a place where there were no signs, where the soft, unbroken snow seemed to advertise solidity beneath, the man broke through. It was not deep. He wetted himself halfway to the knees before he floundered out to the firm crust.

He was angry, and cursed his luck aloud. He had hoped to get into camp with the boys at six o'clock, and this would delay him an hour, for he would have to build a fire and dry out his foot-gear. This was imperative at that low temperature—he knew that much; and he turned aside to the bank, which he

4. TO BUILD A FIRE

climbed. On top, tangled in the underbrush about the trunks of several small spruce trees, was a high-water deposit of dry firewood—sticks and twigs, principally, but also larger portions of seasoned branches and fine, dry, last-year's grasses. He threw down several large pieces on top of the snow. This served for a foundation and prevented the young flame from drowning itself in the snow it otherwise would melt. The flame he got by touching a match to a small shred of birch bark that he took from his pocket. This burned even more readily than paper. Placing it on the foundation, he fed the young flame with wisps of dry grass and with the tiniest dry twigs.

He worked slowly and carefully, keenly aware of his danger. Gradually, as the flame grew stronger, he increased the size of the twigs with which he fed it. He squatted in the snow, pulling the twigs out from their entanglement in the brush and feeding directly to the flame. He knew there must be no failure. When it is seventy-five below zero, a man must not fail in his first attempt to build a fire—that is, if his feet are wet. If his feet are dry, and he fails, he can run along the trail for half a mile and restore his circulation. But the circulation of wet and freezing feet cannot be restored by running when it is seventy-five below. No matter how fast he runs, the wet feet will freeze the harder.

All this the man knew. The old-timer on Sulphur Creek had told him about it the previous fall, and now he was appreciating the advice. Already all sensation had gone out of his feet. To build the fire he had been forced to removed[1] his mittens, and the fingers had quickly gone numb. His pace of four miles an hour had kept his heart pumping blood to the surface of his body and to all the extremities. But the instant he stopped, the action of the pump eased down. The cold of space smote the unprotected tip of the planet, and he, being on that unprotected tip, received the full force of the blow. The blood of his body recoiled before it. The blood was alive, like the dog, and like the dog it wanted to hide away and cover itself up from the fearful cold. So long as he

---

1 原文为removed，此处疑为remove。

walked four miles an hour, he pumped that blood, willy-nilly, to the surface; but now, it ebbed away and sank down into the recesses of his body. The extremities were the first to feel its absence. His wet feet froze the faster, and his exposed fingers numbed the faster; though they had not yet begun to freeze. Nose and cheeks were already freezing, while the skin of all his body chilled as it lost its blood.

But he was safe. Toes and nose and cheeks would be only touched by the frost, for the fire was beginning to burn with strength. He was feeding it with twigs the size of his finger. In another minute he would be able to feed it with branches the size of his wrist, and then he could remove his wet foot-gear and, while it dried, he could keep his naked feet warm by the fire, rubbing them at first, of course, with snow. The fire was a success. He was safe. He remembered the advice of the old-timer on Sulphur Creek, and smiled. The old-timer had been very serious in laying down the law that no man must travel alone in the Klondike after fifty below. Well, here he was; he had had the accident; he was alone; and he had saved himself. Those old-timers were rather womanish, some of them, he thought. All a man had to do was to keep his head; and he was all right. Any man who was a man could travel alone. But it was surprising, the rapidity with which his cheeks and nose were freezing. And he had not thought his fingers could go lifeless in so short a time. Lifeless they were, for he could scarcely make them move together to grip a twig, and they seemed remote from his body and from him. When he touched a twig, he had to look and see whether or not he had hold of it. The wires were pretty well down between him and his finger-ends.

All of which counted for little. There was the fire, snapping and crackling and promising life with every dancing flame. He started to untie his moccasins. They were coated with ice; the thick German socks were like sheaths of iron halfway to the knees; and the mocassin strings were like rods of steel all twisted and knotted as by some conflagration. For a moment he tugged with his numbed fingers, then, realizing the folly of it, he drew his sheath-knife.

But before he could cut the strings, it happened. It was his own fault or, rather, his mistake. He should not have built the fire under the spruce tree. He should have built it in the open. But it had been easier to pull the twigs from the brush and drop them directly on the fire. Now the tree under which he had done this carried a weight of snow on its boughs. No wind had blown for weeks, and each bough was fully freighted. Each time he had pulled a twig he had communicated a slight agitation to the tree—an imperceptible agitation, so far as he was concerned, but an agitation sufficient to bring about the disaster. High up in the tree one bough capsized its load of snow. This fell on the boughs beneath, capsizing them. This process continued, spreading out and involving the whole tree. It grew like an avalanche, and it descended without warning upon the man and the fire, and the fire was blotted out! Where it had burned was a mantle of fresh and disordered snow.

The man was shocked. It was as though he had just heard his own sentence of death. For a moment he sat and stared at the spot where the fire had been. Then he grew very calm. Perhaps the old-timer on Sulphur Creek was right. If he had only had a trail-mate he would have been in no danger now. The trail-mate could have built the fire. Well, it was up to him to build the fire over again, and this second time there must be no failure. Even if he succeeded, he would most likely lose some toes. His feet must be badly frozen by now, and there would be some time before the second fire was ready.

Such were his thoughts, but he did not sit and think them. He was busy all the time they were passing through his mind. He made a new foundation for a fire, this time in the open, where no treacherous tree could blot it out. Next, he gathered dry grasses and tiny twigs from the high-water flotsam. He could not bring his fingers together to pull them out, but he was able to gather them by the handful. In this way he got many rotten twigs and bits of green moss that were undesirable, but it was the best he could do. He worked methodically, even collecting an armful of the larger branches to be used later when the fire gathered strength. And all the while the dog sat and watched him, a certain yearning wistfulness in its eyes, for it looked upon him as the fire-provider, and the fire was slow in coming.

When all was ready, the man reached in his pocket for a second piece of birch bark. He knew the bark was there, and, though he could not feel it with his fingers, he could hear its crisp rustling as he fumbled for it. Try as he would, he could not clutch hold of it. And all the time, in his consciousness, was the knowledge that each instant his feet were freezing. This thought tended to put him in a panic, but he fought against it and kept calm. He pulled on his mittens with his teeth, and threshed his arms back and forth, beating his hands with all his might against his sides. He did this sitting down, and he stood up to do it; and all the while the dog sat in the snow, its wolf-brush of a tail curled around warmly over its forefeet, its sharp wolf-ears pricked forward intently as it watched the man. And the man, as he beat and threshed with his arms and hands, felt a great surge of envy as he regarded the creature that was warm and secure in its natural covering.

After a time he was aware of the first far-away signals of sensation in his beaten fingers. The faint tingling grew stronger till it evolved into a stinging ache that was excruciating, but which the man hailed with satisfaction. He stripped the mitten from his right hand and fetched forth the birch bark. The exposed fingers were quickly going numb again. Next he brought out his bunch of sulphur matches. But the tremendous cold had already driven the life out of his fingers. In his effort to separate one match from the others, the whole bunch fell in the snow. He tried to pick it out of the snow, but failed. The dead fingers could neither touch nor clutch. He was very careful. He drove the thought of his freezing feet, and nose, and cheeks, out of his mind, devoting his whole soul to the matches. He watched, using the sense of vision in place of touch, and when he saw his fingers on each side the bunch, he closed them—that is, he willed to

4. TO BUILD A FIRE

close them, for the wires were drawn, and the fingers did not obey. He pulled the mitten on the right hand, and beat it fiercely against his knee. Then, with both mittened hands he scooped the bunch of matches, along with much snow, into his lap. Yet he was no better off.

After some manipulation he managed to get the bunch between the heels of his mittened hands. In this fashion he carried it to his mouth. The ice crackled and snapped when by a violent effort he opened his mouth. He drew the lower jaw in, curled the upper lip out of the way, and scraped the bunch with his upper teeth in order to separate a match. He succeeded in getting one, which he dropped on his lap. He was no better off. He could not pick it up. Then he devised a way. He picked it up in his teeth and scratched it on his leg. Twenty times he scratched before he succeeded in lighting it. As it flamed he held it with his teeth to the birch bark. But the burning brimstone went up his nostrils and into his lungs, causing him to cough spasmodically. The match fell into the snow and went out.

The old-timer on Sulphur Creek was right, he thought in the moment of controlled despair that ensued: after fifty below, a man should travel with a partner. He beat his hands, but failed in exciting any sensation. Suddenly he bared both hands, removing the mittens with his teeth. He caught the whole bunch between the heels of his hands. His arm-muscles not being frozen enabled him to press the hand-heels tightly against the matches. Then he scratched the bunch along his leg. It flared into flame, seventy sulphur matches at once! There was no wind to blow them out. He kept his head to one side to escape the strangling fumes, and held the blazing bunch to the birch bark. As he so held it, he became aware of sensation in his hand. His flesh was burning. He could smell it. Deep down below the surface he could feel it. The sensation developed into pain that grew acute. And still he endured it, holding the flame of the matches clumsily to the bark that would not light readily because his own burning hands were in the way, absorbing most of the flame.

At last, when he could endure no more, he jerked his hands apart. The blazing matches fell sizzling into the snow, but the birch bark was alight. He began laying dry grasses and the tiniest twigs on the flame. He could not pick and choose, for he had to lift the fuel between the heels of his hands. Small pieces of rotten wood and green moss clung to the twigs, and he bit them off as well as he could with his teeth. He cherished the flame carefully and awkwardly. It meant life, and it must not perish. The withdrawal of blood from the surface of his body now made him begin to shiver, and he grew more awkward. A large piece of green moss fell squarely on the little fire. He tried to poke it out with his fingers, but his shivering frame made him poke too far, and he disrupted the nucleus of the little fire, the burning grasses and tiny twigs separating and scattering. He tried to poke them together again, but in spite of the tenseness of the effort, his shivering got away with him, and the twigs were hopelessly scattered. Each twig gushed a puff of smoke and went out. The fire-provider had failed. As he looked apathetically about him, his eyes chanced on the dog, sitting across the ruins of the fire from him, in the snow, making restless, hunching movements, slightly lifting one forefoot and then the other, shifting its weight back and forth on them with wistful eagerness.

The sight of the dog put a wild idea into his head. He remembered the tale of the man, caught in a blizzard, who killed a steer and crawled inside the carcass, and so was saved. He would kill the dog and bury his hands in the warm body until the numbness went out of them. Then he could build another fire. He spoke to the dog, calling it to him; but in his voice was a strange note of fear that frightened the animal, who had never known the man to speak in such way before. Something was the matter, and its suspicious nature sensed danger—it knew not what danger, but somewhere, somehow, in its brain arose an apprehension of the man. It flattened its ears down at the sound of the man's voice, and its restless, hunching movements and the liftings and shiftings of its forefeet became more pronounced; but it would not come to the man. He got on

4. TO BUILD A FIRE

his hands and knees and crawled toward the dog. This unusual posture again excited suspicion, and the animal sidled mincingly away.

The man sat up in the snow for a moment and struggled for calmness. Then he pulled on his mittens, by means of his teeth, and got upon his feet. He glanced down at first in order to assure himself that he was really standing up, for the absence of sensation in his feet left him unrelated to the earth. His erect position in itself started to drive the webs of suspicion from the dog's mind; and when he spoke peremptorily, with the sound of whiplashes in his voice, the dog rendered its customary allegiance and came to him. As it came within reaching distance, the man lost his control. His arms flashed out to the dog, and he experienced genuine surprise when he discovered that his hands could not clutch, that there was neither bend nor feeling in the lingers. He had forgotten for the moment that they were frozen and that they were freezing more and more. All this happened quickly, and before the animal could get away, he encircled its body with his arms. He sat down in the snow, and in this fashion held the dog, while it snarled and whined and struggled.

But it was all he could do, hold its body encircled in his arms and sit there. He realized that he could not kill the dog. There was no way to do it. With his helpless hands he could neither draw nor hold his sheath-knife nor throttle the animal. He released it, and it plunged wildly away, with tail between its legs, and still snarling. It halted forty feet away and surveyed him curiously, with ears sharply pricked forward. The man looked down at his hands in order to locate them, and found them hanging on the ends of his arms. It struck him as curious that one should have to use his eyes in order to find out where his hands were. He began threshing his arms back and forth, beating the mittened hands against his sides. He did this for five minutes, violently, and his heart pumped enough blood up to the surface to put a stop to his shivering. But no sensation was aroused in the hands. He had an impression that they hung like weights on the ends of his arms, but when he tried to run the impression down, he could not find it.

A certain fear of death, dull and oppressive, came to him. This fear quickly became poignant as he realized that it was no longer a mere matter of freezing his fingers and toes, or of losing his hands and feet, but that it was a matter of life and death with the chances against him. This threw him into a panic, and he turned and ran up the creek-bed along the old, dim trail. The dog joined in behind and kept up with him. He ran blindly, without intention, in fear such as he had never known in his life. Slowly, as he plowed and floundered through the snow, he began to see things again—the banks of the creek, the old timber-jams, the leafless aspens, and the sky. The running made him feel better. He did not shiver. Maybe, if he ran on, his feet would thaw out; and, anyway, if he ran far enough, he would reach camp and the boys. Without doubt he would lose some fingers and toes and some of his face; but the boys would take care of him, and save the rest of him when he got there. And at the same time there was another thought in his mind that said he would never get to the camp and the boys; that it was too many miles away, that the freezing had too great a start on him, and that he would soon be stiff and dead. This thought he kept in the background and refused to consider. Sometimes it pushed itself forward and demanded to be heard, but he thrust it back and strove to think of other things.

It struck him as curious that he could run at all on feet so frozen that he could not feel them when they struck the earth and took the weight of his body. He seemed to himself to skim along the surface, and to have no connexion with the earth. Somewhere he had once seen a winged Mercury, and he wondered if Mercury felt as he felt when skimming over the earth.

His theory of running until he reached camp and the boys had one flaw in it: he lacked the endurance. Several times he stumbled, and finally he tottered, crumpled up, and fell. When he tried to rise, he failed. He must sit and rest, he decided, and next time he would merely walk and keep on going. As he sat and regained his breath, he noted that he was feeling quite warm and comfortable.

4. TO BUILD A FIRE

He was not shivering, and it even seemed that a warm glow had come to his chest and trunk. And yet, when he touched his nose or cheeks, there was no sensation. Running would not thaw them out. Nor would it thaw out his hands and feet. Then the thought came to him that the frozen portions of his body must be extending. He tried to keep this thought down, to forget it, to think of something else; he was aware of the panicky feeling that it caused, and he was afraid of the panic. But the thought asserted itself, and persisted, until it produced a vision of his body totally frozen. This was too much, and he made another wild run along the trail. Once he slowed down to a walk, but the thought of the freezing extending itself made him run again.

And all the time the dog ran with him, at his heels. When he fell down a second time, it curled its tail over its forefeet and sat in front of him, facing him, curiously eager and intent. The warmth and security of the animal angered him, and he cursed it till it flattened down its ears appeasingly. This time the shivering came more quickly upon the man. He was losing in his battle with the frost. It was creeping into his body from all sides. The thought of it drove him on, but he ran no more than a hundred feet, when he staggered and pitched headlong. It was his last panic. When he had recovered his breath and control, he sat up and entertained in his mind the conception of meeting death with dignity. However, the conception did not come to him in such terms. His idea of it was that he had been making a fool of himself, running around like a chicken with its head cut off—such was the simile that occurred to him. Well, he was bound to freeze anyway, and he might as well take it decently. With this new-found peace of mind came the first glimmerings of drowsiness. A good idea, he thought, to sleep off to death. It was like taking an anaesthetic. Freezing was not so bad as people thought. There were lots worse ways to die.

He pictured the boys finding his body next day. Suddenly he found himself with them, coming along the trail and looking for himself. And, still with them, he came around a turn in the trail and found himself lying in the snow. He did not belong with himself any more, for even then he was out of himself, standing with the boys and looking at himself in the snow. It certainly was cold, was his thought. When he got back to the States he could tell the folks what real cold was. He drifted on from this to a vision of the old-timer on Sulphur Creek. He could see him quite clearly, warm and comfortable, and smoking a pipe.

'You were right, old hoss; you were right,' the man mumbled to the old-timer of Sulphur Creek.

Then the man drowsed off into what seemed to him the most comfortable and satisfying sleep he had ever known. The dog sat facing him and waiting. The brief day drew to a close in a long, slow twilight. There were no signs of a fire to be made, and, besides, never in the dog's experience had it known a man to sit like that in the snow and make no fire. As the twilight drew on, its eager yearning for the fire mastered it, and with a great lifting and shifting of forefeet, it whined softly, then flattened its ears down in anticipation of being chidden by the man. But the man remained silent. Later, the dog whined loudly. And still later it crept close to the man and caught the scent of death. This made the animal bristle and back away. A little longer it delayed, howling under the stars that leaped and danced and shone brightly in the cold sky. Then it turned and trotted up the trail in the direction of the camp it knew, where were the other food-providers and fire-providers.

作品赏析

一、作者与情节

杰克·伦敦（Jack London，1876—1916）是近代美国伟大的现实主义作家，也被称为"美国无产阶级文学之父"。

他的原名叫作约翰·格里菲斯·伦敦（John Griffith London），1876年出生于旧金山，1916年在他位于加州的"美丽农场"病逝，年仅40岁。

4. TO BUILD A FIRE

　　杰克·伦敦的母亲来自一个非常富有的家庭，在婚前生下杰克·伦敦，他的父亲则身份不明。在他出生的那一年，他母亲嫁给了残废退伍军人约翰·伦敦。他家几经搬迁，最后定居于奥克兰市。

　　杰克·伦敦家境贫寒，少年时被迫去工厂做工。他从事过各种体力劳动，也曾去日本海岸捕猎海豹。1893年回国后，曾参加失业工人前往华盛顿请愿的游行。之后到处流浪，还曾进过监狱。1896年，他考入加州大学伯克利分校，但由于经济拮据，在1897年辍学。

　　为了避免一辈子从事体力劳动，杰克·伦敦勤奋写作，力图成为一名作家。初期的努力并没有获得成功。大学辍学后，在克朗代克淘金热潮中，21岁的他来到育空地区。后来，他以育空地区为背景创作了若干作品，声名鹊起，成为一名职业作家。

　　1904年，他曾到日本对日俄战争进行报道。四个月内，他被日本政府逮捕三次，最后一次还是在老罗斯福总统介入后才获得释放。

　　杰克·伦敦很早就接触了社会主义思想，经常到街头宣传，被人们称为"奥克兰市的社会主义男孩"。而且，他还代表社会主义政党多次参加政治竞选。他成为知名作家后，也经常利用自己的名望，大力宣传社会主义。

　　杰克·伦敦还在争取女性选举权、推动禁酒运动、反对虐待动物等方面作出了贡献。此外，他还是电影业和商品代言方面的先锋。

　　他对农业很感兴趣，曾买下一块近7000亩的土地，将其命名为"美丽农场"。他想将农场建设成一个能自给自足的世外桃源。他努力写作的部分原因在于他需要挣钱来支撑这个农场。

　　基于他在育空地区、太平洋和城市的生活体验，杰克·伦敦的作品主要探讨了人与大自然的斗争以及人与社会的斗争。前者属于自然主义文学，描写在原始艰苦的自然环境中，人或者动物强大的求生本能和付出的艰巨的努力。后者属于现实主义文学，描写工人阶级的痛苦和挣扎，揭露资本主义社会的黑暗。

　　杰克·伦敦深受尼采、马克思、达尔文、斯宾塞等思想家的影响。这些哲学家的思想在他的作品中共存，但是，占据主导地位的常是个人主义思想，尤其是尼采的超人主义。

　　杰克·伦敦是个多产的作家，共创作了近20部长篇小说、100多部短篇小说，以及一些其他类型的作品。其中，著名的中短篇小说有《野性的呼唤》（*The Call of the Wild*）、《生火》、《热爱生命》（"Love of Life"）和《北方的奥德赛》（"An Odyssey of the North"）；著名的长篇小说有《白牙》（*White Fang*）、《海狼》（*The Sea-Wolf*）、《铁蹄》（*The Iron Heel*）和《马丁·伊登》（*Martin Eden*）。另外，长篇报告文学作品《深渊中的人们》（*The People of the Abyss*）和论文集《阶级间的战争》（*The War of the Classes*）也很有价值。

小说《生火》讲述了主人公和他的几个儿子在严寒中前往亨德森河河汊左岸的一处已经开发的地方的故事。他的儿子们从印第安河一带出发，应该已经到达营地，而他则绕道去调研是否可能在来年春天将育空河中岛屿上的木材运出去销售。

上午9点，他已经调查完毕，动身前往营地。他爬上育空河的河岸，朝着亨德森河走去。一条狗陪伴着他。

他于10点到达亨德森河。他一路上小心翼翼，因为虽然河流已经结冰，但是两岸山坡的泉水可能会顺势流到河中，在冰面上形成积水。他遇到几处危险，不过都安全避开了。有一次，他把狗推过去试探，结果狗打湿了前腿，意味着危险。

正如计划的那样，他在12点半到达亨德森河的河汊。他生了一堆火，吃完午饭，抽了一会儿烟斗，起身继续赶路。

亨德森河左边的岔流仿佛很安全，半小时内没有发现任何泉水的痕迹。但是，在一个没有丝毫异样的地方，他突然踩进一个水坑，打湿了半条裤腿。

他迅速上岸生火取暖，以便烤干打湿的裤腿。火堆搭在树下，他从树下的灌木丛抽取枯枝直接烧火。火势越烧越旺，他似乎化险为夷。此时，他又想起那位来自硫酸河的老前辈关于不要独自旅行的警告，心中不免感到几分得意。突然，树上的积雪塌落下来，将篝火扑灭了。原来抽取树枝破坏了树上积雪的稳定性。

震惊过后，他很快恢复镇静，到空旷处重新生火。但刺骨的严寒已使他的手指变得麻木。好不容易将桦树皮和火柴掏出来，火柴却掉到雪地上。他用两个手掌合抔起火柴，用牙齿咬住一根火柴在腿上划燃。但是，烟火冲进他的鼻腔，他只好放弃。

最后，他脱掉手套，用两只手握住一把火柴，在腿上全部划燃，将桦树皮点燃。一块很大的青苔掉进火堆。他试图取出青苔，又搅散了火芯，火堆熄灭了。

此时，他想杀掉狗来暖手，但是狗侧身跑开了。他站起来恢复专横的语气后，狗顺从地来到他身边。但他意识到自己已经没有能力杀死这条狗了，只好将它放开。

他感到非常恐惧，开始狂奔，希望能够恢复知觉，或者能够跑到营地。但是，他很快累倒在地。休息一会后，他重新开始奔跑，但很快再次倒下。

至此，他彻底放弃挣扎，改而思考如何有尊严地面对死亡。他开始产生幻觉，昏睡了过去。他的狗嗅到死亡的味道，在寂静的雪野，望着星空凄凉地嚎叫。它等了一会儿，孤单地朝营地奔去。

二、人物与主题

这部小说的主要人物只有主人公一人。不过，他的狗、大自然以及那位来自硫酸河的老前辈，也是重要的角色。

主人公应该是一个美国人。他之前经历过两次极寒天气，气温分别是零下46摄氏度和零下47摄氏度。这是他第一次到育空地区。他似乎思想简单，情感淡薄。最初，这位男子对独自旅行很自信，甚至在初步生火成功后还有点自鸣得意。面对各种问题和危险时，他镇定、理智。生火无望，他为了生存进行了勇敢的搏斗。最后，面对死亡，他留住了自己的尊严。

大自然美丽动人，但同时也冷漠危险。主人公推断当时的气温至少零下58摄氏度。一旦停止走动，只需片刻，脸庞和手脚就会失去知觉。同时，一路潜伏着泉水坑，上面还覆盖着薄冰或雪花。那条狗比它的主人有着更加敏锐的直觉，感觉这个季节根本不适合外出。它对大自然也更加敬畏，因此得以保全性命。来自硫酸河的那位老前辈，虽然没有狗的强大直觉，但他吸取经验教训，学会了敬畏自然。

这篇小说通过描写一位旅人与自然对抗并最终失败的故事，似乎是在提醒人类要敬畏自然，遵循自然法则，但同时也赞美了人类勇敢无畏、顽强拼搏的精神。

文艺复兴和宗教改革解放了欧洲人的精神，蒸汽机及后续发明解放了欧洲人的身体，工业革命让欧洲人日益富足。他们在全世界的贪婪殖民和疯狂掠夺则使欧洲一夜暴富。这一切都让欧洲人信心膨胀。而美国人则更加自命不凡。美国人有着强烈的宗教情结，自封为上帝钦定的领袖民族。这个英国殖民者、侵略者建立的国家，不断侵略和掠夺当地人民的土地，大肆屠杀当地人民。到20世纪初，美国领土横跨北美大陆，综合国力也赶超前宗主国大英帝国，成为无冕之王。仅是领土扩张就使美国人信心爆棚。杰克·伦敦所在的时代，虽然北美洲已被瓜分完毕，美国的拓疆时代结束，但侵略成性的美国人对"边疆"和"西部"仍然非常痴迷。所以，当遥远极寒的育空地区富含金矿的消息传出，美国人自然蜂拥而至。

但是，大自然时而婀娜多姿，柔情万种，时而面目狰狞，残酷无情。小说对这种残酷进行了大量的描写：主人公吐的口水会在落地前结冰，嘴里流出的烟汁挂成冰凌，甚至呼出的空气都会变成霜沫。在这种极端严寒的天气里，一旦停止运动，体表就会迅速失温，尤其手脚会转瞬麻木。没有火堆，连吃饭都成问题。而且路上布满陷阱。后来，由于他打湿裤脚，且好一阵没有运动，所以无论如何跑动或挥舞手臂，也无法恢复手脚的知觉。零下58度以下能让无数生命的火焰黯然熄灭。在杰克·伦敦的许多极地小说和海洋小说中，大自然的凶恶随处可见。比如，《白牙》里那些异常凶猛的群狼在恶劣的自然环境里，生活艰辛，经常饥肠辘辘，甚至饿死。

所以，人类应该敬畏自然，道法自然。但是，人类古老的直觉早已退化，转而过分迷信自己的理智，并进而滋生骄傲情绪。一个月里都没有人经过亨德森河河道，说明天气过分寒冷，没人冒险外出。但是，主人公似乎对自己的旅行胸有成竹。他制订了明确的计划，一开始进展顺利。即便打湿裤腿后，他仍然镇定自信。眼见火堆越燃越旺，他甚至有点得意忘形，对老前辈的忠告感到不屑。结果，因为没有遵循自然法则，他错误地将火堆搭在树下，导致火堆被落雪扑灭，最终为自己的傲慢付出了生命的代价。

主人公的狗与他形成鲜明的对比。狗不知道温度度数，也读不懂温度计。当然，狗更没有主人们拥有的火柴以及各种工具。但正因如此，虽然不及野生的狼，驯养的狗相比人类来说，还是较好地保留了原始的直觉，尤其是对自然力量的了解和畏惧。这只狗基于本能，觉得应该顺应自然，找个暖和的地方躲过寒冬，而不是傲慢地挑战自然。但是，即便主人能听懂狗语，想必只会对狗的意见嗤之以鼻。狗的自知之明保全了自己的性命。

　　类似地，来自硫酸河的那位老前辈也能够清醒地认识到自然的强大和人类的脆弱。饱经风霜的他曾经警告主人公不要在育空地区的冬季独自旅行，可惜主人公只是在临死前才认识到老人的正确，并在幻觉中真诚地承认自己的错误。

　　同时，小说也是对人类谋求生存、捍卫生命的拼搏精神的一曲赞歌。一路上，一处接一处的陷阱充满凶险的算计；极寒虎视眈眈，随时准备夺走他手脚的知觉。他机智对付，勇敢抵抗，进行了艰苦卓绝的斗争。火堆熄灭后，主人公意识到他可能将失去生命。但他继续顽强抗争，不言放弃，一直坚持到体力耗尽为止。虽然主人公莽撞无知，但他为了生存而与大自然展开殊死搏斗、绝不认输的精神却值得赞美。主人公身陷绝境，没有祈祷神灵庇佑，而是沉着勇敢地抗争，最后选择有尊严地面对死亡，尤其令人深思，让人敬佩。

　　作者没有介绍主人公的名字，也没有描写他的长相和体格特征。但从他的行走速度，倒是能够推断他体格强健。这么一个强壮的男子，似乎可以代表当时自信的美国人。

　　在这部作品里，达尔文、斯宾塞等人的进化论和尼采的超人主义对作者的影响跃然纸上。适者生存，但主人公既不够了解自然，又不够敬畏自然，所以被大自然淘汰。尼采式的英雄无须遵循庸人的规则在意弱者是否道德。主人公跟这种英雄，倒也有几分神似。

三、结构与技巧

　　对于这部作品，值得关注的是它的情节构造、描写和自然主义风格等特点。

　　小说采用比较传统的叙事策略，依时间顺序展开叙述。不过，值得注意的是，作者经常通过主人公的视角对周围的景物进行描写。比如对育空河和雪原生动逼真的描写。

　　首先，故事的情节跌宕起伏，故事引人入胜。

　　主人公的儿子们沿着传统路线前往营地，应该已经到达，而主人公却绕道调查林木情况。故事的发展路线就此清楚呈现，读者期待这位旅人与他的儿子们顺利会师。虽然小路上的陷阱一个接一个，天气异常寒冷，但主人公身手矫健，时速超过4英里。而且，他已经顺利穿越两条河的分隔地带，来到彻底冻结的亨德森河。至此，一切顺风顺水。

　　但读者终于等来了一点波折：河道上那些隐秘的泉水坑，是一道道陷阱，准备随时吞噬主人公和他的狗。虽然主人公狠心让自己的狗去探路，好在这狗本能强大，成功自救。接下来，主人公谨小慎微，读者提心吊胆，主人公最终按时安全到达河汊。就在惬意、轻松的时候，主人公发现自己双手麻木，虽已掏出午餐却无法进食。生火后，他幸福地吃饭抽烟，随后进入左边的岔河，半小时没有泉水的痕迹，他觉得胜利在望。

　　可就在此时，悲剧发生了。生火成功后，重回愉快气氛，汉子甚至得意扬扬。但是，大自然很快给他上了最后一课，留给读者一个悲伤凄婉、扼腕深思的故事结局。安全和危险、愉快和担心交错，不断切换，甚至在曲折中结尾，使故事一波三折。这种吸引力是伟大文学作品的基本特征。如果丧失了这种吸引力，就失去了读者。

　　其次，这部小说的描写功夫独到，精妙绝伦。

　　静态描写数量不多，但栩栩如生，令人震撼。"他举目远望，无论北方还是南方，但见连绵白雪，唯有一根黑色的发丝，从南面弯来拐去，绕过长满云杉的岛屿，继续向北弯来拐去，消失在另一个长满云杉的岛屿背后。"无疑，那根发丝就是育空地区的南北大道。又比如，虽然是中午，天空清朗，但"地球的表面高高凸起，害得亨德森河难见天日"。这是对北极圈特殊气候的生动描写。这些细腻逼真的文字，与人物刻画有机结合，推动了情节发展、丰富了人物形象。

　　小说在动作描写上展现了深厚的功力。作者对这位男子生火过程的描写，令人难忘。为了生火吃饭，"他大步走来走去，同时不断跺脚舞臂，直到确信重新感到暖意方才停下"。打湿裤腿后，他再次生火。点燃火苗后，"他用一束一束的干草和最细的干树枝喂养幼弱的火苗"。当然，主人公最后一次生火的画面更是如在眼前。首先，他去捡拾柴火，但是，"他无法聚拢手指将柴火单根拔出"，只得"一把一把地扯出来"。然后，他伸手去兜里掏出桦树皮，可是，尽管听到树皮碰到手指发出的哗啦哗啦的响声，却"无论如何努力，他都无法抓住它"。手指已经完全麻木，他只能用牙齿咬住火柴划燃。"他用力张嘴的时候，嘴巴周围的冰发出噼噼啪啪的响声。"接下来，"他用牙齿咬住一根火柴，在腿上划擦"。火苗熄灭后,"他冷漠地环顾四周,眼光不经意间落在那只狗的身上……"这些动作描写简洁明了,具体生动,使故事扣人心弦。

这部作品的心理描写也很精彩。"河岸很陡峭,他爬上顶部后停下喘息。同时,他看了下手表上的时间,以此作为停歇的借口。"可见,这个男子非常自信和要强。这种自信在多处得到体现,比如,"但是气温不是问题","他将在6点前到达营地"。面临危险时,他十分镇静。比如,他打湿裤腿后,没有丝毫慌乱,而是小心谨慎、有条不紊地生火。积雪扑灭火堆后,他知道自己的手脚时刻都在冻结。"这个想法让他有点惊慌,所以,他与之抗争,保持镇静。"实际上,后来生火无望,他在奔跑时,仍然能够抵抗绝望情绪,保持镇静。面对死亡,他的惊恐和绝望都是"有节制的"。当他放弃抗争时,"脸上露出那么一种微笑"。他决定"不妨体面地接受死亡",觉得在睡眠中死去"是个不错的主意"。作者主要通过动作描写和转述人物的心声的形式来进行心理描写。这些心理描写入木三分,使人物形象格外鲜活丰满。

最后,这部小说具有浓郁的自然主义风格。文学上的自然主义要求忠实记录自然并揭示事物之间的内在联系。而本篇作品在这两方面都有上乘表现。

作者在描写景物的时候,尽量通过人物的视角或者感受来表现,从而与人物甚至整个故事保持相当的距离。在叙述人物行为时,不带任何修饰和夸张;对人物的语言,几乎没有记录,从而确保不会失真。对人物的心理描写多借助动作描写和心声转述来进行。叙事口吻客观冷静,甚至冷淡疏远。

作品不但似水墨描摹,在细节上也多有真实呈现。主人公没有名字,但是,作品中的地名,比如Dawson、Nulato、St. Michael、Henderson Creek和Sulphur Creek等,应该都是真实的地名。作者对育空地区的天气描写,也非常客观真实。育空河、亨德森河、河汊等地相互之间的距离,火柴的根数以及主人公行走的速度和耗时等都十分具体精确。这一切都使故事读来特别真实,犹如一篇纪实文学。

主人公没有洞察到自然规律,生火失败。他没有认识到,自己抽取枯枝的行为会破坏积雪的平衡。也就是说,他没有把握自然界里各种事物之间的关系。另外,主人公准备杀死他的狗的时候,没有一丝道德上的检讨。这也非常符合自然主义摒弃道德判断的做法。

Suggested Readings

1. Auerbach, Jonathan. *Male Call: Becoming Jack London*. Durham, NC: Duke University Press, 1996.
2. Beauchamp, Gorman. *Jack London*. San Bernardino, CA: Borgo Press, 1984.
3. Berton, Pierre. *Klondike: The Last Great Gold Rush 1896—1899*, Revised Edition. Toronto: Anchor Canada, 2001.
4. Bloom, Harold, ed. *Jack London (Bloom's Modern Critical Views)*. Broomall, PA: Chelsea House Publishers, 2011.
5. Hedrick, Joan D. *Solitary Comrade: Jack London and His Work*. Chapel Hill, NC: University of North Carolina Press, 1982.
6. Lawlor, Mary. *Recalling the Wild: Naturalism and the Closing of the American West*. New Brunswick, NJ: Rutgers University Press, 2000.
7. London, Jack. *"Love of Life," and Other Stories*. Whitefish, MT: Kessinger Publishing, 2004.
8. London, Jack. *Martin Eden*. London: Penguin Books, 1994.
9. London, Jack. *"Revolution," and Other Essays*. Ithaca, NY: Cornell University Library, 2010.
10. London, Jack. *The Call of the Wild, White Fang, and Other Stories*. Beijing: Foreign Languages and Research Press, 1997.
11. London, Jack. *The Collected Science Fiction & Fantasy of Jack London: Before Adam and Other Stories*. East Yorkshire: Leonaur Publishing, 2005.
12. London, Jack. *The People of the Abyss*. Newburyport, MA: Journeyman Press, 1978.
13. London, Jack. *The Sea Wolf*. Whitefish, MT: Kessinger Publishing, 2010.
14. London, Jack. *War of the Classes*. Charleston, NC: BiblioBazaar, 2008.
15. Lundquist, James. *Jack London: Adventures, Ideas, and Fiction*. New York: Ungar, 1987.
16. Reesman, Jeanne Campbell. *Jack London: A Study of the Short Fiction*. New York: Twayne Publishers, 1999.

4. TO BUILD A FIRE

Questions for Reflection

1. What are the personality traits of the protagonist of this short story? Support your opinion with evidence. What might be the reason that the author tells very little about who the protagonist is, not even mentioning his name?

2. What might be the theme of the short story? What's your opinion of the two philosophies on the relationship between man and nature: "conformity to nature" and "man can conquer nature"? What may this story reveal about Jack London's philosophy and values?

3. How does the protagonist contrast with his dog in the story?

4. What are the characteristics of the description in the story?

5. Why is this short story regarded as a typical work of naturalism?

Questions for Discussion

What are the common topics for Jack London's literary works? What literary techniques are usually employed in his works? What do you know about the U.S. territorial expansion, the California Gold Rush, the Klondike Gold Rush, and the Yukon Territory?

（周家辉　撰写）

5. HILLS LIKE WHITE ELEPHANTS

By Ernest Hemingway, 1927

The hills across the valley of the Ebro were long and white. On this side there was no shade and no trees and the station was between two lines of rails in the sun. Close against the side of the station there was the warm shadow of the building and a curtain, made of strings of bamboo beads, hung across the open door into the bar, to keep out flies. The American and the girl with him sat at a table in the shade, outside the building. It was very hot and the express from Barcelona would come in forty minutes. It stopped at this junction for two minutes and went on to Madrid.

"What should we drink? " the girl asked. She had taken off her hat and put it on the table.

"It's pretty hot, " the man said.

"Let's drink beer."

"Dos cervezas," the man said into the curtain.

"Big ones?" a woman asked from the doorway.

"Yes. Two big ones."

The woman brought two glasses of beer and two felt pads. She put the felt pads and the beer glasses on the table and looked at the man and the girl. The girl was looking off at the line of hills. They were white in the sun and the country was brown and dry.

5. HILLS LIKE WHITE ELEPHANTS

"They look like white elephants," she said.

"I've never seen one." The man drank his beer.

"No, you wouldn't have."

"I might have," the man said. 'just because you say I wouldn't have doesn't prove anything."

The girl looked at the bead curtain. "They've painted something on it," she said. "What does it say?"

"Anis del Toro. It's a drink."

"Could we try it?"

The man called "Listen" through the curtain.

The woman came out from the bar.

"Four reales."

"We want two Anis del Toro."

"With water?"

"Do you want it with water?"

"I don't know," the girl said. "Is it good with water?"

"It's all right."

"You want them with water?" asked the woman.

"Yes, with water."

"It tastes like liquorice," the girl said and put the glass down.

"That's the way with everything."

"Yes," said the girl. "Everything tastes of liquorice. Especially all the things you've waited so long for, like absinthe."

"Oh, cut it out."

"You started it," the girl said. "I was being amused. I was having a fine time."

"Well, let's try and have a fine time."

"All right. I was trying. I said the mountains looked like white elephants. Wasn't that bright?"

"That was bright."

"I wanted to try this new drink. That's all we do, isn't it—look at things and try new drinks?"

"I guess so."

The girl looked across at the hills.

"They're lovely hills," she said. "They don't really look like white elephants. I just meant the coloring of their skin through the trees."

"Should we have another drink?"

"All right."

The warm wind blew the bead curtain against the table.

"The beer's nice and cool," the man said.

"It's lovely," the girl said.

"It's really an awfully simple operation, Jig," the man said. "It's not really an operation at all."

The girl looked at the ground the table legs rested on.

"I know you wouldn't mind it, Jig. It's really not anything. It's just to let the air in."

The girl did not say anything.

"I'll go with you and I'll stay with you all the time. They just let the air in and then it's all perfectly natural."

"Then what will we do afterwards?"

"We'll be fine afterwards. Just like we were before."

"What makes you think so?"

"That's the only thing that bothers us. It's the only thing that's made us unhappy."

The girl looked at the bead curtain, put her hand out and took hold of two of the strings of beads.

"And you think then we'll be all right and be happy."

"I know we will. You don't have to be afraid. I've known lots of people that

5. HILLS LIKE WHITE ELEPHANTS

have done it."

"So have I," said the girl. "And afterward they were all so happy."

"Well," the man said, "if you don't want to you don't have to. I wouldn't have you do it if you didn't want to. But I know it's perfectly simple."

"And you really want to?"

"I think it's the best thing to do. But I don't want you to do it if you don't really want to."

"And if I do it you'll be happy and things will be like they were and you'll love me?"

"I love you now. You know I love you."

"I know. But if I do it, then it will be nice again if I say things are like white elephants, and you'll like it?"

"I'll love it. I love it now but I just can't think about it. You know how I get when I worry."

"If I do it you won't ever worry?"

"I won't worry about that because it's perfectly simple."

"Then I'll do it. Because I don't care about me."

"What do you mean?"

"I don't care about me."

"Well, I care about you."

"Oh, yes. But I don't care about me. And I'll do it and then everything will be fine."

"I don't want you to do it if you feel that way."

The girl stood up and walked to the end of the station. Across, on the other side, were fields of grain and trees along the banks of the Ebro. Far away, beyond the river, were mountains. The shadow of a cloud moved across the field of grain and she saw the river through the trees.

"And we could have all this," she said. "And we could have everything and every day we make it more impossible."

"What did you say?"

"I said we could have everything."

"We can have everything."

"No, we can't."

"We can have the whole world."

"No, we can't." "We can go everywhere."

"No, we can't. It isn't ours any more."

"It's ours."

"No, it isn't. And once they take it away, you never get it back."

"But they haven't taken it away."

"We'll wait and see."

"Come on back in the shade," he said. "You mustn't feel that way."

"I don't feel any way," the girl said. "I just know things."

"I don't want you to do anything that you don't want to do—"

"Nor that isn't good for me," she said. "I know. Could we have another beer?"

"All right. But you've got to realize—"

"I realize," the girl said. "Can't we maybe stop talking?"

They sat down at the table and the girl looked across at the hills on the dry side of the valley and the man looked at her and at the table.

"You've got to realize," he said, "that I don't want you to do it if you don't want to. I'm perfectly willing to go through with it if it means anything to you."

"Doesn't it mean anything to you? We could get along."

"Of course it does. But I don't want anybody but you. I don't want anyone else. And I know it's perfectly simple."

"Yes, you know it's perfectly simple."

"It's all right for you to say that, but I do know it."

"Would you do something for me now?"

"I'd do anything for you."

"Would you please please please please please please please stop talking?"

He did not say anything but looked at the bags against the wall of the station. There were labels on them from all the hotels where they had spent nights.

"But I don't want you to," he said, "I don't care anything about it."

"I'll scream," the girl said.

The woman came out through the curtains with two glasses of beer and put them down on the damp felt pads.

"The train comes in five minutes," she said.

"What did she say?" asked the girl.

"That the train is coming in five minutes."

The girl smiled brightly at the woman, to thank her.

"I'd better take the bags over to the other side of the station," the man said. She smiled at him.

"All right. Then come back and we'll finish the beer."

He picked up the two heavy bags and carried them around the station to the other tracks. He looked up the tracks but could not see the train. Coming back, he walked through the bar-room, where people waiting for the train were drinking. He drank an Anis at the bar and looked at the people. They were all waiting reasonably for the train. He went out through the bead curtain. She was sitting at the table and smiled at him.

"Do you feel better?" he asked.

"I feel fine," she said. "There's nothing wrong with me. I feel fine."

作品赏析

一、作家介绍

欧内斯特·海明威（Ernest Hemingway，1899—1961），美国20世纪二三十年代迷惘的一代的代表作家，被称为美国20世纪上半叶最有才华的天才小说家。

海明威一生创作了很多脍炙人口的作品，尤其以长篇小说和短篇小说闻名于世。

海明威的创作与他的人生经历是分不开的，特别是他的战争经历和记者生涯，对他的创作影响极大。海明威于1899年出生于美国北部伊利诺伊州奥克帕克村的一个中产阶级家庭，父亲是当地著名的外科大夫，母亲上层社会家庭出身。他的父亲喜欢狩猎和钓鱼，母亲有较高的音乐修养。这些都在不同程度上影响了海明威。在海明威的人生中，战争对他创作的影响极大。他经历了第一次世界大战、西班牙内战和第二次世界大战，他的多部小说都与战争相关。

首先我们来看一下第一次世界大战对他的影响。1917年夏天，海明威高中毕业。那是第一次世界大战最激烈的一年。海明威于1918年5月参加了美国红十字会战地救护队，担任车队司机，被授予中尉军衔。他6月随救护队开赴欧洲战场，进入意大利境内，一个月后被炮弹炸伤，在医院治疗了三个月。奥匈帝国投降后，意大利政府授予海明威军功奖章、银质奖章和勇敢奖章各一枚。1919年1月，海明威带着满身伤返回美国，战争给他的心灵留下了难以治愈的创伤，他感到忧郁、空虚和茫然。

基于第一次世界大战的经历，海明威创作了两部十分重要的反战小说《太阳照样升起》（*The Sun Also Rises*）和《永别了，武器》（*A Farewell to Arms*）。

海明威在战争中，看到了一个混乱纷争的世界，他将这一切写进了小说，这些故事充满了孤独、死亡和危险。

在经历第一次世界大战后，海明威于1926年发表了《太阳照样升起》。这一作品发表后，海明威开始有了国际知名度。小说以第一次世界大战之后流落在欧洲的青年男女为描写对象，反映他们憎恨战争，无法消除心中的创伤，心情苦闷、迷茫，又找不到出路的思想情绪。战争毁灭了无辜人民的生命，也摧毁了整整一代人的精神。

1929年海明威又发表了《永别了武器》，这部小说直接描写战争，揭露了战争对人们的摧残，同时也戳穿了美国参战舆论的欺骗性和虚伪性。这两部作品奠定了海明威在文学界的地位，使他成为迷惘的一代最具代表性的作家。

1936年7月，西班牙内战爆发，海明威不仅个人捐款，还公开筹款，积极支持西班牙共和政府。他还受"北美报业同盟"委派，先后4次到西班牙内战第一线报道西班牙人民的英雄事迹。后来他直接参加了国际纵队，与佛朗哥法西斯军队作战，直到内战结束才撤离回国。西班牙内战是海明威创作战争小说的新契机、新源泉。由于战争的性质不同，海明威对战争的认识不同，因此他的态度和行动也大有不同。

1938年，海明威创作了剧作《第五纵队》（*The Fifth Column*），这是他唯一的剧本。这部剧作的主人公美国军官菲利普·罗林斯（Philip Rawlings）在西班牙共和军担任反间谍工作的故事，他为保卫共和政府和首都马德里，破获敌特组织，一举歼灭第五纵队，为共和事业作出了贡献。剧中的主人公拥有崇高的生活理想和奋斗目标，把自己的一切与西班牙民族解放事业紧紧联系在一起。

1940年，海明威发表了长篇小说《丧钟为谁而鸣》（*For Whom the Bell Tolls*）。小说里的主人公不再是厌倦战争的迷惘者，而是一个有意志、有信念、有理想、有抱负的革命战士。罗伯特·乔丹（Robert Jordan）认识到自己从事的是一场反对法西斯主义的正义战争，他是为人民而战。这样的转变与海明威参加西班牙内战的经历是分不开的。

1939年第二次世界大战爆发，海明威又一次积极投入战争。1941年春天，他赴亚洲采访，并到过中国。1941年12月珍珠港事件后美国宣布参战，海明威将自己的游艇改装成巡逻艇，为美国政府提供了许多情报。1944年，他随美军在法国北部登陆，率领一支先遣队投入解放巴黎的战斗。在第二次世界大战期间，海明威多次受伤，曾因飞机失事得了严重的脑震荡。

第二次世界大战以后，特别是到了20世纪50年代，海明威虽然还在坚持创作，但作品的境界和力量似乎无法与过去媲美。这个时期他继续发扬顽强的拼搏精神，但同时也陷入悲观主义，把人生看作是一场残酷的搏斗，学会主宰人生则是人类无法抗拒的命运。不过正当人们都以为他江郎才尽时，他发表了人生后期最重要的一部中篇小说《老人与海》（*The Old Man and the Sea*）。在这部作品里面，他塑造了老渔夫桑提亚哥（Santiago）的形象，这一形象也成了海明威笔下最具代表性或者是最具有特色的硬汉形象。通过这一形象，他一方面歌颂了人类的伟大力量，另一方面又对命运捉弄下必然失败的人生表现出无可奈何的绝望情绪。海明威认为，人即使面对失败，也要不失尊严，勇敢而不妥协，要保持一种重压下的优雅。海明威式的准则英雄或者硬汉形象，一个重要的特点就是能维持重压下的优雅风度。

很多人说海明威的一生就是传奇的一生。遗憾的是，海明威在1961年7月2日用猎枪结束了自己62岁的生命，不过他那些经久传世的作品一直在续写他的传奇。

二、故事与人物

小说《白象似的群山》是海明威在1927年创作的，收入短篇小说集《没有女人的男人们》（*Men Without Women*）。

小说中的故事发生在西班牙北部一个名不见经传的小火车站。故事的两个主要人物在车站酒吧外阴凉处的一张桌子旁喝酒聊天，等待从巴塞罗那开来的火车，火车还有40分钟才进站。故事主要讲述了二人等车的这40分钟内的对话。他们边喝酒边聊天，表面云淡风轻，对话显得轻松随意，但各自内心却波涛汹涌，因为他们讨论的话题是女子是否应该堕胎。我们需要注意的是，这个故事从头到尾一直没有明确指出他们所说的话题是堕胎。这一重要信息需要读者从二人的对话中推测出来。这一故事情节的设置显然体现了海明威的冰山原则。在这个故事中，男女主人公最大的冲突，可能来自不同的选择。男主人公似乎想继续以前的生活，孩子对于他来说是一个不必要的负担，因此希望女方打掉，而女人似乎向往一种新的生活，把孩子视作开始新生活的契机，因此希望能够留下孩子。

在这个作品里，主要人物只有两个：一个是没有姓名的美国人，另一个是跟他在一起喝酒的女人，名字叫吉格（Jig）。次要人物有酒吧的女酒保，以及在酒吧喝酒、等火车的人们。对这些次要人物，小说没有花多余的笔墨去描绘。

小说男主人公来自美国，他的姓名从头到尾都没提及，这么做是为了体现那个时代美国人所具有的特征，也就是说所有美国的年轻人都跟这个美国男人一样，他们是迷惘的。我们从他的旅行包上贴着的旅馆标签就能够看出，男女主人公过着居无定所、漂泊不定的生活，他们不知道前方的路要如何走，生活该如何继续，完全失去了方向，前途一片迷茫。

女主人公叫吉格，相比于男主人公来说，她的形象更加立体。因为怀孕，她希望结束之前的漂泊生活，希望留下孩子，拥抱新的生活。然而，当她与男主人公交谈后，她彻底陷入了绝望和痛苦，因为男主人公一门心思希望她把孩子打掉，这样才能继续他们以往的生活。

5. HILLS LIKE WHITE ELEPHANTS

  第一次世界大战给年轻人带来的影响是难以抹去的，尤其是战后，世界的改变和年轻人的想象完全不同，他们发现了虚假的繁荣掩盖的社会问题。不但自然生态和社会生态出现了危机，更重要的是人的精神生态出现了前所未有的危机。战争摧毁了世界，摧毁了人们的信仰，因此作为个体的人有一种无力感，处于迷茫之中，对未来不再抱有希望，彻底迷失了自我。

  整篇小说基本是由对话构成，读者只能通过人物的对话来判断人物的特点。在小说中，男主人公形象相对扁平，因为他始终如一，几乎没有任何变化，在对话中始终是冷漠、理性的。

  男人在对话中表现得十分理性，说话始终围绕一个主题，那就是劝说女人堕胎，无论女人如何转换、回避话题，男人总能够回到堕胎这个主题，以至于女人最后忍无可忍，请求他，甚至是呵斥他，让他不要再继续说下去了。我们在读这篇文章的过程中会看到，关于堕胎这样重大的决定，男子佯装关心女人的感受，但实际上，他从头至尾一直非常冷漠地劝说女人，逼迫女方自己作出堕胎的决定。他们的对话中多次出现这样的话语："这真的只是一个非常简单的手术""这事实上根本不算是手术""我会跟着你，而且会一直陪着你，他们只是让空气进去，然后就一切都很正常了"。他用这种轻松简单的语气来劝说女子做堕胎手术这样的大事，从而形成一种张力，更加凸显出男人的自私与冷漠。即使在女人情绪失控，连续说出7个"please"的情况下，他还能保持冷静，佯装关心和尊重。

  男主人公似乎代表战后这个冷漠的世界，没有意义，没有希望，无情地夺走人们视为珍宝的东西。而女主人公似乎还试图与这个冷漠的世界协商，寻找生命的意义，然而她最终也以失败告终，因为整个世界就是冷漠和无意义的。女主人公吉格一开始对新生活是有所幻想的，她总是望向远处的山峦，且非常有想象力地把连绵的群山比作白色的大象。在她与男子谈话的过程中，虽然男子的表现一直冷漠理性，但吉格却把自己的希望、不满、抱怨、愤怒全都表达了出来。在对话中，吉格试图以连绵的群山像白色的大象来劝说男子开始新生活，但没有得到回应。之后她在对话中不断向男人发出质问，并且大量使用了反讽，这些都表现出了吉格丰富的情感。与美国男人的冷漠和理性对比，吉格依然感情丰富，有爱，她似乎是非理性的。

海明威认为生活会毫无理由地伤害我们，而且是以最痛的方式来伤害我们，如果我们爱上什么，我们就会失去什么，因为生活一定会夺走它。所以要生活在这个冷漠的世界，人也必须冷漠，不能表露情感，不能在意任何事物，这样才能够生存，因为但凡表达出爱，但凡在意任何事物，生活就会将它夺走。吉格的绝望源于她对生活还有希望，还有爱，然而最终命运似乎也会夺去她所珍惜的东西，使她陷入无尽的绝望之中。

三、创作技巧与主题

海明威在短篇小说《死在午后》（"Death in the Afternoon"）中提出了自己的"冰山原则"："如果一位散文作家对于他想写的东西心中有数，那么他可以省略他所知道的东西，而读者呢，只要作者写得足够真实，就会强烈地感觉到他所省略的东西，好像作者已经写了出来一样，冰山在海里移动，很庄严宏伟，这是因为它只有1/8露出水面。"[1] 简单来说，海明威认为冰山之所以雄伟庄严，是因为7/8是在水面以下，那么写作就应该遵循这个冰山原理，作者可以省去所知道的一切，让作品只露出1/8，让丰富深厚的意义蕴藏在水面以下的7/8。

海明威在创作中一直遵循和实践这一冰山理论，我们可以从他的文体风格、叙事技巧、象征手法等方面看出来。

首先我们来简单看一下文体风格。海明威作品的文体风格，具有电报式语言的简洁、生动和直接的特点，但同时又不乏优美含蓄，主要以短句为主。海明威这样的文体风格主要与他的记者经历有关。

他高中毕业就到《堪萨斯明星报》，后来又到《多伦多明星报》当记者，西班牙内战、第二次世界大战期间都当过战地记者。他早期做记者时曾在C. G. 惠灵顿的指导下写作。惠灵顿认为，记者应该用简短有力的语句写出即时、直观的文章，应少用形容词和术语，后来海明威又在安德森（Sherwood Anderson）、庞德（Ezra Pound）和斯泰因（Gertrude Stein）的影响下，开始广泛阅读现代作家的作品。因此，无论是他的记者经历，还是现代派作家，都对他的文体风格有很大的影响。

---

[1] Ernest Hemingway, "Death in the Afternoon", Ernest Hemingway, *Death in the Afternoon*. New York: Charles Scribner's Sons, 1932, p. 192.

5. HILLS LIKE WHITE ELEPHANTS

  海明威的叙事技巧风格独特，是他对冰山原理的实践结果。他主要采用客观、真实的有限叙事策略，使故事叙述尽可能冷静客观，不让主观判断干扰故事叙述的发展，让人物按照客观逻辑采取行动。海明威还特别关注象征手法的使用。学界普遍认为他对象征的使用，丰富了作品的意义，使作品具有独特的深刻性和生动性，简单的意象下面蕴藏了深厚的意义。我们以《白象似的群山》为例。

  《白象似的群山》以一种含蓄的戏剧性对话贯穿始终，作者选用了外聚焦的叙述视角。外聚焦与零聚焦和内聚焦相比，叙述者的视野受到相当大的限制，比人物知道的信息还要少。因为叙述者犹如一位客观、冷漠的观察者，从头到尾不流露一丝感情色彩，没有任何分析和评价，就像一台摄像机——它拍到什么，读者就看到什么。叙述者不透露任何人物的内心，人物的思想感情只能靠读者通过叙述者的客观描述去推测和想象。

  值得注意的是，虽然从整篇小说来看，叙述者主要是采用了外视角，他没有进入任何一个人物的内心，读者无法看到人物的内心想法，但偶尔叙述者会借助人物的视角来看周围的世界，虽然只是发生短暂的视角转换，但如果仔细阅读小说就会发现男女主人公视点的冲突和差异。两个人物观察世界的角度、对待生活的态度不同，关心和关注的事物则不同，这便产生了视点上的差异。小说中两个人物的视点总是错位的。可以说只要是在文中出现视点差异的地方，就能看到他们的矛盾和冲突。

  小说中女主人公总是望向远处的群山和自然景致，因为那象征着"生命"和"新的生活"。小说开篇写道："年轻女子正在眺望远处那一线连绵的群山。群山在阳光下是白色的，而田野则是褐色而干燥的一片。"女子说"它们看上去像是白色的大象呢"。这是女子第一次提到连绵的群山像白色的大象。白象这一意象起源于印度。在印度社会中，白象被视为造物主，是神圣不可侵犯的，是非常珍贵的。此处吉格是在通过谈论外部自然界的山峦，借助白象的意象，映射自己腹中的胎儿，她非常看重这个宝贵的生命。然而男方却将白象当作昂贵而无用的东西，这是白象的另一个意思。对他来说，孩子是个沉重的包袱，所以男人的视点一直放在眼前的女人和事物上，他总是回避和佯装听不懂女方的话，一门心思劝吉格堕胎。因此当女人说群山像白象时，他只说"我可从来没见过大象"。两个人物关心的事物不同，选择不同，视点不同，从而男人看不到女人看到的"生命和希望"，他只关注眼前的"死亡"。他们的视点或看法，对未来的选择，就像小说中的两条铁轨一样，永不相交。

小说后面多次提到年轻女子望着远处的群山，望着远处的"稻田、树木、河流、连绵的山峦"，这些都是生命和希望的象征。文中也明确提到"年轻女子眺望着远处干涸的河谷和群山时，男子则看着她和桌子"。可见，男人一直只关心眼下劝说女子堕胎的事情，他们的视点有差异，因此年轻女子看到的那些象征着生命和希望的意象，男子都看不到，他只是一味以各种方式暗示或逼迫女人作出堕胎的决定。当女人用7个"please"呵斥他不要再继续说下去不然她要尖叫时，男子的视角转移到"靠在车站墙边的那些包。包上贴着他们曾经过夜的所有旅店的标签"上。行李包象征着两人过去的生活，当男人最后提起两件沉重的行李时，我们知道他选择了继续以往的生活。

小说的结尾意味深长，男人"在吧台边喝了一杯茴香酒，看了看那些人，他们都在耐心地等待着火车"。作者在这里，专门用"waiting reasonably"来强调等车的人都是理性的，这似乎是暗示，女人刚才情绪失控，不够理性。男人的理性和冷漠似乎也得到了这个世界的回应，因为其他所有乘客跟他一样。此时，当他再看向女主人公时，"她正坐在桌旁，对着他微笑"。女人似乎恢复了男人所期待的那种理性，微笑以对，而男子也因她的微笑而误以为她"好了一点"，所以他问女子"你好点了吗？"，女子回答，"我觉得很好，我什么毛病也没有。我觉得很好"。女人重复了两遍"我觉得很好"，表现出对人生的彻底绝望。这似乎是一句反讽，又似乎是女人对自己的安慰和催眠，她似乎只能跟别人一样"恢复理性"、没有感情，才能与这个冷漠、无意义的世界相处。

Suggested Readings

1. Benson, Jackson J., ed. *New Critical Approaches to the Short Stories of Ernest Hemingway*. Durham: Duke University Press, 1990.

2. Bloom, Harold, ed. *Modern Critical Views: Ernest Hemingway*. New York: Chelsea House, 1985.

3. Donaldson, Scott, ed. *The Cambridge Companion to Ernest Hemingway*.

Cambridge: Cambridge University Press, 1996.
4. Flora, Joseph M., ed. *Ernest Hemingway: A Study of the Short Fiction*. Boston: Twayne, 1989.
5. Hemingway, Ernest. *A Farewell to Arms*. New York: Charles Scribner's Sons, 1929.
6. Hemingway, Ernest. *Death in the Afternoon*. New York: Charles Scribner's Sons, 1932.
7. Hemingway, Ernest. *For Whom the Bell Tolls*. New York: Charles Scribner's Sons, 1940.
8. Hemingway, Ernest. *Men without Women*. New York: Charles Scribner's Sons, 1929.
9. Hemingway, Ernest. *The Complete Short Stories of Ernest Hemingway*. New York: Charles Scribner's Sons, 2003.
10. Hemingway, Ernest. *The Old Man and the Sea*. New York: Charles Scribner's Sons, 1952.
11. Hemingway, Ernest. *The Sun Also Rises*. New York: Charles Scribner's Sons, 1926.
12. Lee, A. Robert, ed. *Ernest Hemingway: New Critical Essays*. London & New York: Vision and Barnes and Noble, 1983.
13. Meyers, Jeffrey, ed. *Hemingway: The Critical Heritage*. London: Routledge and Kegan Paul, 1982.
14. Oliver, Charles M. *Critical Companion to Ernest Hemingway: A Literary Reference to His Life and Work*. New York: Facts on File, Inc., 2007.
15. Wagner-Martin, Linda, ed. *A Historical Guide to Ernest Hemingway*. New York: Oxford University Press, 2000.
16. Wagner-Martin, Linda. *Ernest Hemingway: A Literary Life*. New York: Palgrave Macmillan, 2007.

Questions for Reflection

1. Please comment on the external focalization in the story.

2. What is the meaning of the title of the story?

3. What is the main topic discussed in the dialogue between the hero and heroine of the story? How do they respond to this topic differently?

4. How does the short story reflect Hemingway's iceberg principle?

5. From the end of the story, what choices can we infer the heroine may make in the end and why?

Question for Discussion

The short story was rejected by editors several times and was not well received for a long time. Why is it that since the end of the last century, academics have come to regard it as a modernist masterpiece and one of Hemingway's most important short stories?

（方小莉　撰写）

6. THE ICE PALACE

By F. Scott Fitzgerald, 1920

The sunlight dripped over the house like golden paint over an art jar, and the freckling shadows here and there only intensified the rigor of the bath of light. The Butterworth and Larkin houses flanking were intrenched behind great stodgy trees; only the Happer house took the full sun, and all day long faced the dusty road-street with a tolerant kindly patience. This was the city of Tarleton in southernmost Georgia, September afternoon.

Up in her bedroom window Sally Carrol Happer rested her nineteen-year-old chin on a fifty-two-year-old sill and watched Clark Darrow's ancient Ford turn the corner. The car was hot—being partly metallic it retained all the heat it absorbed or evolved—and Clark Darrow sitting bolt upright at the wheel wore a pained, strained expression as though he considered himself a spare part, and rather likely to break. He laboriously crossed two dust ruts, the wheels squeaking indignantly at the encounter, and then with a terrifying expression he gave the steering-gear a final wrench and deposited self and car approximately in front of the Happer steps. There was a plaintive heaving sound, a death-rattle, followed by a short silence; and then the air was rent by a startling whistle.

Sally Carrol gazed down sleepily. She started to yawn, but finding this quite impossible unless she raised her chin from the window-sill, changed her mind and continued silently to regard the car, whose owner sat brilliantly if perfunctorily at attention as he waited for an answer to his signal. After a moment the whistle once more split the dusty air.

"Good mawnin'."

With difficulty Clark twisted his tall body round and bent a distorted glance on the window.

" ' 'Tain't mawnin', Sally Carrol."

"Isn't it, sure enough?"

"What you doin'?"

"Eatin' 'n apple."

"Come on go swimmin'—want to?"

"Reckon so."

"How 'bout hurryin' up?"

"Sure enough."

Sally Carrol sighed voluminously and raised herself with profound inertia from the floor, where she had been occupied in alternately destroying parts of a green apple and painting paper dolls for her younger sister. She approached a mirror, regarded her expression with a pleased and pleasant languor, dabbed two spots of rouge on her lips and a grain of powder on her nose, and covered her bobbed corn-colored hair with a rose-littered sunbonnet. Then she kicked over the painting water, said, "Oh, damn!"—but let it lay—and left the room.

"How you, Clark?" she inquired a minute later as she slipped nimbly over the side of the car.

"Mighty fine, Sally Carrol."

"Where we go swimmin'?"

"Out to Walley's Pool. Told Marylyn we'd call by an' get her an' Joe Ewing."

Clark was dark and lean, and when on foot was rather inclined to stoop. His eyes were ominous and his expression somewhat petulant except when startlingly illuminated by one of his frequent smiles. Clark had "a income"—just

6. THE ICE PALACE

enough to keep himself in ease and his car in gasolene—and he had spent the two years since he graduated from Georgia Tech in dozing round the lazy streets of his home town, discussing how he could best invest his capital for an immediate fortune.

Hanging round he found not at all difficult; a crowd of little girls had grown up beautifully, the amazing Sally Carrol foremost among them; and they enjoyed being swum with and danced with and made love to in the flower-filled summery evenings—and they all liked Clark immensely. When feminine company palled there were half a dozen other youths who were always just about to do something, and meanwhile were quite willing to join him in a few holes of golf, or a game of billiards, or the consumption of a quart of "hard yella licker." Every once in a while one of these contemporaries made a farewell round of calls before going up to New York or Philadelphia or Pittsburgh to go into business, but mostly they just stayed round in this languid paradise of dreamy skies and firefly evenings and noisy niggery street fairs—and especially of gracious, soft-voiced girls, who were brought up on memories instead of money.

The Ford having been excited into a sort of restless resentful life, Clark and Sally Carrol rolled and rattled down Valley Avenue into Jefferson Street, where the dust road became a pavement; along opiate Millicent Place, where there were half a dozen prosperous, substantial mansions; and on into the down-town section. Driving was perilous here, for it was shopping time; the population idled casually across the streets and a drove of low-moaning oxen were being urged along in front of a placid street-car; even the shops seemed only yawning their doors and blinking their windows in the sunshine before retiring into a state of utter and finite coma.

"Sally Carrol," said Clark suddenly, "it a fact that you're engaged?"

She looked at him quickly.

"Where'd you hear that?"

"Sure enough, you engaged?"

" 'At's a nice question!"

"Girl told me you were engaged to a Yankee you met up in Asheville last summer."

Sally Carrol sighed.

"Never saw such an old town for rumors."

"Don't marry a Yankee, Sally Carrol. We need you round here."

Sally Carrol was silent a moment.

"Clark," she demanded suddenly, "who on earth shall I marry?"

"I offer my services."

"Honey, you couldn't support a wife," she answered cheerfully. "Anyway, I know you too well to fall in love with you."

" 'At doesn't mean you ought to marry a Yankee," he persisted.

"S'pose I love him?"

He shook his head.

"You couldn't. He'd be a lot different from us, every way."

He broke off as he halted the car in front of a rambling, dilapidated house. Marylyn Wade and Joe Ewing appeared in the doorway.

" 'Lo, Sally Carrol."

"Hi!"

"How you-all?"

"Sally Carrol," demanded Marylyn as they started off again, "you engaged?"

"Lawdy, where'd all this start? Can't I look at a man 'thout everybody in town engagin' me to him?"

Clark stared straight in front of him at a bolt on the clattering wind-shield.

"Sally Carrol," he said with a curious intensity, "don't you like us?"

"What?"

"Us down here?"

"Why, Clark, you know I do. I adore all you boys."

6. THE ICE PALACE

"Then why you gettin' engaged to a Yankee?"

"Clark, I don't know. I'm not sure what I'll do, but—well, I want to go places and see people. I want my mind to grow. I want to live where things happen on a big scale."

"What you mean?"

"Oh, Clark, I love you, and I love Joe here, and Ben Arrot, and you-all, but you'll—you'll—"

"We'll all be failures?"

"Yes. I don't mean only money failures, but just sort of—of ineffectual and sad, and—oh, how can I tell you?"

"You mean because we stay here in Tarleton?"

"Yes, Clark; and because you like it and never want to change things or think or go ahead."

He nodded and she reached over and pressed his hand.

"Clark," she said softly, "I wouldn't change you for the world. You're sweet the way you are. The things that'll make you fail I'll love always—the living in the past, the lazy days and nights you have, and all your carelessness and generosity."

"But you're goin' away?"

"Yes—because I couldn't ever marry you. You've a place in my heart no one else ever could have, but tied down here I'd get restless. I'd feel I was—wastin' myself. There's two sides to me, you see. There's the sleepy old side you love; an' there's a sort of energy—the feelin' that makes me do wild things. That's the part of me that may be useful somewhere, that'll last when I'm not beautiful any more."

She broke off with characteristic suddenness and sighed, "Oh, sweet cooky!" as her mood changed.

Half closing her eyes and tipping back her head till it rested on the seat-back she let the savory breeze fan her eyes and ripple the fluffy curls of her bobbed hair. They were in the country now, hurrying between tangled growths of bright-green coppice and grass and tall trees that sent sprays of foliage to hang a cool welcome over the road. Here and there they passed a battered Negro cabin, its oldest white-haired inhabitant smoking a corncob pipe beside the door, and half a dozen scantily clothed pickaninnies parading tattered dolls on the wild-grown grass in front. Farther out were lazy cotton-fields, where even the workers seemed intangible shadows lent by the sun to the earth, not for toil, but to while away some age-old tradition in the golden September fields. And round the drowsy picturesqueness, over the trees and shacks and muddy rivers, flowed the heat, never hostile, only comforting, like a great warm nourishing bosom for the infant earth.

"Sally Carrol, we're here!"

"Poor chile's soun' asleep."

"Honey, you dead at last outa sheer laziness?"

"Water, Sally Carrol! Cool water waitin' for you!"

Her eyes opened sleepily.

"Hi!" she murmured, smiling.

II

In November Harry Bellamy, tall, broad, and brisk, came down from his Northern city to spend four days. His intention was to settle a matter that had been hanging fire since he and Sally Carrol had met in Asheville, North Carolina, in midsummer. The settlement took only a quiet afternoon and an evening in front of a glowing open fire, for Harry Bellamy had everything she wanted; and, besides, she loved him—loved him with that side of her she kept especially for loving. Sally Carrol had several rather clearly defined sides.

On his last afternoon they walked, and she found their steps tending half-unconsciously toward one of her favorite haunts, the cemetery. When it came in sight, gray-white and golden-green under the cheerful late sun, she paused,

6. THE ICE PALACE

irresolute, by the iron gate.

"Are you mournful by nature, Harry?" she asked with a faint smile.

"Mournful? Not I."

"Then let's go in here. It depresses some folks, but I like it."

They passed through the gateway and followed a path that led through a wavy valley of graves—dusty-gray and mouldy for the fifties; quaintly carved with flowers and jars for the seventies; ornate and hideous for the nineties, with fat marble cherubs lying in sodden sleep on stone pillows, and great impossible growths of nameless granite flowers. Occasionally they saw a kneeling figure with tributary flowers, but over most of the graves lay silence and withered leaves with only the fragrance that their own shadowy memories could waken in living minds.

They reached the top of a hill where they were fronted by a tall, round head-stone, freckled with dark spots of damp and half grown over with vines.

"Margery Lee," she read; "1844—1873. Wasn't she nice? She died when she was twenty-nine. Dear Margery Lee," she added softly. "Can't you see her, Harry?"

"Yes, Sally Carrol."

He felt a little hand insert itself into his.

"She was dark, I think; and she always wore her hair with a ribbon in it, and gorgeous hoop-skirts of Alice blue and old rose."

"Yes."

"Oh, she was sweet, Harry! And she was the sort of girl born to stand on a wide, pillared porch and welcome folks in. I think perhaps a lot of men went away to war meanin' to come back to her; but maybe none of 'em ever did."

He stooped down close to the stone, hunting for any record of marriage.

"There's nothing here to show."

"Of course not. How could there be anything there better than just 'Margery Lee,' and that eloquent date?"

She drew close to him and an unexpected lump came into his throat as her yellow hair brushed his cheek.

"You see how she was, don't you, Harry?"

"I see," he agreed gently. "I see through your precious eyes. You're beautiful now, so I know she must have been."

Silent and close they stood, and he could feel her shoulders trembling a little. An ambling breeze swept up the hill and stirred the brim of her floppidy hat.

"Let's go down there!"

She was pointing to a flat stretch on the other side of the hill where along the green turf were a thousand grayish-white crosses stretching in endless, ordered rows like the stacked arms of a battalion.

"Those are the Confederate dead," said Sally Carrol simply.

They walked along and read the inscriptions, always only a name and a date, sometimes quite indecipherable.

"The last row is the saddest—see, 'way over there. Every cross has just a date on it, and the word 'Unknown.'"

She looked at him and her eyes brimmed with tears.

"I can't tell you how real it is to me, darling—if you don't know."

"How you feel about it is beautiful to me."

"No, no, it's not me, it's them—that old time that I've tried to have live in me. These were just men, unimportant evidently or they wouldn't have been 'unknown'; but they died for the most beautiful thing in the world—the dead South. You see," she continued, her voice still husky, her eyes glistening with tears, "people have these dreams they fasten onto things, and I've always grown up with that dream. It was so easy because it was all dead and there weren't any disillusions comin' to me. I've tried in a way to live up to those past standards of noblesse oblige—there's just the last remnants of it, you know, like the roses of an old garden dying all round us—streaks of strange courtliness and chivalry

6. THE ICE PALACE

in some of these boys an' stories I used to hear from a Confederate soldier who lived next door, and a few old darkies. Oh, Harry, there was something, there was something! I couldn't ever make you understand, but it was there."

"I understand," he assured her again quietly.

Sally Carrol smiled and dried her eyes on the tip of a handkerchief protruding from his breast pocket.

"You don't feel depressed, do you, lover? Even when I cry I'm happy here, and I get a sort of strength from it."

Hand in hand they turned and walked slowly away. Finding soft grass she drew him down to a seat beside her with their backs against the remnants of a low broken wall.

"Wish those three old women would clear out," he complained. "I want to kiss you, Sally Carrol."

"Me, too."

They waited impatiently for the three bent figures to move off, and then she kissed him until the sky seemed to fade out and all her smiles and tears to vanish in an ecstasy of eternal seconds.

Afterward they walked slowly back together, while on the corners twilight played at somnolent black-and-white checkers with the end of day.

"You'll be up about mid-January," he said, "and you've got to stay a month at least. It'll be slick. There's a winter carnival on, and if you've never really seen snow it'll be like fairy-land to you. There'll be skating and skiing and tobogganing and sleigh-riding, and all sorts of torchlight parades on snowshoes. They haven't had one for years, so they're going to make it a knock-out."

"Will I be cold, Harry?" she asked suddenly.

"You certainly won't. You may freeze your nose, but you won't be shivery cold. It's hard and dry, you know."

"I guess I'm a summer child. I don't like any cold I've ever seen."

She broke off, and they were both silent for a minute.

"Sally Carrol," he said very slowly, "what do you say to—March?"

"I say I love you."

"March?"

"March, Harry."

III

All night in the Pullman it was very cold. She rang for the porter to ask for another blanket, and when he couldn't give her one she tried vainly, by squeezing down into the bottom of her berth and doubling back the bedclothes, to snatch a few hours' sleep. She wanted to look her best in the morning.

She rose at six and sliding uncomfortably into her clothes stumbled up to the diner for a cup of coffee. The snow had filtered into the vestibules and covered the floor with a slippery coating. It was intriguing, this cold, it crept in everywhere. Her breath was quite visible and she blew into the air with a naive enjoyment. Seated in the diner she stared out the window at white hills and valleys and scattered pines whose every branch was a green platter for a cold feast of snow. Sometimes a solitary farmhouse would fly by, ugly and bleak and lone on the white waste; and with each one she had an instant of chill compassion for the souls shut in there waiting for spring.

As she left the diner and swayed back into the Pullman she experienced a surging rush of energy and wondered if she was feeling the bracing air of which Harry had spoken. This was the North, the North—her land now!

"Then blow, ye winds, heigho!
A-roving I will go,"

she chanted exultantly to herself.

"What's 'at?" inquired the porter politely.

"I said: 'Brush me off.'"

6. THE ICE PALACE

The long wires of the telegraph-poles doubled; two tracks ran up beside the train—three—four; came a succession of white-roofed houses, a glimpse of a trolley-car with frosted windows, streets—more streets—the city.

She stood for a dazed moment in the frosty station before she saw three fur-bundled figures descending upon her.

"There she is!"

"Oh, Sally Carrol!"

Sally Carrol dropped her bag.

"Hi!"

A faintly familiar icy-cold face kissed her, and then she was in a group of faces all apparently emitting great clouds of heavy smoke; she was shaking hands. There were Gordon, a short, eager man of thirty who looked like an amateur knocked-about model for Harry, and his wife, Myra, a listless lady with flaxen hair under a fur automobile cap. Almost immediately Sally Carrol thought of her as vaguely Scandinavian. A cheerful chauffeur adopted her bag, and amid ricochets of half-phrases, exclamations, and perfunctory listless "my dears" from Myra, they swept each other from the station.

Then they were in a sedan bound through a crooked succession of snowy streets where dozens of little boys were hitching sleds behind grocery wagons and automobiles.

"Oh," cried Sally Carrol, "I want to do that! Can we, Harry?"

"That's for kids. But we might—"

"It looks like such a circus!" she said regretfully.

Home was a rambling frame house set on a white lap of snow, and there she met a big, gray-haired man of whom she approved, and a lady who was like an egg, and who kissed her—these were Harry's parents. There was a breathless indescribable hour crammed full of half-sentences, hot water, bacon and eggs and confusion; and after that she was alone with Harry in the library, asking him if she dared smoke.

It was a large room with a Madonna over the fireplace and rows upon rows of books in covers of light gold and dark gold and shiny red. All the chairs had little lace squares where one's head should rest, the couch was just comfortable, the books looked as if they had been read—some—and Sally Carrol had an instantaneous vision of the battered old library at home, with her father's huge medical books, and the oil-paintings of her three great-uncles, and the old couch that had been mended up for forty-five years and was still luxurious to dream in. This room struck her as being neither attractive nor particularly otherwise. It was simply a room with a lot of fairly expensive things in it that all looked about fifteen years old.

"What do you think of it up here?" demanded Harry eagerly. "Does it surprise you? Is it what you expected, I mean?"

"You are, Harry," she said quietly, and reached out her arms to him.

But after a brief kiss he seemed anxious to extort enthusiasm from her.

"The town, I mean. Do you like it? Can you feel the pep in the air?"

"Oh, Harry," she laughed, "you'll have to give me time. You can't just fling questions at me."

She puffed at her cigarette with a sigh of contentment.

"One thing I want to ask you," he began rather apologetically. "You Southerners put quite an emphasis on family, and all that—not that it isn't quite all right, but you'll find it a little different here. I mean—you'll notice a lot of things that'll seem to you sort of vulgar display at first, Sally Carrol; but just remember that this is a three-generation town. Everybody has a father, and about half of us have grandfathers. Back of that we don't go."

"Of course," she murmured.

"Our grandfathers, you see, founded the place, and a lot of them had to take some pretty queer jobs while they were doing the founding. For instance, there's one woman who at present is about the social model for the town; well, her father was the first public ash man—things like that."

6. THE ICE PALACE

"Why," said Sally Carrol, puzzled, "did you s'pose I was goin' to make remarks about people?"

"Not at all," interrupted Harry, "and I'm not apologizing for any one either. It's just that—well, a Southern girl came up here last summer and said some unfortunate things, and—oh, I just thought I'd tell you."

Sally Carrol felt suddenly indignant—as though she had been unjustly spanked—but Harry evidently considered the subject closed, for he went on with a great surge of enthusiasm.

"It's carnival time, you know. First in ten years. And there's an ice palace they're building now that's the first they've had since eighty-five. Built out of blocks of the clearest ice they could find—on a tremendous scale."

She rose and walking to the window pushed aside the heavy Turkish portières and looked out.

"Oh!" she cried suddenly. "There's two little boys makin' a snow man! Harry, do you reckon I can go out an' help 'em?"

"You dream! Come here and kiss me."

She left the window rather reluctantly.

"I don't guess this is a very kissable climate, is it? I mean, it makes you so you don't want to sit round, doesn't it?"

"We're not going to. I've got a vacation for the first week you're here, and there's a dinner-dance to-night."

"Oh, Harry," she confessed, subsiding in a heap, half in his lap, half in the pillows, "I sure do feel confused. I haven't got an idea whether I'll like it or not, an' I don't know what people expect, or anythin'. You'll have to tell me, honey."

"I'll tell you," he said softly, "if you'll just tell me you're glad to be here."

"Glad—just awful glad!" she whispered, insinuating herself into his arms in her own peculiar way. "Where you are is home for me, Harry."

And as she said this she had the feeling for almost the first time in her life that she was acting a part.

That night, amid the gleaming candles of a dinner-party, where the men seemed to do most of the talking while the girls sat in a haughty and expensive aloofness, even Harry's presence on her left failed to make her feel at home.

"They're a good-looking crowd, don't you think?" he demanded. "Just look round. There's Spud Hubbard, tackle at Princeton last year, and Junie Morton—he and the red-haired fellow next to him were both Yale hockey captains; Junie was in my class. Why, the best athletes in the world come from these states round here. This is a man's country, I tell you. Look at John J. Fishburn!"

"Who's he?" asked Sally Carrol innocently.

"Don't you know?"

"I've heard the name."

"Greatest wheat man in the Northwest, and one of the greatest financiers in the country."

She turned suddenly to a voice on her right.

"I guess they forgot to introduce us. My name's Roger Patton."

"My name is Sally Carrol Happer," she said graciously.

"Yes, I know. Harry told me you were coming."

"You a relative?"

"No, I'm a professor."

"Oh," she laughed.

"At the university. You're from the South, aren't you?"

"Yes; Tarleton, Georgia."

She liked him immediately—a reddish-brown mustache under watery blue eyes that had something in them that these other eyes lacked, some quality of appreciation. They exchanged stray sentences through dinner, and she made up her mind to see him again.

After coffee she was introduced to numerous good-looking young men who danced with conscious precision and seemed to take it for granted that she wanted to talk about nothing except Harry.

6. THE ICE PALACE

"Heavens," she thought, "they talk as if my being engaged made me older than they are—as if I'd tell their mothers on them!"

In the South an engaged girl, even a young married woman, expected the same amount of half-affectionate badinage and flattery that would be accorded a débutante, but here all that seemed banned. One young man, after getting well started on the subject of Sally Carrol's eyes, and how they had allured him ever since she entered the room, went into a violent confusion when he found she was visiting the Bellamys—was Harry's fiancée. He seemed to feel as though he had made some risqué and inexcusable blunder, became immediately formal, and left her at the first opportunity.

She was rather glad when Roger Patton cut in on her and suggested that they sit out a while.

"Well," he inquired, blinking cheerily, "how's Carmen from the South?"

"Mighty fine. How's—how's Dangerous Dan McGrew? Sorry, but he's the only Northerner I know much about."

He seemed to enjoy that.

"Of course," he confessed, "as a professor of literature I'm not supposed to have read Dangerous Dan McGrew."

"Are you a native?"

"No, I'm a Philadelphian. Imported from Harvard to teach French. But I've been here ten years."

"Nine years, three hundred an' sixty-four days longer than me."

"Like it here?"

"Uh-huh. Sure do!"

"Really?"

"Well, why not? Don't I look as if I were havin' a good time?"

"I saw you look out the window a minute ago—and shiver."

"Just my imagination," laughed Sally Carrol. "I'm used to havin' everythin' quiet outside, an' sometimes I look out an' see a flurry of snow, an' it's just as if somethin' dead was movin'."

He nodded appreciatively.

"Ever been North before?"

"Spent two Julys in Asheville, North Carolina."

"Nice-looking crowd, aren't they?" suggested Patton, indicating the swirling floor.

Sally Carrol started. This had been Harry's remark.

"Sure are! They're—canine."

"What?"

She flushed.

"I'm sorry; that sounded worse than I meant it. You see, I always think of people as feline or canine, irrespective of sex."

"Which are you?"

"I'm feline. So are you. So are most Southern men an' most of these girls here."

"What's Harry?"

"Harry's canine distinctly. All the men I've met to-night seem to be canine."

"What does 'canine' imply? A certain conscious masculinity as opposed to subtlety?"

"Reckon so. I never analyzed it—only I just look at people an' say 'canine' or 'feline' right off. It's right absurd, I guess."

"Not at all. I'm interested. I used to have a theory about these people. I think they're freezing up."

"What?"

"I think they're growing like Swedes—Ibsenesque, you know. Very gradually getting gloomy and melancholy. It's these long winters. Ever read any Ibsen?"

She shook her head.

"Well, you find in his characters a certain brooding rigidity. They're righteous, narrow, and cheerless, without infinite possibilities for great sorrow or joy."

"Without smiles or tears?"

"Exactly. That's my theory. You see there are thousands of Swedes up here. They come, I imagine, because the climate is very much like their own, and there's been a gradual mingling. There're probably not half a dozen here tonight, but—we've had four Swedish governors. Am I boring you?"

"I'm mighty interested."

"Your future sister-in-law is half Swedish. Personally I like her, but my theory is that Swedes react rather badly on us as a whole. Scandinavians, you know, have the largest suicide rate in the world."

"Why do you live here if it's so depressing?"

"Oh, it doesn't get me. I'm pretty well cloistered, and I suppose books mean more than people to me anyway."

"But writers all speak about the South being tragic. You know—Spanish señoritas, black hair and daggers an' haunting music."

He shook his head.

"No, the Northern races are the tragic races—they don't indulge in the cheering luxury of tears."

Sally Carrol thought of her graveyard. She supposed that that was vaguely what she had meant when she said it didn't depress her.

"The Italians are about the gayest people in the world—but it's a dull subject," he broke off. "Anyway, I want to tell you you're marrying a pretty fine man."

Sally Carrol was moved by an impulse of confidence.

"I know. I'm the sort of person who wants to be taken care of after a certain point, and I feel sure I will be."

"Shall we dance? You know," he continued as they rose, "it's encouraging to find a girl who knows what she's marrying for. Nine-tenths of them think of it as a sort of walking into a moving-picture sunset."

She laughed, and liked him immensely.

Two hours later on the way home she nestled near Harry in the back seat.

"Oh, Harry," she whispered, "it's so co-old!"

"But it's warm in here, darling girl."

"But outside it's cold; and oh, that howling wind!"

She buried her face deep in his fur coat and trembled involuntarily as his cold lips kissed the tip of her ear.

IV

The first week of her visit passed in a whirl. She had her promised toboggan-ride at the back of an automobile through a chill January twilight. Swathed in furs she put in a morning tobogganing on the country-club hill; even tried skiing, to sail through the air for a glorious moment and then land in a tangled laughing bundle on a soft snowdrift. She liked all the winter sports, except an afternoon spent snow-shoeing over a glaring plain under pale yellow sunshine, but she soon realized that these things were for children—that she was being humored and that the enjoyment round her was only a reflection of her own.

At first the Bellamy family puzzled her. The men were reliable and she liked them; to Mr. Bellamy especially, with his iron-gray hair and energetic dignity, she took an immediate fancy, once she found that he was born in Kentucky; this made of him a link between the old life and the new. But toward the women she felt a definite hostility. Myra, her future sister-in-law, seemed the essence of spiritless conventionality. Her conversation was so utterly devoid of personality that Sally Carrol, who came from a country where a certain amount of charm and assurance could be taken for granted in the women, was inclined to despise her.

"If those women aren't beautiful," she thought, "they're nothing. They just fade out when you look at them. They're glorified domestics. Men are the centre

6. THE ICE PALACE

of every mixed group."

Lastly there was Mrs. Bellamy, whom Sally Carrol detested. The first day's impression of an egg had been confirmed—an egg with a cracked, veiny voice and such an ungracious dumpiness of carriage that Sally Carrol felt that if she once fell she would surely scramble. In addition, Mrs. Bellamy seemed to typify the town in being innately hostile to strangers. She called Sally Carrol "Sally," and could not be persuaded that the double name was anything more than a tedious, ridiculous nickname. To Sally Carrol this shortening of her name was like presenting her to the public half clothed. She loved "Sally Carrol"; she loathed "Sally." She knew also that Harry's mother disapproved of her bobbed hair; and she had never dared smoke down-stairs after that first day when Mrs. Bellamy had come into the library sniffing violently.

Of all the men she met she preferred Roger Patton, who was a frequent visitor at the house. He never again alluded to the Ibsenesque tendency of the populace, but when he came in one day and found her curled upon the sofa bent over "Peer Gynt," he laughed and told her to forget what he'd said—that it was all rot.

And then one afternoon in her second week she and Harry hovered on the edge of a dangerously steep quarrel. She considered that he precipitated it entirely, though the Serbia in the case was an unknown man who had not had his trousers pressed.

They had been walking homeward between mounds of high-piled snow and under a sun which Sally Carrol scarcely recognized. They passed a little girl done up in gray wool until she resembled a small Teddy bear, and Sally Carrol could not resist a gasp of maternal appreciation.

"Look! Harry!"

"What?"

"That little girl—did you see her face?"

"Yes, why?"

"It was red as a little strawberry. Oh, she was cute!"

"Why, your own face is almost as red as that already! Everybody's healthy here. We're out in the cold as soon as we're old enough to walk. Wonderful climate!"

She looked at him and had to agree. He was mighty healthy-looking; so was his brother. And she had noticed the new red in her own cheeks that very morning.

Suddenly their glances were caught and held, and they stared for a moment at the street-corner ahead of them. A man was standing there, his knees bent, his eyes gazing upward with a tense expression as though he were about to make a leap toward the chilly sky. And then they both exploded into a shout of laughter, for coming closer they discovered it had been a ludicrous momentary illusion produced by the extreme bagginess of the man's trousers.

"Reckon that's one on us," she laughed.

"He must be a Southerner, judging by those trousers," suggested Harry mischievously.

"Why, Harry!"

Her surprised look must have irritated him.

"Those damn Southerners!"

Sally Carrol's eyes flashed.

"Don't call 'em that!"

"I'm sorry, dear," said Harry, malignantly apologetic, "but you know what I think of them. They're sort of—sort of degenerates—not at all like the old Southerners. They've lived so long down there with all the colored people that they've gotten lazy and shiftless."

"Hush your mouth, Harry!" she cried angrily. "They're not! They may be lazy—anybody would be in that climate—but they're my best friends, an' I don't want to hear 'em criticised in any such sweepin' way. Some of 'em are the finest men in the world."

6. THE ICE PALACE

"Oh, I know. They're all right when they come North to college, but of all the hangdog, ill-dressed, slovenly lot I ever saw, a bunch of small-town Southerners are the worst!"

Sally Carrol was clinching her gloved hands and biting her lip furiously.

"Why," continued Harry, "there was one in my class at New Haven, and we all thought that at last we'd found the true type of Southern aristocrat, but it turned out that he wasn't an aristocrat at all—just the son of a Northern carpetbagger, who owned about all the cotton round Mobile."

"A Southerner wouldn't talk the way you're talking now," she said evenly.

"They haven't the energy!"

"Or the somethin' else."

"I'm sorry, Sally Carrol, but I've heard you say yourself that you'd never marry—"

"That's quite different. I told you I wouldn't want to tie my life to any of the boys that are round Tarleton now, but I never made any sweepin' generalities."

They walked along in silence.

"I probably spread it on a bit thick, Sally Carrol. I'm sorry."

She nodded but made no answer. Five minutes later as they stood in the hallway she suddenly threw her arms round him.

"Oh, Harry," she cried, her eyes brimming with tears, "let's get married next week. I'm afraid of having fusses like that. I'm afraid, Harry. It wouldn't be that way if we were married."

But Harry, being in the wrong, was still irritated.

"That'd be idiotic. We decided on March."

The tears in Sally Carrol's eyes faded; her expression hardened slightly.

"Very well—I suppose I shouldn't have said that."

Harry melted.

"Dear little nut!" he cried. "Come and kiss me and let's forget."

That very night at the end of a vaudeville performance the orchestra played

"Dixie" and Sally Carrol felt something stronger and more enduring than her tears and smiles of the day brim up inside her. She leaned forward gripping the arms of her chair until her face grew crimson.

"Sort of get you, dear?" whispered Harry.

But she did not hear him. To the spirited throb of the violins and the inspiring beat of the kettledrums her own old ghosts were marching by and on into the darkness, and as fifes whistled and sighed in the low encore they seemed so nearly out of sight that she could have waved good-by.

>"Away, away,
>
>>Away down South in Dixie!
>
>Away, away,
>
>>Away down South in Dixie!"

V

It was a particularly cold night. A sudden thaw had nearly cleared the streets the day before, but now they were traversed again with a powdery wraith of loose snow that travelled in wavy lines before the feet of the wind, and filled the lower air with a fine-particled mist. There was no sky—only a dark, ominous tent that draped in the tops of the streets and was in reality a vast approaching army of snowflakes—while over it all, chilling away the comfort from the brown-and-green glow of lighted windows and muffling the steady trot of the horse pulling their sleigh, interminably washed the north wind. It was a dismal town after all, she thought—dismal.

Sometimes at night it had seemed to her as though no one lived here—they had all gone long ago—leaving lighted houses to be covered in time by tombing heaps of sleet. Oh, if there should be snow on her grave! To be beneath great piles of it all winter long, where even her headstone would be a light shadow against light shadows. Her grave—a grave that should be flower-strewn and

6. THE ICE PALACE

washed with sun and rain.

She thought again of those isolated country houses that her train had passed, and of the life there the long winter through—the ceaseless glare through the windows, the crust forming on the soft drifts of snow, finally the slow, cheerless melting, and the harsh spring of which Roger Patton had told her. Her spring—to lose it forever—with its lilacs and the lazy sweetness it stirred in her heart. She was laying away that spring—afterward she would lay away that sweetness.

With a gradual insistence the storm broke. Sally Carrol felt a film of flakes melt quickly on her eyelashes, and Harry reached over a furry arm and drew down her complicated flannel cap. Then the small flakes came in skirmish-line, and the horse bent his neck patiently as a transparency of white appeared momentarily on his coat.

"Oh, he's cold, Harry," she said quickly.

"Who? The horse? Oh, no, he isn't. He likes it!"

After another ten minutes they turned a corner and came in sight of their destination. On a tall hill outlined in vivid glaring green against the wintry sky, stood the ice palace. It was three stories in the air, with battlements and embrasures and narrow icicled windows, and the innumerable electric lights inside made a gorgeous transparency of the great central hall. Sally Carrol clutched Harry's hand under the fur robe.

"It's beautiful!" he cried excitedly. "My golly, it's beautiful, isn't it! They haven't had one here since eighty-five!"

Somehow the notion of there not having been one since eighty-five oppressed her. Ice was a ghost, and this mansion of it was surely peopled by those shades of the eighties, with pale faces and blurred snow-filled hair.

"Come on, dear," said Harry.

She followed him out of the sleigh and waited while he hitched the horse. A party of four—Gordon, Myra, Roger Patton, and another girl—drew up beside them with a mighty jingle of bells. There was quite a crowd already, bundled in fur or sheepskin, shouting and calling to each other as they moved through the snow, which was now so thick that people could scarcely be distinguished a few yards away.

"It's a hundred and seventy feet tall," Harry was saying to a muffled figure beside him as they trudged toward the entrance, "covers six thousand square yards."

She caught snatches of conversation: "One main hall"—"walls twenty to forty inches thick"—"and the ice cave has almost a mile of—"—"this Canuck who built it—"

They found their way inside, and dazed by the magic of the great crystal walls Sally Carrol found herself repeating over and over two lines from "Kubla Khan":

>"It was a miracle of rare device,
>A sunny pleasure-dome with caves of ice!"

In the great glittering cavern with the dark shut out she took a seat on a wooden bench, and the evening's oppression lifted. Harry was right—it was beautiful; and her gaze travelled the smooth surface of the walls, the blocks for which had been selected for their purity and clearness to obtain this opalescent, translucent effect.

"Look! Here we go—oh, boy!" cried Harry.

A band in a far corner struck up "Hail, Hail, the Gang's All Here!" which echoed over to them in wild muddled acoustics, and then the lights suddenly went out; silence seemed to flow down the icy sides and sweep over them. Sally Carrol could still see her white breath in the darkness, and a dim row of pale faces over on the other side.

The music eased to a sighing complaint, and from outside drifted in the

6. THE ICE PALACE

full-throated resonant chant of the marching clubs. It grew louder like some pæan of a viking tribe traversing an ancient wild; it swelled—they were coming nearer; then a row of torches appeared, and another and another, and keeping time with their moccasined feet a long column of gray-mackinawed figures swept in, snowshoes slung at their shoulders, torches soaring and flickering as their voices rose along the great walls.

The gray column ended and another followed, the light streaming luridly this time over red toboggan caps and flaming crimson mackinaws, and as they entered they took up the refrain; then came a long platoon of blue and white, of green, of white, of brown and yellow.

"Those white ones are the Wacouta Club," whispered Harry eagerly. "Those are the men you've met round at dances."

The volume of the voices grew; the great cavern was a phantasmagoria of torches waving in great banks of fire, of colors and the rhythm of soft-leather steps. The leading column turned and halted, platoon deployed in front of platoon until the whole procession made a solid flag of flame, and then from thousands of voices burst a mighty shout that filled the air like a crash of thunder, and sent the torches wavering. It was magnificent, it was tremendous! To Sally Carrol it was the North offering sacrifice on some mighty altar to the gray pagan God of Snow. As the shout died the band struck up again and there came more singing, and then long reverberating cheers by each club. She sat very quiet listening while the staccato cries rent the stillness; and then she started, for there was a volley of explosion, and great clouds of smoke went up here and there through the cavern—the flash-light photographers at work—and the council was over. With the band at their head the clubs formed in column once more, took up their chant, and began to march out.

"Come on!" shouted Harry. "We want to see the labyrinths down-stairs before they turn the lights off!"

They all rose and started toward the chute—Harry and Sally Carrol in the lead, her little mitten buried in his big fur gantlet. At the bottom of the chute was a long empty room of ice, with the ceiling so low that they had to stoop—and their hands were parted. Before she realized what he intended Harry had darted down one of the half-dozen glittering passages that opened into the room and was only a vague receding blot against the green shimmer.

"Harry!" she called.

"Come on!" he cried back.

She looked round the empty chamber; the rest of the party had evidently decided to go home, were already outside somewhere in the blundering snow. She hesitated and then darted in after Harry.

"Harry!" she shouted.

She had reached a turning-point thirty feet down; she heard a faint muffled answer far to the left, and with a touch of panic fled toward it. She passed another turning, two more yawning alleys.

"Harry!"

No answer. She started to run straight forward, and then turned like lightning and sped back the way she had come, enveloped in a sudden icy terror.

She reached a turn—was it here?—took the left and came to what should have been the outlet into the long, low room, but it was only another glittering passage with darkness at the end. She called again, but the walls gave back a flat, lifeless echo with no reverberations. Retracing her steps she turned another corner, this time following a wide passage. It was like the green lane between the parted waters of the Red Sea, like a damp vault connecting empty tombs.

She slipped a little now as she walked, for ice had formed on the bottom of her overshoes; she had to run her gloves along the half-slippery, half-sticky walls to keep her balance.

"Harry!"

Still no answer. The sound she made bounced mockingly down to the end

6. THE ICE PALACE

of the passage.

Then on an instant the lights went out, and she was in complete darkness. She gave a small, frightened cry, and sank down into a cold little heap on the ice. She felt her left knee do something as she fell, but she scarcely noticed it as some deep terror far greater than any fear of being lost settled upon her. She was alone with this presence that came out of the North, the dreary loneliness that rose from ice-bound whalers in the Arctic seas, from smokeless, trackless wastes where were strewn the whitened bones of adventure. It was an icy breath of death; it was rolling down low across the land to clutch at her.

With a furious, despairing energy she rose again and started blindly down the darkness. She must get out. She might be lost in here for days, freeze to death and lie embedded in the ice like corpses she had read of, kept perfectly preserved until the melting of a glacier. Harry probably thought she had left with the others—he had gone by now; no one would know until late next day. She reached pitifully for the wall. Forty inches thick, they had said—forty inches thick!

"Oh!"

On both sides of her along the walls she felt things creeping, damp souls that haunted this palace, this town, this North.

"Oh, send somebody—send somebody!" she cried aloud.

Clark Darrow—he would understand; or Joe Ewing; she couldn't be left here to wander forever—to be frozen, heart, body, and soul. This her—this Sally Carrol! Why, she was a happy thing. She was a happy little girl. She liked warmth and summer and Dixie. These things were foreign—foreign.

"You're not crying," something said aloud. "You'll never cry any more. Your tears would just freeze; all tears freeze up here!"

She sprawled full length on the ice.

"Oh, God!" she faltered.

A long single file of minutes went by, and with a great weariness she felt her eyes closing. Then some one seemed to sit down near her and take her face in warm, soft hands. She looked up gratefully.

"Why, it's Margery Lee," she crooned softly to herself. "I knew you'd come." It really was Margery Lee, and she was just as Sally Carrol had known she would be, with a young, white brow, and wide, welcoming eyes, and a hoop-skirt of some soft material that was quite comforting to rest on.

"Margery Lee."

It was getting darker now and darker—all those tombstones ought to be repainted, sure enough, only that would spoil 'em, of course. Still, you ought to be able to see 'em.

Then after a succession of moments that went fast and then slow, but seemed to be ultimately resolving themselves into a multitude of blurred rays converging toward a pale-yellow sun, she heard a great cracking noise break her new-found stillness.

It was the sun, it was a light; a torch, and a torch beyond that, and another one, and voices; a face took flesh below the torch, heavy arms raised her, and she felt something on her cheek—it felt wet. Some one had seized her and was rubbing her face with snow. How ridiculous—with snow!

"Sally Carrol! Sally Carrol!"

It was Dangerous Dan McGrew; and two other faces she didn't know.

"Child, child! We've been looking for you two hours! Harry's half-crazy!"

Things came rushing back into place—the singing, the torches, the great shout of the marching clubs. She squirmed in Patton's arms and gave a long, low cry.

"Oh, I want to get out of here! I'm going back home. Take me home"—her voice rose to a scream that sent a chill to Harry's heart as he came racing down the next passage—"to-morrow!" she cried with delirious, unrestrained passion—"To-morrow! To-morrow! To-morrow!"

6. THE ICE PALACE

VI

The wealth of golden sunlight poured a quite enervating yet oddly comforting heat over the house where day long it faced the dusty stretch of road. Two birds were making a great to-do in a cool spot found among the branches of a tree next door, and down the street a colored woman was announcing herself melodiously as a purveyor of strawberries. It was April afternoon.

Sally Carrol Happer, resting her chin on her arm, and her arm on an old window-seat, gazed sleepily down over the spangled dust whence the heat waves were rising for the first time this spring. She was watching a very ancient Ford turn a perilous corner and rattle and groan to a jolting stop at the end of the walk. She made no sound, and in a minute a strident familiar whistle rent the air. Sally Carrol smiled and blinked.

"Good mawnin'."

A head appeared tortuously from under the cartop below.

" 'Tain't mawnin', Sally Carrol."

"Sure enough!" she said in affected surprise. "I guess maybe not."

"What you doin'?"

"Eatin' green peach. 'Spect to die any minute."

Clark twisted himself a last impossible notch to get a view of her face.

"Water's warm as a kettla steam, Sally Carrol. Wanta go swimmin'?"

"Hate to move," sighed Sally Carrol lazily, "but I reckon so."

作品赏析

一、作家介绍

菲茨杰拉德（F. Scott Fitzgerald，1896—1940）是美国20世纪与福克纳、海明威齐名的著名小说家，迷惘的一代的杰出代表、爵士乐时代和"喧嚣的二十年代"（"The Roaring Twenties"）的最佳代言人。在他44岁的短暂人生中，在作为职业作家的二十余年里，他创作了《人间天堂》（*This Side of Paradise*，

1920)、《漂亮冤家》(The Beautiful and Damned, 1922)、《了不起的盖茨比》(The Great Gatsby, 1925)、《夜色温柔》(Tender Is the Night, 1934)、《最后一位君子》(The Last Tycoon, 生前未完成) 五部长篇小说，出版了短篇小说集《新潮女郎与哲学家》(Flappers and Philosophers, 1920)、《爵士时代的故事》(Tales of the Jazz Age, 1922)、《所有悲伤的年轻人》(All the Sad Young Men, 1926)、《清晨的起床号》(Taps at Reville, 1935)，一部剧本《蔬菜》(The Vegetable, 1923)，一部自传散文集《崩溃》(The Crack-Up, 1945)。他一生共创作了178篇短篇小说[1]，其中有8部公认的名篇，它们是《重访巴比伦》("Babylon Revisited")、《赦罪》("Absolution")、《阔少爷》("The Rich Boy")、《冰宫》、《五一节》("May Day")、《冬天的梦》("Winter Dreams")、《一颗像里茨饭店那么大的钻石》("The Diamond as Big as the Ritz")、《疯狂的星期天》("Crazy Sunday")。在他的长篇小说中，《了不起的盖茨比》《夜色温柔》和《最后一位君子》被公认为他最好的作品，评论界评价极高。哈罗德·布鲁姆 (Harold Bloom) 的《西方正典》(The West Canon: The Books and school of the Ages) 的附录"经典书目"中收录了他的《了不起的盖茨比》《夜色温柔》《重访巴比伦及其他故事》三部作品[2]，就是对他长篇和短篇小说创作的充分肯定。《了不起的盖茨比》可能是全世界读者都十分熟悉的菲茨杰拉德的代表作，它是对20世纪20年代美国历史以及美国梦破碎主题的最忠实的呈现，在著名的1998年现代图书馆20世纪100部最佳英语小说榜中高居第二位，仅次于《尤利西斯》，可以说是评论家眼里最有影响力的美国小说，菲茨杰拉德本人说它"大概可以称得上是有史以来写得最精彩的美国小说之一"[3]。虽然这部小说在市场上没有取得《人间天堂》和《漂亮冤家》那样巨大的商业成功，不过它获得的评价却超过了前两部小说。著名作家伊迪斯·华顿 (Edith Wharton)、薇拉·凯瑟 (Willa Cather)、格特鲁德·斯

1　其中部分短篇小说是菲茨杰拉德去世后经人整理发表的。数据来源参见：Jackson R. Bryer, ed., *New Essays on F. Scott Fitzgerald's Neglected Stories*, Columbia & London: University of Missouri Press, 1996, p. 4.

2　Harold Bloom, *The Western Canon: The Books and School of the Ages*, New York, San Diego, London: Harcourt Brace & Company, 1994, p. 562.

3　John Kuehl and Jackson R. Bryer, eds., *Dear Scott/Dear Max: The Fitzgerald-Perkins Correspondence*, New York: Charles Scribner's Sons, 1971, p. 76.

6. THE ICE PALACE

泰因（Gertrude Stein）、T. S. 艾略特（T. S. Elliot），著名评论家埃德蒙·威尔逊（Edmund Wilson）和范怀克·布鲁克斯（Van Wyck Brooks）等人，甚至连向来对人苛刻的海明威也纷纷写信给菲茨杰拉德，高度评价这部小说。例如，斯泰因称他"用笔创造了一个现代世界，一个现代的纵酒宴乐的祭祀仪式"[1]。威尔逊认为这是他写得最出色的一部作品[2]。艾略特在写给菲茨杰拉德的信中，对《了不起的盖茨比》作出了常为人们引用的评价："在我若干年里所拜读过的新小说中，无论是英国小说还是美国小说，我感觉这部作品是最有趣味、最令人振奋的……事实上，在我看来，这是美国小说自亨利·詹姆斯以来所迈出的第一步。"[3] 同样，虽然不乏各种批评声音，但《夜色温柔》和《最后一位君子》也受到了文学圈和评论界的广泛好评。

为了更好地理解菲茨杰拉德的小说，有必要先简要回顾他的生平，因为他的创作和人生是密不可分的，可以说，他的每部作品都或多或少有自传的成分。他生于明尼苏达州的首府圣保罗，父母都是罗马天主教徒。父亲在一家小公司工作，母亲出生于一个殷实的爱尔兰移民家庭。菲茨杰拉德的父亲在经商上屡屡失败，家庭的经济来源一度主要依靠母亲继承的遗产。不过他有一定的文学修养，常常给儿子阅读诗歌，诸如爱伦·坡和拜伦的诗歌，从小培养儿子对文学的兴趣。深受南方贵族传统影响的他还常跟儿子讲南北战争的故事。菲茨杰拉德从小就显示出对文学的喜爱，10岁开始写侦探小说。他17岁进入普林斯顿大学，在大学里他的学习成绩并不好，却对写作和体育极感兴趣。他与后来成为文学界名人的约翰·皮尔·毕晓普（John Peale Bishop）和埃德蒙·威尔逊是同学兼朋友。他加入文学社团"三角俱乐部"（Triangle Club），积极向文学刊物《普林斯顿之虎》（*The Princeton Tiger*）和《拿骚文学杂志》（*The Nassau Literary Magazine*）投稿。大学里的这些文学活动为将来成为职业作家的菲茨杰拉德奠定了基础。1917年他离校入伍，被派驻亚拉巴马州首府蒙哥马利任陆军中尉。但还

1　Edmund Wilson, ed., *F. Scott Fitzgerald: The Crack-Up*, New York: New Directions Books, 1993, p. 308.
2　Edmund Wilson, *Letters on Literature and Politics: 1912—1972*, New York: Farrar, Straus and Giroux, 1977, p. 121.
3　Edmund Wilson, ed., *F. Scott Fitzgerald: The Crack-Up*, New York: New Directions Books, 1993, p. 310.

未出征,第一次世界大战结束,因此他未出国参战。在这期间,他在一场舞会上认识了当地大法官的女儿珊尔达·塞耶(Zelda Sayre)。珊尔达是亚拉巴马州著名的美女,而菲茨杰拉德是英俊帅气的军官。两人一见钟情,很快就相恋,接着订婚。菲茨杰拉德退伍后在纽约的一家广告公司工作,收入微薄。尽管他几次到蒙哥马利去求婚,珊尔达都未应允。1919年6月珊尔达解除了与他的婚约。这给菲茨杰拉德很大的打击,于是,他辞职回到家乡圣保罗,潜心修改他的长篇小说《浪漫的自私主义者》(*The Romantic Egoists*),并改名为《人间天堂》。他把书稿给了斯克里布纳出版社的编辑珀金斯,珀金斯答应他在1920年春出版。同时,他的《头与肩》("Head and Shoulders")和《冰宫》等6篇短篇小说被当时最畅销的杂志《星期六晚邮报》(*The Saturday Evening Post*)接受,获得了可观的稿费。在他几次赴蒙哥马利后,1920年1月珊尔达与他恢复婚约。不久《人间天堂》出版,几天后这对金童玉女就在纽约圣帕特里克教堂举行了婚礼。他们婚礼的时间也恰好是"喧嚣的二十年代",即菲茨杰拉德自己命名的"爵士时代"("The Jazz Age")的开始。他本人成了爵士时代的代言人和象征。第一部长篇小说《人间天堂》的发表对他的人生和事业都是关键的一步。这部小说给他带来了可观的收入,也给他带来了巨大的名声。当时新人的第一部小说能卖到5000册就是最好的了,而他的这部作品在出版一星期后销量就超过20 000册。他的短篇小说的稿酬也由每篇30美元猛涨至1000美元。此时,菲茨杰拉德从一位业余作者转变为一位职业作家。他写道:"每天早上醒来都是面对一个难以形容的辉煌并且充满希望的世界。"[1] 读者不妨想象一下,在普通人大学刚毕业的不满24岁的年纪,菲茨杰拉德可以说就已经登上了人生的巅峰,金钱、美女、名望和文学的理想,一位成功人士的一切,他似乎都拥有了。不过,他的人生轨迹,从一夜成名又回落到后来的籍籍无名,反差巨大,而这也是我们在理解《了不起的盖茨比》的主题时不得不考虑的因素。此后菲茨杰拉德夫妇往返于欧洲与美国之间,在法国南部的里维埃拉海滨地区,珊尔达遇上了一位法国飞行员,两人相恋。怒不可遏的菲茨杰拉德提出要与该飞行员对决,而后者躲避了。珊尔达为此曾提出要离婚。最后菲茨杰拉德劝阻珊尔达,两人重归于好。这场风波给他们的

---

[1] Mathew J. Bruccoli, et al. eds., *F. Scott Fitzgerald on Authorship*, Columbia, SC: University of South Carolina Press, 1996, p.160.

6. THE ICE PALACE

婚姻带来了难以弥合的裂痕，也被写进了菲茨杰拉德后来的小说《夜色温柔》和珊尔达唯一的长篇小说《留住我的华尔兹》（*Save Me the Waltz*）中。1925年春，菲茨杰拉德一家移居巴黎，在那里他与海明威初次见面，当时见面的情况后来海明威在回忆录《流动的盛宴》（*A Movable Feast*）中有描述。从此菲茨杰拉德与海明威开始了长期而曲折的友谊。尽管当时海明威在文学界还是一个无名之辈，但是菲茨杰拉德十分欣赏海明威的人格和文学才能，竭力帮助海明威。他向编辑珀金斯大力推荐海明威，为他的第一部长篇小说《太阳照样升起》提出了长达10页的修改润色意见，海明威也根据他的意见做了修改。他还把海明威介绍给文学界的朋友。但是海明威却在作品中多次显露出对菲茨杰拉德的藐视和嘲讽态度。他们这种不对等的友谊和相互影响成了文学界至今仍津津乐道的话题和批评家研究的一个重要课题。[1] 1927年菲茨杰拉德应邀去好莱坞创作剧本，结识了年轻的女明星路易·莫兰（Louis Moran），这使珊尔达萌生醋意。1929春季他们第四度赴欧洲。此时海明威也在法国，菲茨杰拉德与他交往密切，珊尔达怀疑他们有同性恋关系，菲茨杰拉德夫妇的婚姻危机进一步加深。1930年珊尔达精神病发作，先后到巴黎和瑞士治疗。为了支付珊尔达治病和女儿斯科蒂（Frances Scott Fitzgerlad，昵称"Scottie"）在巴黎上学的费用，菲茨杰拉德拼命写作，这一时期他的稿酬达到了高峰，仅1931年就达37 599美元[2]，而那时一辆普通福特轿车也不过一百多美元。可是，到了1937年菲茨杰拉德就已是分文无收、债台高筑了，负债达22 000美元。[3] 此后他第三次去好莱坞，在一次聚会上与来自英国的专栏作家希拉·格雷厄姆（Sheilah Graham）相识，二人后来发展为情人关系。格雷厄姆在回忆录《心爱的异端》（*Beloved Infidel*）中披露了菲茨杰拉德最后几年同她一起生活的情况。1939年在格雷厄姆的鼓励下，菲茨杰拉德开始创作《最后一位君子》。菲茨杰拉德在1940年12月21日因心脏病在格雷厄姆家中离奇去世，当然也有不少人认为他早逝的原因可能与海明威一样，更多是他的酗酒。具

1　程锡麟等著，《菲茨杰拉德学术史研究》，南京：译林出版社，2014年，第207页。

2　Mathew J. Bruccoli, *Some Sort of Epic Grandeur: The Life of F. Scott Fitzgerald*, New York: Harcourt Brace Jovanovich, 1981, p. 308.

3　程锡麟等著，《菲茨杰拉德学术史研究》，南京：译林出版社，2014年，第211页。

有讽刺意味的是,他对名声十分在乎,却在声誉处于最低谷时去世。他在死之前也认为自己是一个失败者。不过,著名诗人斯蒂芬·文森特·贝内特(Stephen Vincent Benét)在评论《最后一位君子》时这样号召我们向菲茨杰拉德脱帽致敬:"先生们,现在你们可以摘下帽子了,我想你们最好这样做。这不是一个传说,这是一种声誉,并且客观地看,它将是我们时代最稳固的声誉之一。"[1] 贝内特的这一结论已经并且还将继续被历史证实。

二、情节与人物

《冰宫》是菲茨杰拉德最早的短篇小说之一,发表在1920年5月22日的《星期六晚邮报》上,后来收录在《新潮女郎与哲学家》中,是他的八部名篇之一。菲茨杰拉德以职业创作为生,虽然他的稿费非常可观,但他们夫妇的生活十分铺张浪费,总是入不敷出,而菲茨杰拉德对待创作的态度又近乎苛刻,从他一生仅有四部长篇面世就可以看出来。于是,他在谋生与创作之间选择了以短篇小说养长篇小说的模式,短篇向杂志投稿,有了足够稿费后再积极构思长篇。因此,他自己一直是蔑视短篇小说的,甚至将不得不写短篇类比为娼妓行为。不过,随着20世纪90年代第三波菲茨杰拉德复兴的到来,评论界对他的短篇小说也开始了更深入的研究,从总体上肯定了这些作品的艺术成就。

故事开始于南方佐治亚州塔尔顿市一个9月的下午,19岁的女主人公莎莉·卡罗尔·哈珀睡眼惺忪,头枕着卧室的窗口跟朋友克拉克·戴罗打招呼,并答应跟他和其他一些朋友一起去游泳。大家都很关心哈珀跟一位扬基佬订婚的事情。她说尽管她很爱大家,但却不太可能留在慵懒的塔尔顿,因为她想去"有许多大事发生的地方"。在她的身上有两面性,一面是旧的慵懒的南方,另一面又充满能量,想要证明自己即使美貌不在了,也能"在某个地方有用"。哈珀身上的这种两面性,也可以从她的举止体现出来,她虽然是典型的南方美女,却也留短发、抽烟。

故事的第二部分讲述哈珀的未婚夫哈里·贝拉米从北方来访,他们一起去哈珀最喜欢的墓地散步。在那里她深情地向贝拉米讲述了一位生于1844年、死于

---

1 Henry Claridge, ed., *F. Scott Fitzgerald: Critical Assessments*, Vol. 3, Near Robertsbridge, UK: Helm Information, 1991, p. 257.

6. THE ICE PALACE

1873年的韶华早逝的黑人女孩玛格瑞·李的故事。她的讲述充满了理想化的色彩，也获得了贝拉米的认同。接着他们来到一片南方邦联军无名士兵墓地，哈珀认为他们"为了世界上最美好的事情而死"，虽然具有悲剧色彩，却赋予了她以力量。他们讨论了哈珀次年1月去北方拜访的事，贝拉米告诉她那里"就像童话世界"，而哈珀却十分担心寒冷的天气，因为她是"属于夏天的孩子"。

第三部分讲述哈珀乘列车前往北方，这是一次寒冷而痛苦的经历。贝拉米、贝拉米的父母以及兄嫂高登和迈拉到车站接她。在贝拉米家，哈珀注意到了他家的书房与自己家南方的书房的不同，前者摆放着不满15年历史的昂贵用品，而自家的书房则充满了家族记忆和历史。尽管她很爱贝拉米，但她与贝拉米在对南方家庭的理解上产生了分歧。在当天晚上的宴会上，哈珀被介绍给了贝拉米家的众多朋友，这些人她都没什么印象和好感，不过却立刻喜欢上了罗杰·帕顿，他是从哈佛大学过来在当地大学教法语的文学教授。哈珀告诉他，北方的小伙子都是犬科动物，而她、帕顿和南方的很多人都是猫科动物。帕顿则告诉她，北方人都是"冰冻人"，他们不少人是瑞典后裔，北方人越来越像斯堪的纳维亚人了。

第四部分讲述哈珀来北方一周后的故事。她玩了北方孩子们常玩的冰雪游戏，不过却越来越感到与这里的一切格格不入。在她看来，北方人对"陌生人有着天生的敌视"，她喜欢贝拉米先生，瞧不上未来的嫂嫂迈拉，讨厌贝拉米夫人，因为贝拉米夫人看不惯她抽烟、留短发，还老是直呼其名"莎莉"。在所有人中她最喜欢罗杰·帕顿。不久后的一天下午，因贝拉米对街头一位邂逅的南方男子充满偏见的评价，哈珀跟贝拉米爆发了激烈的冲突。争吵结束后，哈珀建议他们立即结婚，但贝拉米依然坚持原定的婚期不变。当天晚上，歌舞表演结束后，乐队奏起的"前进，前进，唱着《迪克西》一路南行"的南军进行曲，又勾起了哈珀的思乡情绪。

在第五部分，哈珀、贝拉米和镇上的人们一起去参观高达50余米、占地5000多平方米的宏伟的冰宫。她和贝拉米等人走散了，迷失在冰冷、漆黑的冰宫里。哈珀惊恐万分，担心自己会冻死在冰宫里。在绝望之际，她想到了温暖好客的南方，想到了家乡的朋友，也仿佛看到了玛格瑞·李的魂灵守在自己身旁。当罗杰·帕顿救醒她以后，哈珀终于情绪失控，歇斯底里地要求把自己送回南方。

第六部分仿佛又回到了开头一幕，在金色骄阳笼罩下的慵懒的南方，哈珀在窗前看着戴罗驾驶着他那破旧的福特汽车来到房前，邀请她一起去游泳。

三、主题与技巧

菲茨杰拉德作为职业作家从年少成名到穷困潦倒的跌宕人生，正好见证了美国从第一次世界大战后的繁荣到经济萧条的历史过程。而他绝对是这一时期的最佳见证人之一，他最深切地感受到了时代的脉动，同时又带着最尖锐的反思来抨击美国现代社会的弊端，为美国梦书写它的挽歌。因此，了解菲茨杰拉德的作品，就需要了解他的人生，以及他所代表的那个时代。这种深入时代又超然其外的双重视角，今天已成为评论界公认的菲茨杰拉德最了不起的地方。他的作品中那些常见的主题，如金钱、美女、爱情、婚姻、浪费、青年文化、消费主义、南北战争，以及带着浪漫主义与挽歌情愫的优美怀旧的文字，既是他自己的人生总结，也是那个时代的缩影。罗纳德·伯曼（Ronald Berman）称"菲茨杰拉德是美国景象第一流的观察家"。亨利·丹·派珀（Henry Dan Piper）在评论《了不起的盖茨比》时则明确指出："他的小说比许多正统历史学家的事实性陈述使我们更接近于那个世界。"[1] 莱昂内尔·特里林（Lionel Trilling）更把他与歌德相提并论。[2]

《冰宫》的核心主题是南北冲突。首先，故事的开头和结尾与标题形成了强烈反差，在金色骄阳笼罩下的慵懒的南方小镇塔尔顿，主人公哈珀那"19岁的下巴枕在52岁的窗台"，看着戴罗那辆吱嘎作响的福特车费力地开到自家门口。哈珀打招呼说"早上好"，戴罗回答说"已经不是早上了"。时间在哈珀的发愣打盹中不知不觉地溜走，她却一点也不在乎，而她身边的朋友也都在这节奏缓慢的生活中胸无大志地慢慢消磨时光。在故事结尾处，当戴罗问她在干什么时，哈珀甚至心满意足地说"在等死"，连去游泳"都不想动"。这是一幅南方人慵懒、友好、与世无争、怡然自得的生活画卷。而在哈里·贝拉米所代表的北方，到处都是冰天雪地，人们裹在厚厚的皮衣里，他们虽然拥有新鲜的事物和现代文明，却犹如生活在冰窟里。在哈珀眼里，宏伟壮丽的冰宫犹如北方民族在一个巨大的

---

[1] Henry Dan Piper, *Fitzgerald's "The Great Gatsby": The Novel, The Critics, The Background*, New York: Charles Scribner's Sons, 1970, p.1.

[2] Alfred Kazin, ed. *F. Scott Fitzgerald: The Man and His Work*, New York: Collier Books, 1962, p. 202.

6. THE ICE PALACE

祭坛上向他们那灰色的异教雪神供上祭品（...the North offering sacrifice on some mighty altar to the gray pagan God of Snow）。她孤身一人迷失在这个北方的迷宫里，如冰冻的北冰洋上的捕鲸人一般孤独寂寥，如堆积着探险者的累累白骨的荒原一般凄清寒凉。一阵寒彻心扉的死亡气息，正从地下翻卷而来，要将她俘获：

"She was alone with this presence that came out of the North, the dreary loneliness that rose from ice-bound whalers in the Arctic seas, from smokeless, trackless wastes where were strewn the whitened bones of adventure. It was an icy breath of death; it was rolling down low across the land to clutch at her."

她的北方之行，最后被证明是一场噩梦般的经历。她的心最终只属于夏天般温暖的南方，那里有骄阳、朋友，整天无所事事，也有她的玛格瑞·李、邦联军无名士兵墓和承载着数代人历史记忆的日常事物。菲茨杰拉德为什么如此在乎南北冲突呢？罗纳德·伯曼指出，菲茨杰拉德笔下的东和北是与西和南对立的。东部的纽约代表了进步的市场价值，而南方则代表了发展中不可避免的传统的失落。[1]《冰宫》里的哈珀·哈珀重返塔里顿的墓地，是因为墓地沉淀了历史的厚重，代表了人性化的历史，颠覆了美国人认为历史就是进步的观点。

菲茨杰拉德的文字精练优美，描写生动传神，结构安排独具匠心，体现了作家对待文学创作的严谨态度，《冰宫》也不例外。如故事开头的一段："阳光照射在房屋上，宛如涂抹在艺术陶罐上的金黄色油彩。那些到处可见、明暗相间的阳光斑点，仅仅增强了沐浴日光的严酷感。巴特沃恩和拉金家房子的侧面为大树的阴影遮盖，只有哈珀家的房子才全然沐浴在日光之中。这所房子整天对着尘土飞扬的行人汽车道，仿佛显现出一种温和的忍耐力，忍耐着阳光的烤晒。这是乔治亚州最南面的塔伦顿市。这时的时间是九月的一个下午。"[2]

---

[1] Ronald Berman, *Modernity and Progress: Fitzgerald, Hemingway, Orwell*, Tuscaloosa: University of Alabama Press, 2005, p. 17.

[2] 〔美国〕司各特·菲茨杰拉德，《冰宫》，苏珊译，《当代外国文学》，1990年第3期，第96页。

The sunlight dripped over the house like golden paint over an art jar, and the freckling shadows here and there only intensified the rigor of the bath of light. The Butterworth and Larkin houses flanking were intrenched behind great stodgy trees; only the Happer house took the full sun, and all day long faced the dusty road-street with a tolerant kindly patience. This was the city of Tarleton in southernmost Georgia, September afternoon.

寥寥数语生动地交代了故事发生的时间、地点与氛围。在结构上，第一、六部分是呼应，形成首尾循环；第一、二部分和三、四和五、六部分构成了故事的起承转合关系。整个故事形成了一个有机整体，故事高潮"迷失在冰宫里"的那一部分，又正如一些评论家指出的那样，颇有梦境的意味，似乎是受到了济慈和乔叟梦幻诗的影响。而哈珀的形象，尤其是她在冰宫中的歇斯底里，显然是以珊尔达为原型的。因此，曾经对他的《人间天堂》大加挞伐的海伍德·布龙也不得不说："《冰宫》让我们马上确信：菲茨杰拉德确实有内容要表达，而且知道如何表达这些内容。"[1]

Suggested Readings

1. Berman, Ronald. *The Great Gatsby and Modern Times.* Urbana: University of Illinois Press, 1994.

2. Bloom, Harold, ed. *F. Scott Fitzgerald's Short Stories.* New York: Bloom's Literary Criticism, 2011.

3. Bruccoli, Mathew J. *Some Sort of Epic Grandeur: The Life of F. Scott Fitzgerald.* New York: Harcourt Brace Jovanovich, 1981.

4. Bryer, Jackson R. ed. *New Essays on F. Scott Fitzgerald's Neglected Stories.* Columbia & London: University of Missouri Press, 1996.

5. Cowley, Malcolm. *Exile's Return.* New York: Viking, 1934/1963.

6. Curnutt, Kirk. *The Cambridge Introduction to F. Scott Fitzgerald.* New York:

---

[1] Jackson R. Bryer, ed., *F. Scott Fitzgerald: The Critical Reception*, New York: Burt Franklin, 1978, pp. 45-46.

6. THE ICE PALACE

Cambridge University Press, 2007.

7. Donaldson, Scott. *Fitzgerald and Hemingway: Works and Days*. New York: Columbia University Press, 2009.
8. Fitzgerald, F. Scott. *Flappers and Philosophers*. New York, London, Toronto, Sydney: Pocket Books, 1920.
9. Fitzgerald, F. Scott. *Tales of the Jazz Age*. New York: Charles Scribner's Sons, 1922.
10. Fitzgerald, F. Scott. *Tender Is the Night*. New York: Charles Scribner's Sons, 1934.
11. Fitzgerald, F. Scott. *The Great Gatsby*. New York: Charles Scribners, 1925.
12. Fitzgerald, F. Scott. *The Stories of F. Scott Fitzgerald*. Ed. Malcolm Cowley. New York: Charles Scribner's Sons, 1951.
13. Fitzgerald, F. Scott. *This Side of Paradise*. New York: Charles Scribner's Sons, 1920.
14. Kazin, Alfred, ed. *F. Scott Fitzgerald: The Man and His Work*. New York: Collier Books, 1962.
15. Kuehl, John. *F. Scott Fitzgerald: A Study of the Short Fiction*. Boston: Twayne, 1991.
16. Mizener, Arthur. *The Far Side of Paradise: A Biography of F. Scott Fitzgerald*. Boston: Houghton Mifflin, 1951
17. 程锡麟等著：《菲茨杰拉德学术史研究》，南京：译林出版社，2014年。

Questions for Reflection

1. What is "the Lost Generation"? Why is *The Great Gatsby* an illustration of the disillusionment of the American dream?

2. Why is F. Scott Fitzgerald hailed as a first-class observer of the American society? Why do we have to know about his life when reading his works?

3. Who are the characters in "The Ice Palace"? What personality traits do they have?

4. Why does the author mention Margery Lee and the cemetery? What is the symbolic meaning of the ice palace?

5. How does the story reflect south-north differences? Why does the author accentuate such differences?

Question for Discussion

Fitzgerald has always belittled short stories, considering them worthless compared with novels. What is your assessment of his "The Ice Palace"?

（王安　撰写）

7. A ROSE FOR EMILY

By William Faulkner, 1930

I

When Miss Emily Grierson died, our whole town went to her funeral: the men through a sort of respectful affection for a fallen monument, the women mostly out of curiosity to see the inside of her house, which no one save an old man-servant—a combined gardener and cook—had seen in at least ten years.

It was a big, squarish frame house that had once been white, decorated with cupolas and spires and scrolled balconies in the heavily lightsome style of the seventies, set on what had once been our most select street. But garages and cotton gins had encroached and obliterated even the august names of that neighborhood; only Miss Emily's house was left, lifting its stubborn and coquettish decay above the cotton wagons and the gasoline pumps—an eyesore among eyesores. And now Miss Emily had gone to join the representatives of those august names where they lay in the cedar-bemused cemetery among the ranked and anonymous graves of Union and Confederate soldiers who fell at the battle of Jefferson.

Alive, Miss Emily had been a tradition, a duty, and a care; a sort of hereditary obligation upon the town, dating from that day in 1894 when Colonel Sartoris, the mayor—he who fathered the edict that no Negro woman should appear on the streets without an apron—remitted her taxes, the dispensation dating from the death of her father on into perpetuity. Not that Miss Emily would have accepted charity. Colonel Sartoris invented an involved tale to the effect that Miss Emily's father had loaned money to the town, which the town, as a matter of business, preferred this way of repaying. Only a man of Colonel Sartoris' generation and thought could have invented it, and only a woman could have believed it.

When the next generation, with its more modern ideas, became mayors and aldermen, this arrangement created some little dissatisfaction. On the first of the year they mailed her a tax notice. February came, and there was no reply. They wrote her a formal letter, asking her to call at the sheriff's office at her convenience. A week later the mayor wrote her himself, offering to call or to send his car for her, and received in reply a note on paper of an archaic shape, in a thin, flowing calligraphy in faded ink, to the effect that she no longer went out at all. The tax notice was also enclosed, without comment.

They called a special meeting of the Board of Aldermen. A deputation waited upon her, knocked at the door through which no visitor had passed since she ceased giving china-painting lessons eight or ten years earlier. They were admitted by the old Negro into a dim hall from which a stairway mounted into still more shadow. It smelled of dust and disuse—a close, dank smell. The Negro led them into the parlor. It was furnished in heavy, leather-covered furniture. When the Negro opened the blinds of one window, they could see that the leather was cracked; and when they sat down, a faint dust rose sluggishly about their thighs, spinning with slow motes in the single sun-ray. On a tarnished gilt easel before the fireplace stood a crayon portrait of Miss Emily's father.

They rose when she entered—a small, fat woman in black, with a thin gold chain descending to her waist and vanishing into her belt, leaning on an ebony cane with a tarnished gold head. Her skeleton was small and spare; perhaps that was why what would have been merely plumpness in another was obesity in her. She looked bloated, like a body long submerged in motionless water, and of that pallid hue. Her eyes, lost in the fatty ridges of her face, looked like two small pieces of coal pressed into a lump of dough as they moved from one face to another while the visitors stated their errand.

She did not ask them to sit. She just stood in the door and listened quietly until the spokesman came to a stumbling halt. Then they could hear the invisible watch ticking at the end of the gold chain.

Her voice was dry and cold. "I have no taxes in Jefferson. Colonel Sartoris explained it to me. Perhaps one of you can gain access to the city records and satisfy yourselves."

"But we have. We are the city authorities, Miss Emily. Didn't you get a notice from the sheriff, signed by him?"

"I received a paper, yes," Miss Emily said. "Perhaps he considers himself the sheriff ...I have no taxes in Jefferson."

"But there is nothing on the books to show that, you see. We must go by the—"

"See Colonel Sartoris. I have no taxes in Jefferson."

"But, Miss Emily—"

"See Colonel Sartoris. " (Colonel Sartoris had been dead almost ten years.) "I have no taxes in Jefferson. Tobe!" The Negro appeared. "Show these gentlemen out."

II

So she vanquished them, horse and foot, just as she had vanquished their fathers thirty years before about the smell.

That was two years after her father's death and a short time after her sweetheart—the one we believed would marry her—had deserted her. After her father's death she went out very little; after her sweetheart went away, people hardly saw her at all. A few of the ladies had the temerity to call, but were not received, and the only sign of life about the place was the Negro man—a young man then—going in and out with a market basket.

"Just as if a man—any man—could keep a kitchen properly," the ladies said; so they were not surprised when the smell developed. It was another link between the gross, teeming world and the high and mighty Griersons.

A neighbor, a woman, complained to the mayor, Judge Stevens, eighty years old.

"But what will you have me do about it, madam?" he said.

"Why, send her word to stop it," the woman said. "Isn't there a law?"

"I'm sure that won't be necessary," Judge Stevens said. "It's probably just a snake or a rat that nigger of hers killed in the yard. I'll speak to him about it."

The next day he received two more complaints, one from a man who came in diffident deprecation. "We really must do something about it, Judge. I'd be the last one in the world to bother Miss Emily, but we've got to do something." That night the Board of Aldermen met—three graybeards and one younger man, a member of the rising generation.

"It's simple enough," he said. "Send her word to have her place cleaned up. Give her a certain time to do it in, and if she don't..."

"Dammit, sir," Judge Stevens said, "will you accuse a lady to her face of smelling bad?"

So the next night, after midnight, four men crossed Miss Emily's lawn and slunk about the house like burglars, sniffing along the base of the brickwork and at the cellar openings while one of them performed a regular sowing motion with his hand out of a sack slung from his shoulder. They broke open the cellar door and sprinkled lime there, and in all the outbuildings. As they recrossed the lawn, a window that had been dark was lighted and Miss Emily sat in it, the light behind her, and her upright torso motionless as that of an idol. They crept quietly across the lawn and into the shadow of the locusts that lined the street. After a week or two the smell went away.

That was when people had begun to feel really sorry for her. People in our town, remembering how old lady Wyatt, her great-aunt, had gone completely crazy at last, believed that the Griersons held themselves a little too high for what they really were. None of the young men were quite good enough for Miss Emily and such. We had long thought of them as a tableau, Miss Emily a slender figure in white in the background, her father a spraddled silhouette in the foreground, his back to her and clutching a horsewhip, the two of them framed by the back-flung front door. So when she got to be thirty and was still single, we were not pleased exactly, but vindicated; even with insanity in the family she wouldn't have turned down all of her chances if they had really materialized.

When her father died, it got about that the house was all that was left to her; and in a way, people were glad. At last they could pity Miss Emily. Being left alone, and a pauper, she had become humanized. Now she too would know the old thrill and the old despair of a penny more or less.

The day after his death all the ladies prepared to call at the house and offer condolence and aid, as is our custom. Miss Emily met them at the door, dressed as usual and with no trace of grief on her face. She told them that her father was not dead. She did that for three days, with the ministers calling on her, and the doctors, trying to persuade her to let them dispose of the body. Just as they were about to resort to law and force, she broke down, and they buried her father quickly.

We did not say she was crazy then. We believed she had to do that. We remembered all the young men her father had driven away, and we knew that with nothing left, she would have to cling to that which had robbed her, as people will.

III

She was sick for a long time. When we saw her again, her hair was cut short, making her look like a girl, with a vague resemblance to those angels in colored church windows—sort of tragic and serene.

The town had just let the contracts for paving the sidewalks, and in the summer after her father's death they began the work. The construction company came with niggers and mules and machinery, and a foreman named Homer Barron, a Yankee—a big, dark, ready man, with a big voice and eyes lighter than his face. The little boys would follow in groups to hear him cuss the niggers, and the niggers singing in time to the rise and fall of picks. Pretty soon he knew everybody in town. Whenever you heard a lot of laughing anywhere about the square, Homer Barron would be in the center of the group. Presently we began to see him and Miss Emily on Sunday afternoons driving in the yellow-wheeled buggy and the matched team of bays from the livery stable.

At first we were glad that Miss Emily would have an interest, because the ladies all said, "Of course a Grierson would not think seriously of a Northerner, a day laborer." But there were still others, older people, who said that even grief could not cause a real lady to forget *noblesse oblige*—without calling it *noblesse oblige*. They just said, "Poor Emily. Her kinsfolk should come to her." She had some kin in Alabama; but years ago her father had fallen out with them over the estate of old lady Wyatt, the crazy woman, and there was no communication between the two families. They had not even been represented at the funeral.

And as soon as the old people said, "Poor Emily," the whispering began. "Do you suppose it's really so?" they said to one another. "Of course it is. What else could…" This behind their hands; rustling of craned silk and satin behind jalousies closed upon the sun of Sunday afternoon as the thin, swift clop-clop-clop of the matched team passed: "Poor Emily."

She carried her head high enough—even when we believed that she was fallen. It was as if she demanded more than ever the recognition of her dignity as the last Grierson; as if it had wanted that touch of earthiness to reaffirm her imperviousness. Like when she bought the rat poison, the arsenic. That was over a year after they had begun to say "Poor Emily," and while the two female cousins were visiting her.

"I want some poison," she said to the druggist. She was over thirty then, still a slight woman, though thinner than usual, with cold, haughty black eyes in a face the flesh of which was strained across the temples and about the eyesockets as you imagine a lighthouse-keeper's face ought to look. "I want some poison," she said.

"Yes, Miss Emily. What kind? For rats and such? I'd recom—"

"I want the best you have. I don't care what kind."

The druggist named several. "They'll kill anything up to an elephant. But what you want is—"

"Arsenic," Miss Emily said. "Is that a good one?"

"Is...arsenic? Yes, ma'am. But what you want—"

"I want arsenic."

The druggist looked down at her. She looked back at him, erect, her face like a strained flag. "Why, of course," the druggist said. "If that's what you want. But the law requires you to tell what you are going to use it for."

Miss Emily just stared at him, her head tilted back in order to look him eye for eye, until he looked away and went and got the arsenic and wrapped it up. The Negro delivery boy brought her the package; the druggist didn't come back. When she opened the package at home there was written on the box, under the skull and bones: "For rats."

IV

So the next day we all said, "She will kill herself"; and we said it would be the best thing. When she had first begun to be seen with Homer Barron, we had said, "She will marry him." Then we said, "She will persuade him yet," because Homer himself had remarked—he liked men, and it was known that he drank with the younger men in the Elks' Club—that he was not a marrying man. Later we said, "Poor Emily" behind the jalousies as they passed on Sunday afternoon in the glittering buggy, Miss Emily with her head high and Homer Barron with his hat cocked and a cigar in his teeth, reins and whip in a yellow glove.

Then some of the ladies began to say that it was a disgrace to the town and a bad example to the young people. The men did not want to interfere, but at last the ladies forced the Baptist minister—Miss Emily's people were Episcopal—to call upon her. He would never divulge what happened during that interview, but he refused to go back again. The next Sunday they again drove about the streets, and the following day the minister's wife wrote to Miss Emily's relations in Alabama.

So she had blood-kin under her roof again and we sat back to watch developments. At first nothing happened. Then we were sure that they were to be married. We learned that Miss Emily had been to the jeweler's and ordered a man's toilet set in silver, with the letters H. B. on each piece. Two days later we learned that she had bought a complete outfit of men's clothing, including a nightshirt, and we said, "They are married." We were really glad. We were glad because the two female cousins were even more Grierson than Miss Emily had ever been.

So we were not surprised when Homer Barron—the streets had been finished some time since—was gone. We were a little disappointed that there was not a public blowing-off, but we believed that he had gone on to prepare for Miss Emily's coming, or to give her a chance to get rid of the cousins. (By that time it was a cabal, and we were all Miss Emily's allies to help circumvent the cousins.) Sure enough, after another week they departed. And, as we had expected all along, within three days Homer Barron was back in town. A neighbor saw the Negro man admit him at the kitchen door at dusk one evening.

And that was the last we saw of Homer Barron. And of Miss Emily for some time. The Negro man went in and out with the market basket, but the front door remained closed. Now and then we would see her at a window for a moment, as the men did that night when they sprinkled the lime, but for almost six months she did not appear on the streets. Then we knew that this was to be expected too; as if that quality of her father which had thwarted her woman's life so many times had been too virulent and too furious to die.

When we next saw Miss Emily, she had grown fat and her hair was turning gray. During the next few years it grew grayer and grayer until it attained an even pepper-and-salt iron-gray, when it ceased turning. Up to the day of her death at seventy-four it was still that vigorous iron-gray, like the hair of an active man.

From that time on her front door remained closed, save for a period of six or seven years, when she was about forty, during which she gave lessons in china-painting. She fitted up a studio in one of the downstairs rooms, where the daughters and granddaughters of Colonel Sartoris' contemporaries were sent to her with the same regularity and in the same spirit that they were sent to church on Sundays with a twenty-five-cent piece for the collection plate. Meanwhile her taxes had been remitted.

Then the newer generation became the backbone and the spirit of the town, and the painting pupils grew up and fell away and did not send their children to her with boxes of color and tedious brushes and pictures cut from the ladies' magazines. The front door closed upon the last one and remained closed for good. When the town got free postal delivery, Miss Emily alone refused to let them fasten the metal numbers above her door and attach a mailbox to it. She would not listen to them.

Daily, monthly, yearly we watched the Negro grow grayer and more stooped, going in and out with the market basket. Each December we sent her a tax notice, which would be returned by the post office a week later, unclaimed. Now and then we would see her in one of the downstairs windows—she had evidently shut up the top floor of the house—like the carven torso of an idol in a niche, looking or not looking at us, we could never tell which. Thus she passed from generation to generation—dear, inescapable, impervious, tranquil, and perverse.

And so she died. Fell ill in the house filled with dust and shadows, with only a doddering Negro man to wait on her. We did not even know she was sick; we had long since given up trying to get any information from the Negro. He talked to no one, probably not even to her, for his voice had grown harsh and rusty, as if from disuse.

She died in one of the downstairs rooms, in a heavy walnut bed with a curtain, her gray head propped on a pillow yellow and moldy with age and lack of sunlight.

V

The Negro met the first of the ladies at the front door and let them in, with their hushed, sibilant voices and their quick, curious glances, and then he disappeared. He walked right through the house and out the back and was not seen again.

The two female cousins came at once. They held the funeral on the second day, with the town coming to look at Miss Emily beneath a mass of bought flowers, with the crayon face of her father musing profoundly above the bier and the ladies sibilant and macabre; and the very old men—some in their brushed Confederate uniforms—on the porch and the lawn, talking of Miss Emily as if she had been a contemporary of theirs, believing that they had danced with her and courted her perhaps, confusing time with its mathematical progression, as the old do, to whom all the past is not a diminishing road but, instead, a huge meadow which no winter ever quite touches, divided from them now by the narrow bottle-neck of the most recent decade of years.

Already we knew that there was one room in that region above stairs which no one had seen in forty years, and which would have to be forced. They waited until Miss Emily was decently in the ground before they opened it.

The violence of breaking down the door seemed to fill this room with pervading dust. A thin, acrid pall as of the tomb seemed to lie everywhere upon this room decked and furnished as for a bridal: upon the valance curtains of faded rose color, upon the rose-shaded lights, upon the dressing table, upon the delicate array of crystal and the man's toilet things backed with tarnished silver, silver so tarnished that the monogram was obscured. Among them lay a collar and tie, as if they had just been removed, which, lifted, left upon the surface a pale crescent in the dust. Upon a chair hung the suit, carefully folded; beneath it the two mute shoes and the discarded socks.

The man himself lay in the bed.

For a long while we just stood there, looking down at the profound and fleshless grin. The body had apparently once lain in the attitude of an embrace, but now the long sleep that outlasts love, that conquers even the grimace of love, had cuckolded him. What was left of him, rotted beneath what was left of the nightshirt, had become inextricable from the bed in which he lay; and upon him and upon the pillow beside him lay that even coating of the patient and biding dust.

Then we noticed that in the second pillow was the indentation of a head. One of us lifted something from it, and leaning forward, that faint and invisible dust dry and acrid in the nostrils, we saw a long strand of iron-gray hair.

作品赏析

一、作家与作品简介

如果说福克纳（William Faulkner，1897—1962）是20世纪美国最伟大的小说家，估计不会有多少人反对。这位诺贝尔文学奖得主（1949年）一生创作了18部小说、3部短篇小说集，包括《沙特里斯》（Sartoris，1929）、《喧哗与骚动》（The Sound and the Fury，1929）、《我弥留之际》（As I Lay Dying，1930）、《圣殿》（Sanctuary，1931）、《押沙龙，押沙龙！》（Absalom, Absalom!，1936）、《去吧，摩西》（Go Down, Moses，1942）等著名小说。哈罗德·布鲁姆的《西方正典：伟大作家和不朽作品》收录了福克纳8部作品，这是罕见的。这8部作品是《喧哗与骚动》、《押沙龙，押沙龙！》、《我弥留之际》、《圣殿》、《八月之光》（Light in August）、《野棕榈》（The Wild Palms）、《短篇小说集》（Collected Stories）、《村子》（The Hamlet）[1]。

福克纳也是美国南方文艺复兴（Southern Renaissance）的代表人物。他的作品大多以美国南方为题材，以自己的出生地为原型。他在一系列作品中虚构出"约克纳帕特法县"（Yoknapatawpha county），以此描绘美国南方的兴衰荣辱——约克纳帕特法传奇。值得注意的是，福克纳以美国南方为题材的小说，其意义并不限于美国南方，他笔下的美国南方历史可以看作人类经历的一个缩影。作为一名现代主义作家，福克纳对人性、对文明的发展、对人类的命运都进行了深刻的思考和反省。这也是为什么来自不同时代和不同社会的读者都能从其作品中获得反思的原因。

福克纳是一位文学艺术大师。他有一个观点，认为作家不应直接干预小说的叙事，而应给予小说人物最大限度的独立性，这就是所谓的"作者的超脱"（authorial transcendence）。这样做，一方面是使得小说人物形象更加丰满和逼真，使得情节发展更有内在驱动力，而非作者的意志，进而有助于探索和表现人生内在的无限的发展可能性——这也是福克纳认为的作家的首要责任所在；另一方面也使得读者能够充分发挥自己的想象力和判断力，以达成一种认知和

---

1 Harold Bloom, *The Western Canon: The Books and School of the Ages*, New York, San Diego, London: Harcourt Brace & Company, 1994, p. 563.

审美的体验。与"作者的超脱"相关的,是福克纳经常通过一个"不可靠叙述者"(unreliable narrator)来讲故事,有时还采用多角度的叙述方法(multiple points of view),在同一部小说中使用多个不同的叙述者。[1]另外,福克纳经常打破传统的时空观念,在其作品中常常出现时间和地点都不同的场面的"并置"(juxtaposition)。福克纳在文学的形式和语言方面,还有其他很多创新,限于篇幅,这里不再赘述。

《献给爱米莉的玫瑰》堪称福克纳最脍炙人口的短篇小说,它从题材、人物、主题、形式技巧等各个方面都鲜明地反映出福克纳作品的风格,因此,从该小说入手,有助于我们深入了解福克纳这位伟大的作家。

《献给爱米莉的玫瑰》讲述了一个带有神秘和恐怖色彩的哥特式(gothic)故事(美国南方文学中常有这种哥特式风格)。故事的背景是20世纪二三十年代美国南方小镇杰佛森,这也是福克纳虚构世界"约克纳帕特法县"的县治。主人公爱米莉小姐是小镇上最后一个贵族家庭格里尔森家的唯一传人。爱米莉长期生活在南方父权制家庭的阴影下,当她父亲去世时,年过三十的她依然待字闺中。这时,她认识了来小镇修路的北方佬荷默,两人开始频繁约会,进而谈婚论嫁。此事招来了镇上人的反对,人们认为爱米莉小姐的行为有辱"贵人举止",他们竭力阻挠,并找来爱米莉的贵族亲戚对她施加压力。于是,悲剧发生了。爱米莉买来毒药,毒死了荷默,并藏尸家中。此后,爱米莉闭门谢客达半年之久,等到她再度出门时,她的头发开始变得灰白。渐渐地,她不再出门,又过了五六年,迫于生计,爱米莉开始在家里开设儿童绘画班,绘画班持续了7年,直到镇上的人不再送孩子们来学画画。自此,有10年之久,爱米莉和镇上的人断绝了联系。她去世前最后一次和外人接触,是镇上的官员们亲自上门收税时,爱米莉让官员们大败而归。当74岁的爱米莉小姐去世后,镇上的人为她举办了隆重的葬礼,终于走进她的房子,看到了楼上那个40年间没有外人涉足的房间——床上赫然躺着荷默的尸体,枕头上还有一绺铁灰色的头发。

---

1 李宜燮、常耀信主编,《美国文学选读(下册)》,天津:南开大学出版社,2010年,第241-242页。

二、情节与人物

在鉴赏小说的时候,我们需要注意情节和故事的区别。故事(story)是指按时间先后顺序发生的一系列事件,而情节(plot)是作家对故事的艺术性处理,主要表现在对事件的取舍以及对事件发生时间的重新安排上。为了便于说明,我们先将这篇小说涉及的相关事件以时间顺序大致列出来:

1862——爱米莉出生。

1893——爱米莉的父亲去世,爱米莉病倒,爱米莉被赦免交税。

1894——爱米莉与荷默交往。

1895——爱米莉买鼠药;荷默最后一次进入爱米莉家;爱米莉家散发出臭味,镇上派人在房子周围偷偷撒石灰;爱米莉闭门6个月(此时她"过了30岁")。

1896—1898——爱米莉重新出现,头发开始变灰。

1899——爱米莉开始闭门不出,长达5年。

1903——爱米莉开始在家开绘画班,长达7年(此时她"大约40岁")。

1911——爱米莉停止教画画,从此与世隔绝。

1922——镇上官员就税收问题登门拜访(爱米莉最后一次接触外人)。

1936——爱米莉去世(74岁),葬礼,镇上人进入爱米莉家,黑人托比出走。[1]

请注意,这样的故事时间线是在文本细读的基础上总结出来的,从中我们可以看到福克纳在情节处理上的匠心独运。首先,在事件的选择上,虽然小说是关于爱米莉一生的故事,但作者并未平铺直叙,面面俱到,而是着重选择那些具有重要意义的事件进行浓墨重彩的叙述。例如,爱米莉父亲去世后发生的一系列事件无疑是爱米莉一生中的最重要的转折点,也是整个悲剧的中心事件。以此为核心,其他事件被有选择地纳入故事框架之中。其次,在对故事叙述的时间顺序上,福克纳打乱了事件发生的先后顺序。小说一开始就是爱米莉的葬礼,在这短短的第一段里,我们看到镇上"所有人"都参加了葬礼,我们看到爱米莉被形容为"一座倒下的纪念碑",我们知道"至少10年"没人进过爱米莉的房子,除了

---

[1] 具体的时间顺序也可参见程锡麟,《献给爱米莉的玫瑰在哪里——〈献给爱米莉的玫瑰〉叙事策略分析》,《外国文学评论》,2005年第3期,第71-72页。

一个"年迈的男仆"。寥寥数行立即勾起了读者的好奇心。这个神秘的爱米莉到底是谁呢?我们像镇上那些"好奇的"女人们一样,也想去格里尔森家的宅子里一窥究竟。然而,我们必须等到最后,等到小说结尾,才能知道那幢房子里藏着怎样的秘密。当高潮来临真相大白之时,故事也就戛然而止。

古希腊哲学家亚里士多德在谈论悲剧的时候曾说,悲剧的两大要素是情节和人物,而这两者又是相辅相成的;人物是"行动中的人",情节的发展推动着人物性格的发展,而人物的性格也会影响甚至决定情节的走向。[1]有什么样的人,才会有什么样的所作所为;而只有通过其所作所为,我们才能知道他是怎样一个人。因此,小说人物的性格一定要经历变化和发展,否则人物形象就会是我们称为"静态"或"扁平"的人物。就阅读《献给爱米莉的玫瑰》这篇小说而言,一个至关重要的问题就是:爱米莉何以从一个大家闺秀演变成一个毒杀情人并藏尸家中的恶魔般的人物?

在回答这个问题之前,还有一个问题需要注意,这就是关于文学作品的"真实性"问题。我们经常说,文学应该源于生活,贴近生活,忠实于生活。这话没错。然而,在文学作品的人物塑造(characterization)中,我们又经常看到优秀作家创造出一个个特立独行、惊世骇俗、难以置信的诡异甚至疯狂的人物,这些人物毫无疑问是我们在现实生活中很难看到的。我们不禁要问,这样的人物是否"真实"?亚里士多德说过,文学作品的"真实"不在于照搬现实生活,而是应该遵循情节发展的"可然或必然的原则"[2],也就是说应该符合事物发展的内在逻辑;用现在的话说,文学作品所追求的是"艺术的真实",从这个意义上讲,文学不仅源于生活,而且高于生活。一个优秀的作家的才能恰恰表现在将貌似不可信的人物塑造得合情合理,使读者读来有意料之外又在情理之中的感觉。因此,在研究爱米莉这个人物的时候,我们必须结合故事情节,认真分析她的行为动机(motive),分析她在一系列冲突(conflicts)中的性格变化,进而领会她"疯狂"背后的意义(significance)。可以说,没有冲突,就没有人物。冲突表现在各种相互关系上:与环境、与社会、与他人、与自己等。在《献给爱米莉的玫瑰》中,各种各样的冲突交织在一起,我们可以以此为线索来分析爱米莉这个

---

1 亚里士多德著,《诗学》,陈中梅译注,北京:商务印书馆,1996年,第38页。
2 同上,第75页。

人物的性格发展。

　　第一，爱米莉与她父亲的关系。爱米莉的家庭是小镇上最后的贵族家庭，她的父亲是一个骄横跋扈的父权制家长。我们在小说中没有看到爱米莉的母亲，只知道爱米莉是在父亲的阴影下长大的，只知道她的父亲控制了她的全部生活，把她的追求者全部赶走，剥夺了她自由追求个人幸福的权利，使得爱米莉在父亲去世时虽然已年届三十还孑然一身。这对于爱米莉的性格养成无疑产生了十分重要的影响。首先，贵族家庭的出身和教养使得爱米莉小姐性格孤傲，看不起阶级地位比她低下的小镇上的普通人，这持续到即便是当他父亲去世后，她失去了所有经济来源沦为贫困人口时。其次，长期生活在封闭环境中使爱米莉缺少与人交流的机会和能力，她越来越孤僻。最后，生命中的头三十年囚徒般的生活给她留下了严重的精神创伤。当她父亲去世时，她精神崩溃，不让别人把尸体带走。小说里说："我们还记得她父亲赶走了所有的青年男子，我们也知道她现在已经一无所有，只好像人们常常所做的一样，死死拖住抢走了她一切的那个人。"这里描述了一种被囚禁者与囚禁者的共生关系，也就是所谓的"斯德哥尔摩综合征"。这是一个长期失去自由意志的人的表现，这样的创伤对未来成长的破坏性影响是无可估量的；也许有人会从此一蹶不振，完全沉沦下去，但也有像爱米莉这种生性倔强的人，会因此而激发出更加强烈的追求个人自由和幸福的渴望。爱米莉后来为了留住荷默而不惜用鼠药毒死他，这样的因为害怕失去而采取的极端举动不能不说是和爱米莉过去的创伤有着巨大的关联。

　　第二，爱米莉与镇上人的关系。这个问题更加复杂，因为"镇上的人"涉及几代人，他们对爱米莉的态度也是不同的；爱米莉与镇上人的关系不仅体现了不同阶级之间的冲突，而且体现了不同时代的冲突。爱米莉是小镇上"最后"一个贵族家庭的千金小姐，这意味着她生长在一个新旧交替的时代，而在某种程度上，她也是这样一个时代的牺牲品。虽然小说没有涉及，但我们可以推算出，爱米莉正好出生在美国南北战争初期，美国南方发生了天翻地覆的变化：奴隶制废除，贵族阶级没落，南方重建，等等。但是，需要注意的是，思想观念的变化往往滞后于政治和经济的变化。因此，虽然内战以后南方的传统观念受到冲击甚至动摇，但根深蒂固的传统仍在影响人们的思想和行为。最为明显的例子就是南方的种族隔离和种族歧视法律直到奴隶制被废除了一百年以后，才在20世纪中叶被彻底废除。小说中忠心耿耿的黑人仆人托比，很有可能就是在奴隶制废除以后仍然选择继续待在格里尔森家帮佣的。所以，尽管南方的贵族阶级像格里尔森家那幢房子那样颓败，但作为小镇上唯一的贵族传人的爱米莉小姐在镇上人眼里"始终是一个传统的化身，是义务的象征，也是人们关注的对象"。可以说，爱米莉就是衰落的南方传统的象征。

在小说中，我们看到至少有三代人。第一代是爱米莉的父辈沙托里斯上校那一代。他们念念不忘南方往日的辉煌（如爱米莉葬礼上那些曾参加过南北战争的老人），他们以小镇上拥有格里尔森这样的贵族家庭为荣，对爱米莉小姐尊敬有加，时时维护她的贵族颜面。沙托里斯上校在爱米莉父亲去世后以非常体面的方式免去了爱米莉将来的税赋，就是一个绝好的例子。但是，也恰恰是这一代人最为强烈地反对爱米莉与北方佬荷默的交往，他们写信从亚拉巴马州招来爱米莉的贵族亲戚，他们对爱米莉的恋爱生活的干涉与爱米莉父亲对她生活的控制如出一辙。"他们时时维护她的贵族颜面"，其实质是维护爱米莉小姐所代表的南方贵族传统。

小镇的第二代是一个过渡代，他们和爱米莉是同一代人，对爱米莉持爱恨交加的态度，也就是对南方传统的矛盾态度。他们一方面认同爱米莉所代表的传统，视爱米莉为小镇的宝贵遗产，他们在爱米莉因生活拮据而在家开班教画画的时候，主动送自己的孩子去学画画。另一方面，他们又看不惯爱米莉又穷又傲慢的样子，更不像老一代人那样无怨无悔地关爱爱米莉，认为"只有沙托里斯一代的人以及像沙多里斯一样头脑的人才能编得出来、也只有妇道人家才会相信的"为了照顾爱米莉的面子那个免除她税赋的借口。当爱米莉与荷默约会的时候，他们在背后指指点点，认为"这会给镇上带来耻辱，会给年轻人树立坏榜样"。而当爱米莉与她的亚拉巴马亲戚抗争的时候，他们又站在爱米莉一边，把她视为家庭的一员，当然还因为那两个贵族亲戚"甚至比爱米莉更加像格里尔森家的人"。在爱米莉与荷默约会的问题上，他们"起初都高兴地看到爱米丽小姐多少有了一点寄托，因为妇女们都说：'格里尔森家的人绝对不会真的看中一个北方佬'"，然而当他们发现爱米莉在谈婚论嫁了，就立刻加入众口铄金的行列，宁愿牺牲爱米莉的个人幸福，也要维护她身上所代表的南方旧传统。在小说中，当镇上的人知道爱米莉小姐去药店买了鼠药，"第二天我们大家都说：'她要自杀了'。我们也都说这是再好没有的事"。可以说，他们和老一代是造成最后悲剧的主要推动力量。

小镇的第三代是新生代，他们对旧南方传统的感情淡漠，开始把爱米莉小姐当成普通人，尽管爱米莉小姐身上的贵族气质和气场仍然可以令他们胆寒。他们不想再给爱米莉特殊待遇，开始上门向她收税了。他们也不再为了救济爱米莉而把自己的孩子送去她家学画画。

第三，爱米莉与荷默的关系。北方佬荷默的出现是爱米莉悲剧人生中的重要转折点，也是整个悲剧的导火索。爱米莉的父亲去世后，她大病了一场，"当我们再次见到她时，她的头发已经剪短，看上去像个姑娘"。这是小说中一个重要的细节，它说明爱米莉心中重新燃起生活的激情；她挣脱了父权制的桎梏，终于有机会追求自由的生活了。荷默就是在这个时候闯入爱米莉的生活的。那么，高傲的爱米莉怎么会看得上北方佬荷默呢？小说里讲道："（荷默）个子高大，皮肤黝黑，精明强干，声音洪亮，双眼比脸色浅淡。一群群孩子跟在他身后听他用不堪入耳的话责骂黑人……没有多少时候，全镇的人他都认识了。随便什么时候人们要是在广场上的什么地方听见呵呵大笑的声音，荷默·伯隆肯定是在人群的中心。"粗野、开朗、善于交际的荷默正好和爱米莉相反，正好是她生活中缺少的。也许她过去的生活太过文雅、太过谨慎，也太过压抑，荷默就像一阵来自北方的清风，一扫没落贵族家庭生活的陈腐之气。与其说爱米莉被荷默这个人所吸引，毋宁说她是被荷默所代表的那种自由无羁的生活所吸引。当然，我们从中也可感受到爱米莉那种特立独行、敢作敢为的个性。接下来发生的事情是可以预料到的，爱米莉和荷默的约会招来了镇上人的流言蜚语和干涉反对，他们甚至从亚拉巴马州叫来爱米莉的贵族亲戚对她施加压力。在巨大压力面前，爱米莉展现出倔强不屈的性格，"她把头抬得高高的——甚至当我们深信她已经堕落了的时候也是如此"。倒是荷默不堪压力，临阵退缩了，也许是迫于压力，也许他本来就没有真正爱过爱米莉，他和爱米莉约会不过是出于追求南方贵族小姐的猎奇心理，也或许两种因素都有；但无论如何，始乱终弃给他带来了杀身之祸，因为他所面对的是再度处于精神崩溃边缘的爱米莉。

综上所述，爱米莉这一人物形象的塑造是在一系列矛盾冲突中完成的。爱米莉与父亲的关系体现了她与父权制的冲突，爱米莉与镇上人的关系体现了在不同阶级之间、不同时代之间、传统与现实之间的冲突，爱米莉与荷默的关系则体现了南方与北方的冲突。我们看到爱米莉处在多种冲突的交织点上，最终悲剧的发生不可避免。

三、不可靠叙述者与小说篇名

在这篇小说中，主人公毒杀情人的故事就足以令读者骇然，但更为震撼的情节是爱米莉小姐藏尸家中长达40年之久。我们不禁要问：这么长时间难道没人发现吗？或者，已经有人发现却隐瞒不报？这个问题就涉及讲故事的人——叙述者。

在这篇小说中，叙述者是第一人称复数"我们"。但这里的"我们"显然不是一个实指，也并不代表镇上所有的人。首先，叙述者"我们"代表的是镇上的男人，因为小说里的女人都是"好打听的"、轻信的、喜欢搬弄是非的，字里行间透露出浓浓的性别歧视。其次，叙述者"我们"代表的是小镇上的第二代人，即爱米莉的同代人，因为当说到第一代和第三代的时候，叙述者使用的是排他的口吻。即使把叙述者"我们"缩小到小镇上第二代男人这个较小的范围，这依然是个模糊的群体概念。因为如前所述，小镇上的第二代人是过渡的一代，其中个体之间在思想认识上的差异必定很大，所谓"我们"的看法顶多只能代表这中间相对普遍的看法。那么，为什么不用"我们"中间具体的某个人作为故事的叙述者呢？在很多文学作品我们不是经常见到这样的第一人称叙述者"我"吗？这个问题，我们稍后再来解答。现在我们需要追问：叙述者"我们"是否知道爱米莉家中藏有荷默的尸体？

答案是肯定的。尽管叙述者没有明说，但小说作者已在很多细节处暗示读者：叙述者知而不报。首先，叙述者"我们"知道爱米莉小姐买了毒药，也看见荷默最后一次进入她家里，后来爱米莉小姐没有自杀，而荷默却不见了，然后爱米莉的家里散发出臭味，这一系列事件难道还不足以引起镇上的人的怀疑吗？再者，叙述者说："不时我们在楼底下的一个窗口——她显然是把楼上封闭起来了——见到她的身影"；"我们已经知道，楼上那块地方有一个房间，四十年来从没有人见到过，要进去得把门撬开。他们等到爱米丽小姐安葬之后，才设法去开门"。很明显，镇上的人早就怀疑荷默的尸体就在格里尔森房子的顶楼上，他们一直等到安葬完爱米莉小姐,这才迫不及待地破门而入,以证实自己的猜测。这是一个近乎恐怖的事实:全镇的人集体缄默,成为谋杀犯的包庇者,而且——在长达40年的时间里,镇上的人明知楼上停着死尸,还送自己的小孩去爱米莉家学画画,竟长达7年之久!

这样一个不可靠叙述者说明了什么?首先,这是一种保护,使爱米莉小姐免受牢狱之灾,从而可以安度余生,这体现了镇上人对爱米莉所代表的行将就寝的南方旧传统的一种呵护。其次,这是一种避责。所谓不知者不罪。叙述者以一种貌似袖手旁观的姿态,故意作出不知真相的样子,目的是避免卷入一桩谋杀案之中。这让我们想到之前的问题:为什么叙述者不是一个实指的个人,而是一个虚指的、模糊的群体"我们"?因为"我们"是模糊的,是不容易具体锁定的,而且"我们"是一个群体,所谓法不责众。最后,这是一种隐约的自白和忏悔。之所以这么说,是因为叙述者并非一味隐瞒或者扭曲事实,他已经足够坦诚,他给出的细节足以让读者了解真相,他只是没有把真相直接公开说出口。但无论如何,这种行为已经可以被视为一种自白和忏悔,它透露出叙述者怀有的某种负罪感,反映出镇上的人意识到了在爱米莉的悲剧中自己实在是难逃罪责。最后这一点,与接下来我们要说到的篇名和作者的态度也有关联。

小说的篇名叫"献给爱米莉的玫瑰",但在小说中我们并没有看到玫瑰,只是在停放着死尸、原本布置为婚房的房间里,我们看到"败了色的玫瑰色窗帘,玫瑰色的灯罩"。那么,作者为什么为这篇小说取名叫"献给爱米莉的玫瑰"?

我们知道,玫瑰是爱和爱情的象征,进而代表着婚姻和幸福生活,特别是对于那个年代像爱米莉这样的贵族小姐而言。然而,爱米莉小姐生前没有获得她所渴望得到的"玫瑰"。作者以"献给爱米莉的玫瑰"来命名该小说,毫无疑问表达了"纪念"和"缅怀"之意:既然爱米莉小姐生前没有得到"玫瑰",那就让我们以此文作为一枝玫瑰送给她,以寄托我们对爱米莉小姐以及她所代表的南方传统的哀思。这样的篇名既可以视为作者态度的表现,也可视为作为自白者的叙述人的情感流露。篇名所寄托的哀思必定是十分复杂的情感,它包含了缅怀、同情、敬佩、忏悔,甚至赎罪。作为一个悲剧人物,爱米莉小姐是值得同情的,因为她和被她毒杀的荷默一样,都是那个社会和时代的牺牲品;她甚至也是值得敬佩的,就像一个悲剧英雄(tragic hero),她以弱小的身躯,单枪匹马挑战整个社会，她从不退缩，也从不乞求怜悯，在她那可怕的极端自尊、独立的人格中，我们看到了令人敬畏的尊严和勇气——"高贵，宁静，无法逃避，无法接近，怪僻乖张"。

Suggested Readings

1. Baker, Charles. *William Faulkner's Postcolonial South*. New York: Peter Lang, 2000.
2. Bloom, Harold. *William Faulkner*. New York: Bloom's Literary Criticism, 2008.
3. Brooks, Cleanth. *William Faulkner: The Yoknapatawpha Country*. Batom Rouge: Louisiana State University Press, 1963.
4. Cowley, Malcolm. *The Faulkner-Cowley File: Letters and Memories, 1944—1962*. London: Chatto & Windus, 1966.
5. Faulkner, William. *As I Lay Dying: The Corrected Text*. New York: Vintage International, 1990.
6. Faulkner, William. *Collected Stories*. New York: Random House, 1950.
7. Faulkner, William. *Light in August: The Corrected Text*. New York: Vintage International, 1990.
8. Faulkner, William. *The Sound and the Fury: The Corrected Text*. New York: Vintage International, 1990.
9. Heller, Terry. *The Telltale Hair: A Critical Study of William Faulkner's "A Rose for Emily"*. Tucson, AZ: University of Arizona, 1972.
10. Millgate, Michael. *Achievement of Willaim Faulkner*. Athens, GA: University of Georgia Press, 1989.
11. Minter, David. *William Faulkner: His Life and Work*. Baltimore: Johns Hopkins University Press, 1980.
12. Moreland, Richard C. *Faulkner and Modernism: Rereading and Rewriting*. Madison: University of Wisconsin Press, 1990.
13. Tindall, George Brown. *The Emergence of the New South, 1913—1945*. Baton Rouge: Louisiana State University Press, 1967.

14. Wadlington, Warwick. *Reading Faulknerian Tradegy*. Ithaca, NY: Cornell University Press, 1987.
15. Warren, Robert Penn, ed. *Faulkner: A Collection of Critical Essays*. Englewood Cliffs, NJ: Prentice-Hall, 1966.
16. Weinstein, Philip M., ed. *The Cambridge Campanion to William Faulkn*er. Cambridge: Cambridge University Press, 1995.
17. Zender, Karl F. *The Crossing of the Ways: William Faulkner, the South and the Modern World*. New Brunswick: Rutgers University Press, 1989.

Questions for Reflection

1. Why does Miss Emily commit the monstrous act? Is her act supported with proper motives?

2. What are the dominant features in Miss Emily's character?

3. How do the townspeople look at Miss Emily? Are their attitudes toward her contradictory?

4. Who is the narrator? Is the narrator reliable?

5. Would you regard Miss Emily as a tragic hero? How do you look at Miss Emily's tragedy?

Question for Discussion

Why does Faulkner deliberately break the timeline of the story in "A Rose for Emily"? Please arrange the major events in Emily's life in chronological order.

（陈杰　撰写）

8. THE MAN WHO WAS ALMOST A MAN

By Richard Wright, 1940

Dave struck out across the fields, looking homeward through paling light. Whut's the use talkin wid em niggers in the field? Anyhow, his mother was putting supper on the table. Them niggers can't understan nothing. One of these days he was going to get a gun and practice shooting, then they couldn't talk to him as though he were a little boy. He slowed, looking at the ground. Shucks, Ah ain scareda them even ef they are biggern me! Aw, Ah know whut Ahma do. Ahm going by ol Joe's sto n git that Sears Roebuck catlog n look at them guns. Mebbe Ma will lemme buy one when she gits mah pay from ol man Hawkins. Ahma beg her t gimme some money. Ahm ol ernough to hava gun. Ahm seventeen. Almost a man. He strode, feeling his long loose-jointed limbs. Shucks, a man oughta hava little gun aftah he done worked hard all day.

He came in sight of Joe's store. A yellow lantern glowed on the front porch. He mounted steps and went through the screen door, hearing it bang behind him. There was a strong smell of coal oil and mackerel fish. He felt very confident until he saw fat Joe walk in through the rear door, then his courage began to ooze.

"Howdy, Dave! Whutcha want?"

"How yuh, Mistah Joe? Aw, Ah don wanna buy nothing. Ah jus wanted t see ef yuhd lemme look at tha catlog erwhile."

"Sure! You wanna see it here?"

"Nawsuh. Ah wants t take it home wid me. Ah'll bring it back termorrow when Ah come in from the fiels."

"You plannin on buying something?"

"Yessuh."

"Your ma lettin you have your own money now?"

"Shucks. Mistah Joe, Ahm gittin t be a man like anybody else!"

Joe laughed and wiped his greasy white face with a red bandanna.

"What you plannin on buyin?"

Dave looked at the floor, scratched his head, scratched his thigh, and smiled. Then he looked up shyly.

"Ah'll tell yuh, Mistah Joe, ef yuh promise yuh won't tell."

"I promise."

"Waal, Ahma buy a gun."

"A gun? Whut you want with a gun?"

"Ah wanna keep it."

"You ain't nothing but a boy. You don't need a gun."

"Aw, lemme have the catlog, Mistah Joe. Ah'll bring it back."

Joe walked through the rear door. Dave was elated. He looked around at barrels of sugar and flour. He heard Joe coming back. He craned his neck to see if he were bringing the book. Yeah, he's got it. Gawddog, he's got it!

"Here, but be sure you bring it back. It's the only one I got."

"Sho, Mistah Joe."

"Say, if you wanna buy a gun, why don't you buy one from me? I gotta gun to sell."

"Will it shoot?"

"Sure it'll shoot."

"Whut kind is it?"

"Oh, it's kinda old ... a left-hand Wheeler. A pistol. A big one."

8. THE MAN WHO WAS ALMOST A MAN

"Is it got bullets in it?"

"It's loaded."

"Kin Ah see it?"

"Where's your money?"

"What yuh wan fer it?"

"I'll let you have it for two dollars."

"Just two dollahs? Shucks, Ah could buy tha when Ah git mah pay."

"I'll have it here when you want it."

"Awright, suh. Ah be in fer it."

He went through the door, hearing it slam again behind him. Ahma git some money from Ma n buy me a gun! Only two dollahs! He tucked the thick catalogue under his arm and hurried.

"Where yuh been, boy?" His mother held a steaming dish of black-eyed peas.

"Aw, Ma, Ah jus stopped down the road t talk wid the boys."

"Yuh know bettah t keep suppah waiting."

He sat down, resting the catalogue on the edge of the table.

"Yuh git up from there and git to the well n wash yoself! Ah ain feedin no hogs in mah house!"

She grabbed his shoulder and pushed him. He stumbled out of the room, then came back to get the catalogue.

"Whut this?"

"Aw, Ma, it's jusa catlog."

"Who yuh git it from?"

"From Joe, down at the sto."

"Waal, thas good. We kin use it in the outhouse."

"Naw, Ma." He grabbed for it. "Gimme ma catlog, Ma."

She held onto it and glared at him.

"Quit hollerin at me! Whut's wrong wid yuh? Yuh crazy?"

"But Ma, please. It ain mine! It's Joe's! He tol me t bring it back t im termorrow."

She gave up the book. He stumbled down the back steps, hugging the thick book under his arm. When he had splashed water on his face and hands, he groped back to the kitchen and fumbled in a corner for the towel. He bumped into a chair; it clattered to the floor. The catalogue sprawled at his feet. When he had dried his eyes he snatched up the book and held it again under his arm. His mother stood watching him.

"Now, ef yuh gonna act a fool over that ol book, Ah'll take it n burn it up."

"Naw, Ma, please."

"Waal, set down n be still!"

He sat down and drew the oil lamp close. He thumbed page after page, unaware of the food his mother set on the table. His father came in. Then his small brother.

"Whutcha got there, Dave?" his father asked.

"Jusa catlog," he answered, not looking up.

"Yeah, here they is!" His eyes glowed at blue-and-black revolvers. He glanced up, feeling sudden guilt. His father was watching him. He eased the book under the table and rested it on his knees. After the blessing was asked, he ate. He scooped up peas and swallowed fat meat without chewing. Buttermilk helped to wash it down. He did not want to mention money before his father. He would do much better by cornering his mother when she was alone. He looked at his father uneasily out of the edge of his eye.

"Boy, how come yuh don quit foolin wid tha book n eat yo suppah?"

"Yessuh."

"How you n ol man Hawkins gitten erlong?"

"Suh?"

"Can't yuh hear? Why don yuh lissen? Ah ast you how wuz yuh n ol man Hawkins gittin erlong?"

8. THE MAN WHO WAS ALMOST A MAN

"Oh, swell, Pa. Ah plows mo lan than anybody over there."

"Waal, yuh oughta keep yo mind on whut yuh doin."

"Yessuh."

He poured his plate full of molasses and sopped it up slowly with a chunk of cornbread. When his father and brother had left the kitchen, he still sat and looked again at the guns in the catalogue, longing to muster courage enough to present his case to his mother. Lawd, ef Ah only had tha pretty one! He could almost feel the slickness of the weapon with his fingers. If he had a gun like that he would polish it and keep it shining so it would never rust. N Ah'd keep it loaded, by Gawd!

"Ma?" His voice was hesitant.

"Hunh?"

"Ol man Hawkins give yuh mah money yit?"

"Yeah, but ain no usa yuh thinking about throwin nona it erway. Ahm keeping tha money sos yuh kin have cloes t go to school this winter. "

He rose and went to her side with the open catalogue in his palms. She was washing dishes, her head bent low over a pan. Shyly he raised the book. When he spoke, his voice was husky, faint.

"Ma, Gawd knows Ah wans one of these."

"One of whut?" she asked, not raising her eyes.

"One of these," he said again, not daring even to point. She glanced up at the page, then at him with wide eyes.

"Nigger, is yuh gone plumb crazy?"

"Aw, Ma—"

"Git outta here! Don yuh talk t me bout no gun! Yuh a fool!"

"Ma, Ah kin buy one fer two dollahs."

"Not ef Ah knows it, yuh ain!"

"But yuh promised me one—"

"Ah don care what Ah promised! Yuh ain nothing but a boy yit!"

"Ma, ef yuh lemme buy one Ah'll *never* ast yuh fer nothing no mo."

"Ah tol yuh t git outta here! Yuh ain gonna toucha penny of tha money fer no gun! Thas how come Ah has Mistah Hawkins t pay yo wages t me, cause Ah knows yuh ain got no sense."

"But, Ma, we needa gun. Pa ain got no gun. We needa gun in the house. Yuh kin never tell whut might happen."

"Now don yuh try to maka fool outta me, boy! Ef we did hava gun, yuh wouldn't have it!"

He laid the catalogue down and slipped his arm around her waist.

"Aw, Ma, Ah done worked hard alla summer n ain ast yuh fer nothing, is Ah, now?"

"Thas whut yuh spose t do!"

"But Ma, Ah wans a gun. Yuh kin lemme have two dollahs outta mah money. Please, Ma. I kin give it to Pa… Please, Ma! Ah loves yuh, Ma."

When she spoke her voice came soft and low.

"What yu wan wida gun, Dave? Yuh don need no gun. Yuh'll git in trouble. N ef yo pa jus thought Ah let yuh have money t buy a gun he'd hava fit."

"Ah'll hide it, Ma. It ain but two dollahs."

"Lawd, chil, whut's wrong wid yuh?"

"Ain nothin wrong, Ma. Ahm almos a man now. Ah wans a gun."

"Who gonna sell yuh a gun?"

"Ol Joe at the sto."

"N it don cos but two dollahs?"

"Thas all, Ma. Jus two dollahs. Please, Ma."

She was stacking the plates away; her hands moved slowly, reflectively. Dave kept an anxious silence. Finally, she turned to him.

"Ah'll let yuh git tha gun ef yuh promise me one thing."

"Whut's tha, Ma?"

"Yuh bring it straight back t me, yuh hear? It be fer Pa."

8. THE MAN WHO WAS ALMOST A MAN

"Yessum! Lemme go now, Ma."

She stooped, turned slightly to one side, raised the hem of her dress, rolled down the top of her stocking, and came up with a slender wad of bills.

"Here," she said. "Lawd knows yuh don need no gun. But yer pa does. Yuh bring it right back t me, yuh hear? Ahma put it up. Now ef yuh don, Ahma have yuh pa lick yuh so hard yuh won fergit it."

"Yessum."

He took the money, ran down the steps, and across the yard.

"Dave! Yuuuuu h Daaaaave!"

He heard, but he was not going to stop now. "Naw, Lawd!"

The first movement he made the following morning was to reach under his pillow for the gun. In the gray light of dawn he held it loosely, feeling a sense of power. Could kill a man with a gun like this. Kill anybody, black or white. And if he were holding his gun in his hand, nobody could run over him; they would have to respect him. It was a big gun, with a long barrel and a heavy handle. He raised and lowered it in his hand, marveling at its weight.

He had not come straight home with it as his mother had asked; instead he had stayed out in the fields, holding the weapon in his hand, aiming it now and then at some imaginary foe. But he had not fired it; he had been afraid that his father might hear. Also he was not sure he knew how to fire it.

To avoid surrendering the pistol he had not come into the house until he knew that they were all asleep. When his mother had tiptoed to his bedside late that night and demanded the gun, he had first played possum; then he had told her that the gun was hidden outdoors, that he would bring it to her in the morning. Now he lay turning it slowly in his hands. He broke it, took out the cartridges, felt them, and then put them back.

He slid out of bed, got a long strip of old flannel from a trunk, wrapped the gun in it, and tied it to his naked thigh while it was still loaded. He did not go in to breakfast. Even though it was not yet daylight, he started for Jim Hawkins' plantation. Just as the sun was rising he reached the barns where the mules and plows were kept.

"Hey! That you, Dave?"

He turned. Jim Hawkins stood eying him suspiciously.

"What're yuh doing here so early?"

"Ah didn't know Ah wuz gittin up so early, Mistah Hawkins. Ah wuz fixin t hitch up ol Jenny n take her t the fiels."

"Good. Since you're so early, how about plowing that stretch down by the woods?"

"Suits me, Mistah Hawkins."

"O.K. Go to it!"

He hitched Jenny to a plow and started across the fields. Hot dog! This was just what he wanted. If he could get down by the woods, he could shoot his gun and nobody would hear. He walked behind the plow, hearing the traces creaking, feeling the gun tied tight to his thigh.

When he reached the woods, he plowed two whole rows before he decided to take out the gun. Finally, he stopped, looked in all directions, then untied the gun and held it in his hand. He turned to the mule and smiled.

"Know whut this is, Jenny? Naw, yuh wouldn know! Yuhs jusa ol mule! Anyhow, this is a gun, n it kin shoot, by Gawd!"

He held the gun at arm's length. Whut t hell, Ahma shoot this thing! He looked at Jenny again.

"Lissen here, Jenny! When Ah pull this ol trigger, Ah don wan yuh to run n acka fool now!"

Jenny stood with head down, her short ears pricked straight. Dave walked off about twenty feet, held the gun far out from him at arm's length, and turned his head. Hell, he told himself, Ah ain afraid. The gun felt loose in his fingers; he waved it wildly for a moment. Then he shut his eyes and tightened his

8. THE MAN WHO WAS ALMOST A MAN

forefinger. Bloom! A report half deafened him and he thought his right hand was torn from his arm. He heard Jenny whinnying and galloping over the field, and he found himself on his knees, squeezing his fingers hard between his legs. His hand was numb; he jammed it into his mouth, trying to warm it, trying to stop the pain. The gun lay at his feet. He did not quite know what had happened. He stood up and stared at the gun as though it were a living thing. He gritted his teeth and kicked the gun. Yuh almos broke mah arm! He turned to look for Jenny; she was far over the fields, tossing her head and kicking wildly.

"Hol on there, ol mule!"

When he caught up with her she stood trembling, walling her big white eyes at him. The plow was far away; the traces had broken. Then Dave stopped short, looking, not believing. Jenny was bleeding. Her left side was red and wet with blood. He went closer. Lawd, have mercy! Wondah did Ah shoot this mule? He grabbed for Jenny's mane. She flinched, snorted, whirled, tossing her head.

"Hol on now! Hol on."

Then he saw the hole in Jenny's side, right between the ribs. It was round, wet, red. A crimson stream streaked down the front leg, flowing fast. Good Gawd! Ah wuzn't shootin at tha mule. He felt panic. He knew he had to stop that blood, or Jenny would bleed to death. He had never seen so much blood in all his life. He chased the mule for half a mile, trying to catch her. Finally she stopped, breathing hard, stumpy tail half arched. He caught her mane and led her back to where the plough and gun lay. Then he stooped and grabbed handfuls of damp black earth and tried to plug the bullet hole. Jenny shuddered, whinnied, and broke from him.

"Hol on! Hol on now!"

He tried to plug it again, but blood came anyhow. His fingers were hot and sticky. He rubbed dirt into his palms, trying to dry them. Then again he attempted to plug the bullet hole, but Jenny shied away, kicking her heels high. He stood helpless. He had to do something. He ran at Jenny; she dodged him. He watched a red stream of blood flow down Jenny's leg and form a bright pool at her feet.

"Jenny...Jenny," he called weakly.

His lips trembled. She's bleeding t death! He looked in the direction of home, wanting to go back, wanting to get help. But he saw the pistol lying in the damp black clay. He had a queer feeling that if he only did something, this would not be; Jenny would not be there bleeding to death.

When he went to her this time, she did not move. She stood with sleepy, dreamy eyes; and when he touched her she gave a low-pitched whinny and knelt to the ground, her front knees slopping in blood.

"Jenny... Jenny..." he whispered.

For a long time she held her neck erect; then her head sank, slowly. Her ribs swelled with a mighty heave and she went over.

Dave's stomach felt empty, very empty. He picked up the gun and held it gingerly between his thumb and forefinger. He buried it at the foot of a tree. He took a stick and tried to cover the pool of blood with dirt—but what was the use? There was Jenny lying with her mouth open and her eyes walled and glassy. He could not tell Jim Hawkins he had shot his mule. But he had to tell something. Yeah, Ah'll tell em Jenny started gittin will n fell on the joint of the plow.... But that would hardly happen to a mule. He walked across the field slowly, head down.

It was sunset. Two of Jim Hawkins' men were over near the edge of the woods digging a hole in which to bury Jenny. Dave was surrounded by a knot of people, all of whom were looking down at the dead mule.

"I don't see how in the world it happened," said Jim Hawkins for the tenth time.

8. THE MAN WHO WAS ALMOST A MAN

The crowd parted and Dave's mother, father, and small brother pushed into the center.

"Where Dave?" his mother called.

"There he is," said Jim Hawkins.

His mother grabbed him.

"Whut happened, Dave? Whut yuh done?"

"Nothin."

"C mon, boy, talk," his father said.

Dave took a deep breath and told the story he knew nobody believed.

"Waal," he drawled. "Ah brung ol Jenny down here sos Ah could do mah plowin. Ah plowed bout two rows, just like yuh see." He stopped and pointed at the long rows of upturned earth. "Then somethin musta been wrong wid ol Jenny. She wouldn ack right a-tall. She started snortin n kickin her heels. Ah tried t hol her, but she pulled erway, rearin n goin in. Then when the point of the plow was stickin up in the air, she swung erroun n twisted herself back on it... She stuck herself n started t bleed. N fo Ah could do anything, she wuz dead."

"Did you ever hear of anything like that in all your life?" asked Jim Hawkins.

There were white and black standing in the crowd. They murmured. Dave's mother came close to him and looked hard into his face. "Tell the truth, Dave," she said.

"Looks like a bullet hole to me," said one man.

"Dave, whut yuh do wid tha gun?" his mother asked.

The crowd surged in, looking at him. He jammed his hands into his pockets, shook his head slowly from left to right, and backed away. His eyes were wide and painful.

"Did he hava gun?" asked Jim Hawkins.

"By Gawd, Ah tol yuh tha wuz a gun wound," said a man, slapping his thigh.

His father caught his shoulders and shook him till his teeth rattled.

"Tell whut happened, yuh rascal! Tell whut ..."

Dave looked at Jenny's stiff legs and began to cry.

"Whut yuh do wid tha gun?" his mother asked.

"Whut wuz he doin wida gun?" his father asked.

"Come on and tell the truth," said Hawkins. "Ain't nobody going to hurt you ..."

His mother crowded close to him.

"Did yuh shoot tha mule, Dave?"

Dave cried, seeing blurred white and black faces.

"Ahh ddinn gggo tt sshooot hher... Ah ssswear ffo Gawd Ahh ddin.... Ah wuz a-tryin t ssssee ef the old gggun would sshoot—"

"Where yuh git the gun from?" his father asked.

"Ah got it from Joe, at the sto."

"Where yuh git the money?"

"Ma give it t me."

"He kept worryin me, Bob. Ah had t. Ah tol im t bring the gun right back t me ... It was fer yuh, the gun."

"But how yuh happen to shoot that mule?" asked Jim Hawkins.

"Ah wuzn shootin at the mule, Mistah Hawkins. The gun jumped when Ah pulled the trigger... N fo Ah knowed anythin Jenny was there a-bleedin."

Somebody in the crowd laughed. Jim Hawkins walked close to Dave and looked into his face.

"Well, looks like you have bought you a mule, Dave."

"Ah swear fo Gawd. Ah didn go t kill the mule, Mistah Hawkins!"

"But you killed her!"

All the crowd was laughing now. They stood on tiptoe and poked heads over one another's shoulders.

8. THE MAN WHO WAS ALMOST A MAN

"Well, boy, looks like yuh done bought a dead mule! Hahaha!"

"Ain tha ershame."

"Hohohohoho."

Dave stood, head down, twisting his feet in the dirt.

"Well, you needn't worry about it, Bob," said Jim Hawkins to Dave's father. "Just let the boy keep on working and pay me two dollars a month."

"What yuh wan fer yo mule, Mistah Hawkins?"

Jim Hawkins screwed up his eyes.

"Fifty dollars."

"Whut yuh do wid tha gun?" Dave's father demanded.

Dave said nothing.

"Yuh wan me t take a tree n beat yuh till yuh talk!"

"Nawsuh!"

"Whut yuh do wid it?"

"Ah throwed it erway."

"Where?"

"Ah... Ah throwed it in the creek."

"Waal, c mon home. N firs thing in the mawnin git to tha creek n fin tha gun."

"Yessuh."

"Whut yuh pay fer it?"

"Two dollahs."

"Take tha gun n git yo money back n carry it t Mistah Hawkins, yuh hear? N don fergit Ahma lam you black bottom good fer this! Now march yosef on home, suh!"

Dave turned and walked slowly. He heard people laughing. Dave glared, his eyes welling with tears. Hot anger bubbled in him. Then he swallowed and stumbled on.

That night Dave did not sleep. He was glad that he had gotten out of killing the mule so easily, but he was hurt. Something hot seemed to turn over inside him each time he remembered how they had laughed. He tossed on his bed, feeling his hard pillow. *N Pa says he's gonna beat me...* He remembered other beatings, and his back quivered. *Naw, naw, Ah sho don wan im t beat me tha way no mo. Dam em all!* Nobody ever gave him anything. All he did was work. *They treat me like a mule, n then they beat me.* He gritted his teeth. *N Ma had t tell on me.*

Well, if he had to, he would take old man Hawkins that two dollars. But that meant selling the gun. And he wanted to keep that gun. Fifty dollars for a dead mule.

He turned over, thinking how he had fired the gun. He had an itch to fire it again. *Ef other men kin shoota gun, by Gawd, Ah kin!* He was still, listening. *Mebbe they all sleepin now.* The house was still. He heard the soft breathing of his brother. *Yes, now!* He would go down and get that gun and see if he could fire it! He eased out of bed and slipped into overalls.

The moon was bright. He ran almost all the way to the edge of the woods. He stumbled over the ground, looking for the spot where he had buried the gun. *Yeah, here it is.* Like a hungry dog scratching for a bone, he pawed it up. He puffed his black cheeks and blew dirt from the trigger and barrel. He broke it and found four cartridges unshot. He looked around; the fields were filled with silence and moonlight. He clutched the gun stiff and hard in his fingers. But, as soon as he wanted to pull the trigger, he shut his eyes and turned his head. *Naw, Ah can't shoot wid mah eyes closed n mah head turned.* With effort he held his eyes open; then he squeezed. *Blooooom!* He was stiff, not breathing. The gun was still in his hands. *Dammit, he'd done it!* He fired again. *Blooooom! He smiled. Blooooom! Blooooom! Click, click.* There! It was empty. If anybody could shoot a gun, he could. He put the gun into his hip pocket and started across the fields.

When he reached the top of a ridge he stood straight and proud in the

8. THE MAN WHO WAS ALMOST A MAN

moonlight, looking at Jim Hawkins' big white house, feeling the gun sagging in his pocket. Lawd, ef Ah had just one mo bullet Ah'd taka shot at tha house. Ah'd like t scare ol man Hawkins jusa little... Jusa enough t let im know Dave Saunders is a man.

To his left the road curved, running to the tracks of the Illinois Central. He jerked his head, listening. From far off came a faint *hoooof-hoooof; hoooof-hoooof; hoooof-hoooof....* He stood rigid. Two dollahs a mont. Les see now... Tha means it'll take bout two years. Shucks! Ah'll be dam!

He started down the road, toward the tracks. Yeah, here she comes! He stood beside the track and held himself stiffly. Here she comes, erroun the ben... C mon, yuh slow poke! C mon! He had his hand on his gun; something quivered in his stomach. Then the train thundered past, the gray and brown box cars rumbling and clinking. He gripped the gun tightly; then he jerked his hand out of his pocket. Ah betcha Bill wouldn't do it! Ah betcha... The cars slid past, steel grinding upon steel. Ahm ridin yuh ternight, so hep me Gawd! He was hot all over. He hesitated just a moment; then he grabbed, pulled atop a car, and lay flat. He felt his pocket; the gun was still there. Ahead the long rails were glinting in the moonlight, stretching away, away to somewhere, somewhere where he could be a man...

作品赏析

一、作家及作品介绍

理查德·赖特（Richard Wright, 1908—1960），美国20世纪著名的小说家、短篇小说家、政治评论家、剧作家、诗人和散文作家。他拒绝满足读者时至今日仍有的对非裔美国作家的要求，并坚持表达非裔美国人的声音，为后来的作家树立了榜样，影响了托尼·莫里森等一系列美国黑人作家，使其可以随心所欲地写作，而不必担心需要向主流阅读公众解释作品中有时晦涩难懂的含义。赖特的反抗精神为非裔美国作家的写作创造了更多的可能性。赖特出生在密西西比州纳切斯附近的一个农场。他的母亲埃拉·威尔逊·赖特（Ella Wilson Wright）是一名教师，父亲内森（Nathan Wright）是一名佃农。在赖特6岁时，他的父亲抛弃了这个家庭，这使得他的母亲不得不去从事低薪工作，而赖特和他的弟弟莱昂经常因为没有食物而饿肚子。他8岁左右，他妈妈带着一家人搬到了住在阿肯色州的伊莱恩的姐姐那里一起生活。但是好景不长，赖特的叔叔因经营酒类生意被白人嫉妒，最终惨遭杀害，他们得知这一消息后只能连夜逃走。赖特的家人最终回到了密西西比州，由于母亲生病，他们只能与祖母一起生活，被迫忍受祖母的宗教狂热。因为家庭不断迁徙和贫困的经济状况，赖特从未接受正规教育。但他自己并未放弃读书，从15岁起就开进行广泛的阅读，从H. L. 门肯（H. L. Mencken）、费奥多尔·米哈伊洛维奇·陀思妥耶夫斯基（Fyodor Mikhailovich Dostoevsky）、辛克莱·刘易斯（Sinclair Lewis）、舍伍德·安德森（Sherwood Anderson），到西奥多·德莱塞（Theodore Dreiser），这些作家都对他后来的写作和生活产生了一定的影响。

理查德·赖特对后世的影响主要始于1940年出版的《土生子》（*Native Son*）。小说出版的意义在于它的内容具有新的、大胆的反抗性，以及它被"每月一书"俱乐部采用，这标志着自19世纪逃亡奴隶叙事以来，主流阅读公众第一次愿意倾听一个非裔美国作家的声音。赖特对非裔美国人生活的理解植根于他的南方背景。他写的第一本书《汤姆大叔的孩子》（*Uncle Tom's Children*, 1938），是一本短篇小说集，源于他对作为一个年轻黑人男性在南方成长的意义的理解和认识。其导言"The Ethics of Living Jim Crow"（1940年与第五个短篇小说一起添加），构成了他后来自传《黑孩子》（*Black Boy*, 1945）的核心，而联结这两部作品的是《土生子》。虽然赖特的兴趣主要在于揭露和攻击白人的压迫，但他也有兴趣揭开日常生活中除种族以外的奴役和压迫黑人的因素，而正统的基督教就是其中最重要的一个。他深信，是这种信仰安抚了黑人，使他们屈服。

《土生子》和《黑孩子》两部作品带给他成功后，理查德·赖特却于1947年和他的第二任妻子和女儿举家搬到了法国巴黎。定居巴黎可以看作是赖特开始新生活的尝试，尽管赖特作为有史以来最著名的黑人作家之一取得了成功，但他仍然感到被种族主义造成的紧张局势所困扰。在纽约，他不可能自由自在地生活，因为他还是没有被看作是一个伟大的作家，而只是被看作是一个伟大的黑人作家。他觉得在欧洲，特别是在法国，他可以不受那些感情的影响而生活，而这些感情让他回想起在南方成长时的恐惧和痛苦。巴黎曾是其他失意的美国作家的家，也许它也可以成为他的家。

　　法国知识分子对赖特的写作产生了很大影响，特别是存在主义者让·保罗·萨特（Jean-Paul Sartre）、西蒙娜·德·波伏娃（Simone de Beauvoir）和阿尔伯特·加缪（Albert Camus），这在他之后的小说中可以明显看到，例如《局外人》（*The Outsider*，1953）、《野蛮假期》（*Savage Holiday*，1954）和《没完没了的梦》（*The Long Dream*，1958）。这些作品都带有浓厚的存在主义和心理分析的色彩，但是这些小说都未产生像他的早期作品那样重大的影响。赖特的短篇小说集《八个男人》（*Eight Men*，1961）是在其去世后出版的。

　　除了小说，赖特还写了数百首俳句诗，其遗作于2000年出版。赖特也创作了很多非虚构作品，包括《1200万黑人的声音：美国黑人的民俗史》（*12 Million Black Voices: A Folk History of the Negro in the United States*，1941）。他还写了游记《黑人的力量》（*Black Power*，1954）、《色幕》（*The Color Curtain*，1956）、《异教徒的西班牙》（*Pagan Spain*，1957）、《白人们，听着！》（*White Man, Listen!*，1957）。这些作品都从不同方面展示了作者本人对于解决黑人身份危机、重新书写黑人历史和反抗种族压迫的尝试。

　　理查德·赖特对美国文学产生了不可估量的影响。他证明了一个非裔美国人确实可以成为一个具有国际声誉和地位的重要作家。他为非裔美国作家探索了此前未曾见过或不为人知的可能性。他的影响不仅仅局限在作家之间，他充分展示了黑人作家的成功是可能的。由于赖特在文学史上的地位及其作品的广泛影响，许多人将其视为20世纪最伟大的作家之一。

　　《即将成人》（"The Man Who Was Almost a Man"）是收录在《八个男人》中的一篇短篇小说。小说的背景似乎与密西西比州纳切斯附近的乡村地区有很多相似之处，小说里的主人公就出生在极端贫困、家庭混乱和充满白人暴力的环境中，在那里度过了自己的童年和青春时期，并最终离开家乡，踏上未知的旅途。[1]

二、小说背景与人物关系

小说发生在20世纪30年代的美国南方密西西比附近的乡村，主人公戴维·桑德斯是一位在农场干活的17岁黑人男孩。小说讲述了主人公戴维想要通过拥有一把枪以表明自己是一个男人而不再是一个男孩的故事。想要更好地理解这部短篇小说，读者首先要对当时美国的社会历史背景，尤其是涉及种族方面的背景，有一个大致的了解。"吉姆·克劳法案"（Jim Crow Laws）是1876至1965年间美国南部各州实行的种族隔离法案的总称，而小说恰恰是发生在这段时间内。当时美国存在的种族不平等的状况，使得小说主人公戴维想要成为男人的愿望几乎成为不可能完成的任务。

许多学者指出，"吉姆·克劳法案"给那些想要努力成为一个真正意义上的人的黑人来说带来了一个悖论。一方面，"'吉姆·克劳法案'坚持认为，黑人不是完整意义上的人，实际上，他们不可能成为正常的人。另一方面，尽管'吉姆·克劳法案'坚持黑人作为人的天然缺陷，它却要求他们遵守为符合社会标准的完整的人而制定的行为准则"[2]。小说主人公戴维的愿望就体现了这个悖论的后一方面，即成为一个被社会认可的人，而不再受肤色和种族问题的困扰。对于小说主人公戴维最终是否达到了这一目的，存在很多争议。一方面，有很多学者认为戴维射杀骡子珍妮这一举动虽然是无意的，却最终导致其有意地离家出走，这些有意无意的行为都可以看作是对白人统治的反抗，而这些反抗和最后的离家出走使戴维成长为一个真正的男人。只有离开这样一个充满种族压迫和不平等的环境，戴维才有可能成为一个真正意义上的人。"我们对当时美国社会存在的种族歧视情况的了解使我们清楚地认识到，在当时的美国要寻找到一个不存在种族歧视的地方是不可能的。如果成为一个真正的人是要获得社会对其人格的认可和

---

1 作家及作品介绍参考：William Andrews, Frances Smith Foster, and Trudier Harris, eds. *The Concise Oxford Companion to African American Literature*, New York: Oxford University Press, 2001, pp. 447-449; Wilfred Samuels, ed. *Encyclopedia of African-American Literature*, New York: Facts On File, Inc., 2007, pp. 566-568.

2 Marlon B. Ross, *Manning the Race: Reforming Black Men in the Jim Crow Era*, New York: New York University Press, 2004, pp. 1-2.

8. THE MAN WHO WAS ALMOST A MAN

尊重，那么戴维的命运很可能像《宠儿》（*Beloved*）中的保罗·D一样，从一个地方流浪到另一个地方，而自己始终无法像一个真正的人那样生活。"[1]作者本人尽管是当时最成功的黑人作家，但也只有逃离美国去欧洲寻求这样一个不存在种族歧视的家园。在20世纪的美国，火车的终点很可能意味着主人公戴维作为男人生涯的终结。

在当时的美国社会，黑人作为一个群体受到来自白人的压迫和剥削，但是对于黑人个体来说，其往往还要面对除种族因素之外的多方面的压迫，当然这些压迫的根源在一定意义上被认为是肤色。小说的主人公戴维，一个17岁的黑人男孩，就面对来自当地白人、家庭、经济，甚至是黑人种族内部的多重压迫，而戴维的境遇实际上也反映了当时美国所有黑人的遭遇和生活状态。分析小说主人公戴维和其他人物之间的关系可以更好地帮助我们理解戴维想要成为男人这一渴望的不可能。小说开篇简明扼要地交代了故事背景和主人公的基本情况，并且点名戴维想要通过拥有枪支来成为男人这一贯穿小说的主要冲突。与此同时，读者首先看到的是戴维和当地其他黑人男性之间的关系，而戴维对其他黑人男性的态度从他当时的内心想法就可以清楚看到："和这些田野里的黑鬼交谈有什么意义？……这些黑鬼什么都不懂。"戴维想要一把枪以成为一个男人的愿望好像直接来源于其他黑人男性对他的压迫，而非来自白人的压迫。"这几天，他想要搞到一支手枪并练习射击，这样他们就不能像同小孩子讲话一样同他讲话了。"而这里的"他们"很明显是指前面提到的在田野的那些"黑鬼"。这里我们可以清楚地看到，一个黑人哪怕是在自己的黑人社区之中，也不会被当作一个真正意义上的人来看待。

在戴维和小说其他人物的关系中我们可以看到，他永远都只被当成一个男孩，而不是一个男人。小说中出现的第二种关系就是戴维和杂货店老板白人老乔的关系。在戴维和老乔的短暂交谈中，这个白人胖老头似乎是个和蔼可亲的人，但无论如何老乔也是一个白人。在他面前，戴维仅有的一点勇气和信心也消失得无影无踪。当戴维提出他要买一把枪的时候，老乔的回应像其他人一样："你只

---

[1] Kevin Brown, "Both Boy and Man; Neither Boy Nor Man: Liminality in Richard Wright's 'the Man Who Was Almost a Man'", *Midwest Quarterly*, Vol. 60, No. 4 (Summer 2019), pp. 436-437.

是个小孩。你不需要枪。"但戴维说服了他以两美元的价格卖给自己一把左轮手枪。戴维的勇气和试图从老乔这里买枪的行为证明他与其他黑人的不同。小说中戴维一直处于一种不安和亢奋的精神状态，这种状态和其他黑人的屈服和顺从的态度形成了强烈的对比。

小说中的第三组关系是戴维和父亲、母亲之间的关系，当戴维走进家门的那一刻，读者可以明确地感觉到白人的统治在这里并没有结束，只不过换了一种形式内化为黑人之间的统治。戴维在父母的眼中正如大家可以预料到的一样，也只是一个孩子。戴维面对父母的态度则更像一个孩子，他不敢看父亲的眼睛，只敢用余光观察父亲的反应，他甚至不敢让父亲知道自己要买枪的事情。戴维向母亲要钱的时候，他只能不断请求，为了从母亲那里得到两美元，最后只能撒谎要把买来的枪交给父亲，而他每天辛苦劳作的收入都由母亲保管。

小说中出现的最后一组关系就是戴维与雇主霍金斯之间的关系。霍金斯作为一个农场主，是一个典型的南方白人男性。在霍金斯面前，戴维更是一个彻头彻尾的孩子。

从小说发生的背景和主人公戴维与其他人物之间的关系我们可以看到，主人公戴维想要通过拥有一把枪而成为男人的愿望是不可能实现的，尽管小说结尾戴维跳上火车远走他乡，但是等待他的只不过是另外一个充满种族歧视的地方和一段段不平等的关系，他则永远只能是一个男孩而不是一个男人。

三、小说主题与象征手法

《即将成人》是收录在《八个男人》中的第一篇短篇小说，在一定程度上为后面的作品树立了一个基本的框架。《即将成人》是一部成长小说，小说的主题是黑人在当时的美国社会面临的身份危机和种族压迫[1]，以及在这样的情况下黑人如何从少年走向成年，如何从男孩成长为男人。在小说中我们可以同时看到作者对白人的压迫、黑人的软弱和屈服的批判与反思。黑人的软弱和屈服在一定程度上是一种畸形的存在，并在某种程度上成为白人的共谋。要理解小说主

---

[1] Donald Secreast, "Using Scene Structure to Explore Character Complexity in Richard Wright's 'the Man Who Was Almost a Man'", *Virginia English Journal*, Vol. 62, No. 2 (Fall-Winter 2012), pp. 44-47.

8. THE MAN WHO WAS ALMOST A MAN

题，一方面应该了解上一部分小说背景，另一方面要了解文学传统，尤其是美国白人男性的文学传统中涉及成长主题的部分。把这篇短篇小说和同时期的经典白人作家的作品，比如福克纳、海明威，或者早期的经典作品，比如库柏，进行比较可以帮助我们更好地把握小说主题。在这些白人男性涉及成长主题的经典的作品中，也像《即将成人》一样，主人公都要经历一个成人仪式（the Rite of Passage），而成人仪式往往是射杀动物这样的狩猎行为。在白人作家的成长小说中，对动物甚至是人的狩猎成功往往象征着主人公的成熟，而在黑人作家的作品中，这样的行为对于黑人主人公来讲是不可能的。但在《即将成人》这部短篇小说中，一方面，我们可以看到理查德·赖特对于这一普遍的狩猎行为的成功戏仿（Parody），另一方面，我们也可以看到作者对当时社会中白人和黑人成长之间存在的差异的批判与反思。

小说中有很多具有象征意义的行为和场景。小说的主题在主人公戴维渴望一把枪和得到枪后射杀骡子珍妮这两个极具象征意义的行为中得到了充分的展示。首先，从主人公渴望获得一把枪从而成为一个男人的行为，我们可以清楚地认识到枪这一外在物品并不能改变一个人的社会身份和地位，但是小说对这一行为的三种不同的态度——渴望、反对和无视，却可以准确地反映出当时黑人成长过程中的一些基本方面。主人公对于拥有枪支的渴望也就是其"对于成为一个被社会认可和尊重的男人的渴望""而枪本身作为一种暴力武器，同时具有反抗压迫和保卫自身的功能"。[1] 从小说中我们似乎可以意识到作者对于获取枪支这一行为的道德上的支持。因为作者清楚地知道，在当时的社会背景下，黑人想要成为真正意义上的人只有反抗。与主人公戴维想要获取枪支的渴望直接相对的是其他黑人，包括他的父母。而小说中的白人对这一行为却持中立或者更确切地说是无视的态度。在其他黑人看来，他们并不需要枪这种东西，这也就在一定程度上反映了他们对于压迫的屈服与顺从，失去了戴维身上所具有的反抗精神。这就是为什么在小说中我们可以感觉到戴维相对于白人来说似乎更加反感和厌恶其他黑人。白人对于戴维想要获取枪支这一行为的无视态度也是源于黑人身上普遍存在的屈

---

[1] John E. Loftis, "Domestic Prey: Richard Wright's Parody of the Hunt Tradition in 'the Man Who Was Almost a Man'", *Studies in Short Fiction*, Vol. 23, No. 4 (Fall 1986), p. 439.

服和逆来顺受的态度，这样的态度使得白人认为少数黑人的反抗行为可笑，不值一提，而在小说的结尾部分我们可以清楚地看到白人甚至是黑人对戴维的嘲笑和讽刺。小说中戴维几次提到他的父亲没有枪，而这从戴维对于成为一个男人的标准来看，侧面反映了父亲在戴维心中并不是一个真正的男人。戴维想要获取枪支的愿望和他无意中射杀骡子珍妮，再到他克服开枪的恐惧，都反映了他身上的反抗精神。

小说的高潮就是主人公戴维对骡子珍妮的射杀，这一行为可以看作是作者对其他白人成长小说狩猎主题的戏仿。在当时的社会背景下，与其他白人不同的是，黑人的成长并没有榜样和历史可以遵循，只能靠自己摸索。在其他白人的成长小说中，主人公的狩猎行为或者开枪动作，都是在长辈的指导下进行的，这些悉心的教导和完善的文化机制使得成长成为一种自然而然的过程。与此相反，小说主人公戴维在成长的过程中除了找不到学习的榜样和目标，还要遇到重重阻碍。在这样一个白人统治的社会，黑人个体遇到的压迫往往都是双重甚至是多重的，只有打破这些束缚，才能真正成长为一个自由的人。射杀骡子珍妮的这一行为，尽管是无意的，也往往在隐喻意义上被解读为戴维对白人统治的反抗。其中一种解读是：珍妮是珍妮弗（Jennifer）的缩写，这一名字又来源威尔士语"格温"（gwen，白色的含义），因此珍妮是白人社会的象征，而戴维射杀珍妮这一举动可以看作是推翻白人统治的行为。由于其中的逻辑过于牵强，大多数学者对这种解读持保留意见。戴维射杀骡子珍妮这一行为更多地被解读为：一方面是戴维对白人压迫者的反抗，因为珍妮是白人雇主的财产，而破坏财产是一种明显的反抗行为；另一方面，珍妮这头骡子象征着黑人身上奴性的一面，而射杀珍妮可以看作戴维杀死自己身上奴性的一面，表明自己不愿再像骡子一样为白人干活。[1] 因此，戴维射杀骡子珍妮的这一行为并不像他看起来那样是一个意外。这一"无意的错误的"行为使得戴维最终有意地跳上火车去远方寻找自由平等的生活。虽然这一开放性结尾对戴维是否已经成为一个男人并没有给出一个确切的答案，但其中对未来生活的希望是不言而喻的。

1　John E. Loftis, "Domestic Prey: Richard Wright's Parody of the Hunt Tradition in 'the Man Who Was Almost a Man'", *Studies in Short Fiction*, Vol. 23, No. 4 (Fall 1986), p. 439.

8. THE MAN WHO WAS ALMOST A MAN

Suggested Readings

1. Bell, Michael Davitt. *Culture, Genre, and Literary Vocation: Selected Essays on American Literature*. Chicago, ILL.: University of Chicago Press, 2001.
2. Butler, Robert. *Native Son: The Emergence of a New Black Hero*. Boston: Twayne Press, 1991.
3. Chabot, C. Barry. *Writers for the Nation: American Literary Modernism*. Tuscaloosa: University of Alabama Press, 1997
4. Relyea, Sarah. *Outsider Citizens: The Remaking of Postwar Identity in Wright, Beauvoir, and Baldwin*. New York: Routledge, 2006.
5. Wright, Richard. *Native Son: The Restored Text*. New York: Perennial Classics, 1998.

Questions for Reflection

1. Why does the main character Dave want to buy a gun?
2. How do you interpret Dave's act of shooting Jenny the mule?
3. What other oppressions does Dave suffer from besides the oppression from the white man?
4. What are Dave's acts of resistance to oppression?
5. Is the protagonist's resistance to oppression successful?

Question for Discussion

Please have a discussion on the topic of racial discrimination in American society based on the short story, especially on the possible oppressions suffered by the blacks.

（方小莉　撰写）

9. THEFT

By Katherine Anne Porter, 1930

She had the purse in her hand when she came in. Standing in the middle of the floor, holding her bathrobe around her and trailing a damp towel in one hand, she surveyed the immediate past and remembered everything clearly. Yes, she had opened the flap and spread it out on the bench after she had dried the purse with her handkerchief.

She had intended to take the Elevated, and naturally she looked in her purse to make certain she had the fare, and was pleased to find forty cents in the coin envelope. She was going to pay her own fare, too, even if Camilo did have the habit of seeing her up the steps and dropping a nickel in the machine before he gave the turnstile a little push and sent her through it with a bow. Camilo by a series of compromises had managed to make effective a fairly complete set of the smaller courtesies, ignoring the larger and more troublesome ones. She had walked with him to the station in a pouring rain, because she knew he was almost as poor as she was, and when he insisted on a taxi, she was firm and said, "You know it simply will not do." He was wearing a new hat of a pretty biscuit shade, for it never occurred to him to buy anything of a practical colour; he had put it on for the first time and the rain was spoiling it. She kept thinking, "But this is dreadful, where will he get another?" and compared it with Eddie's hats that always seemed to be precisely seven years old and as if they had been

9. THEFT

quite purposely left out in the rain, and they sat with a careless and incidental rightness on Eddie. But Camilo was far different, if he wore a shabby hat it would be merely shabby on him, and he would lose his spirits over it. If she had not feared Camilo would take it badly, for he insisted on the practise of his little ceremonies up to the point he had fixed for them, she would have said to him as they left Thora's house, "Do go home. I can surely reach the station by myself."

"It is written that we must be rained upon to-night," said Camilo, "so let it be together."

At the foot of the platform stairway she staggered slightly — they were both nicely set up on Thora's cocktails — and said: "At least, Camilo, do me the favor not to climb these stairs in your present state, since for you it is only a matter of coming down again at once, and you'll certainly break your neck."

He made three quick bows, he was Spanish, and leaped off through the rainy darkness. She stood watching him, for he was a very graceful young man, thinking that to-morrow morning he would gaze soberly at his spoiled hat and soggy shoes and possibly associate her with his misery. And as she watched, he stopped at the far corner and took off his hat and hid it under his overcoat. She felt she had betrayed him by seeing, because he would have been humiliated if he thought she even suspected him of trying to save his hat.

Roger's voice sounded over her shoulder above the clang of the rain falling on the stairway shed, wanting to know what she was doing out in the rain at this time of night, and did she take herself for a duck? His long, imperturbable face was streaming with water, and he tapped a bulging spot on the breast of his buttoned-up overcoat: "Hat," he said. "Come on, let's take a taxi."

She settled back against Roger's arm which he laid around her shoulders, and with the gesture they exchanged a glance full of long amiable associations, then she looked through the window at the rain changing the shapes of everything, and the colours. The taxi dodged in and out between the pillars of the Elevated, skidding slightly on every curve, and she said: "The more it skids the calmer I feel, so I really must be drunk."

"You must be," said Roger. "This bird is a homicidal maniac, and I could do with a cocktail myself this minute."

They waited on the traffic at Fortieth Street and Sixth Avenue, and three boys walked before the nose of the taxi. Under the globes of light they were cheerful scarecrows, all very thin and wearing very seedy snappy-cut suits and gay neckties. They were not very sober either, and they stood for a moment wobbling in front of the car, and there was an argument going on among them. They leaned toward each other as if they were getting ready to sing, and the first one said: "When I get married it won't be jus' for getting married, I'm gonna marry for *love,* see?" and the second one said, "Aw, gwan and tell that stuff to *her,* why'nt yuh?" and the third one gave a kind of hoot, and said, "Hell, dis guy? Wot the hell's he got?" and the first one said: "Aaah, shurrup yuh mush, I got plenty." Then they all squealed and scrambled across the street beating the third one on the back and pushing him around.

"Nuts," commented Roger, "pure nuts."

Two girls went skittering by in short transparent raincoats, one green, one red, their heads tucked against the drive of the rain. One of them was saying to the other, "Yes, I know all about *that.* But what about me? You're always so sorry for *him...*" and they ran on with their little pelican legs flashing back and forth.

The taxi backed up suddenly and leaped forward again, and after a while Roger said: "I had a letter from Stella to-day, and she'll be home on the 26th, so I suppose she's made up her mind and it's all settled."

"I had a sort of letter to-day too," she said. "I think it is time for you and Stella to do something definite."

When the taxi stopped on the corner of West Fifty-third Street, Roger said, "I've just enough if you'll add ten cents," so she opened her purse and gave him a dime, and he said, "That's beautiful, that purse."

9. THEFT

"It's a birthday present," she told him, "and I like it. How's your show coming?"

"Oh, still hanging on, I guess. I don't go near the place. Nothing sold yet. I mean to keep right on the way I'm going and they can take it or leave it. I'm through with the argument."

"It's absolutely a matter of holding out, isn't it?"

"Holding out's the tough part."

"Good-night, Roger."

"Good-night, you should take aspirin and push yourself into a tub of hot water, you look as though you're catching cold."

"I will."

With the purse under her arm she went upstairs, and on the first landing Bill heard her step and poked his head out with his hair tumbled and his eyes red, and he said: "For Christ's sake come in and have a drink with me. I've had some bad news."

"You're perfectly sopping," said Bill. They had two drinks, and Bill told how the director had thrown his play out after the cast had been picked over twice, and had gone through three rehearsals. "I said to him, 'I didn't say it was a masterpiece, I said it was a good show.' And he said, 'It just doesn't *play*, do you see? It needs a doctor.' So I'm stuck, absolutely stuck," said Bill, on the edge of weeping again. "I've been crying," he told her, "in my cups." And he went on to ask her if she realized that his wife was ruining him with her extravagance. "I send her ten dollars every week of my unhappy life, and I don't really have to. She threatens to jail me if I don't, but she can't do it. God, let her try it after the way she treated me! She's no right to alimony, and she knows it. But I send it because I can't bear to see anybody suffer. And I'm way behind on the piano and the victrola, both — "

"Well, this is a pretty rug, anyhow," she said.

Bill stared at it and blew his nose. "I got it at Ricci's for ninety-five dollars," he said. "Ricci said it once belonged to Marie Dressler and cost fifteen hundred dollars, but there's a burnt place on it. Can you beat that?"

"No," she said.

They had another drink and she went to her apartment on the floor above, and there, she now remembered distinctly, she had taken the letter out of the purse before she spread the purse out to dry.

She had sat down and read the letter over again: but there were phrases that insisted on being read many times, they had a life of their own separate from the others, and when she tried to read past and around them, they moved with the movement of her eyes, and she could not escape them... "thinking about you more than I mean to ... yes, I even talk about you... why were you so anxious to destroy... even if I could see you now I would not.. . not worth all this abominable ... the end ..."

Carefully she tore the letter into narrow strips and touched a lighted match to them in the coal grate.

Early the next morning she was in the bath tub when the janitress knocked and then came in, calling out that she wished to examine the radiators before she started the furnace going for the winter. After moving about the room for a few minutes, the janitress went out closing the door very sharply.

She came out of the bathroom to get a cigarette from the package in the purse. The purse was gone. She dressed and made coffee, and sat by the window while she drank it. Certainly the janitress had taken the purse, and certainly it would be impossible to get it back without a great deal of ridiculous excitement. Then let it go. With this decision of her mind, there rose coincidentally in her blood a deep almost murderous anger. She set the cup carefully in the centre of the table, and walked unsteadily downstairs, three long flights and a short hall and a steep short flight into the basement, where the janitress, her face streaked with coal dust, was shaking up the furnace. "Will you please give me back my purse? There isn't any money in it. It was a present, and I don't want to lose it."

9. THEFT

The janitress turned without straightening up and peered at her with hot flickering eyes, a red light reflected from the furnace in them. "What do you mean, your purse?"

"The gold cloth purse you took from the wooden bench in my room," she said. "I must have it back."

"Before God I never laid eyes on your purse, and that's the holy truth," said the janitress.

"Oh, well then, keep it," she said, but in a very bitter voice, "keep it if you want it so much." And she walked away.

She remembered how she had never locked a door in her life, on some principle of rejection in her that made her uncomfortable in the ownership of things, and her paradoxical boast before the warnings of her friends, that she had never lost a penny by theft; and she had been pleased with the bleak humility of this concrete example designed to illustrate and justify a certain fixed, otherwise baseless and general faith which ordered the movements of her life without regard to her will in the matter.

In this moment she felt that she had been robbed of an enormous number of valuable things, whether material or intangible: things lost or broken by her own fault, things she had forgotten and left in houses when she moved: books borrowed and not returned, journeys she had planned and had not made, words she had waited to hear spoken to her and had not heard, and the words she had meant to answer with bitter alternatives and intolerable substitutes worse than nothing, and yet inescapable: the long patient suffering of dying friendships and the dark inexplicable death of love — all that she had had, and all that she had missed, were lost together, and were twice lost in this landslide of remembered losses.

The janitress was following her upstairs with her purse in her hand and the same deep red fire flickering in her eyes. The janitress thrust the purse towards her while they were still a half dozen steps apart, and said: "Don't never tell on me. I musta been crazy. I get crazy in the head sometimes, I swear I do. My son can tell you."

She took the purse after a moment, and the janitress went on: "I got a niece who is going on seventeen, and she's a nice girl and I thought I'd give it to her. She needs a pretty purse. I musta been crazy, I thought maybe you wouldn't mind, you leave things around and don't seem to notice much."

She said: "I missed this because it was a present to me from some one …"

The janitress said: "He'd get you another if you lost this one. My niece is young and needs pretty things, we oughta give the young ones a chance. She's got young men after her maybe will want to marry her. She oughta have nice things. She needs them bad right now. You're a grown woman, you've had your chance, you ought to know how it is!"

She held the purse out to the janitress saying: "You don't know what you're talking about. Here, take it, I've changed my mind. I really don't want it."

The janitress looked up at her with hatred and said: "I don't want it either now. My niece is young and pretty, she don't need fixin' up to be pretty, she's young and pretty anyhow! I guess you need it worse than she does!"

"It wasn't really yours in the first place," she said, turning away. "You mustn't talk as if I had stolen it from you."

"It's not from me, it's from her you're stealing it," said the janitress, and went back downstairs.

She laid the purse on the table and sat down with the cup of chilled coffee, and thought. I was right not to be afraid of any thief but myself, who will end by leaving me nothing.

作品赏析

一、作家与作品介绍

凯瑟琳·安·波特（Katherine Anne Porter，1890—1980），美国20世纪杰出

9. THEFT

的小说家，评论界公认的文体家，与威廉·福克纳、罗伯特·潘·沃伦（Robert Penn Warren）、艾伦·退特（Allen Tate）等同属美国南方作家群，以写短篇小说著称。波特生于得克萨斯州印第安河市一个天主教家庭，幼年丧母，由祖母抚养成人。她16岁结婚，但两次婚姻均以离异告终。她虽未受过高等教育，但被许多大学授予荣誉学位并被邀请去讲学，1958年她继威廉·福克纳之后被聘为弗吉尼亚大学驻校作家。她曾先后获得欧·亨利奖、普利策奖、全国图书奖等小说类大奖。

波特是位创作态度十分严谨的作家，对每篇作品字斟句酌，反复修改，绝不轻易发表，唯一的长篇小说从构思到发表花了22年的时间。《诺顿美国文学选集》称波特的"每一篇小说都是一部融合精湛技艺和深邃情感的杰作"[1]。她一生只发表过一部长篇小说《愚人船》（Ship of Fools，1962）、一部文学评论集《过去的日子》（The Days Before，1953）、一部回忆录《千古奇冤》（The Never-Ending Wrong，1977），以及27篇中短篇小说，分别收录在《开花的犹大树》（Flowering Judas，1930）、《斜塔及其他》（The Leaning Tower and Other Stories，1944）、《灰色骑士灰色马》（Pale Horse, Pale Rider，1939）等集子中。波特的作品以细腻生动的笔触反映了人们的思想感情和社会生活。在谈到自己的创作意图时，她说，"我一向致力于发现和了解人的动机和感情，并将我的心灵所能感受到的人际关系和人的经历加以提炼。……我热切地关注着那些生活在迁徙和灾难中的人们"[2]。她力图表现新旧秩序的冲突、传统与变革的矛盾以及人的理想与现实之间的裂痕，以揭示现代"荒原"中存在的问题——人无法按照自己的梦想去生活。波特作品的主人公多为女性，她们受到男权社会的不公正待遇，或隐遁，或抗争，体现了现代女性在西方文明逐渐衰落下的生存困境，因此，她也是女性主义研究中的一位重要作家。波特尤其擅长刻画人物内心深处的精神困境，被誉为对人类心灵进行"精雕细刻的艺术家"[3]。她的名作《愚人

---

[1] Mary Loeffelholz, ed., *The Norton Anthology of American Literature*, 7th edition, Vol. D, New York & London: W. W. Norton & Company, 2007, p. 1690.
[2] 李宜燮、常耀信主编，《美国文学选读（下册）》，天津：南开大学出版社，2010年，第368页。
[3] 〔美〕凯·安·波特著，《波特中短篇小说集》，鹿金等译，上海：上海译文出版社，1984年，第1页。

船》通过描写一艘由墨西哥开往德国的客船上形形色色的乘客的故事，揭示了20世纪西方社会人的劣根性，并指出这正是滋生纳粹主义的土壤。她的短篇小说《开花的犹大树》以20世纪初的墨西哥为背景，借用《圣经》中犹大背叛耶稣的故事，讲述了美国姑娘劳拉、革命者布拉乔尼、欧亨尼奥等人物之间不同程度的背叛。小说人物性格刻画细致，语言优美，主题深刻，是20世纪以来美国最优秀的短篇小说之一，也是被各类文集收录最多的波特的短篇小说之一。本书以她另一部短篇《偷窃》为例来和读者一起体会波特那细腻的文笔、高超的叙事技巧和深刻的主题。

《偷窃》是波特创作于1930年的一部著名的短篇小说。故事发生在美国经济大萧条之后的20世纪30年代的纽约，作家运用意识流的手法，紧紧围绕钱包丢失这一线索，从女主人公"她"的视角回忆了钱包丢失前后的人物与事件。从"她"的回溯性叙事中，我们不难发现，"她"是一位中产阶级的女性作家和评论家，与作家波特的经历类似。当"她"从浴室里出来时，突然发现钱包不见了。"她"站在屋里，仔细回想钱包丢失前后的每个细节。"她"想到了卡米洛，二人从托拉家的鸡尾酒会回来，卡米洛曾送"她"到高架铁路的闸机口，那时钱包还在。"她"想到了罗杰，在雨中罗杰陪"她"一起打车回公寓，"她"还替罗杰支付了车费。"她"想到了邻居比尔，想向他讨回欠自己的钱，比尔却向"她"诉苦。回到家中，"她"把钱包打开晾干时，还从钱包里取出了男朋友的分手信重读了一遍。第二天早上，"她"从浴室出来，发现钱包被女看门人偷走了。当"她"要求看门人归还钱包时，看门人先是否认，接着又说是为了自己的侄女才拿的。看门人反过来指责女主人公偷了她侄女的东西，最后主人公意识到，她应该害怕的不是小偷，而是她自己。

二、人物与主题

小说中的主要人物有女主人公"她"、卡米洛、罗杰、比尔和女看门人。"她"是作家兼评论家，但手头并不宽裕。从"她"与朋友的交往可以看出，"她"比较软弱，总是处处迁就、退让，为别人着想。卡米洛是"她"的朋友，主动送"她"到车站，他对女士殷勤，但手头拮据，因为他总是做些帮别人投硬币之类的小事，却付不起给女主人公的出租车费。卡米洛彬彬有礼，颇有绅士风

9. THEFT

度,目送"她"进了车站后,为了不让雨淋湿帽子,偷偷地把帽子取下来藏进衣服里,而"她"则心怀愧疚,假装没看见,以免被发现后伤了他的自尊心。罗杰是"她"的异性好友,剧作家,他们之间的关系很亲密,或许有成为男女朋友的可能,因为"她"在出租车上把头靠在罗杰的肩膀上,而车经过第六大道四十街口时,他们看到的三男两女似乎都在谈论着爱情。罗杰刚刚收到了女友的分手信,没有足够的钱支付出租车费,他们两人一起凑够了车费。回到家后"她"由罗杰想到自己也收到了一封分手信。此时,读者难免会猜测:故事在提到卡米洛的帽子时拿艾迪的帽子进行过比较,这位艾迪会不会是给"她"写分手信的男友?在回自己公寓的楼梯口,邻居比尔听到了"她"的脚步声,请"她"进去喝两杯,向"她"哭诉自己的剧本遭拒还要支付离婚赡养费的事,打消了"她"向他索要拖欠的稿费的念头,而实际上从比尔花了95美元买了一张二手地毯可以看出,比尔其实并不穷,只是不想还钱而已,他是一个善于撒谎的卑鄙的伪君子。女看门人明明趁"她"洗澡的时候偷拿了钱包,但在"她"的质问下却拒不承认,于是"她"打算息事宁人,不再计较。这时"她"脑子里出现了自己一生中曾经失去的美好的东西。女看门人怒气冲冲地归还了她的钱包,还数落了她一顿。最后她终于明白,"她"应该担心的不是偷窃,而是自己的一味隐忍。这些人中,卡米洛是一位死要面子活受罪的潦倒绅士,罗杰是她亲密而穷困潦倒的异性好友,比尔是一个卑鄙的伪君子,看门人则是一位满腹怨气、爱贪小便宜的底层妇女。"她"从一味忍让到逐渐醒悟,故事以钱包失窃为线索串起了"她"曾失去的金钱、友谊、爱情和事业。

《偷窃》看似讲述了生活中一桩平淡无奇的小事,但波特了不起的地方在于,她能够从日常生活的点滴小事中挖掘深刻的主题。这个故事中的主人公是一位无名无姓的"她","她"可以看作美国经济大萧条时期普通中产阶级尤其是中产女性的化身。当然,更进一步地看,"她"以自己细腻、敏感的所见、所闻、所思、所悟深刻揭示了经济萧条背景下普通人的失落、女性意识的觉醒、不同社会阶层以及理想与现实之间的冲突等多种主题。

首先,小说深刻反映了经济危机对普通人的冲击。"她"被偷窃的不仅是钱包,更是友情、爱情、事业与理想。从故事的讲述来看,"她"经济拮据,人生失意、苦闷,但又得不到理解和同情。"她"身边有四个男人和一个女人,卡米洛代表的是友谊的脆弱。他颇有绅士风度，矜持，好面子，不过囊中羞涩，英雄气短，不仅帮不上忙，还泥菩萨过河自身难保。罗杰和艾迪代表的爱情在经济危机下不堪一击。罗杰同样颇有绅士风度，陪她坐出租回家，却需要"她"共担车费，他们在车上举止亲昵，不过听到大街上三男两女的交谈，涉及的都是难以实现的爱情和婚姻。罗杰收到了女朋友的分手信，"她"也收到了艾迪推卸责任的分手信。显然，"她"是情场上的失意者。比尔是故事中最富有的人，他和"她"都算是作家，却睁着眼睛说瞎话，故意拖欠"她"的稿费。从这一层面看，"她"的事业也不如意。女守门人偷了钱包，却反过来愤愤不平地指责"她"，她们同属女人，都不富裕，虽然阶层不同，却互相猜忌，缺乏基本的信任。"她"在处处碰壁之后，意识到自己丢失的不仅仅是一个钱包，而是被剥夺了的更多的东西，包括财产、友谊、爱情、事业和理想。于是"她"想到曾经丢失的"她搬家时遗忘的东西，她借出却没有归还的书，她计划已久但却没有实现的旅行，那些她期待却没有听到的话语，那些她本想回复的话语"等，不禁悲从心起。

其次，小说生动地刻画了一位心思敏锐的女性在钱包丢失前后的思想变化，揭示了"她"从妥协、退让到逐渐觉醒的过程。从前面的分析可以看出，虽然生活早已虐"她"千百遍，"她"却依然忍辱负重。钱包的失窃，以及与女看门人针锋相对的正面交锋，让我们看到，"她"终于克服了逆来顺受的软弱，坚持拿回了属于自己的东西，"她"也逐渐意识到，"她"在生活中失去了那么多，原因在于女性自身的一味退让和妥协，因此，"她"觉醒过来，意识到只有不迷失自己，做到自立自强，才不会被他人偷去宝贵的东西。

最后，小说不仅以小见大地展示了经济萧条时期美国社会中各阶层普遍的失意潦倒和苦闷彷徨，还影射了男性与女性，以及不同阶层女性之间的冲突，揭示出理想与现实之间的巨大差距。男人对女人爱情的背叛，中产阶级普遍的一贫如洗、钱包的失窃，以及"她"与女看门人之间的互相指责，都指向了失窃背后的元凶——经济萧条。在这一背景下，所有的人，包括"她"、卡米洛、罗杰、比尔、女看门人，都被偷走了生活中宝贵的东西，他们都是"20世纪30年代的美国"这一更广泛意义上的"盗窃行为"的受害者。因此，在阅读时我们不难发现字里行间始终有种看似平静而又难以排解的怨愤。

三、结构与技巧

正如前文所述,波特在主题处理上善于在平凡中显深刻,于平静中见惊奇,这种以小博大的高超技巧也体现在小说的结构与技巧上。

首先,这篇小说的结构极为精密,可谓丝丝入扣,绝无一个多余的词语、一句多余的句子。整篇故事可以分为两个部分,四幕场景,各部分各场景之间的转换,都紧紧围绕题眼"钱包"展开。

第一部分采用的是倒叙,这部分大多是意识流,包括卡米洛车站送别、罗杰陪"她"回家、比尔拦"她"诉苦三幕场景,讲述"她"沐浴后发现钱包失窃,拼命想回忆起自己在哪里弄丢了钱包,这非常符合失窃事件发生后人们的正常反应。我们都知道,当生活中某个重要的东西突然不见了,人的本能反应肯定是绞尽脑汁,赶紧想想这个东西最近出现在哪个地方,跟哪些人和事有关。于是,"她"由钱包联想到了卡米洛送她去车站时"她"曾从里面掏钱付费,联想到了罗杰陪"她"坐出租车回五十三街附近的公寓时曾打开钱包,帮他付了10美分,联想到了"她"腋下夹着钱包上楼时被比尔拦下一起喝酒。在这一过程中,"她"的思绪发散开来,进一步想到了与这些人有关的细节。可以说,"钱包"就像是波特看似漫不经心的讲述中的节点和枢纽,而整个故事中,那些性格鲜明的人物,都以这一枢纽为中心,被有机地一个个串联在一起。第二部分接着故事开头"她"沐浴后发现钱包不见了讲起,中间穿插着"她"的大段思想活动,主要讲述"她"和女看门人围绕钱包丢失的交锋。这一部分塑造了一位顺手牵羊、不肯认错还强词夺理的女看门人形象。可以说,在整篇故事中,所有的情节都和"钱包"有着密切的关联,波特最高明的地方,就在于围绕着钱包丢失这一小事,描绘了当时人们普遍的生存状态。

其次,波特精密的安排还体现在"她"在对意象的处理上。除了前面提到的核心意象"钱包",小说中还有一个突出的意象"帽子",这两个意象都具有深刻的隐含意义。我们知道,帽子在当时的美国社会,代表着男人在社交场合中的形象和地位,与正装一样重要。从一个人所戴的帽子,可以看出他的地位高低和财富多寡。卡米洛戴着一顶寒酸的、淡褐色的新帽子,不过显然帽子的颜色有些不搭调,多半是为了省钱买的打折货,他第一次戴这顶帽子,就让雨水给糟蹋了。女主人公心里清楚这顶帽子对卡米洛的重要性,因此她不断自责:

"这可真糟,他到哪里去再买一顶?"("But this is dreadful, where will he get another?")为了表现自己的绅士风度,卡米洛不愿当着"她"的面脱下帽子,直到目送"她"远去,才偷偷在角落里摘下帽子,藏在衣服里。他以为女主人公看不到这一幕,不料"她"早已看在眼里,并对此深感内疚,觉得自己仿佛背叛了朋友。从卡米洛的帽子,"她"想到了艾迪的帽子,虽然不像卡米洛那样不得体,但艾迪的帽子总是看起来好像用了整整七年。"她"也想到了罗杰在大雨中与"她"见面,同样也将帽子严严实实地藏在外套里。从对卡米洛、罗杰和艾迪的帽子的描绘,我们不难发现,当时美国中产阶级的经济状况显然是比较糟糕的,他们甚至没有钱来买一顶体面的帽子;当然也可以说,他们为了强装绅士,死要面子活受罪,非要戴上一顶帽子,显得虚伪了些。

最后,这篇小说的叙述视角和意识流手法的运用非常成功。故事采用了独特的第三人称有限视角来讲述,既具有第三人称全知叙述自由观察人物的全景外部视野,也可以深入人物内心。因此读者不难发现,叙述者总能引导读者自由地在"她"的人生与"她"的内心世界之间切换,不留任何痕迹。故事一开篇"她"在洗浴后发现钱包失窃,立即由此展开回忆,将读者直接带入"她"的思维活动,让读者跟着"她"自己去体验生活,没有加入作者的任何评论。这一叙述方式更多的是展示而非叙述,在牢牢抓住读者的同时,作者又很快将读者带入故事世界,让读者和"她"一起去看,去听,去感受,因此具有更强烈的身临其境感,增加了叙述的力量和可信度。

故事的讲述主要借助人物的意识流展开,由于是第三人称全知视角和人物有限视角的结合,因此运用最多的是类似旁白的自由间接引语,而不是直接暴露人物混乱无序的无意识活动。如小说一开始,"她刚进来的时候,一只手里还拿着钱包。她站在地板中央,身上披着浴衣,一只手提着条湿毛巾,仔细思量刚刚发生的事情,一切都记得清清楚楚。不错,她用手帕揩干钱包后,把钱包盖子打开,摊在长凳上。"(She had the purse in her hand when she came in. Standing in the middle of the floor, holding her bathrobe around her and trailing a damp towel in one hand, she surveyed the immediate past and remembered everything clearly. Yes, she had opened the flap and spread it out on the bench after she had dried the purse with her handkerchief.)前面两句交代了故事的起因,第三句则以自由间接引用不动声色

9. THEFT

地引导读者进入"她"的回忆。当女看门人矢口否认偷窃一事,拒绝交还钱包,"她"终于按捺不住失意和委屈的情绪,一下子爆发出来。这时作者以完整的两段话,细致地描述了"她"心理的微妙变化:"她记得,她心里有一种抗拒的原则,使她觉得拥有东西是让人不舒服的事,所以她一生从不锁门,而且在朋友们警告她时,还自相矛盾地夸口说她从来没有因为被窃而丢失过一分钱。她曾经对这个具体的例子所反映出来的那种完全逆来顺受的态度感到高兴,因为这正好说明是某种根深蒂固的、否则就无法解释的普遍信念,再不以她的意志为转移,来指挥着她生活中的一举一动。"(She remembered how she had never locked a door in her life, on some principle of rejection in her that made her uncomfortable in the ownership of things, and her paradoxical boast before the warnings of her friends, that she had never lost a penny by theft; and she had been pleased with the bleak humility of this concrete example designed to illustrate and justify a certain fixed, otherwise baseless and general faith which ordered the movements of her life without regard to her will in the matter.)"她"觉得自己失去了大量宝贵的东西,"她"曾拥有的一切、"她"向往过的一切,全都失去了。钱包的失窃令"她"联想到了自己以前曾失去的东西,而在回想这一切的时候,"她"感到怅然若失,这无疑是双重意义上的失落,因为钱包的丢失不仅意味着失去财物,还意味着尊严、信任、感情和个性的丧失。

波特的小说往往描写日常生活中平淡无奇的小事,没有曲折离奇的情节,也没有惊天动地的结局,但她总是能以一位女性作家细腻敏锐的观察来以小见大揭示更为深邃的主题。她精心安排结构,在惜墨如金的文字中,编织进一个个看似漫不经心的细节,丝丝入扣,娓娓道来,看似平常,实则巧妙,展现了作家极为高超的叙述技巧。《偷窃》堪称一件文字考究、描写细腻、思想深邃、风格优美的精雕细琢的艺术品。

Suggested Readings

1. DeMouy, Jane Krause. *Katherine Anne Porter's Women*. Austin: University of Texas Press, 1983.
2. Givner, Joan. *Katherine Anne Porter: A Life*. New York: Simon & Schuster, 1982.

3. Porter, Katherine Anne. *The Collected Stories of Katherine Ann Porter*. New York: Harcourt, Brace & World, 1965.

4. Unrue, Darlene Harbour. *Truth and Vision in Katherine Anne Porter's Fiction*. Athens, GA: University of Georgia Press, 1985.

5. Unrue, Darlene Harbour. *Understanding Katherine Anne Porter*. Columbia, SC: University of South Carolina Press, 1988.

6. Warren, Robert Penn, ed. *Katherine Anne Porter: A Collection of Critical Essays*. Englewood Cliffs, NJ: Prentice-Hall, Inc., 1979.

7. West, Ray B. *Katherine Anne Porter*. Minneapolis: University of Minnesota Press, 1963.

8. 〔美〕凯·安·波特著：《波特中短篇小说集》，鹿金等译，上海：上海译文出版社，1984年。

Questions for Reflection

1. How much do you know about Katherine Anne Porter's famous short story "The Flowering Judas"?

2. How do you understand the structural function and symbolic meanings of the "purse" and the "hat" in the story?

3. What are the personality traits of the main characters in the story? Why is the narrator an unnamed "she"?

4. How do you understand the title "Theft"? What things has she been stolen?

5. Find in the story places where stream-of-consciousness is used. How memory and reality are seamlessly connected in the story?

Question for Discussion

Why do we say "Theft" manifests Katherine Anne Porter's superb craftswomanship?

（王安　撰写）

10. THE ENORMOUS RADIO

By John Cheever, 1947

Jim and Irene Westcott were the kind of people who seem to strike that satisfactory average of income, endeavor, and respectability that is reached by the statistical reports in college alumni bulletins. They were the parents of two young children, they had been married nine years, they lived on the twelfth floor of an apartment house near Sutton Place, they went to the theatre on an average of 10.3 times a year, and they hoped someday to live in Westchester. Irene Westcott was a pleasant, rather plain girl with soft brown hair and a wide, fine forehead upon which nothing at all had been written, and in the cold weather she wore a coat of fitch skins dyed to resemble mink. You could not say that Jim Westcott looked younger than he was, but you could at least say of him that he seemed to feel younger. He wore his graying hair cut very short, he dressed in the kind of clothes his class had worn at Andover, and his manner was earnest, vehement, and intentionally naïve. The Westcotts differed from their friends, their classmates, and their neighbors only in an interest they shared in serious music. They went to a great many concerts—although they seldom mentioned this to anyone—and they spent a good deal of time listening to music on the radio.

Their radio was an old instrument, sensitive, unpredictable, and beyond repair. Neither of them understood the mechanics of radio—or of any of the other appliances that surrounded them—and when the instrument faltered, Jim would strike the side of the cabinet with his hand. This sometimes helped. One Sunday afternoon, in the middle of a Schubert quartet, the music faded away altogether. Jim struck the cabinet repeatedly, but there was no response; the Schubert was lost to them forever. He promised to buy Irene a new radio, and on Monday when he came home from work he told her that he had got one. He refused to describe it, and said it would be a surprise for her when it came.

The radio was delivered at the kitchen door the following afternoon, and with the assistance of her maid and the handyman Irene uncrated it and brought it into the living room. She was struck at once with the physical ugliness of the large gumwood cabinet. Irene was proud of her living room, she had chosen its furnishings and colors as carefully as she chose her clothes, and now it seemed to her that the new radio stood among her intimate possessions like an aggressive intruder. She was confounded by the number of dials and switches on the instrument panel, and she studied them thoroughly before she put the plug into a wall socket and turned the radio on. The dials flooded with a malevolent green light, and in the distance she heard the music of a piano quintet. The quintet was in the distance for only an instant; it bore down upon her with a speed greater than light and filled the apartment with the noise of music amplified so mightily that it knocked a china ornament from a table to the floor. She rushed to the instrument and reduced the volume. The violent forces that were snared in the ugly gumwood cabinet made her uneasy. Her children came home from school then, and she took them to the Park. It was not until later in the afternoon that she was able to return to the radio.

The maid had given the children their suppers and was supervising their baths when Irene turned on the radio, reduced the volume, and sat down to listen to a Mozart quintet that she knew and enjoyed. The music came through clearly. The new instrument had a much purer tone, she thought, than the old one. She decided that tone was most important and that she could conceal the

10. THE ENORMOUS RADIO

cabinet behind a sofa. But as soon as she had made her peace with the radio, the interference began. A crackling sound like the noise of a burning powder fuse began to accompany the singing of the strings. Beyond the music, there was a rustling that reminded Irene unpleasantly of the sea, and as the quintet progressed, these noises were joined by many others. She tried all the dials and switches but nothing dimmed the interference, and she sat down, disappointed and bewildered, and tried to trace the flight of the melody. The elevator shaft in her building ran beside the living-room wall, and it was the noise of the elevator that gave her a clue to the character of the static. The rattling of the elevator cables and the opening and closing of the elevator doors were reproduced in her loudspeaker, and, realizing that the radio was sensitive to electrical currents of all sorts, she began to discern through the Mozart the ringing of telephone bells, the dialing of phones, and the lamentation of a vacuum cleaner. By listening more carefully, she was able to distinguish doorbells, elevator bells, electric razors, and Waring mixers, whose sounds had been picked up from the apartments that surrounded hers and transmitted through her loudspeaker. The powerful and ugly instrument, with its mistaken sensitivity to discord, was more than she could hope to master, so she turned the thing off and went into the nursery to see her children.

When Jim Westcott came home that night, he went to the radio confidently and worked the controls. He had the same sort of experience Irene had had. A man was speaking on the station Jim had chosen, and his voice swung instantly from the distance into a force so powerful that it shook the apartment. Jim turned the volume control and reduced the voice. Then, a minute or two later, the interference began. The ringing of telephones and doorbells set in, joined by the rasp of the elevator doors and the whir of cooking appliances. The character of the noise had changed since Irene had tried the radio earlier; the last of the electric razors was being unplugged, the vacuum cleaners had all been returned to their closets, and the static reflected that change in pace that overtakes the city after the sun goes down. He fiddled with the knobs but couldn't get rid of the noises, so he turned the radio off and told Irene that in the morning he'd call the people who had sold it to him and give them hell.

The following afternoon, when Irene returned to the apartment from a luncheon date, the maid told her that a man had come and fixed the radio. Irene went into the living room before she took off her hat or her furs and tried the instrument. From the loudspeaker came a recording of the "Missouri Waltz." It reminded her of the thin, scratchy music from an old-fashioned phonograph that she sometimes heard across the lake where she spent her summers. She waited until the waltz had finished, expecting an explanation of the recording, but there was none. The music was followed by silence, and then the plaintive and scratchy record was repeated. She turned the dial and got a satisfactory burst of Caucasian music—the thump of bare feet in the dust and the rattle of coin jewelry—but in the background she could hear the ringing of bells and a confusion of voices. Her children came home from school then, and she turned off the radio and went to the nursery.

When Jim came home that night, he was tired, and he took a bath and changed his clothes. Then he joined Irene in the living room. He had just turned on the radio when the maid announced dinner, so he left it on, and he and Irene went to the table.

Jim was too tired to make even a pretense of sociability, and there was nothing about the dinner to hold Irene's interest, so her attention wandered from the food to the deposits of silver polish on the candlesticks and from there to the music in the other room. She listened for a few minutes to a Chopin prelude and then was surprised to hear a man's voice break in. "For Christ's sake, Kathy," he said, "do you always have to play the piano when I get home?" The music stopped abruptly. "It's the only chance I have," a woman said. "I'm at the office all day." "So am I," the man said. He added something obscene about an upright piano, and slammed a door. The passionate and melancholy music

10. THE ENORMOUS RADIO

began again.

"Did you hear that?" Irene asked.

"What?" Jim was eating his dessert.

"The radio. A man said something while the music was still going on—something dirty."

"It's probably a play."

"I don't think it is a play," Irene said.

They left the table and took their coffee into the living room. Irene asked Jim to try another station. He turned the knob. "Have you seen my garters?" a man asked. "Button me up," a woman said. "Have you seen my garters?" the man said again. "Just button me up and I'll find your garters," the woman said. Jim shifted to another station. "I wish you wouldn't leave apple cores in the ashtrays," a man said. "I hate the smell."

"This is strange," Jim said.

"Isn't it?" Irene said.

Jim turned the knob again. " 'On the coast of Coromandel where the early pumpkins blow,' " a woman with a pronounced English accent said. " 'in the middle of the woods lived the Yonghy-Bonghy-Bò. Two old chairs, and half a candle, one old jug without a handle...' "

"My God!" Irene cried. "That's the Sweeneys' nurse."

" 'These were all his worldly goods,' " the British voice continued.

"Turn that thing off," Irene said. "Maybe they can hear *us*." Jim switched the radio off. "That was Miss Armstrong, the Sweeneys' nurse," Irene said. "She must be reading to the little girl. They live in 17-B. I've talked with Miss Armstrong in the Park. I know her voice very well. We must be getting other people's apartments."

"That's impossible," Jim said.

"Well, that was the Sweeneys' nurse," Irene said hotly. "I know her voice. I know it very well. I'm wondering if they can hear us."

Jim turned the switch. First from a distance and then nearer, nearer, as if borne on the wind, came the pure accents of the Sweeneys' nurse again: " *'Lady Jingly! Lady Jingly!'* "she said, " *'sitting where the pumpkins blow, will you come and be my wife? said the Yonghy- Bonghy-Bò...'* "

Jim went over to the radio and said "Hello" loudly into the speaker.

" *'I am tired of living singly,'* " the nurse went on, " *'on this coast so wild and shingly, I'm a-weary of my life; if you'll come and he my wife, quite serene would he my life...'* "

"I guess she can't hear us," Irene said. "Try something else."

Jim turned to another station, and the living room was filled with the uproar of a cocktail party that had overshot its mark. Someone was playing the piano and singing the "Whiffenpoof Song," and the voices that surrounded the piano were vehement and happy. "Eat some more sandwiches," a woman shrieked. There were screams of laughter and a dish of some sort crashed to the floor.

"Those must be the Fullers, in 11-E," Irene said. "I knew they were giving a party this afternoon. I saw her in the liquor store. Isn't this too divine? Try something else. See if you can get those people in 18-C."

The Westcotts overheard that evening a monologue on salmon fishing in Canada, a bridge game, running comments on home movies of what had apparently been a fortnight at Sea Island, and a bitter family quarrel about an overdraft at the bank. They turned off their radio at midnight and went to bed, weak with laughter. Sometime in the night, their son began to call for a glass of water and Irene got one and took it to his room. It was very early. All the lights in the neighborhood were extinguished, and from the boy's window she could see the empty street. She went into the living room and tried the radio. There was some faint coughing, a moan, and then a man spoke. "Are you all right, darling?" he asked. "Yes," a woman said wearily. "Yes, I'm all right, I guess," and then she added with great feeling, "But, you know, Charlie, I don't feel like

10. THE ENORMOUS RADIO

myself any more. Sometimes there are about fifteen or twenty minutes in the week when I feel like myself I don't like to go to another doctor, because the doctor's bills are so awful already, but I just don't feel like myself, Charlie. I just never feel like myself." They were not young, Irene thought. She guessed from the timbre of their voices that they were middle-aged. The restrained melancholy of the dialogue and the draft from the bedroom window made her shiver, and she went back to bed.

The following morning, Irene cooked breakfast for the family—the maid didn't come up from her room in the basement until ten—braided her daughter's hair, and waited at the door until her children and her husband had been carried away in the elevator. Then she went into the living room and tried the radio. "I don't want to go to school," a child screamed. "I hate school. I won't go to school. I hate school." "You will go to school," an enraged woman said. "We paid eight hundred dollars to get you into that school and you'll go if it kills you." The next number on the dial produced the worn record of the "Missouri Waltz." Irene shifted the control and invaded the privacy of several breakfast tables. She overheard demonstrations of indigestion, carnal love, abysmal vanity, faith, and despair. Irene's life was nearly as simple and sheltered as it appeared to be, and the forthright and sometimes brutal language that came from the loudspeaker that morning astonished and troubled her. She continued to listen until her maid came in. Then she turned off the radio quickly, since this insight, she realized, was a furtive one.

Irene had a luncheon date with a friend that day, and she left her apartment at a little after twelve. There were a number of women in the elevator when it stopped at her floor. She stared at their handsome and impassive faces, their furs, and the cloth flowers in their hats. Which one of them had been to Sea Island? she wondered. Which one had overdrawn her bank account? The elevator stopped at the tenth floor and a woman with a pair of Skye terriers joined them. Her hair was rigged high on her head and she wore a mink cape. She was humming the "Missouri Waltz."

Irene had two Martinis at lunch, and she looked searchingly at her friend and wondered what her secrets were. They had intended to go shopping after lunch, but Irene excused herself and went home. She told the maid that she was not to be disturbed; then she went into the living room, closed the doors, and switched on the radio. She heard, in the course of the afternoon, the halting conversation of a woman entertaining her aunt, the hysterical conclusion of a luncheon party, and a hostess briefing her maid about some cocktail guests. "Don't give the best Scotch to anyone who hasn't white hair," the hostess said. "See if you can get rid of that liver paste before you pass those hot things, and could you lend me five dollars? I want to tip the elevator man."

As the afternoon waned, the conversations increased in intensity. From where Irene sat, she could see the open sky above the East River. There were hundreds of clouds in the sky, as though the south wind had broken the winter into pieces and were blowing it north, and on her radio she could hear the arrival of cocktail guests and the return of children and businessmen from their schools and offices. "I found a good-sized diamond on the bathroom floor this morning," a woman said. "It must have fallen out of that bracelet Mrs. Dunston was wearing last night." "We'll sell it," a man said. "Take it down to the jeweler on Madison Avenue and sell it. Mrs. Dunston won't know the difference, and we could use a couple of hundred bucks... " " 'Oranges and lemons, say the bells of St. Clement's,' " the Sweeneys' nurse sang. " 'Halfpence and farthings, say the bells of St. Martin's. When will you pay me? say the bells at old Bailey...'" "It's not a hat," a woman cried, and at her back roared a cocktail party. "It's not a hat, it's a love affair. That's what Walter Florell said. He said it's not a hat, it's a love affair," and then, in a lower voice, the same woman added, "Talk to somebody, for Christ's sake, honey, talk to somebody. If she catches you standing here not talking to anybody, she'll take us off her invitation list, and I

10. THE ENORMOUS RADIO

love these parties."

The Westcotts were going out for dinner that night, and when Jim came home, Irene was dressing. She seemed sad and vague, and he brought her a drink. They were dining with friends in the neighborhood, and they walked to where they were going. The sky was broad and filled with light. It was one of those splendid spring evenings that excite memory and desire, and the air that touched their hands and faces felt very soft. A Salvation Army band was on the corner playing "Jesus Is Sweeter." Irene drew on her husband's arm and held him there for a minute, to hear the music. "They're really such nice people, aren't they?" she said. "They have such nice faces. Actually, they're so much nicer than a lot of the people we know." She took a bill from her purse and walked over and dropped it into the tambourine. There was in her face, when she returned to her husband, a look of radiant melancholy that he was not familiar with. And her conduct at the dinner party that night seemed strange to him, too. She interrupted her hostess rudely and stared at the people across the table from her with an intensity for which she would have punished her children.

It was still mild when they walked home from the party, and Irene looked up at the spring stars. " 'How far that little candle throws its beams,' " she exclaimed. " 'So shines a good deed in a naughty world.' " She waited that night until Jim had fallen asleep, and then went into the living room and turned on the radio.

Jim came home at about six the next night. Emma, the maid, let him in, and he had taken off his hat and was taking off his coat when Irene ran into the hall. Her face was shining with tears and her hair was disordered. "Go up to 16-C, Jim!" she screamed. "Don't take off your coat. Go up to 16-C. Mr. Osborn's beating his wife. They've been quarreling since four o'clock, and now he's hitting her. Go up there and stop him."

From the radio in the living room, Jim heard screams, obscenities, and thuds. "You know you don't have to listen to this sort of thing," he said. He strode into the living room and turned the switch. "It's indecent," he said. "It's like looking in windows. You know you don't have to listen to this sort of thing. You can turn it off."

"Oh, it's so horrible, it's so dreadful," Irene was sobbing. "I've been listening all day, and it's so depressing."

"Well, if it's so depressing, why do you listen to it? I bought this damned radio to give you some pleasure," he said. "I paid a great deal of money for it. I thought it might make you happy. I wanted to make you happy."

"Don't, don't, don't, don't quarrel with me," she moaned, and laid her head on his shoulder. "All the others have been quarreling all day. Everybody's been quarreling. They're all worried about money. Mrs. Hutchinson's mother is dying of cancer in Florida and they don't have enough money to send her to the Mayo Clinic. At least, Mr. Hutchinson says they don't have enough money. And some woman in this building is having an affair with the handyman—with that hideous handyman. It's too disgusting. And Mrs. Melville has heart trouble and Mr. Hendricks is going to lose his job in April and Mrs. Hendricks is horrid about the whole thing and that girl who plays the 'Missouri Waltz' is a whore, a common whore, and the elevator man has tuberculosis and Mr. Osborn has been beating Mrs. Osborn." She wailed, she trembled with grief and checked the stream of tears down her face with the heel of her palm.

"Well, why do you have to listen?" Jim asked again. "Why do you have to listen to this stuff if it makes you so miserable?"

"Oh, don't, don't, don't," she cried. "Life is too terrible, too sordid and awful. But we've never been like that, have we, darling? Have we? I mean, we've always been good and decent and loving to one another, haven't we? And we have two children, two beautiful children. Our lives aren't sordid, are they, darling? Are they?" She flung her arms around his neck and drew his face down

10. THE ENORMOUS RADIO

to hers. "We're happy, aren't we, darling? We are happy, aren't we?"

"Of course we're happy," he said tiredly. He began to surrender his resentment. "Of course we're happy. I'll have that damned radio fixed or taken away tomorrow." He stroked her soft hair. "My poor girl," he said.

"You love me, don't you?" she asked. "And we're not hypercritical or worried about money or dishonest, are we?"

"No, darling," he said.

A man came in the morning and fixed the radio. Irene turned it on cautiously and was happy to hear a California-wine commercial and a recording of Beethoven's Ninth Symphony, including Schiller's "Ode to Joy." She kept the radio on all day and nothing untoward came from the speaker.

A Spanish suite was being played when Jim came home. "Is everything all right?" he asked. His face was pale, she thought. They had some cocktails and went in to dinner to the "Anvil Chorus" from *Il Trovatore*. This was followed by Debussy's "La Mer."

"I paid the bill for the radio today," Jim said. "It cost four hundred dollars. I hope you'll get some enjoyment out of it."

"Oh, I'm sure I will," Irene said.

"Four hundred dollars is a good deal more than I can afford," he went on. "I wanted to get something that you'd enjoy. It's the last extravagance we'll be able to indulge in this year. I see that you haven't paid your clothing bills yet. I saw them on your dressing table." He looked directly at her. "Why did you tell me you'd paid them? Why did you lie to me?"

"I just didn't want you to worry, Jim," she said. She drank some water. "I'll be able to pay my bills out of this month's allowance. There were the slipcovers last month, and that party."

"You've got to learn to handle the money I give you a little more intelligently, Irene," he said. "You've got to understand that we won't have as much money this year as we had last. I had a very sobering talk with Mitchell today. No one is buying anything. We're spending all our time promoting new issues, and you know how long that takes. I'm not getting any younger, you know. I'm thirty-seven. My hair will be gray next year. I haven't done as well as I'd hoped to do. And I don't suppose things will get any better."

"Yes, dear," she said.

"We've got to start cutting down," Jim said. "We've got to think of the children. To be perfectly frank with you, I worry about money a great deal. I'm not at all sure of the future. No one is. If anything should happen to me, there's the insurance, but that wouldn't go very far today. I've worked awfully hard to give you and the children a comfortable life," he said bitterly. "I don't like to see all of my energies, all of my youth, wasted in fur coats and radios and slipcovers and—"

"Please, Jim," she said. "Please. They'll hear us."

"*Who'll hear us*? Emma can't hear us."

"The radio."

"Oh, I'm sick!" he shouted. "I'm sick to death of your apprehensiveness. The radio can't hear us. Nobody can hear us. And what if they can hear us? Who cares?"

Irene got up from the table and went into the living room. Jim went to the door and shouted at her from there. "Why are you so Christly all of a sudden? What's turned you overnight into a convent girl? You stole your mother's jewelry before they probated her will. You never gave your sister a cent of that money that was intended for her—not even when she needed it. You made Grace Howland's life miserable, and where was all your piety and your virtue when you went to that abortionist? I'll never forget how cool you were. You packed your bag and went off to have that child murdered as if you were going to Nassau. If you'd had any reasons, if you'd had any good reasons—"

Irene stood for a minute before the hideous cabinet, disgraced and sickened, but she held her hand on the switch before she extinguished the music and the voices, hoping that the instrument might speak to her kindly, that she might hear the Sweeneys' nurse. Jim continued to shout at her from the door. The voice on the radio was suave and non-committal. "An early-morning railroad disaster in Tokyo," the loudspeaker said, "killed twenty-nine people. A fire in a Catholic hospital near Buffalo for the care of blind children was extinguished early this morning by nuns. The temperature is forty-seven. The humidity is eighty-nine."

作品赏析

一、作家与故事情节

约翰·威廉·契弗（John William Cheever, 1912—1982），出生于马萨诸塞州，是美国著名的小说家。

契弗的父亲是一名富裕的鞋商，在大萧条中几近破产，进而消沉酗酒。契弗没有上过大学，靠自学成才。他从少年时代就开始创作，立志成为一名作家。他居住在波士顿和纽约一带，很多时光都在位于纽约的Yaddo艺术家和作家社区度过。1942年，他应征入伍，参加了第二次世界大战。战后，除了一直努力进行文学创作之外，他还担任过杂志编辑、创作培训营讲师和志愿消防员。1974年，他成为波士顿大学的一名教授。

1941年，他与大他7岁的玛丽·温特尼兹（Mary Winternitz）结婚。他妻子的父亲是耶鲁大学医学院院长，祖父是电话发明者贝尔的助手。两人育有三个小孩。虽然没有离婚，但是因契弗酗酒和婚外情等问题，他们的夫妻关系并不和睦。

契弗被公认为20世纪最重要的短篇小说家之一，被美国作家埃尔莫尔·伦纳德（Elmore Leonard）称为"郊区契诃夫"（the Chekov of the suburbs）[1]。

---

[1] Martin Chilton, *"John Cheever: 'the Chekhov of the suburbs'"*, The Daily Telegraph, UK. October 15, 2015. https://www.telegraph.co.uk/books/authors/john-cheever-master-of-the-short-story/.

他的作品通常以纽约郊区为背景，针砭愚蠢、压抑、毫无创意的中产阶级枯燥得令人窒息的生活。他对中产阶级的沉闷生活的批判登峰造极，所以，同时代的美国作家约翰·厄普代克（John Updike）评价契弗时说："约翰·契弗通常被称为郊区题材作家，但是很多人都写过这个题材。唯独契弗能够从中提炼出作品背景的原型。"[1]

除了上述主题，契弗作品主要探讨另外两种主题。一是揭示人性的两面性：或者是外表光鲜与内心龌龊之间的反差，或者是人格极端不同的角色之间的矛盾；二是表达对悠久的文化传统和强烈的社区意识的怀旧情绪。

契弗的短篇小说，题材真实亲切，情节紧凑，意味深长，触动心灵，深受读者喜爱。他曾经获得过"普利策小说奖""本杰明·富兰克林奖""欧·亨利奖""国家图书奖""国家文学奖章"等各种嘉奖和荣誉。

契弗著名的短篇小说有《巨型收音机》（"The Enormous Radio"）、《再见吧，弟弟》（"Goodbye, My Brother"）、《乡下丈夫》（"The Country Husband"）和《游泳者》（"The Swimmer"）。他的长篇小说主要有《沃普萧纪事》（*The Wapshot Chronicle*）和《沃普萧丑闻》（*The Wapshot Scandal*）。

在小说《巨型收音机》中，作者首先大致介绍了吉姆·韦斯科特和艾琳·韦斯科特夫妇的情况。他俩大学毕业，是典型的中产阶级。他们喜欢古典音乐，经常收听电台的相关节目。但是，一个星期天，收音机突然坏了。第二天，吉姆下班回来告诉艾琳，他已经订购了一台新的收音机。星期二下午，收音机送来了。艾琳刚开始摆弄这台新设备，这时两个孩子回来了，她只得停下，陪他们去公园玩耍。

女佣安排孩子们吃完晚饭，并监督他们洗澡，艾琳则在试听新的收音机。不久，收音机开始出现噪音，而且噪音种类越来越多：电梯门开关的响声、电话铃声、剃须刀的嗡鸣、吸尘器的啸叫，不一而足。晚些时候，吉姆回家调试了一阵，但噪声依旧。他关掉收音机，说明天去找卖家理论。

1　Tacalino, Rob. "The 20th-Century American Short Story: Three Authors, Three Generations." *Bookmarks Magazine*, May/June 2006: 29. Web. August 24, 2021. https://www.bookmarksmagazine.com/uploads/1/2/3/6/123678800/twentiethcenturyshortstory-20060506.pdf. Reagan, Mary. "The Archetypal Significance of John Cheever's 'The Swimmer.'" Web. August 24, 2021. https://digital.library.txstate.edu/handle/10877/5527

10. THE ENORMOUS RADIO

星期三下午，艾琳跟朋友在外面吃完午饭后回家，女佣告诉她师傅已经修过收音机了。刚开始挺好的，但很快就传来铃声以及一团扭曲的人声。晚上，艾琳一边吃饭一边听音乐，突然，她听到一对男女在争吵。吉姆和艾琳离开餐桌，凑近细听。吉姆旋转按钮，另一对夫妻的对话传来，继续旋转，他们听见斯维尼（Sweeney）家保姆正在朗读童话故事。艾琳在公园见过这位保姆，对她的声音很熟悉，一下子就辨认出来了。夫妻俩听到深夜才停，凌晨时分，艾琳给孩子送水后又开始偷听。

星期四早上送别丈夫、孩子后，艾琳马上打开收音机，直到女佣进来才关掉。中午，她赴约跟朋友一起吃午饭。在电梯里，她瞪着几位外表优雅的女子，寻思着刚才唱歌的是哪位，刚才吵架的又是哪位。吃完饭，她提前结束约会，回来继续偷听，并且告诉女佣不准打扰。晚上他们夫妇跟朋友一起在附近吃饭。他们路过街边布道的救世军时，艾琳捐了一些钱。吃晚饭的时候，艾琳举止粗鲁。

星期五晚上，吉姆下班回家，艾琳叫他赶快去邻居奥斯本（Osborn）家阻止他打他老婆。吉姆劝艾琳别再偷听了，艾琳则不断央求丈夫不要和自己争吵。

星期六上午，收音机真的修好了。吉姆回家告诉艾琳，这台收音机花了400美元，这一年不能再有其他奢侈消费了。吉姆接着质问艾琳为什么还没有付清衣服的账单，还要撒谎隐瞒。接着吉姆诉说挣钱的艰辛和对未来的焦虑，提醒艾琳要勤俭持家。

艾琳叫吉姆不要说下去，因为她担心收音机会听到，邻居也会听到。吉姆怒火中烧，站在客厅门口不断数落艾琳。艾琳在客厅听了大约一分钟电台节目后，关掉了收音机。

二、人物与主题

这篇小说的主要人物是艾琳·韦斯科特和丈夫吉姆·韦斯科特。其他人物有他们家的女佣、他俩的孩子、跟他们一起吃饭的朋友、修理收音机的师傅等。

艾琳是一位家庭主妇，两个孩子的妈妈。虽然相貌平平，穿着仿貂皮，但是保养得很好，应该略显年轻，而且家里还雇了一名女佣。特别的是，她跟丈夫非常喜欢古典音乐，会不时参加音乐演奏会。可见，她过着滋润优越的物质和文化生活，堪称郊区中产阶级幸福生活的典型。

由于收音机出现故障，他们能够从收音机听到邻居家的动静。艾琳非常好奇邻居们隐藏在外表后面的真实生活，逮着机会就偷听，相当痴迷。艾琳是一个多愁善感的人，通过偷听，她了解到邻居们的各种烦恼和丑闻，这些真实情况让她感到诧异、压抑和苦闷，同时产生了隐隐的不安。艾琳还是一个自我感觉良好、情绪化的人，她对邻居们的丑陋和堕落感到失望和愤怒，进而觉得世界充满丑恶。她对邻居们，或者说世人，既怜悯又鄙夷，所以，她捐钱给救世军，却又粗鲁地对待他人，甚至她的朋友。

随着对邻居生活的了解日益增加，她心中隐隐的不安逐渐明显和强烈起来，她变得敏感脆弱，渴望能够确认自己的生活是安全幸福的；但是，他们的家境其实是窘迫和令人焦虑的，而她自己的人品也充满瑕疵，面对这样的真相，她感到沮丧、痛苦和无助。

吉姆37岁，负责挣钱养家，他辛苦打拼，却觉得自己的职业和收入前景黯淡。同时，他对社会现实也更加熟悉，所以他对邻居们的秘密兴趣不大。平时他表情严肃，刻意掩饰，表现潇洒，其实，他长期以来感到沮丧和焦虑。

这部短篇小说虽然也涉及中产阶级的攀比、嫉妒和自卑心理，但其主题是揭穿美国长期流行的关于中产阶级富裕优雅的幸福生活的神话，暴露他们困顿、苦闷、压抑、焦虑和堕落的真实生活，启迪美国社会进行自我检讨。作品主要通过描绘主人公艾琳的心理和情感历程来表现这一主题。

小说开篇特意指出，艾琳和吉姆一家是标准的中产阶级，具有典型代表意义。"吉姆·韦斯科特和艾琳·韦斯科特夫妇的收入、事业和社会地位正好相当于各种大学校友简报统计出来的、表明能够过得不错的那个平均数。"他们跟朋友、同学、邻居的唯一区别"在于他们对严肃音乐的兴趣"。

他们住在纽约郊区的一栋公寓楼12层，并希望有朝一日能够搬进一个他们心仪的小区。丈夫吉姆上班养家，妻子艾琳在家照顾两个孩子；他们还雇了一名女佣帮忙。艾琳精力充沛，"宽大、光滑的前额看不出一丝皱纹"，吉姆也拥有比实际年龄年轻的心态。读者似乎看到了一个熟悉的中产阶级幸福家庭。而且，此时的艾琳，跟大多数人一样，相信有关中产阶级美好生活的神话，她觉得幸福满足，同时也认为邻居们跟她一样幸福。

但是，偷听了邻居的生活，她首先认识到，这些表面上光鲜、愉快的邻居，

10. THE ENORMOUS RADIO

其实生活困苦，精神荒芜，道德沦丧。自然，她听到的各种居家动静，内容无所不包，但主旋律却是负面的：家庭争吵此起彼伏，聚会的嘈杂是这些中产阶级富裕生活的伪装，掩饰着他们的财务窘态，更掩藏着各种丑陋和堕落；有人捡到邻居的钻石后决定私吞、看不起病、失业、婚外情、卖淫，各种困顿和丑陋，不一而足。那位保姆朗读童话的声音算是例外。

艾琳因此对邻居和朋友满心怀疑和鄙夷。在电梯里，她开始怀疑那些漂亮优雅的女子，尤其那位穿着真正貂皮的年轻女子，她甚至猜想一起吃饭的朋友肯定也藏掖着不可告人的秘密。晚上和丈夫与朋友聚餐席间，她举止粗鲁，毫不尊重他人，因为那些人形象体面但内心腐败，根本不配得到她的尊重。

愤世嫉俗的同时，她心情沉重，悲天悯人。经过沿街布道的救世军时，她拉着丈夫倾听良久，还捐钱赞助，她感叹道："他们是真正的好人，对吧？"似乎天下好人难寻，只剩下她和这些同道的教会人士。晚饭后出来散步，她举头仰望星空，借用莎士比亚的话感叹道："一支小小的蜡烛，它的光照耀得多么远！""一件善事也正像这支蜡烛一样，在这个罪恶的世界里，发出巨大的光辉！"

唏嘘之余，她为自己感到庆幸，因为他们夫妻恩爱和睦，经济宽裕，但是她很快进一步认识到，她自己的家庭存在同样的问题。丈夫语气稍显严厉，建议她别再偷听邻居生活，并指出这种行为并不高尚。艾琳顿时感到危机逼近，害怕重复邻居家的那些争吵，她赶紧苦苦哀求。吉姆感到无奈，只好安抚她。后来，吉姆责备她没有支付衣服的账单还撒谎，然后告诉艾琳，自己身心疲惫，前途暗淡，提醒艾琳节约开支。此时，艾琳幻想的和睦和宽裕被击得粉碎。

艾琳最终认识到，自己也是腐败堕落的。当丈夫述说自己的压抑和焦虑时，艾琳惊慌失措，请求吉姆不要再说，因为她害怕收音机会听到，邻居会听到。吉姆本来就对艾琳突如其来的自视清高和悲天悯人感到迷惑和反感，此时，艾琳的虚伪更让他怒不可遏，他高声数落艾琳，指出她的各种自私和堕落，尤其是她兴高采烈地去堕胎这件事。艾琳终于意识到，自己跟那些令人鄙夷的邻居们并无二致。

艾琳感到压抑、痛苦和绝望，听着电台的节目，她希望听到保姆朗读的童话，获得一丝安慰，但只听见主持人语气平淡地报道着新闻：东京早晨发生列车事故，死亡29人；布法罗附近的盲童医院的火灾已被修女扑灭；当前气温华氏47度，湿度89；灾难重重的世界、丑陋的社会、绝望的自己，又要熬过冰冷、沉闷的一天。

至此，艾琳完成了对邻居、她的家庭以及她本人的真实面目的认知。通过揭示艾琳的认知历程，作者揭示了美国中产阶级的真实生态。

三、结构与技巧

这部小说采用第三人称的叙事角度，按照时间顺序进行叙述。作品结构自然、简单，但是紧凑精致，具有明显的蒙太奇效果，主要由主人公艾琳的几个生活场面、她从收音机听到的各种邻居情况、她由此产生的心理反应等组成。表面上看，故事的线索是收音机的故障及对故障的处理，故事因收音机故障引起，又以关掉收音机结尾，结构颇为巧妙。但故事发展的真正逻辑是艾琳的认知和情感过程。艾琳逐步认识到了邻居、她的家庭和她本人的真实状况，而读者则认识到整个中产阶级甚至整个美国社会的真实面目。故事在艾琳和丈夫的争吵中结束。

至于创作技巧，可以关注这部作品中的语言风格、以小见大的表现方式、心理描写、象征、对比和反衬、反讽、巧妙结尾等特色。

小说叙述语言简单直接，作者很少使用过多的形容词和副词进行修饰和点缀。比如，在描述吉姆的疲惫时，作者只是直白地写道：他"太累了，连假装礼貌的心情都没有"，没有进一步渲染。当艾琳和朋友吃完晚饭出来仰望星空时，作者对天空的描述只用了"缀满星星的"一个单词，并没有对天空的各种情景进行描述来衬托艾琳的澎湃心潮。这种文风使叙述特别清新明了、酣畅淋漓，而且，这种白描风格的描述，让作品读来十分真实和亲切。

作者擅长从细节入手，以小见大，这个特点在这部作品中得到了充分体现。收音机出现故障，是生活中的一件微不足道的事情，而正是这个细节串起整个故事，几处细节充分表明了吉姆和艾琳夫妇的生活状况和社会地位。例如，"她对装饰和颜色的选择，就如她对衣服的挑选一样挑剔"；那曲音乐让艾琳想起"她每逢夏季前往度假的湖畔"的对岸传来的那种旧式留音机发出的音乐。艾琳心态的发展变化，不是通过直接的陈述和分析来表达，而是通过各种细节来表现的。再如，她对邻居和朋友的粗鲁无礼生动地展示了她对这些人的怀疑和鄙夷。她给救世军捐款，评论他们，并在晚饭后吟诵莎士比亚的诗句，这些都很委婉地表露了她自视清高、悲天悯人的情怀。作者通过这些细节，塑造出艾琳幸福、高贵的形象，为后文揭穿真相进行铺垫。作者正是凭借各种细节，冷静地一层一层地剥掉中产阶级的伪装，揭示出真实面目。比起直接评论和说教，这种启发使读者对主题的理解更加深刻。

这部小说对主人公艾琳的心路历程进行了鞭辟入里的剖析，但是，作者主要采取动作和语言描写来表现。比如，看见救世军布道，艾琳拉着丈夫伫立静听，丈夫感到诧异和扭捏，可以看出，艾琳夫妇跟他们的邻居一样，通常也是冷漠麻木的；又比如，当吉姆语气稍微严厉的时候，艾琳连续使用很多个"不要"来哀求他别再说下去，艾琳力图维持自己对幸福的幻想的心理跃然纸上。

作品屡次使用象征手法。收音机、保姆朗读的童话、聚会和结尾都富含象征意义。"她立刻被这个硕大的橡木箱子的丑陋外表惊呆了"，这个丑陋的收音机象征着中产阶级生活，尤其是他们的道德和精神生活的本来面目。保姆朗读的童话则代表纯洁和美好，代表艾琳寻求的安慰。邻居家里举行的各种聚会是中产阶级生活的外在伪装。结尾处，艾琳怀着沮丧和绝望的心情，关掉收音机，这犹如说她认清真相后，不忍再继续直视丑陋的生活。

这部小说在多处使用对比和反衬的写作手法。吉姆和艾琳在思想认识上构成鲜明对比。吉姆在外打拼，对社会和人性的阴暗面自然有较多了解，所以对邻居的丑陋和困顿并不觉得新鲜，也不想偷听这些事情。但是家庭主妇艾琳一直生活在温室和想象中，文中写道，"艾琳的生活几乎就像看上去那样简单和与世隔绝"，所以，她对这些事情感到好奇，而且在知道这些事情很普遍后，她感到非常震惊和压抑。保姆朗读童话的声音与公寓的主旋律形成对比和反衬，童话的纯真、善良和快乐，使这些中产阶级虚张声势的嘈杂和鬼鬼祟祟的心声显得更加虚伪、浅薄和龌龊。吉姆责骂艾琳时道出了艾琳的真实人格，这与她的自我认知和自我标榜形成强烈对比，这一真相反衬出艾琳的脆弱和虚荣，使艾琳的人物形象变得特别圆满和鲜活。丑陋的收音机和艾琳精致的房间装饰也形成对比，分别代表着他们生活的实质和外表。

反讽也是这部作品的一个突出特点。小说开篇，读者看到一对幸福的中产阶级夫妇，接着，和艾琳夫妇一起，读者了解到那些邻居的各种不堪。艾琳从此自视与众不同，对邻居既同情又鄙视，她的清高甚至从道德层面上升到宗教层面。但是，作品用各种生活细节撕掉艾琳的层层伪装，暴露了她的家庭和她本人的真实面目：自诩高尚，却不断偷听邻居；自诩富足，却拖欠账单不付；自诩恩爱，却对丈夫撒谎。不但艾琳如此，她的邻居们也是一样，表面上穿金戴银，别墅度假，举办各种聚会，一派繁荣，但实际上各种财务问题缠身；表面上体面斯文，但实际上腐朽堕落。作品是对艾琳以及整个中产阶级的一则辛辣的讽刺，更是对美国社会敲响的警钟。

小说的结尾非常巧妙，别具特色。电台的新闻节目暗示着，这个世界正如艾琳现在明白的那样充满丑陋和痛苦，同时也反映了艾琳当时绝望和无助的心境。小说情节以收音机故障为开端，以主人公关掉收音机为结尾，使整个故事浑然一体。故事在吉姆和艾琳的争吵中收尾，预示着中产阶级那种沉闷困顿的生活在故事结束之后还将延续下去。

Suggested Readings

1. Baumgartner, M. P. *The Moral Order of A Suburb*. New York: Oxford University Press, 1988.
2. Bosha, Francis J. *John Cheever: A Reference Guide*. Boston: G.K. Hall, 1991.
3. Cheever, John. *John Cheever: Collected Stories and Other Writings*. New York: Library of America, 2009.
4. Cheever, John. *The Stories of John Cheever*. New York: Vintage International, 2000.
5. Cheever, John. *Falconer*. New York: Rosetta Books, 2004.
6. Cheever, John. *Bullet Park*. New York: Rosetta Books, 2004.
7. Coale, Samuel. *John Cheever*. New York: Ungar, 1977.
8. Donaldson, Scott. *John Cheever: A Biography*. New York: Random House, 1988.
9. Donaldson, Scott. *John Cheever: A Biography*. New York: Open Road Distribution, 2016.
10. Donaldson, Scott, ed. *Conversations with John Cheever*. Jackson, MS: University Press of Mississippi, 1987.
11. Gerlach, John. "Closure in Modern Fiction: Cheever's 'the Enormous Radio' and

'Artemis, the Honest Well-Digger'." *Modern Fiction Studies* 28 (1982), pp. 145-152.

12. May, Charles. "Chekhov and the Modern Short Story." *A Chekhov Companinon*, ed. Toby W. Clyman. Westport, CT: Greenwood, 1985, pp. 147-163.

13. Meanor, Patrick. *John Cheever Revisited.* Boston: Twayne Publishers, 1995.

14. O'Hara, James E. *John Cheever: A Study of the Short Fiction.* Boston: Twayne Publishers, 1981.

Questions for Reflection

1. Is it viable to break down into rough categories the sounds and voices that Irene, through the radio, overhears from her neighbors?

2. What psychological process has Irene experienced? What may that psychological process suggest about the real situations of the middle class of the U.S. society?

3. When Irene sees a Salvation Army band playing gospel music at a street corner, she stops and holds her husband there to listen to the music. Then she makes a donation, and says to him, "They're really such nice people, aren't they?" How do you understand this comment? Later, walking home from the party, she looks up at the stars and emotionally chants a poem of Shakespeare. What may all these details suggest of her psychology?

4. How do Irene and Jim differ in their attitudes toward their neighbors' secrets? Are there some obvious differences between their personality traits? Why does Irene beg Jim to stop talking about his difficulty and anxiety?

5. Does the radio broadcast at the end of the story have any symbolic meaning?

Questions for Discussion

Why are Irene and Jim typical of the U.S. middle class? What details indicate their middle class status? What is the relationship between the two concepts: "middle class" and the "American Dream"?

（周家辉　撰写）

11. SO MUCH WATER SO CLOSE TO HOME

By Raymond Carver, 1981

My husband eats with a good appetite. But I don't think he's really hungry. He chews, arms on the table, and stares at something across the room. He looks at me and looks away. He wipes his mouth on the napkin. He shrugs, and goes on eating.

"What are you staring at me for?" he says. "What is it?" he says and lays down his fork.

"Was I staring?" I say, and shake my head.

The telephone rings.

"Don't answer it," he says.

"It might be your mother," I say.

"Watch and see," he says.

I pick up the receiver and listen. My husband stops eating.

"What did I tell you?" he says when I hang up. He starts to eat again. Then throws his napkin on his plate. He says, "Goddamn it, why can't people mind their own business? Tell me what I did wrong and I'll listen! I wasn't the only man there. We talked it over and we all decided. We couldn't just turn around. We were five miles from the car. I won't have you passing judgment. Do you hear?"

11. SO MUCH WATER SO CLOSE TO HOME

"You know," I say.

He says, "What do I know, Claire? Tell me what I'm supposed to know. I don't know anything except one thing?" He gives me what he thinks is a meaningful look. "She was dead," he says. "And I'm as sorry as anyone else. But she was dead."

"That's the point," I say.

He raises his hands. He pushes his chair away from the table. He takes out his cigarettes and goes out to the back with a can of beer. I see him sit in the lawn chair and pick up the newspaper again.

His name is in there on the first page. Along with the names of his friends.

I close my eyes and hold on to the sink. Then I rake my arm across the drainboard and send the dishes to the floor.

He doesn't move. I know he's heard. He lifts his head as if still listening. But he doesn't move otherwise. He doesn't turn around.

He and Gordon Johnson and Mel Dorn and Vern Williams, they play poker and bowl and fish. They fish every spring and early summer before visiting relatives can get in the way. They are decent men, family men, men who take care of their jobs. They have sons and daughters who go to school with our son, Dean.

Last Friday these family men left for the Naches River. They parked the car in the mountains and hiked to where they wanted to fish. They carried their bedrolls, their food, their playing cards, their whiskey.

They saw the girl before they set up camp. Mel Dorn found her. No clothes on her at all. She was wedged into some branches that stuck out over the water.

He called the others and they came to look. They talked about what to do. One of the men—my Stuart didn't say which—said they should start back at once. The others stirred the sand with their shoes, said they didn't feel inclined that way. They pleaded fatigue, the late hour, the fact that the girl wasn't going anywhere.

In the end they went ahead and set up the camp. They built a fire and drank their whiskey. When the moon came up, they talked about the girl. Someone said they should keep the body from drifting away. They took their flashlights and went back to the river. One of the men—it might have been Stuart—waded in and got her. He took her by the fingers and pulled her into shore. He got some nylon cord and tied it to her wrist and then looped the rest around a tree.

The next morning they cooked breakfast, drank coffee, and drank whiskey, and then split up to fish. That night they cooked fish, cooked potatoes, drank coffee, drank whiskey, then took their cooking things and eating things back down to the river and washed them where the girl was.

They played some cards later on. Maybe they played until they couldn't see them anymore. Vern Williams went to sleep. But the others told stories. Gordon Johnson said the trout they'd caught were hard because of the terrible coldness of the water.

The next morning they got up late, drank whiskey, fished a little, took down their tents, rolled their sleeping bags, gathered their stuff, and hiked out. They drove until they got to a telephone. It was Stuart who made the call while the others stood around in the sun and listened. He gave the sheriff their names. They had nothing to hide. They weren't ashamed. They said they'd wait until someone could come for better directions and take down their statements.

I was asleep when he got home. But I woke up when I heard him in the kitchen. I found him leaning against the refrigerator with a can of beer. He put his heavy arms around me and rubbed his big hands on my back. In bed he put his hands on me again and then waited as if thinking of something else. I turned and opened my legs. Afterwards, I think he stayed awake.

He was up that morning before I could get out of bed. To see if there was something in the paper, I suppose.

The telephone began ringing right after eight.

11. SO MUCH WATER SO CLOSE TO HOME

"Go to hell!" I heard him shout.

The telephone rang right again.

"I have nothing to add to what I already said to the sheriff!"

He slammed the receiver down.

"What is going on?" I said.

It was then that he told me what I just told you.

I sweep up the broken dishes and go outside. He is lying on his back on the grass now, the newspaper and can of beer within reach.

"Stuart, could we go for a drive?" I say.

He rolls over and looks at me. "We'll pick up some beer," he says. He gets to his feet and touches me on the hip as he goes past. "Give me a minute," he says.

We drive through town without speaking. He stops at a roadside market for beer. I notice a great stack of papers just inside the door. On the top step a fat woman in a print dress holds out a licorice stick to a little girl. Later on, we cross Everson Creek and turn into the picnic grounds. The creek runs under the bridge and into a large pond a few hundred yards away. I can see the men out there. I can see them out there fishing.

So much water so close to home.

I say, "Why did you have to go miles away?"

"Don't rile me," he says.

We sit on a bench in the sun. He opens us cans of beer. He says, "Relax, Claire."

"They said they were innocent. They said they were crazy."

He says, "Who?" He says, "What are you talking about?"

"The Maddox brothers. They killed a girl named Arlene Hubly where I grew up. They cut off her head and threw her into the Cle Elum River. It happened when I was a girl."

"You're going to get me riled," he says.

I look at the creek. I'm right in it, eyes open, face down, staring at the moss on the bottom, dead.

"I don't know what's wrong with you," he says on the way home. "You're getting me more riled by the minute."

There is nothing I can say to him.

He tries to concentrate on the road. But he keeps looking into the rear-view mirror.

He knows.

Stuart believes he is letting me sleep this morning. But I was awake long before the alarm went off. I was thinking, lying on the far side of the bed away from his hairy legs.

He gets Dean off for school, and then he shaves, dresses, and leaves for work. Twice he looks in and clears his throat. But I keep my eyes closed.

In the kitchen I find a note from him. It's signed "Love."

I sit in the breakfast nook and drink coffee and leave a ring on the note. I look at the newspaper and turn it this way and that on the table. Then I skid it close and read what it says. The body has been identified, claimed. But it took some examining it, some putting things into it, some cutting, some weighing, some measuring, some putting things back again and sewing them in.

I sit for a long time holding the newspaper and thinking. Then I call up to get a chair at the hairdresser's.

I sit under the dryer with a magazine on my lap and let Marnie do my nails.

"I am going to a funeral tomorrow," I say.

"I'm sorry to hear that," Marnie says.

"It was a murder," I say.

"That's the worst kind," Marnie says.

11. SO MUCH WATER SO CLOSE TO HOME

"We weren't all that close," I say. "But you know."

"We'll get you fixed up for it," Marnie says.

That night I make my bed on the sofa, and in the morning I get up first. I put on coffee and fix breakfast while he shaves.

He appears in the kitchen doorway, towel over his bare shoulder, appraising.

"Here's coffee," I say. "Eggs'll be ready in a minute."

I wake Dean, and the three of us eat. Whenever Stuart looks at me, I ask Dean if he wants more milk, more toast, etc.

"I'll call you today," Stuart says as he opens the door.

I say, "I don't think I'll be home today."

"All right," he says. "Sure."

I dress carefully. I try on a hat and look at myself in the mirror. I write out a note for Dean.

> *Honey, Mommy has things to do this afternoon, but will be back later. You stay in or be in the backyard until one of us comes home.*
>
> *Love, Mommy*

I look at the word *Love* and then I underline it. Then I see the word *backyard*. Is it one word or two?

I drive through farm country, through fields of oats and sugar beets and past apple orchards, cattle grazing in pastures. Then everything changes, more like shacks than farmhouses and stands of timber instead of orchards. Then mountains, and on the right, far below, I sometimes see the Naches River.

A green pickup comes up behind me and stays behind me for miles. I keep slowing at the wrong times, hoping he will pass. Then I speed up. But this is at the wrong times, too. I grip the wheel until my fingers hurt.

On a long clear stretch he goes past. But he drives along beside for a bit, a crewcut man in a blue workshirt. We look each other over. Then he waves, toots his horn, and pulls on up ahead.

I slow down and find a place. I pull over and shut off the motor. I can hear the river down below the trees. Then I hear the pickup coming back.

I lock the doors and roll up the windows.

"You all right?" the man says. He raps on the glass. "You okay?" He leans his arms on the door and brings his face to the window.

I stare at him. I can't think what else to do.

"Is everything all right in there? How come you're all locked up?"

I shake my head.

"Roll down your window." He shakes his head and looks at the highway and then back at me. "Roll it down now."

"Please," I say, "I have to go."

"Open the door," he says as if he isn't listening. "You're going to choke in there."

He looks at my breasts, my legs. I can tell that's what he's doing.

"Hey, sugar," he says. "I'm just here to help is all."

The casket is closed and covered with floral sprays. The organ starts up the minute I take a seat. People are coming in and finding chairs. There's a boy in flared pants and a yellow short-sleeved shirt. A door opens and the family comes in in a group and moves over to a curtained place off to one side. Chairs creak as everybody gets settled. Directly, a nice blond man in a nice dark suit stands and asks us to bow our heads. He says a prayer for us, the living, and when he finishes, he says a prayer for the soul of the departed.

Along with the others I go past the casket. Then I move out onto the front steps and into the afternoon light. There's a woman who limps as she goes down the stairs ahead of me. On the sidewalk she looks around. "Well, they got him," she says. "If that's any consolation. They arrested him this morning. I heard it on the radio before I come. A boy right here in town."

We move a few steps down the hot sidewalk. People are starting cars. I put out my hand and hold on to a parking meter. Polished hoods and polished fenders. My head swims.

I say, "They have friends, these killers. You can't tell."

"I have known that child since she was a little girl," the woman says. "She used to come over and I'd bake cookies for her and let her eat them in front of the TV."

Back home, Stuart sits at the table with a drink of whiskey in front of him. For a crazy instant I think something's happened to Dean.

"Where is he?" I say. "Where is Dean?"

"Outside," my husband says.

He drains his glass and stands up. He says, "I think I know what you need."

He reaches an arm around my waist and with his other hand he begins to unbutton my jacket and then he goes on to the buttons of my blouse.

"First things first," he says.

He says something else. But I don't need to listen. I can't hear a thing with so much water going.

"That's right," I say, finishing the buttons myself. "Before Dean comes. Hurry."

作品赏析

一、作者与故事情节

雷蒙德·卡弗（Raymond Carver，1938—1988），美国作家、诗人，美国20世纪下半叶最重要的作家之一。卡弗出生于美国俄勒冈州，在华盛顿州长大，因肺癌在华盛顿州去世。

卡弗家庭十分贫寒。他的父亲是锯木厂工人、渔民，是一个酒鬼；他的母亲是服务员、商店销售员。1956年，卡弗在本地高中毕业；1963年，他毕业于加州州立大学洪堡分校。在这之前和之后，他还在加州州立大学奇科分校、萨克拉门托分校，爱荷华大学，以及斯坦福大学学习过。

高中毕业后，卡弗成为一名木材厂工人。他艰难谋生，长期从事各种辛苦、收入微薄的体力工作，如餐厅清洁工、医院守夜门卫、送货工人、仓库搬运工、加油站加油员等；他同时挣扎着进行文学创作。他妻子则当过推销员、服务员、中学教师等帮补家用。1970年，他成为一家协会的教材编辑和公关主任。这是他平生第一份白领工作。他从1971年开始在加州大学圣克鲁兹分校及伯克利分校、得州大学埃尔帕索分校以及纽约州雪城大学任教。

卡弗跟他父亲一样，深受酗酒恶习的困扰。根据卡弗本人回忆，有段时间，他和另一位著名作家契弗在爱荷华创作集训营执教时，两个酒鬼喝酒第一，教书第二，至于写作，则根本没有发生过。[1]

高中毕业的次年，19岁的卡弗与刚从教会学校毕业的16岁的玛丽安·伯克结婚。二人育有两子。他妻子努力养家，支持他上完大学，然后自己再读大学，取得硕士学位，成为一名中学教师。但是，卡弗移情别恋，1982年与妻子离婚，并于1988年再婚。

卡弗观察和记录穷苦大众的"艰难时世"，以简洁却深刻的文学形式呈现给读者。他主要关注美国蓝领阶层的生活，尤其关注社会底层的沮丧、痛苦和迷茫。所以，批评家通常认为，卡弗的作品有两大创作特色，一是简约主义，二是"肮脏现实主义"。[2] 他影响了村上春树、苏童等众多作家。

1961年卡弗发表了他的处女作《愤怒的季节》（"Furious Seasons"）。此后他创作了众多短篇小说和诗歌，以短篇小说闻名。1977年，他的小说集《请你安静一下好不好？》（*Would You Please Be Quiet, Please?*）进入国家图书奖提名短名单，从而奠定了他主流作家的身份。他曾经获得各种文学奖，包括5次"欧·亨利奖"和"普利策小说奖"。美国作家约翰·厄普代克将卡弗的作品

---

[1] Sklenicka, Carol, *Raymond Carver: A Writer's Life*, New York: Charles Scribner's Sons, 2009, p. 253.

[2] Hemmingson, Michael. *The Dirty Realism Duo: Charles Bukowski and Raymond Carver on the Aesthetics of the Ugly*, Rockville, MD: Borgo, 2008, p. 11 and backcover.

11. SO MUCH WATER SO CLOSE TO HOME

《我打电话的地方》("Where I'm Calling From")选入《本世纪美国最佳短篇小说》。[1] 他的其他名篇还有《一件美好的小事》("A Small, Good Thing")、《设身处地替我想想》("Put Yourself in My Shoes")、《你是医生吗？》("Are You a Doctor?")以及本章要讨论的《这么多水，离家这么近》，等等。需要特别说明的是，《这么多水，离家这么近》出版过三个版本，而且相互之间区别很大，这里的讨论针对第二个版本，也就是故事的简约版。

一个星期五的下午，克莱尔的丈夫斯图亚特和三名男子进山露营垂钓，他们来到目的地，在附近的河里发现一具女尸，尸体被倒在河里的树枝卡住。有人提议马上回去报警，但其他三人不同意，最后他们决定按计划安营过夜。晚上，斯图亚特把尸体拖到岸边，用尼龙绳将其固定。从周五晚上到周日上午，他们吃喝玩乐，钓鱼打牌。星期天，他们在回家的路上报警，之后，他们去警察局做笔录。斯图亚特很晚才回家。

星期一早上，斯图亚特起得很早。8点过，他开始接到媒体的采访电话，非常生气。他把周末发生的事情给克莱尔说了一遍。

他们正在吃饭，电话铃响了，斯图亚特叫克莱尔不要接听，但克莱尔说有可能是斯图亚特的妈妈打来的坚持接听。来电的当然是记者。斯图亚特再次申明自己是无辜的，没有做错什么。吃完饭，斯图亚特坐在草坪上喝啤酒。克莱尔心情复杂，突然将碗碟从台面打落一地。

之后，克莱尔和丈夫一起开车兜风散心。他们来到一个路边商场，斯图亚特下车去买啤酒，然后，他们来到野炊区，坐在河边交谈。克莱尔质问丈夫为什么要去那么远的地方钓鱼，丈夫回答说："别烦我！"然后，克莱尔提起她少女时代老家发生的奸杀案。斯图亚特说，克莱尔让他觉得越来越心烦。

几天后，克莱尔通过报纸了解到，警察局已经确认出死者的身份，也了解到次日将为死者举行追悼会。于是她约好美发师做了头发。那天晚上，克莱尔在沙发上过了一晚。

第二天早上，丈夫出门前想和她交流，但她装作睡觉，没有搭理他。给孩子留下一张便条后，克莱尔驱车前去参加死者的追悼会。路上，她觉得一辆皮卡似

---

[1] Updike, John & Katrina Kenison, eds., *The Best American Short Stories of the Century*, Boston & New York: Houghton Mifflin Company, 1999, pp. 581-594.

乎故意尾随她，后来皮卡终于超车走了，她在路边停车熄火。过了一小会儿，她听见皮卡又开回来了，她关紧汽车门窗，拒绝搭理那名男司机。那人表示只是担心她遇到了什么麻烦，但克莱尔觉得他眼睛盯着自己的胸部和大腿，不怀好意。

克莱尔参加完追悼会出来，一个女人告诉她，新闻说凶手已被逮捕，但克莱尔说，说不定还有帮凶逍遥法外。

克莱尔回来的时候，看见斯图亚特坐在桌前，手里端着一杯威士忌，她突然觉得儿子迪恩肯定出事了。斯图亚特告诉她儿子好好的，然后，丈夫一饮而尽，说他明白克莱尔需要什么。说罢，斯图亚特解开妻子外衣的纽扣。克莱尔自己脱掉内衣，与丈夫亲热起来。

二、人物与主题

这篇小说的主要人物是克莱尔，次要人物有她的丈夫斯图亚特、皮卡司机、被害的女孩、美发师、追悼会上与跟克莱尔搭话的妇女，等等。

克莱尔是一名家庭主妇，在少年时代曾经遭受过心理创伤，她缺乏安全感和自信，不善于表达和交流。她有点自我封闭，内心感到孤独恐惧，对他人的戒备心理很强。她很敏感，容易触景生情。

斯图亚特跟他的朋友们一样，是普通中产阶级家庭的养家男人。他们职业体面，人品中规中矩，但是，他们除了挣钱养家，关心自己和家庭之外，对社会和他人态度冷漠。

对这部小说的主题有一种解读是，作品主要揭示了美国社会人与人之间的疏离、冷漠和猜疑，同时也暗示了美国社会普通民众生活艰难、缺乏安全感的冷峻现实；另外，作者似乎认为，回归自然才是解决这些社会问题的有效策略。

首先，在现代社会里，人们感到孤立，缺乏对他人的信任。这篇小说从几个侧面揭示了这个社会问题。

斯图亚特对媒体缺乏信任。当媒体来电询问相关情况的时候，他怀疑媒体采访的动机，不愿意发扬公民精神，配合媒体传播真相，帮助缉拿凶手，而是一味强调自己并不存在过错。读者可以推断，他的朋友们的态度估计也与此类似。

作为叙事者"我"的克莱尔，对那名前来关心、帮助她的皮卡司机充满怀疑。由于她强烈的不安全感和疑心，她感觉那名司机是在故意尾随她。道路变得

11. SO MUCH WATER SO CLOSE TO HOME

宽敞时，皮卡自然地超车离去。此时，克莱尔靠边停车，前面的司机觉得异常，以为克莱尔遇到了麻烦，倒回来关心她，这在人烟稀少的山区公路上，是非常自然的。司机站在车窗外对克莱尔说话，眼光自然会覆盖克莱尔全身，但克莱尔却觉得他盯着她的胸部和大腿，不怀好意。后来，那名司机告诉她自己只是想帮忙，见克莱尔不愿接受帮助便离开了。这个过程充分反映出克莱尔缺乏安全感和怀疑他人的心理状态。

克莱尔也不信任自己的丈夫。克莱尔含沙射影地说斯图亚特"知道真相"，她的意思是说，自己丈夫知道女孩是如何被害死的，甚至可能还亲自参与行凶。丈夫进入路边商店购买啤酒，克莱尔注意到商店门口摆着报纸，她的意思是，丈夫买酒是假，自己心虚需要关注新闻是真，而且，克莱尔还注意到门口一个女人带着一个女孩，她此时应该联想到了那位被害的女孩。他们坐在河边聊天时，她意味深长地问道："这么多水，离家这么近。你们为什么要跑那么远去钓鱼？"这句话清楚地表达了她对丈夫及他的朋友们的怀疑。丈夫开车时，克莱尔觉得丈夫不断偷看后视镜，似乎害怕有警察侦查他。实际上，克莱尔的疑心贯穿整部小说。

甚至，克莱尔还对整个社会都充满怀疑。她在离家去参加追悼会前，给自己的儿子写了张便条，告诉儿子回家后千万不要在屋子前面玩耍，一定要躲在屋里或后院。她觉得社会很危险，所以，当看见丈夫在喝威士忌时，她顿时联想到儿子已经出事。克莱尔这种不安全心理，部分源自她早年的心理创伤，但更多是植根于美国严酷的社会现实。造成这种人际信任缺失的原因在于，人们内心感到孤立，对他人也报以冷漠。这种人际疏离和冷漠在这篇小说里得到诸多体现。

追悼会上，"有个男孩穿着喇叭裤和黄色的短袖衬衫"。这种鲜艳的着装显然表现对死者的冷漠态度。在理发店，克莱尔告诉美发师她次日要去参加一名谋杀案被害人的葬礼，并特意补充说自己并不认识那位死者，此时，美发师不是询问死者的情况以及克莱尔参加葬礼的缘由，而是非常冷漠地说会给克莱尔做好头发。美发师对谋杀案件以及被害人漠不关心，甚至对老顾客克莱尔的心境也置之不理。

当然，这种冷漠在斯图亚特及其朋友们对待死者尸体的态度上，体现得更为淋漓尽致。星期五傍晚他们在营地附近发现尸体，多数人决定继续玩乐，不愿意返回报警。他们的理由居然是天快黑了，需要走五英里才能开上汽车，自己很疲倦，尸体反正不会冲走，等等。总之，他们不愿意牺牲几个小时的娱乐时间来伸张正义，而且他们还在女孩尸体旁边清洗餐具等。一旁的尸体既没有触发他们强烈的伤感和同情，也没有激起他们对凶手的愤恨，更没有唤醒他们对正义的追求。他们对社会、对他人的这种冷漠心理，令人不胜唏嘘。

追根到底，美国过度的个人主义和人民群众艰难的生活状况可能是造成这种冷漠的部分原因。美国社会向来崇尚和宣扬个人主义，有时候这种思想还比较极端，尤其是，社会上层经常以个人主义作遮羞布，掩盖他们拒绝承担社会责任、拒绝帮助贫困群体的自私嘴脸。社会下层人民，自己生活艰难，很多时候自顾不暇，没有心情也没有能力关心别人。也许，对物质享受的过度追求，对精神修养的忽视，畸形的个人主义、严重的贫富分化……才是导致上述社会问题的根本原因。

小说的结尾似乎主张返璞归真，从而解决这些社会问题。斯图亚特说他知道克莱尔需要什么，然后开始和妻子亲热起来。他们之间似乎达成了默契。克莱尔需要丈夫关爱自己，与自己坦诚交流，给自己安全感。夫妻之间，自然应该坦诚相待。人是社会动物，需要相互关心。不同阶层之间，也理应相互提携，社会想必能够一步步杜绝冷漠和孤独。

三、结构与技巧

这部作品的叙事方式颇有特点，整个故事由克莱尔的日常生活若干片段组成，但是在第一个和第三个片段中间插入了她丈夫和朋友们钓鱼并发现女尸的经过，插入的倒叙部分使用过去时态，其余部分全部采用现在时态进行叙述。故事采用第一人称的叙事角度，叙事者是克莱尔。克莱尔早年应该受过心理创伤，而且内心敏感，过度揣测，所以，她是一个不可靠的叙事者，读者难以通过她的观察和记录来构建一个真实的文本世界。现在时态则使作品进一步充满不确定性。因为第一人称的叙事视角本来就受到很大限制，在此基础上使用现在时态，一方面导致叙述缺少那种基于事后思考和总结的成熟理智，另一方面导致叙事者对现实的了解非常受限，与读者处于相同的水平。稍后将要讨论的极端简约的写作风格也会使作品充满不确定性。这种不确定性一方面给读者解读作品造成障碍，另一方面则把阅读过程变成思考、讨论和创造的过程，可以增加读者的阅读兴趣。

就这部作品的第二版即精简版而言，简约主义无疑是其最大的创作特色。这一特色主要体现在两个方面：一是语言的凝练，二是内容的精简。如果将这部作品的三个版本对照阅读，则会发现第二个版本将简约主义发挥到极致，使作品洗尽铅华，显得特别犀利和厚重。

小说语言不施粉黛，言简意赅。整部作品朴实无华，几乎找不到一个"高大上"的单词，也罕见繁复长句。例如，叙事者克莱尔应该对附近的那条河流以及追悼会场景产生强烈感触，普通文学作品多半会对此浓墨重彩地描写一番，但是，卡弗却轻描淡写："这条小溪流经桥下，在百步之外形成一个很大的河湾。"前来哀悼的人们纷纷走进教堂，克莱尔刚落座就听到"风琴开始演奏"，然后看到"人们进来找到椅子"，听到"人们就坐的时候椅子吱嘎吱嘎地响"。这种摹写风格的叙事，恰好符合叙事者的人物设定。她是个家庭主妇，虽然触景生情，但想必也不会用复杂的语言来表达。文中的段落一般比较简短，只记录对话和行动。这种杜绝冗词赘句、排除语言干扰的简约风格，留给读者更多的感动和沉思。

作品内容清新脱俗，嶙峋骨感。对必须保留的内容，比如克莱尔少年时代家乡发生的那件凶案、她理发的过程以及她参加追悼会的过程，作者删繁就简，力求精练。作者把"减法式"写作运用到极致：凶案的内容是一个女孩被奸杀，两兄弟被抓，人们说他俩很疯狂，而他俩一口咬定自己无辜；理发过程则浓缩成一小段对话；追悼会也只是入座、听了两句祷告、经过棺材而已；而且大量使用省略和空缺的手法，例如，作者根本没写克莱尔夫妇平时夫妻关系如何，克莱尔家住在什么样一个城市，她去哪个地方参加追悼会，那地方离她所在城市多远，她做头发和开追悼会是在报案后第几天等信息。作者不会对事件场景进行描写，也不会对人物或事件提出主观分析和评价，更不会对写作主题进行任何阐释，这样，读者可以拥有巨大的想象和解读空间；而且，这种省略和缺省还能赋予作品一种神秘气氛，引发读者思考。

此外，作者的简约风格还体现在这部作品的心理描写和隐喻手法中。这部小说的心理描写和心理剖析别具一格。虽然故事情节由克莱尔的行动和语言推动，但实际上是由她孤独、恐惧和怀疑的心理状态推动的。作者通过语言和行动描写来展示主人公心理，很少直接描述人物的内心活动。克莱尔对丈夫冷漠对待被害女孩的尸体的愤怒，通过她砸碎碗碟的行动表现出来。她对丈夫的怀疑，通过她看到的现象来展示：丈夫到路边商店买酒，她看到的是门口的报纸以及台阶上的女孩；丈夫开车，她看到的是丈夫频繁张望后视镜。她坐在岸边，想象着自己死了，漂在河里的样子。克莱尔认为那名皮卡司机盯着自己胸部和大腿，这表明克莱尔不仅对丈夫而且对整个社会存在疑惧心理。作者使用蕴涵丰富的细节，非常克制地展示主人公的心理，而把剖析人物心理的工作交给读者自己去完成。

在这部作品里，作者使用了若干意象进行隐喻，仅举一例讨论。故事的结尾特别突兀和隐晦，其解读主要取决于对水的寓意的理解。在凶手被抓前，水可能会让克莱尔想到死亡。现在凶手已经被抓，那么，正如标题暗示的那样，水似乎应该代表着快乐，是斯图亚特和朋友们错误地舍近求远、跋山涉水寻找的目标。结尾处，凶手落网，儿子安全，克莱尔的心态想必已经发生很大的改变；同时夫妻关系正在恢复正常，她的内心感到巨大的快乐。小说中水与人物的心理活动形成了相互映衬的关系。

小说里人物之间的对话别具特色，听者要么听不懂，要么没有兴趣，不想听懂。比如，丈夫说那女孩反正都死了，克莱尔说："那正是问题所在。"丈夫显然没有明白克莱尔的意思：你知道那女孩是怎么死了，说不定你还是凶手之一。又比如，克莱尔对理发师说自己并不认识死者时，理发师完全不想听懂。后来克莱尔跟那位妇女说，凶手说不定有帮凶，那人当然听不懂，因为她又不知道克莱尔小时候那个案子。这些对话从一个侧面反映了人与人之间的隔膜和冷淡。

最后，作品中有一处反衬值得注意。四个好朋友，四个分享着友情和温暖的男人，那样冷漠地对待女孩的尸体，简直是对友谊莫大的讽刺，也是人际疏离的绝佳反映。

Suggested Readings

1. Carver, Maryann Burk. *What It Used to Be Like: A Portrait of My Marriage to Raymond Carver*. New York: St. Martin's, 2007.
2. Carver, Raymond. *Will You Please Be Quiet, Please?* New York: McGraw-Hill, 1976.

3. Carver, Raymond. *What We Talk About When We Talk About Love*. New York: Knopf, 1981.
4. Carver, Raymond. *Where I'm Calling From: New and Selected Stories*. New York: Atlantic Monthly, 1988.
5. Carver, Raymond. *Raymond Carver: Collected Stories*. Eds. William Stull and Maureen Carroll. New York: Library of America, 2009.
6. Kleppe, Sandra lee, and Robert Miltner, eds. *New Paths to Raymond Carver: Critical Essays on His Life, Fiction, and Poetry*. Columbia, SC: University of South Carolina Press, 2008.
7. McSweeney, Kerry. *The Realist Short Story of the Powerful Glimpse: Chekhov to Carver*. Columbia SC: University of South Carolina Press, 2007.
8. Nesset, Kirk. *The Stories of Raymond Carver: A Critical Study*. Athens, OH: Ohio University Press, 1995.
9. Plath, James, ed. *Critical Insights: Raymond Carver*. Ipswich, MA: Salem Press, 2013.
10. Saltzman, Arthur M. *Understanding Raymond Carver*. Columbia, SC: University of South Carolina Press, 1988.
11. Sklenicka, Carol. *Raymond Carver: A Writer's Life*. New York: Charles Scribner's Sons, 2009.
12. Zhou, Jingqiong. *Raymond Carver's Short Fiction in the History of Black Humor*. New York: Peter Lang, 2006.

Questions for Reflection

1. How should we readers treat the narrator Claire's various suspicious assumptions about her husband Stuart? What might be the social causes for her suspicion and anxiety?

2. How do Stuart and his friends respond when they come across the body of a dead girl? What does Claire think of their response?

3. What has possibly motivated Claire to attend the funeral of the girl?

4. How do you understand the title and the ending of this story?

5. What possible interpretations can readers make of the theme of the story?

Questions for Discussion

What is "minimalism"? How does it relate to the literary creation by Hemingway and the Modernist poets? How does this short story embody Carver's minimalistic style?

（周家辉　撰写）

12. WHERE ARE YOU GOING, WHERE HAVE YOU BEEN

By Joyce Carol Oates, 1966

To Bob Dylan

Her name was Connie. She was fifteen and she had a quick, nervous giggling habit of craning her neck to glance into mirrors, or checking other people's faces to make sure her own was all right. Her mother, who noticed everything and knew everything and who hadn't much reason any longer to look at her own face, always scolded Connie about it. "Stop gawking at yourself, who are you? You think you're so pretty?" she would say. Connie would raise her eyebrows at these familiar old complaints and look right through her mother, into a shadowy vision of herself as she was right at that moment: she knew she was pretty and that was everything. Her mother had been pretty once too, if you could believe those old snapshots in the album, but now her looks were gone and that was why she was always after Connie.

"Why don't you keep your room clean like your sister? How've you got your hair fixed—what the hell stinks? Hair spray? You don't see your sister using that junk."

Her sister June was twenty-four and still lived at home. She was a secretary in the high school Connie attended, and if that wasn't bad enough—with her in the same building—she was so plain and chunky and steady that Connie had to hear her praised all the time by her mother and her mother's sisters. June did this, June did that, she saved money and helped clean the house and cooked and Connie couldn't do a thing, her mind was all filled with trashy daydreams. Their father was away at work most of the time and when he came home he wanted supper and he read the newspaper at supper and after supper he went to bed. He didn't bother talking much to them, but around his bent head Connie's mother kept picking at her until Connie wished her mother was dead and she herself was dead and it was all over. "She makes me want to throw up sometimes," she complained to her friends. She had a high, breathless, amused voice that made everything she said sound a little forced, whether it was sincere or not.

There was one good thing: June went places with girlfriends of hers, girls who were just as plain and steady as she, and so when Connie wanted to do that her mother had no objections. The father of Connie's best girlfriend drove the girls the three miles to town and left them at a shopping plaza, so that they could walk through the stores or go to a movie, and when he came to pick them up again at eleven he never bothered to ask what they had done.

They must have been familiar sights, walking around the shopping plaza in their shorts and flat ballerina slippers that always scuffed the sidewalk, with charm bracelets jingling on their thin wrists; they would lean together to whisper and laugh secretly if someone passed who amused or interested them. Connie had long dark blond hair that drew anyone's eye to it, and she wore part of it pulled up on her head and puffed out and the rest of it she let fall down her back. She wore a pull-over jersey blouse that looked one way when she was at home and another way when she was away from home. Everything about her had two sides to it, one for home and one for anywhere that was not home: her walk that could be childlike and bobbing, or languid enough to make anyone think she was hearing music in her head, her mouth, which was pale and smirking most of the time, but bright and pink on these evenings out, her

12. WHERE ARE YOU GOING, WHERE HAVE YOU BEEN

laugh, which was cynical and drawling at home—"Ha, ha, very funny"—but high-pitched and nervous anywhere else, like the jingling of the charms on her bracelet.

Sometimes they did go shopping or to a movie, but sometimes they went across the highway, ducking fast across the busy road, to a drive-in restaurant where older kids hung out. The restaurant was shaped like a big bottle, though squatter than a real bottle, and on its cap was a revolving figure of a grinning boy who held a hamburger aloft. One night in midsummer they ran across, breathless with daring, and right away someone leaned out a car window and invited them over, but it was just a boy from high school they didn't like. It made them feel good to be able to ignore him. They went up through the maze of parked and cruising cars to the bright-lit, fly-infested restaurant, their faces pleased and expectant as if they were entering a sacred building that loomed out of the night to give them what haven and blessing they yearned for. They sat at the counter and crossed their legs at the ankles, their thin shoulders rigid with excitement, and listened to the music that made everything so good: the music was always in the background, like music at a church service, it was something to depend upon.

A boy named Eddie came in to talk with them. He sat backwards on his stool, turning himself jerkily around in semicircles and then stopping and turning again, and after a while he asked Connie if she would like something to eat. She said she did and so she tapped her friend's arm on her way out—her friend pulled her face up into a brave droll look—and Connie said she would meet her at eleven, across the way. "I just hate to leave her like that," Connie said earnestly, but the boy said that she wouldn't be alone for long. So they went out to his car, and on the way Connie couldn't help but let her eyes wander over the windshields and faces all around her, her face gleaming with a joy that had nothing to do with Eddie or even this place; it might have been the music. She drew her shoulders up and sucked in her breath with the pure pleasure of being alive, and just at that moment she happened to glance at a face just a few feet from hers. It was a boy with shaggy black hair, in a convertible jalopy painted gold. He stared at her and then his lips widened into a grin. Connie slit her eyes at him and turned away, but she couldn't help glancing back and there he was still watching her. He wagged a finger and laughed and said, "Gonna get you, baby," and Connie turned away again without Eddie noticing anything.

She spent three hours with him, at the restaurant where they ate hamburgers and drank Cokes in wax cups that were always sweating, and then down an alley a mile or so away, and when he left her off at five to eleven only the movie house was still open at the plaza. Her girlfriend was there, talking with a boy. When Connie came up, the two girls smiled at each other and Connie said, "How was the movie?" and the girl said, "*You* should know." They rode off with the girl's father, sleepy and pleased, and Connie couldn't help but look back at the darkened shopping plaza with its big empty parking lot and its signs that were faded and ghostly now, and over at the drive-in restaurant where cars were still circling tirelessly. She couldn't hear the music at this distance.

Next morning June asked her how the movie was and Connie said, "So-so."

She and that girl and occasionally another girl went out several times a week that way, and the rest of the time Connie spent around the house—it was summer vacation—getting in her mother s way and thinking, dreaming, about the boys she met. But all the boys fell back and dissolved into a single face that was not even a face, but an idea, a feeling, mixed up with the urgent insistent pounding of the music and the humid night air of July. Connie's mother kept dragging her back to the daylight by finding things for her to do or saying, suddenly, "What's this about the Pettinger girl?"

And Connie would say nervously, "Oh, her. That dope." She always drew thick clear lines between herself and such girls, and her mother was simple and kind enough to believe her. Her mother was so simple, Connie thought,

12. WHERE ARE YOU GOING, WHERE HAVE YOU BEEN

that it was maybe cruel to fool her so much. Her mother went scuffling around the house in old bedroom slippers and complained over the telephone to one sister about the other, then the other called up and the two of them complained about the third one. If June's name was mentioned her mother's tone was approving, and if Connie's name was mentioned it was disapproving. This did not really mean she disliked Connie and actually Connie thought that her mother preferred her to June because she was prettier, but the two of them kept up a pretense of exasperation, a sense that they were tugging and struggling over something of little value to either of them. Sometimes, over coffee, they were almost friends, but something would come up—some vexation that was like a fly buzzing suddenly around their heads—and their faces went hard with contempt.

One Sunday Connie got up at eleven—none of them bothered with church—and washed her hair so that it could dry all day long, in the sun. Her parents and sister were going to a barbecue at an aunt's house and Connie said no, she wasn't interested, rolling her eyes to let her mother know just what she thought of it. "Stay home alone then," her mother said sharply. Connie sat out back in a lawn chair and watched them drive away, her father quiet and bald, hunched around so that he could back the car out, her mother with a look that was still angry and not at all softened through the windshield, and in the back seat poor old June all dressed up as if she didn't know what a barbecue was, with all the running yelling kids and the flies. Connie sat with her eyes closed in the sun, dreaming and dazed with the warmth about her as if this were a kind of love, the caresses of love, and her mind slipped over onto thoughts of the boy she had been with the night before and how nice he had been, how sweet it always was, not the way someone like June would suppose but sweet, gentle, the way it was in movies and promised in songs; and when she opened her eyes she hardly knew where she was, the back yard ran off into weeds and a fence-line of trees and behind it the sky was perfectly blue and still. The asbestos "ranch house" that was now three years old startled her—it looked small. She shook her head as if to get awake.

It was too hot. She went inside the house and turned on the radio to drown out the quiet. She sat on the edge of her bed, barefoot, and listened for an hour and a half to a program called XYZ Sunday Jamboree, record after record of hard, fast, shrieking songs she sang along with, interspersed by exclamations from "Bobby King": "An' look here, you girls at Napoleon's—Son and Charley want you to pay real close attention to this song coming up!"

And Connie paid close attention herself, bathed in a glow of slow-pulsed joy that seemed to rise mysteriously out of the music itself and lay languidly about the airless little room, breathed in and breathed out with each gentle rise and fall of her chest.

After a while she heard a car coming up the drive. She sat up at once, startled, because it couldn't be her father so soon. The gravel kept crunching all the way in from the road—the driveway was long—and Connie ran to the window. It was a car she didn't know. It was an open jalopy, painted a bright gold that caught the sunlight opaquely. Her heart began to pound and her fingers snatched at her hair, checking it, and she whispered, "Christ. Christ," wondering how bad she looked. The car came to a stop at the side door and the horn sounded four short taps as if this were a signal Connie knew.

She went into the kitchen and approached the door slowly, then hung out the screen door, her bare toes curling down off the step. There were two boys in the car and now she recognized the driver: he had shaggy, shabby black hair that looked crazy as a wig and he was grinning at her.

"I ain't late, am I?" he said.

"Who the hell do you think you are?" Connie said.

"Toldja I'd be out, didn't I?"

"I don't even know who you are."

She spoke sullenly, careful to show no interest or pleasure, and he spoke in a fast bright monotone. Connie looked past him to the other boy, taking her time. He had fair brown hair, with a lock that fell onto his forehead. His sideburns gave him a fierce, embarrassed look, but so far he hadn't even bothered to glance at her. Both boys wore sunglasses. The driver's glasses were metallic and mirrored everything in miniature.

"You wanta come for a ride?" he said.

Connie smirked and let her hair fall loose over one shoulder.

"Don'tcha like my car? New paint job," he said. "Hey."

"What?"

"You're cute."

She pretended to fidget, chasing flies away from the door.

"Don'tcha believe me, or what?" he said.

"Look, I don't even know who you are," Connie said in disgust.

"Hey, Ellie's got a radio, see. Mine's broke down." He lifted his friend's arm and showed her the little transistor the boy was holding, and now Connie began to hear the music. It was the same program that was playing inside the house.

"Bobby King?" she said.

"I listen to him all the time. I think he's great."

"He's kind of great," Connie said reluctantly.

"Listen, that guy's *great*. He knows where the action is."

Connie blushed a little, because the glasses made it impossible for her to see just what this boy was looking at. She couldn't decide if she liked him or if he was just a jerk, and so she dawdled in the doorway and wouldn't come down or go back inside. She said, "What's all that stuff painted on your car?"

"Can'tcha read it?" He opened the door very carefully, as if he was afraid it might fall off. He slid out just as carefully, planting his feet firmly on the ground, the tiny metallic world in his glasses slowing down like gelatine hardening and in the midst of it Connie's bright green blouse. "This here is my name, to begin with, he said. ARNOLD FRIEND was written in tarlike black letters on the side, with a drawing of a round grinning face that reminded Connie of a pumpkin, except it wore sunglasses. "I wanta introduce myself, I'm Arnold Friend and that's my real name and I'm gonna be your friend, honey, and inside the car's Ellie Oscar, he's kinda shy." Ellie brought his transistor radio up to his shoulder and balanced it there. "Now these numbers are a secret code, honey," Arnold Friend explained. He read off the numbers 33, 19, 17 and raised his eyebrows at her to see what she thought of that, but she didn't think much of it. The left rear fender had been smashed and around it was written, on the gleaming gold background: DONE BY CRAZY WOMAN DRIVER. Connie had to laugh at that. Arnold Friend was pleased at her laughter and looked up at her. "Around the other side's a lot more —you wanta come and see them?"

"No."

"Why not?"

"Why should I?"

"Don'tcha wanta see what's on the car? Don'tcha wanta go for a ride?"

"I don't know."

"Why not?"

"I got things to do."

"Like what?"

"Things."

He laughed as if she had said something funny. He slapped his thighs. He was standing in a strange way, leaning back against the car as if he were balancing himself. He wasn't tall, only an inch or so taller than she would be if she came down to him. Connie liked the way he was dressed, which was the way all of them dressed: tight faded jeans stuffed into black, scuffed boots, a belt that pulled his waist in and showed how tan he was, and a white pullover shirt that was a little soiled and showed the hard small muscles of his arms and shoulders. He looked as if he probably did hard work, lifting and carrying things. Even his neck looked muscular. And his face was a familiar face, somehow: the jaw and chin and cheeks slightly darkened, because he hadn't shaved for a day or two, and the nose long and hawklike, sniffing as if she were a treat he was going to gobble up and it was all a joke.

"Connie, you ain't telling the truth. This is your day set aside for a ride with me and you know it," he said, still laughing. The way he straightened and recovered from his fit of laughing showed that it had been all fake.

"How do you know what my name is?" she said suspiciously.

"It's Connie."

"Maybe and maybe not."

"I know my Connie," he said, wagging his finger. Now she remembered him even better, back at the restaurant, and her cheeks warmed at the thought of how she sucked in her breath just at the moment she passed him—how she must have looked to him. And he had remembered her. "Ellie and I come out here especially for you," he said. "Ellie can sit in back. How about it?"

"Where?"

"Where what?"

"Where're we going?"

He looked at her. He took off the sunglasses and she saw how pale the skin around his eyes was, like holes that were not in shadow but instead in light. His eyes were like chips of broken glass that catch the light in an amiable way. He smiled. It was as if the idea of going for a ride somewhere, to someplace, was a new idea to him.

"Just for a ride, Connie sweetheart."

"I never said my name was Connie," she said.

"But I know what it is. I know your name and all about you, lots of things," Arnold Friend said. He had not moved yet but stood still leaning back against the side of his jalopy. "I took a special interest in you, such a pretty girl, and found out all about you like I know your parents and sister are gone somewheres and I know where and how long they're going to be gone, and I know who you were with last night, and your best girl friend's name is Betty. Right?"

He spoke in a simple lilting voice, exactly as if he were reciting the words to a song. His smile assured her that everything was fine. In the car Ellie turned up the volume on his radio and did not bother to look around at them.

"Ellie can sit in the back seat," Arnold Friend said. He indicated his friend with a casual jerk of his chin, as if Ellie did not count and she should not bother with him.

"How'd you find out all that stuff?" Connie said.

"Listen: Betty Schultz and Tony Fitch and Jimmy Pettinger and Nancy Pettinger," he said, in a chant. "Raymond Stanley and Bob Hutter—"

"Do you know all those kids?"

"I know everybody."

"Look, you're kidding. You're not from around here."

"Sure."

"But—how come we never saw you before?"

"Sure you saw me before," he said. He looked down at his boots, as if he were a little offended. "You just don't remember."

"I guess I'd remember you," Connie said.

"Yeah?" He looked up at this, beaming. He was pleased. He began to mark time with the music from Ellie's radio, tapping his fists lightly together. Connie looked away from his smile to the car, which was painted so bright it almost hurt her eyes to look at it. She looked at that name, ARNOLD FRIEND. And up at the front fender was an expression that was familiar—MAN THE FLYING SAUCERS. It was an expression kids had used the year before, but didn't use this year. She looked at it for a while as if the words meant something to her that she did not yet know.

"What're you thinking about? Huh?" Arnold Friend demanded. "Not worried about your hair blowing around in the car, are you?"

12. WHERE ARE YOU GOING, WHERE HAVE YOU BEEN

"No."

"Think I maybe can't drive good?"

"How do I know?"

"You're a hard girl to handle. How come?" he said. "Don't you know I'm your friend? Didn't you see me put my sign in the air when you walked by?"

"What sign?"

"My sign." And he drew an X in the air, leaning out toward her. They were maybe ten feet apart. After his hand fell back to his side the X was still in the air, almost visible. Connie let the screen door close and stood perfectly still inside it, listening to the music from her radio and the boy's blend together. She stared at Arnold Friend. He stood there so stiffly relaxed, pretending to be relaxed, with one hand idly on the door handle as if he were keeping himself up that way and had no intention of ever moving again. She recognized most things about him, the tight jeans that showed his thighs and buttocks and the greasy leather boots and the tight shirt, and even that slippery friendly smile of his, that sleepy dreamy smile that all the boys used to get across ideas they didn't want to put into words. She recognized all this and also the singsong way he talked, slightly mocking, kidding, but serious and a little melancholy, and she recognized the way he tapped one fist against the other in homage to the perpetual music behind him. But all these things did not come together.

She said suddenly, "Hey, how old are you?"

His smiled faded. She could see then that he wasn't a kid, he was much older—thirty, maybe more. At this knowledge her heart began to pound faster.

"That's a crazy thing to ask. Can'tcha see I'm your own age?"

"Like hell you are."

"Or maybe a couple years older, I'm eighteen."

"Eighteen?" she said doubtfully.

He grinned to reassure her and lines appeared at the corners of his mouth. His teeth were big and white. He grinned so broadly his eyes became slits and she saw how thick the lashes were, thick and black as if painted with a black tarlike material. Then he seemed to become embarrassed, abruptly, and looked over his shoulder at Ellie. "*Him,* he's crazy," he said. "Ain't he a riot, he's a nut, a real character." Ellie was still listening to the music. His sunglasses told nothing about what he was thinking. He wore a bright orange shirt unbuttoned halfway to show his chest, which was a pale, bluish chest and not muscular like Arnold Friend's. His shirt collar was turned up all around and the very tips of the collar pointed out past his chin as if they were protecting him. He was pressing the transistor radio up against his ear and sat there in a kind of daze, right in the sun.

"He's kinda strange," Connie said.

"Hey, she says you're kinda strange! Kinda strange!" Arnold Friend cried. He pounded on the car to get Ellie's attention. Ellie turned for the first time and Connie saw with shock that he wasn't a kid either—he had a fair, hairless face, cheeks reddened slightly as if the veins grew too close to the surface of his skin, the face of a forty-year-old baby. Connie felt a wave of dizziness rise in her at this sight and she stared at him as if waiting for something to change the shock of the moment, make it all right again. Ellie's lips kept shaping words, mumbling along with the words blasting in his ear.

"Maybe you two better go away," Connie said faintly.

"What? How come?" Arnold Friend cried. "We come out here to take you for a ride. It's Sunday." He had the voice of the man on the radio now. It was the same voice, Connie thought. "Don'tcha know it's Sunday all day and honey, no matter who you were with last night today you're with Arnold Friend and don't you forget it! —Maybe you better step out here," he said, and this last was in a different voice. It was a little flatter, as if the heat was finally getting to him.

"No. I got things to do."

"Hey."

"You two better leave."

12. WHERE ARE YOU GOING, WHERE HAVE YOU BEEN

"We ain't leaving until you come with us."

"Like hell I am—"

"Connie, don't fool around with me. I mean, I mean, don't fool *around*," he said, shaking his head. He laughed incredulously. He placed his sunglasses on top of his head, carefully, as if he were indeed wearing a wig, and brought the stems down behind his ears. Connie stared at him, another wave of dizziness and fear rising in her so that for a moment he wasn't even in focus but was just a blur, standing there against his gold car, and she had the idea that he had driven up the driveway all right but had come from nowhere before that and belonged nowhere and that everything about him and even about the music that was so familiar to her was only half real.

"If my father comes and sees you—"

"He ain't coming. He's at a barbecue."

"How do you know that?"

"Aunt Tillie's. Right now they're—uh—they're drinking. Sitting around," he said vaguely, squinting as if he were staring all the way to town and over to Aunt Tillie's back yard. Then the vision seemed to get clear and he nodded energetically. "Yeah. Sitting around. There's your sister in a blue dress, huh? And high heels, the poor sad bitch—nothing like you, sweetheart! And your mother's helping some fat woman with the corn, they're cleaning the corn— husking the corn—"

"What fat woman?" Connie cried.

"How do I know what fat woman, I don't know every goddam fat woman in the world!" Arnold Friend laughed.

"Oh, that's Mrs. Hornsby... Who invited her?" Connie said. She felt a little light-headed. Her breath was coming quickly.

"She's too fat. I don't like them fat. I like them the way you are, honey," he said, smiling sleepily at her. They stared at each other for a while, through the screen door. He said softly, "Now, what you're going to do is this: you're going to come out that door. You're going to sit up front with me and Ellie's going to sit in the back, the hell with Ellie, right? This isn't Ellie's date. You're my date. I'm your lover, honey."

"What? You're crazy—"

"Yes, I'm your lover. You don't know what that is but you will," he said. "I know that too. I know all about you. But look: it's real nice and you couldn't ask for nobody better than me, or more polite. I always keep my word. I'll tell you how it is, I'm always nice at first, the first time. I'll hold you so tight you won't think you have to try to get away or pretend anything because you'll know you can't. And I'll come inside you where it's all secret and you'll give in to me and you'll love me—"

"Shut up! You're crazy!" Connie said. She backed away from the door. She put her hands up against her ears as if she'd heard something terrible, something not meant for her. "People don't talk like that, you're crazy," she muttered. Her heart was almost too big now for her chest and its pumping made sweat break out all over her. She looked out to see Arnold Friend pause and then take a step toward the porch lurching. He almost fell. But, like a clever drunken man, he managed to catch his balance. He wobbled in his high boots and grabbed hold of one of the porch posts.

"Honey?" he said. "You still listening?"

"Get the hell out of here!"

"Be nice, honey. Listen."

"I'm going to call the police—"

He wobbled again and out of the side of his mouth came a fast spat curse, an aside not meant for her to hear. But even this "Christ!" sounded forced. Then he began to smile again. She watched this smile come, awkward as if he were smiling from inside a mask. His whole face was a mask, she thought wildly, tanned down to his throat but then running out as if he had plastered makeup on his face but had forgotten about his throat.

"Honey—? Listen, here's how it is. I always tell the truth and I promise you this: I ain't coming in that house after you."

"You better not! I'm going to call the police if you—if you don't—"

"Honey," he said, talking right through her voice, "honey, I m not coming in there but you are coming out here. You know why?"

She was panting. The kitchen looked like a place she had never seen before, some room she had run inside but that wasn't good enough, wasn't going to help her. The kitchen window had never had a curtain, after three years, and there were dishes in the sink for her to do—probably—and if you ran your hand across the table you'd probably feel something sticky there.

"You listening, honey? Hey?"

"—going to call the police—"

"Soon as you touch the phone I don't need to keep my promise and can come inside. You won't want that."

She rushed forward and tried to lock the door. Her fingers were shaking. "But why lock it," Arnold Friend said gently, talking right into her face. "It's just a screen door. It's just nothing." One of his boots was at a strange angle, as if his foot wasn't in it. It pointed out to the left, bent at the ankle. "I mean, anybody can break through a screen door and glass and wood and iron or anything else if he needs to, anybody at all and specially Arnold Friend. If the place got lit up with a fire honey you'd come runnin' out into my arms, right into my arms an' safe at home—like you knew I was your lover and'd stopped fooling around. I don't mind a nice shy girl but I don't like no fooling around." Part of those words were spoken with a slight rhythmic lilt, and Connie somehow recognized them—the echo of a song from last year, about a girl rushing into her boyfriend's arms and coming home again—

Connie stood barefoot on the linoleum floor, staring at him. "What do you want?" she whispered.

"I want you," he said.

"What?"

"Seen you that night and thought, that's the one, yes sir. I never needed to look any more."

"But my father's coming back. He's coming to get me. I had to wash my hair first—" She spoke in a dry, rapid voice, hardly raising it for him to hear.

"No, your Daddy is not coming and yes, you had to wash your hair and you washed it for me. It's nice and shining and all for me, I thank you, sweetheart," he said, with a mock bow, but again he almost lost his balance. He had to bend and adjust his boots. Evidently his feet did not go all the way down; the boots must have been stuffed with something so that he would seem taller. Connie stared out at him and behind him at Ellie in the car, who seemed to be looking off toward Connie's right, into nothing. This Ellie said, pulling the words out of the air one after another as if he were just discovering them, "You want me to pull out the phone?"

"Shut your mouth and keep it shut," Arnold Friend said, his face red from bending over or maybe from embarrassment because Connie had seen his boots. "This ain't none of your business."

"What—what are you doing? What do you want?" Connie said. "If I call the police they'll get you, they'll arrest you—"

"Promise was not to come in unless you touch that phone, and I'll keep that promise," he said. He resumed his erect position and tried to force his shoulders back. He sounded like a hero in a movie, declaring something important. He spoke too loudly and it was as if he were speaking to someone behind Connie. "I ain't made plans for coming in that house where I don't belong but just for you to come out to me, the way you should. Don't you know who I am?"

"You're crazy," she whispered. She backed away from the door but did not want to go into another part of the house, as if this would give him permission to come through the door. "What do you... You're crazy, you..."

"Huh? What're you saying, honey?"

12. WHERE ARE YOU GOING, WHERE HAVE YOU BEEN

Her eyes darted everywhere in the kitchen. She could not remember what it was, this room.

"This is how it is, honey: you come out and we'll drive away, have a nice ride. But if you don't come out we're gonna wait till your people come home and then they're all going to get it."

"You want that telephone pulled out?" Ellie said. He held the radio away from his ear and grimaced, as if without the radio the air was too much for him.

"I toldja shut up, Ellie," Arnold Friend said, "you're deaf, get a hearing aid, right? Fix yourself up. This little girl's no trouble and's gonna be nice to me, so Ellie keep to yourself, this ain't your date—right? Don't hem in on me. Don't hog. Don't crush. Don't bird dog. Don't trail me," he said in a rapid meaningless voice, as if he were running through all the expressions he'd learned but was no longer sure which one of them was in style, then rushing on to new ones, making them up with his eyes closed, "Don't crawl under my fence, don't squeeze in my chipmunk hole, don't sniff my glue, suck my popsicle, keep your own greasy fingers on yourself!" He shaded his eyes and peered in at Connie, who was backed against the kitchen table. "Don't mind him honey he's just a creep. He's a dope. Right? I'm the boy for you, and like I said you come out here nice like a lady and give me your hand, and nobody else gets hurt, I mean, your nice old bald-headed daddy and your mummy and your sister in her high heels. Because listen: why bring them in this?"

"Leave me alone," Connie whispered.

"Hey, you know that old woman down the road, the one with the chickens and stuff—you know her?"

"She's dead!"

"Dead? What? You know her?" Arnold Friend said.

"She's dead—"

"Don't you like her?"

"She's dead—she's—she isn't here any more—"

But don't you like her, I mean, you got something against her? Some grudge or something?" Then his voice dipped as if he were conscious of a rudeness. He touched the sunglasses perched up on top of his head as if to make sure they were still there. "Now you be a good girl."

"What are you going to do?"

"Just two things, or maybe three," Arnold Friend said. "But I promise it won't last long and you'll like me the way you get to like people you're close to. You will. It's all over for you here, so come on out. You don't want your people in any trouble, do you?"

She turned and bumped against a chair or something, hurting her leg, but she ran into the back room and picked up the telephone. Something roared in her ear, a tiny roaring, and she was so sick with fear that she could do nothing but listen to it—the telephone was clammy and very heavy and her fingers groped down to the dial but were too weak to touch it. She began to scream into the phone, into the roaring. She cried out, she cried for her mother, she felt her breath start jerking back and forth in her lungs as if it were something Arnold Friend was stabbing her with again and again with no tenderness. A noisy sorrowful wailing rose all about her and she was locked inside it the way she was locked inside this house.

After a while she could hear again. She was sitting on the floor with her wet back against the wall.

Arnold Friend was saying from the door, "That's a good girl. Put the phone back."

She kicked the phone away from her.

"No, honey. Pick it up. Put it back right."

She picked it up and put it back. The dial tone stopped.

"That's a good girl. Now, you come outside."

She was hollow with what had been fear, but what was now just an emptiness. All that screaming had blasted it out of her. She sat, one leg cramped under her, and deep inside her brain was something like a pinpoint of light that kept going and would not let her relax. She thought, I'm not going to see my mother again. She thought, I'm not going to sleep in my bed again. Her bright green blouse was all wet.

Arnold Friend said, in a gentle-loud voice that was like a stage voice, "The place where you came from ain't there any more, and where you had in mind to go is canceled out. This place you are now—inside your daddy's house—is nothing but a cardboard box I can knock down any time. You know that and always did know it. You hear me?"

She thought, I have got to think. I have got to know what to do.

"We'll go out to a nice field, out in the country here where it smells so nice and it's sunny," Arnold Friend said. "I'll have my arms tight around you so you won't need to try to get away and I'll show you what love is like, what it does. The hell with this house! It looks solid all right," he said. He ran a fingernail down the screen and the noise did not make Connie shiver, as it would have the day before. "Now, put your hand on your heart, honey. Feel that? That feels solid too but we know better, be nice to me, be sweet like you can because what else is there for a girl like you but to be sweet and pretty and give in?—and get away before her people come back?"

She felt her pounding heart. Her hand seemed to enclose it. She thought for the first time in her life that it was nothing that was hers, that belonged to her, but just a pounding, living thing inside this body that wasn't really hers either.

"You don't want them to get hurt," Arnold Friend went on. "Now, get up, honey. Get up all by yourself."

She stood.

"Now, turn this way. That's right. Come over here to me—Ellie, put that away, didn't I tell you? You dope. You miserable creepy dope," Arnold Friend said. His words were not angry but only part of an incantation. The incantation was kindly. "Now come out through the kitchen to me honey, and let's see a smile, try it, you're a brave sweet little girl and now they're eating corn and hot dogs cooked to bursting over an outdoor fire, and they don't know one thing about you and never did and honey, you're better than them because not a one of them would have done this for you."

Connie felt the linoleum under her feet; it was cool. She brushed her hair back out of her eyes. Arnold Friend let go of the post tentatively and opened his arms for her, his elbows pointing in toward each other and his wrists limp, to show that this was an embarrassed embrace and a little mocking, he didn't want to make her self-conscious.

She put out her hand against the screen. She watched herself push the door slowly open as if she were back safe somewhere in the other doorway, watching this body and this head of long hair moving out into the sunlight where Arnold Friend waited.

"My sweet little blue-eyed girl," he said, in a half-sung sigh that had nothing to do with her brown eyes but was taken up just the same by the vast sunlit reaches of the land behind him and on all sides of him, so much land that Connie had never seen before and did not recognize except to know that she was going to it.

作品赏析

一、作家介绍

乔伊斯·卡罗尔·欧茨（Joyce Carol Oates，1938— ），美国当代最多产的小说家、诗人、评论家、剧作家，也是美国当代文坛最有影响力的作家之一，她与菲利普·罗斯（Philip Roth）、村上春树（Murakami Haruki）等人曾同为诺贝尔文学奖的热门候选人。除了曾两度获得诺贝尔文学奖提名外，她还获得过美国国家图书奖、欧·亨利小说奖、法国费米娜文学奖、美国"国家人文奖章"等众多奖项。

12. WHERE ARE YOU GOING, WHERE HAVE YOU BEEN

  欧茨1938年出生于美国纽约州洛克波特市的一个穷苦家庭，父亲是信奉天主教的爱尔兰后裔，一个穷工人，母亲是农民的女儿。她从小被寄养在务农的外祖父家，后来在水牛城附近的高中就读。从高中开始，她对文学产生了浓厚兴趣，阅读了大量的文学作品。20世纪30年代经济大萧条时期家庭的贫苦生活为她以后的文学创作提供了丰富的素材。高中毕业后，欧茨进入锡拉丘兹大学，1960年毕业后考入威斯康辛大学，获得硕士学位。从1962年起，她在底特律大学教英语，同时从事文学创作，后来到赖斯大学攻读博士学位。1967年欧茨和丈夫一起前往加拿大温莎大学任教，两人创办了《安大略评论》。1978年欧茨回到美国，受聘于普林斯顿大学，同年当选为美国文学艺术院院士。[1]

  欧茨的创作最容易被世人记住的特点是她特别高产。自1963年出版第一部小说集《北门边》（*By the North Gate*）以来，欧茨笔耕不辍，经常以每年两三部的速度出版作品。在长达50多年的创作生涯里，她已创作了43部长篇小说、11部中篇小说、39部短篇小说集、8部诗歌集、9部戏剧作品集，以及非虚构文学评论集和回忆录16部，以笔名罗莎蒙德·史密斯（Rosamond Smith）创作的关注身份问题的小说8部，以笔名劳伦·凯利（Lauren Kelly）创作的惊悚小说3部、青少年题材小说6部和儿童绘本3部。长篇小说中比较有名的有《人间乐园》（*A Garden of Earthly Delights*，1967）、《他们》（*them*，1969）、《贝尔弗勒》（*Bellefleur*，1980）、《大瀑布》（*The Falls*，2004）等。美国著名作家约翰·厄普代克在钦佩其多产之外，也对其进行了高度的评价："如果'女文人'这一词组成立的话，那么她无疑是这个国家首当其冲应该享有这一称号的人。"[2] 由于欧茨的作品数量庞大，涉及美国社会文化生活的方方面面，堪称反映美国社会的万花筒。她被评论界誉为"美国的巴尔扎克"和"穿裙子的福克纳"。[3]

  虽然欧茨特别高产，作品的数量多得连名字都很难被读者记住，但在许多读

---

[1] 刘海平、王守仁主编，《新编美国文学史》（第四卷），上海：上海外语教育出版社，2002年，第276-277页。

[2] 转引自肖旭，《乔伊斯·卡罗尔·欧茨在中国的译介与接收研究》，《外国文学动态研究》，2017年第3期，第28页。

[3] 肖旭，《国外乔伊斯·卡罗尔·欧茨研究评析》，李维屏主编，《英美文学研究论丛》第22辑，上海：上海外语教育出版社，2013年，第314页。

者和评论家看来,她之所以了不起主要在于她在短篇小说上取得的成就。欧茨的短篇小说多次获得欧·亨利奖,这些作品不仅颇具实验性,技巧高超,而且紧密结合美国的社会现实,体现了一位严肃作家对道德主题的关切。由于她总是将文学技巧与道德关注巧妙地结合在一起,约翰逊曾总结道,"她的短篇小说是对当代美国心理现状与文化现实的后现代主义的呈现"[1]。

欧茨的小说有不少是关注美国社会的暴力和女性问题的,这也是读者比较容易发现的一个特点。在她的早期作品,如第一部短篇小说集《北门边》、第一部长篇小说《冷得发抖的秋天》(*With Shuddering Fall*, 1964),以及早期代表作《他们》中往往都有吸毒、强奸、卖淫、殴打、凶杀、乱伦、吃人等暴力内容。欧茨与美国女作家弗兰纳里·奥康纳(Mary Flannery O'Connor)一样,敢于直面美国社会日益泛滥的暴力和罪恶,表现出强烈的批判精神和道德关切。同时,欧茨又善于以女性作家特有的细腻和敏感,结合女性的亲身体验,来描写女性人物的命运,探索她们的内心世界。

欧茨的创作时间跨度很大,早期的创作倾向于传统的现实主义技法,这期间的作品大多描写她在农村和底特律的生活,以1969年出版的《他们》为代表。从70年代开始,她的作品中开始大量融入心理分析和意识流的技法,80年代后越发成熟,开始尝试各种形式和体裁上的创新。她有一种"巴尔扎克式的野心",试图在小说的虚构世界里展示美国建国以来的全部历史,如1980年出版的《贝尔弗勒》就是这样一部雄心勃勃的作品。虽然对欧茨贴标签的做法并不妥当,但评论界大多认为,她是一位心理现实主义作家,其小说创作的一个显著特征是大量的心理描写,她在继承马克·吐温、德莱塞、斯坦贝克(John Steinbeck)等作家的批判现实主义传统的同时,还深受福克纳的意识流和哥特式风格的影响,善于揭示人物的内心世界,因此,又以"女版福克纳"之称广为人知。欧茨作品数量众多,创作技法多样,但她受到美国文学传统的影响却是显而易见的,因此有学者认为,与同时代一些后现代主义作家相比,她的文学实验仍趋于保守,她后期的小说无论怎样具有反现实主义或元小说的实验性质,都依旧没有背离传统的模式。不过,不管怎么说,欧茨的作品从总体上看都是严肃的,也有高超的艺术技

---

[1] 转引自肖旭,《国外乔伊斯·卡罗尔·欧茨研究评析》,李维屏主编,《英美文学研究论丛》第22辑,上海:上海外语教育出版社,2013年,第319页。

巧，因此受到了评论界的广泛好评和读者的喜爱。

二、故事与人物

　　欧茨的小说"Where Are You Going, Where Have You Been"标题直译成汉语是"你要去哪里，你去过哪里"，今天一般译为"何去何从"。这篇小说最早发表在1966年的《纪元》（*Epoch*）杂志上，标题下的献词是"致鲍勃·迪伦"，发表后很快成为美国文学中的经典名篇，收录在各类重要的短篇小说选集中，在1986年还改编成电影《甜言蜜语》（*Smooth Talk*），由劳拉·邓恩（Laura Dern）主演。

　　鲍勃·迪伦是美国影响最大的摇滚歌手和民谣艺术家，于2016年获得诺贝尔文学奖，成为该奖设立以来第一位获奖的音乐家。他是美国六七十年代以来的反文化运动、嬉皮士运动等的精神领袖。从小说发表的时间和献词来看，读者应该已经猜到了故事发生的时代背景：没错，那就是乱世出英雄的20世纪60年代，是与美国20世纪20年代类似的动荡时代。我们不妨来看看当时美国的乱象，这对我们理解小说有很大的帮助：1962年古巴导弹危机，1963年肯尼迪总统遇刺，同年马丁·路德·金发表了《我有一个梦想》的演讲，冷战正如火如荼，核恐慌让人们惶惶不可终日，美苏在太空竞赛中你追我赶，美军陷入越战泥沼，妇女解放运动、民权运动不断高涨……这无疑是美国历史上的多事之秋，是一个急剧变动的时代。一方面现代科技迅猛发展、人们的物质生活极大丰富，另一方面各种社会问题不断涌现，两相交织使不少美国青年在理想与现实的冲突中失去了信仰，于是他们纷纷投身各种非主流文化的反战运动、嬉皮士运动等，借助音乐、毒品、性解放、怪异的举止、奇装异服等来发泄自己的苦闷，追求精神的解放。

　　据作家本人透露，《何去何从》中阿诺德·福润德（Arnold Friend）的原型来自1965年《生活》杂志刊登的一个连环杀手查尔斯·施密特（Charles Schmid）。此人是一个油嘴滑舌的无业游民，喜欢编造故事，诱骗未成年少女，跟她们套近乎，然后杀害她们。他相貌英俊，个子不高，打扮入时，喜欢装酷，化妆涂口红，而且为了显高，还在定做的牛仔长靴底部塞上东西。他把自己当成猫王埃尔维斯·普雷斯利（Elvis Presley）。据他案发后交代，他曾诱拐并杀害了三位少女，这个连环杀手后来被人称为"来自图森的花衣风笛手"（The Pied

Piper of Tucson）。欧茨读到这篇报道后想，这样一个有些蹩脚的浪荡子怎么就能骗到这么多女孩子呢？于是她就构思了从受害者康妮（Connie）的角度叙述的这部短篇《何去何从》。

故事的情节并不复杂：15岁的叛逆少女康妮被陌生男子阿诺德·福润德（Arnold Friend）诱拐、侵害。在一次夏夜出游中康妮偶遇一个迷人的帅哥福润德，两人互相多看了一眼，康妮也没放在心上。到了星期天，康妮的家人外出野餐，她独自一人在家，福润德带着自己的小跟班突然开着金色的涂鸦破敞篷车来约她一起出去兜风，以漏洞百出又极富魅力的语言来诱惑她。当康妮从一开始的迷惑不解、不知所措到警觉惶恐、试图报警时，福润德终于凶相毕露，以她和家人的安全相威胁，最后成功迫使她跟他们一起出去。

小说中出现的人物主要有康妮、阿诺德、康妮的母亲、姐姐琼（June）、最要好的朋友贝蒂·舒尔茨（Betty Shultz），以及阿诺德的跟班艾利·奥斯卡（Ellie Oscar）。

康妮是一位住在郊区的叛逆少女，她与家人关系紧张，跟循规蹈矩的24岁姐姐琼形成了鲜明对照；她有点爱慕虚荣，非常在意自己的外表，想去外面的世界冒险，渴望有位白马王子出现在自己的生活中。在一个仲夏夜晚，康妮和她最要好的朋友搭乘朋友父亲的车子去当地的购物中心。其实这只是爱冒险的少女的小把戏，她们并不是要去购物，而是去跟购物中心有一条马路之隔的免下车餐厅（drive-in restaurant）的年长的男子一起寻开心。一个叫艾迪（Eddie）的男孩子跟康妮聊天，约她出去吃饭，在离开汽车餐厅去艾迪的车的途中，康妮瞥见一个坐在有涂鸦的金色敞篷车里的男子，他向康妮微笑，康妮避开他的目光，但又很快回头看了看他。这位陌生男子伸出手指向她比画说，"宝贝儿，你是我的了"。康妮和艾迪在另一家餐厅待了三个小时，然后两人又去了一个无人的巷子。虽然故事没有明确告诉我们二人在小巷子里做了什么，但读者可以推知，康妮和艾迪应该是在偷食禁果。之后康妮和朋友回到购物中心，被朋友的父亲一起接回。这些大概就是康妮暑假期间经常做的事情。

一个星期天的上午，康妮一边洗头，一边听收音机里的音乐节目。康妮的家人都外出野餐了。不久一辆有涂鸦的金色敞篷车停在她家门前按喇叭，车里有两个男子。康妮并未警觉，而是和陌生男子聊起了天。车上播放的音乐和康妮正

12. WHERE ARE YOU GOING, WHERE HAVE YOU BEEN

在听的音乐一样，二人邀请康妮出去兜风。他们一个自称福润德，另一个叫奥斯卡，是福润德的小跟班。福润德说那晚与康妮在免下车餐厅偶遇之后，他已对康妮的一举一动、她的朋友和家人了如指掌。康妮问他有多大年纪，他说跟康妮差不多，但他的相貌明显老得多，30岁上下。康妮逐渐意识到事情不太对劲，阿诺德继续纠缠，言语也越来越轻佻。康妮威胁要报警，但阿诺德以她家人的性命要挟，一步步逼近她，最后迫使她走出了房间。

  连环杀手福润德是小说中的重要人物，他是一个帅气时尚、喜欢装酷、口蜜腹剑的坏蛋，一个像老鹰一般四处寻找猎物的恶魔。值得注意的是，他的名字本身是有特别含义的。他的姓Friend是"朋友"的意思，这是他能诱惑康妮的一个原因，是对康妮遇人不淑、认敌为友的讽刺；另外Friend与Fiend只有一个字母之差，后者意为"恶魔"，是这个人物的真实面目。他是戴着一副朋友面具的魔鬼。另外，其名Arnold一词从词源上讲，意思是"强大的鹰"，在小说中欧茨就把他比喻成四处寻找猎物的鹰，他有一个"长长的鹰一般的鼻子"，说话就像在唱歌，掩盖自己邪恶的用意，使康妮为之着迷，上了他的当。他喜欢装酷，戴着一副墨镜，穿着褪色的牛仔裤和长靴，戴着一顶假发，在风中凌乱，又喜欢音乐，好似一副摇滚歌星的派头。为了显得高大，他在鞋里垫了东西。他开着一辆破旧的满是涂鸦的金色敞篷车，身边跟着一个被他呼来唤去的跟班，还有一台时尚的收音机。这一前卫、叛逆的形象和酷酷的打扮，加上江湖老大的派头，无疑对康妮具有不小的吸引力。小说里，康妮从窗户看到阿诺德突然出现，甚至还有些激动，开始急忙整理发型要准备见这位帅哥。然而在正常人看来，阿诺德的甜言蜜语都是胡扯，他像故交好友一样，直截了当地邀请康妮出去兜风，在她面前用"亲爱的""宝贝儿"等轻浮的字眼故作关爱，在被识破后又死缠烂打、凶相毕露。他似乎拥有一种神秘的力量，像先知一样对康妮及其家人朋友的情况了如指掌，他听的收音机和康妮在家里听的调到了同一个台，他甚至能看清康妮的家人在野餐时的一举一动，让读者感觉他是无所不能的，康妮终究难逃魔掌。在小说的结尾，康妮看见自己的身体走出家门，阳光普照着广阔的大地，而家早已不再是家。

三、主题与技巧

在《何去何从》中，一如在她的其他作品中那样，欧茨表达了对美国社会中的暴力问题、家庭不睦、青少年的叛逆和女性面临的威胁等诸多话题的关注。她主要使用心理现实主义创作手法，借助康妮的视角和心理活动，以一种直接、客观、简洁的风格揭示了美国20世纪60年代面临的众多问题。

不少人在读完这篇故事后都有这样的感受，那就是虽然故事中并没有血腥的暴力场面，也没有激烈的挣扎打斗，但那种与康妮感同身受而又身不由己的恐惧、顺从和认命的感觉，让人不寒而栗。换句话说，当暴力降临的时候，你只能绝望地选择屈服，而一个小小的错误，将导致致命的后果，这种无助才是最令人恐惧的。这也给我们大家提了一个醒：在那些看似彬彬有礼的陌生人中，也许就有道貌岸然的魔鬼杀手。欧茨高明的地方，就在于以看似平淡的语言，将这一现象描写得如此真实。康妮就像我们身边的某个问题少女，她在家里感受不到爱与关怀，渴望冒险，渴望去认识外面的人与世界。然而她不知道的是，外面的世界危机四伏，只因为在汽车餐厅多看了一眼，她就被魔鬼般的福润德盯上并找上门来，最后不得不离开自己的家，跟他上了车。至于她后来受到了怎样非人的折磨、是否香消玉殒，恐怕大家早已有了自己的判断。欧茨对平静中蕴含的巨大恐惧、人在面对暴力时的绝望无助的真实的描写，与海明威在《杀手》中的故事颇有异曲同工之妙。关于美国社会的暴力描写，笔者还推荐大家读读弗兰纳里·奥康纳的《好人难寻》（*A Good Man Is Hard to Find*）和科马克·麦卡锡（Cormac MaCarthy）的《老无所依》（*No Country for Old Men*），后者已被改编成电影。

欧茨是美国当代文坛最著名的女性作家之一，因此，不少评论家认为，她的许多作品都在力图表现女性主义的主题，探讨女性在现代社会的命运。例如，著名女性主义评论家肖沃尔特（Elaine Showalter）就编有一部关于《何去何从》的评论文集，其中有一篇提到了这部小说的女性主义主题。《何去何从》是欧茨被收录最多的短篇，它发表的1966年正值美国女性主义运动第二波浪潮的鼎盛时期。作者通过描写叛逆少女康妮的悲剧命运，反思了父权制社会对女性看不见的压制，以及暴力对女性的身心摧残。有人指出，康妮的父亲是美国父权制度的代表，他作为一家之主，却只关心自己，与妻子、两个女儿形同陌路，体现的是家庭中的父权制冷暴力。小说中康妮的父亲没有名字，这使他的冷暴力具有更普遍

12. WHERE ARE YOU GOING, WHERE HAVE YOU BEEN

的象征意义，代表了社会对女性的冷漠。福润德则以轻浮的语言来诱惑她，以肉体的伤害来威胁她，迫使她投怀送抱，成为他可以任意处置的猎物。更有评论家明确指出，《何去何从》讲述了一个"撒旦引诱夏娃"的故事。这类女性主义的解释不无道理，不过考虑到欧茨本人曾反对给自己贴上女性主义作家的标签，因此我们也需要注意：不要过度解读。[1]

《何去何从》还真实地反映了20世纪60年代青少年的叛逆、离家出走等社会问题。首先，康妮的叛逆是因为她在家里体会不到关爱和温暖。康妮一家是60年代典型的家庭模式，有一个"沉默"的父亲和一个"愤怒"的母亲。父亲"总是在上班，回家了便要吃饭，边吃边看报，吃完了便去睡觉"（Their father was away at work most of the time and when he came home he wanted supper and he read the newspaper at supper and after supper he went to bed）。在康妮最需要关爱和引导的青少年时期，沉默而缺席的父亲显然不利于她人格的成长。父亲对待家人很冷漠，仿佛她们是陌生人，连话都懒得跟她们说。母亲总是拿"相貌平平，又矮又胖"的琼来做康妮的榜样，处处贬低康妮。故事开篇交待了主人公的名字和年龄之后，立即就提到了她爱照镜子的习惯："她习惯于伸长脖子，急促而紧张地傻笑着照镜子，抑或仔细观察别人的脸色，确保自己的样子还行"（…she had a quick nervous giggling habit of craning her neck to glance into mirrors, or checking other people's faces to make sure her own was all right）。然而，她的母亲却总是在她照镜子时挖苦她。在《何去何从》中我们见到了美国现实主义小说中常出现的家庭场景：夫妻疏离，长幼隔阂，家人之间缺乏关爱，大家相互指责，于是我们在小说中读到当父亲沉默不语低头吃饭时，康妮的母亲便老是找茬骂她，骂得康妮恨不得她的母亲死掉她自己也死掉就一了百了了。妻子在丈夫那里得不到关爱就骂康妮，而康妮和"模范姐姐"琼之间也是水火不容，仿佛生活在两个世界的人。

其次，青春期是身份认同形成的关键时期，被父亲忽视、被母亲否定的康妮迫切需要在别人那里得到认同，以确立自己的价值。于是在家庭之外，她会戴上另一张面具，获得另一种不同的身份："她的一切都有两面，一面是在家里

---

[1] 参见顾悦，《鲍勃·迪伦、离家出走与60年代的"决裂"问题：欧茨〈何去何从〉中的家庭系统》，《外国文学》，2017年第5期，第66页。

时的样子,一面是在家以外的一切地方出现的样子"(Everything about her had two sides to it, one for home and one for anywhere that was not home...)。康妮寻求男孩子的欣赏,为的就是获得认同和价值感;一周数次,她和其他姑娘会去"大孩子待的"汽车餐厅,那里对她们而言宛若"圣殿",应许着赐给她们所祈望的平安与祝福,可以让她们"有所依傍"。康妮与大男孩子们鬼混,是因为从他们那里,她可以获得家里得不到的认可和欣赏。尽管康妮家庭并不穷困,但却情感贫瘠,不能从家庭里得到的,她希望从别处获得,而对外部世界的危险她毫无防备。福润德出现时,她的第一反应并非警惕、防卫,而是关心自己样子是否好看,即使福润德的言语恐吓不断升级,她也没有发出任何明确拒绝的信号。阿诺德一边强调她家庭的不幸福,一边又给出幸福的许诺。在阿诺德的威逼利诱下,"她人生第一次想到,没有什么是她自己的,没有什么是属于她的,只是一个撞击的活着的东西,在这个身体中,而这个身体也不是她自己的"(She thought for the first time in her life that it was nothing that was hers, that belonged to her, but just a pounding, living thing inside this body that wasn't really hers either)。最终康妮打开门走向了这位陌生男子,走向"广阔的阳光照耀的大地,在他的身后,在他的四周——如此广阔的大地,康妮从未见过,也从不认得,她只知道,她要去那里"[1](...the vast sunlit reaches of the land behind him and on all sides of him, so much land that Connie had never seen before and did not recognize except to know that she was going to it)。这一段描写充满《圣经》中上帝"应许之地"的意味,因此,康妮的出走简直就是一场"出埃及记"。她离家出走,投向了陌生人的怀抱,也把自己送给了撒旦。

最后我们来简单谈谈大家可能感到困惑的几个问题:欧茨为什么要将故事献给鲍勃·迪伦?小说为什么要起名"何去何从"?结尾处康妮为什么要走向"广阔的阳光照耀的大地"?关于第一个问题,已有不少学者指出了小说与摇滚乐和嬉皮士运动之间的关系,而鲍勃·迪伦无疑是这场运动中影响最大的人物。在小说中,摇滚乐这条线索贯穿始终,康妮痴迷于摇滚乐的魅力,觉得它使一切都显得如此美妙,音乐是她逃避家庭现实的精神寄托,正是因为福润德跟她一样热爱

---

[1] 顾悦,《鲍勃·迪伦、离家出走与60年代的"决裂"问题:欧茨〈何去何来〉中的家庭系统》,《外国文学》,2017年第5期,第65页。

摇滚乐，她便对他产生了好感。第二个问题，欧茨的这篇小说标题可以说体现了作家的精心设计和安排。首先，它很像调皮孩子出门寻找刺激时家长的询问与叮嘱，"你要去哪里呀，你去过哪些地方呀"，一看题目大概就能想到故事是关于青少年成长主题的。其次，题目很像汉语中的对仗，上下句字数完全相等，音韵又朗朗上口，不仅具有民谣歌词的形式美，还像格言警句般暗含深意：这似乎是一个人生哲学的问题：你将何去？又将何从？最后，题目也影射了康妮面临的选择困境。当福润德试图威逼她顺从时曾说，"你来的地方已经不再，你想去的地方已经被取消了"（The place where you came from ain't there any more, and where you had in mind to go is cancelled out）。康妮对自己的未来充满困惑和绝望：她将何去何从？小说的结尾颇有些超现实的意味，就像我们前面在分析福润德的名字所包含的意义时所谈到的那样，在这位大魔头（Arch Fiend）化身为朋友（Friend）的甜言蜜语和威逼利诱之下，康妮似乎已经失去了自我，她的心"只是一个撞击的活着的东西，在这个身体中，而这个身体也不是她自己的"，这时她仿佛灵魂出窍，身心分离，她看到自己的身体打开了门，而灵魂似乎仍在那里。她走向了阿诺德，走向了这位陌生男子，走向了"广阔的阳光照耀的大地，在他的身后，在他的四周——如此广阔的大地，康妮从未见过，也从不认得，她只知道，她要去那里"。显然，这最后一幕确实如一些批评家所说，具有"撒旦引诱夏娃"的超现实的、梦魇般的效果。

Suggested Readings

1. Bloom, Harold. *Joyce Carol Oates.* New York: Chelsea House Publishing, 1987.
2. Cologne-Brookes, Gavin. *Dark Eyes on America: The Novels of Joyce Carol Oates.* Baton Rouge: Louisiana State University Press, 2005.
3. Creighton, Joanne. *Joyce Carol Oates.* Boston: Twayne, 1979.
4. Crighton, Joanee. *Joyce Carol Oates: Novels of the Middle Ages.* Boston: Twayne, 1992.
5. Daly, Brenda. *Lavish Self-Divisions: The Novels of Joyce Carol Oates.* Jackson: University Press of Mississippi, 1996.
6. *A Study Guide for Joyce Carol Oates's "Where Are You Going, Where Have You

Been?", Detroit: Gale, Cengage Learning, 2017.

7. Grant, Mary K. *The Tragic Vision of Joyce Carol Oates*. Durham: Duke University Press, 1978.

8. Johnson, Greg. *Invisible Writer: A Biography of Joyce Carol Oates*. New York: Dutton, 1998.

9. Johnson, Greg. *Joyce Carol Oates: A Study of the Short Fiction*. New York: Twayne, 1994.

10. Johnson, Greg. *Understanding Joyce Carol Oates*. Columbia: University of South Carolina Press, 1987.

11. Millazzo, Lee. *Conversations with Joyce Carol Oates*. Jackson: University Press of Mississippi, 1989.

Questions for Reflection

1. Why was the story dedicated to Bob Dylan? Under what social background did it take place? Why is this significant?

2. What is your first impression of the strange boy "in a convertible jalopy painted gold"? What information does his flirtous greeting "Gonna get you, baby" convey?

3. Why is Connie alone at home? What is her relationship with her family?

4. What is Connie's reaction to Arnold Friend's coercion? Has she undergone any emotional and psychological changes?

5. How do you understand the title of the story?

Questions for Discussion

Why do writers like Joyce Carol Oates, Flannery O'Connor, Cormac McCarthy, et al. are fond of exposing social problems such as violence in the American society in their works? What is your understanding of such literary works about violence?

（王安　撰写）

13. THE SHAWL

By Cynthia Ozick, 1980

Stella, cold, cold, the coldness of hell. How they walked on the roads together, Rosa with Magda curled up between sore breasts, Magda wound up in the shawl. Sometimes Stella carried Magda. But she was jealous of Magda. A thin girl of fourteen, too small, with thin breasts of her own, Stella wanted to be wrapped in a shawl, hidden away, asleep, rocked by the march, a baby, a round infant in arms. Magda took Rosa's nipple, and Rosa never stopped walking, a walking cradle. There was not enough milk; sometimes Magda sucked air; then she screamed. Stella was ravenous. Her knees were tumors on sticks, her elbows chicken bones.

Rosa did not feel hunger; she felt light, not like someone walking but like someone in a faint, in trance, arrested in a fit, someone who is already a floating angel, alert and seeing everything, but in the air, not there, not touching the road. As if teetering on the tips of her fingernails. She looked into Magda's face through a gap in the shawl: a squirrel in a nest, safe, no one could reach her inside the little house of the shawl's windings. The face, very round, a pocket mirror of a face: but it was not Rosa's bleak complexion, dark like cholera, it was another kind of face altogether, eyes blue as air, smooth feathers of hair nearly as yellow as the Star sewn into Rosa's coat. You could think she was one of *their* babies.

Rosa, floating, dreamed of giving Magda away in one of the villages. She could leave the line for a minute and push Magda into the hands of any woman on the side of the road. But if she moved out of line they might shoot. And even if she fled the line for half a second and pushed the shawl-bundle at a stranger, would the woman take it? She might be surprised, or afraid; she might drop the shawl, and Magda would fall out and strike her head and die. The little round head. Such a good child, she gave up screaming, and sucked now only for the taste of the drying nipple itself. The neat grip of the tiny gums. One mite of a tooth tip sticking up in the bottom gum, how shining, an elfin tombstone of white marble gleaming there. Without complaining, Magda relinquished Rosa's teats, first the left, then the right; both were cracked, not a sniff of milk. The duct-crevice extinct, a dead volcano, blind eye, chill hole, so Magda took the corner of the shawl and milked it instead. She sucked and sucked, flooding the threads with wetness. The shawl's good flavor, milk of linen.

It was a magic shawl, it could nourish an infant for three days and three nights. Magda did not die, she stayed alive, although very quiet. A peculiar smell, of cinnamon and almonds, lifted out of her mouth. She held her eyes open every moment, forgetting how to blink or nap, and Rosa and sometimes Stella studied their blueness. On the road they raised one burden of a leg after another and studied Magda's face. "Aryan," Stella said, in a voice grown as thin as a string; and Rosa thought how Stella gazed at Magda like a young cannibal. And the time that Stella said "Aryan," it sounded to Rosa as if Stella had really said "Let us devour her."

But Magda lived to walk. She lived that long, but she did not walk very well, partly because she was only fifteen months old, and partly because the spindles of her legs could not hold up her fat belly. It was fat with air, full and round. Rosa gave almost all her food to Magda, Stella gave nothing; Stella was ravenous, a growing child herself, but not growing much. Stella did not

13. THE SHAWL

menstruate. Rosa did not menstruate. Rosa was ravenous, but also not; she learned from Magda how to drink the taste of a finger in one's mouth. They were in a place without pity, all pity was annihilated in Rosa, she looked at Stella's bones without pity. She was sure that Stella was waiting for Magda to die so she could put her teeth into the little thighs.

Rosa knew Magda was going to die very soon; she should have been dead already, but she had been buried away deep inside the magic shawl, mistaken there for the shivering mound of Rosa's breasts; Rosa clung to the shawl as if it covered only herself. No one took it away from her. Magda was mute. She never cried. Rosa hid her in the barracks, under the shawl, but she knew that one day someone would inform; or one day someone, not even Stella, would steal Magda to eat her. When Magda began to walk, Rosa knew that Magda was going to die very soon, something would happen. She was afraid to fall asleep; she slept with the weight of her thigh on Magda's body; she was afraid she would smother Magda under her thigh. The weight of Rosa was becoming less and less; Rosa and Stella were slowly turning into air.

Magda was quiet, but her eyes were horribly alive, like blue tigers. She watched. Sometimes she laughed—it seemed a laugh, but how could it be? Magda had never seen anyone laugh. Still, Magda laughed at her shawl when the wind blew its corners, the bad wind with pieces of black in it, that made Stella's and Rosa's eyes tear. Magda's eyes were always clear and tearless. She watched like a tiger. She guarded her shawl. No one could touch it; only Rosa could touch it. Stella was not allowed. The shawl was Magda's own baby, her pet, her little sister. She tangled herself up in it and sucked on one of the corners when she wanted to be very still.

Then Stella took the shawl away and made Magda die.

Afterward Stella said: "I was cold."

And afterward she was always cold, always. The cold went into her heart: Rosa saw that Stella's heart was cold. Magda flopped onward with her little pencil legs scribbling this way and that, in search of the shawl; the pencils faltered at the barracks opening, where the light began. Rosa saw and pursued. But already Magda was in the square outside the barracks, in the jolly light. It was the roll-call arena. Every morning Rosa had to conceal Magda under the shawl against a wall of the barracks and go out and stand in the arena with Stella and hundreds of others, sometimes for hours, and Magda, deserted, was quiet under the shawl, sucking on her corner. Every day Magda was silent, and so she did not die. Rosa saw that today Magda was going to die, and at the same time a fearful joy ran in Rosa's two palms, her fingers were on fire, she was astonished, febrile: Magda, in the sunlight, swaying on her pencil legs, was howling. Ever since the drying up of Rosa's nipples, ever since Magda's last scream on the road, Magda had been devoid of any syllable; Magda was a mute. Rosa believed that something had gone wrong with her vocal cords, with her windpipe with the cave of her larynx; Magda was defective, without a voice; perhaps she was deaf; there might be something amiss with her intelligence; Magda was dumb. Even the laugh that came when the ash-stippled wind made a clown out of Magda's shawl was only the air-blown showing of her teeth. Even when the lice, head lice and body lice, crazed her so that she became as wild as one of the big rats that plundered the barracks at daybreak looking for carrion, she rubbed and scratched and kicked and bit and rolled without a whimper. But now Magda's mouth was spilling a long viscous rope of clamor.

"Maaaa—"

It was the first noise Magda had ever sent out from her throat since the drying up of Rosa's nipples.

"Maaaa... aaa!"

Again! Magda was wavering in the perilous sunlight of the arena, scribbling on such pitiful little bent shins. Rosa saw. She saw that Magda was grieving for the loss of her shawl, she saw that Magda was going to die. A tide of commands hammered in Rosa's nipples: Fetch, get, bring! But she did not know which to

13. THE SHAWL

go after first, Magda or the shawl. If she jumped out into the arena to snatch Magda up, the howling would not stop, because Magda would still not have the shawl; but if she ran back into the barracks to find the shawl, and if she found it, and if she came after Magda holding it and shaking it, then she would get Magda back, Magda would put the shawl in her mouth and turn dumb again.

Rosa entered the dark. It was easy to discover the shawl. Stella was heaped under it, asleep in her thin bones. Rosa tore the shawl free and flew—she could fly, she was only air—into the arena. The sunheat murmured of another life, of butterflies in summer. The light was placid, mellow. On the other side of the steel fence, far away, there were green meadows speckled with dandelions and deep-colored violets; beyond them, even farther, innocent tiger lilies, tall, lifting their orange bonnets. In the barracks they spoke of "flowers," of "rain": excrement, thick turd-braids, and the slow stinking maroon waterfall that slunk down from the upper bunks, the stink mixed with a bitter fatty floating smoke that greased Rosa's skin. She stood for an instant at the margin of the arena. Sometimes the electricity inside the fence would seem to hum; even Stella said it was only an imagining, but Rosa heard real sounds in the wire: grainy sad voices. The farther she was from the fence, the more clearly the voices crowded at her. The lamenting voices strummed so convincingly, so passionately, it was impossible to suspect them of being phantoms. The voices told her to hold up the shawl, high; the voices told her to shake it, to whip with it, to unfurl it like a flag. Rosa lifted, shook, whipped, unfurled. Far off, very far, Magda leaned across her air-fed belly, reaching out with the rods of her arms. She was high up, elevated, riding someone's shoulder. But the shoulder that carried Magda was not coming toward Rosa and the shawl, it was drifting away, the speck of Magda was moving more and more into the smoky distance. Above the shoulder a helmet glinted. The light tapped the helmet and sparkled it into a goblet. Below the helmet a black body like a domino and a pair of black boots hurled themselves in the direction of the electrified fence. The electric voices began to chatter wildly. "Maamaa, maaamaaa," they all hummed together. How far Magda was from Rosa now, across the whole square, past a dozen barracks, all the way on the other side! She was no bigger than a moth.

All at once Magda was swimming through the air. The whole of Magda travelled through loftiness. She looked like a butterfly touching a silver vine. And the moment Magda's feathered round head and her pencil legs and balloonish belly and zigzag arms splashed against the fence, the steel voices went mad in their growling, urging Rosa to run and run to the spot where Magda had fallen from her flight against the electrified fence; but of course Rosa did not obey them. She only stood, because if she ran they would shoot, and if she tried to pick up the sticks of Magda's body they would shoot, and if she let the wolf's screech ascending now through the ladder of her skeleton break out, they would shoot; so she took Magda's shawl and filled her own mouth with it, stuffed it in and stuffed it in, until she was swallowing up the wolf's screech and tasting the cinnamon and almond depth of Magda's saliva; and Rosa drank Magda's shawl until it dried.

作品赏析

一、作家与作品介绍

辛西娅·奥兹克（Cynthia Ozick, 1928—），20世纪70年代以来美国最重要的犹太作家之一，她与索尔·贝娄（Saul Bellow）、伯纳德·马拉默德（Bernard Malamud）等美国犹太作家一样，同属美国第二代犹太移民，父母来自俄罗斯，长期接受美国主流文化的熏陶，因此一方面继承了犹太文化传统，另一方面又深切关注美国现实。她于1928年出生在美国纽约，从小就说一口流利的意第绪语。她五岁半到犹太教小学读书，同时也接受美国主流文化的教育，长大后进入亨特大学，成绩优秀。在大学期间曾修希伯来语，后来系统地阅读过有关犹太民族的文学、历史、哲学等著作。1966年奥兹克发表第一篇长篇小说《信任》（*Trust*），引起了评论界的关注。1971年她的中短篇小说集《异教的拉比及其

13. THE SHAWL

他故事》(*The Pagan Rabbi and Other Stories*)出版后,获得了评论界的广泛好评,她逐渐成为当代美国最重要的犹太作家。迄今为止,她已创作了6部长篇小说、7部短篇小说集、7部随笔集和1部戏剧。[1] 奥兹克以中短篇小说见长,文字简练犀利,人物刻画生动鲜明,其显著特点是将美国的现实与犹太传统有机结合,与索尔·贝娄、伯纳德·马拉默德等人的作品一样,兼具美国性和犹太性。她的短篇小说曾多次获奖。1970年,《妒忌,或意第绪语在美国》(*Envy, or Yiddish in America*, 1969)获年度最佳美国短篇小说奖;1971年和1977年,短篇小说集《异教的拉比及其他故事》(1971)和《流血和三部中篇小说》(*Bloodshed and Three Novellas*, 1976)先后获犹太图书协会奖,前者还于1972年获美国全国图书奖提名;1983年,《罗莎》获得美国文学艺术学院和研究院斯特劳斯奖;1984年又获欧·亨利短篇小说奖一等奖。她迄今已有3部短篇小说获欧·亨利短篇小说奖一等奖。1986年,她成为首位获得迈克尔·瑞(Michael Rea)短篇小说终身成就奖的作家;2000年获蓝南基金会小说成就奖。

今天评论界公认,反偶像崇拜是奥兹克作品中将美国现实和犹太性完美结合的出发点。[2] 犹太教是一神教,明确禁止制作和崇拜各种偶像,而在奥兹克看来,美国社会长期受异教徒思想的浸染,物质主义、享乐主义、金钱崇拜盛行,人们过分追求物质上的成功,过分强调个人的奋斗和感官享受,这些正是人们对象征性爱的爱神厄洛斯、象征享乐主义的酒神巴克斯、象征艺术与权力的缪斯和阿波罗等偶像崇拜所带来的恶果,导致美国社会普遍的沦落,呈现出现代社会的荒原景观。

奥兹克的作品具有浓厚的犹太意识,犹太大屠杀是这些作品中反复出现的主题。奥兹克被评论家们称为犹太文学的"代言人和最无畏的作家"[3]。尽管西奥多·阿多诺的名言"奥斯维辛之后,写诗是野蛮的"揭示了大屠杀书写的苍白无力和道德困境,认为"大屠杀只应是留存于档案文献中的历史",但犹

---

1 张晶晶,《辛西娅·奥兹克国内研究综述》,《西藏民族大学学报(哲学社会科学版)》,2016年第2期,第136页。
2 孙鲁瑶,《击碎偶像,终得涅槃——从〈陌生的身体〉看辛西娅欧芝克的反偶像崇拜思想》,《名作欣赏》,2015年第17期,第89-92页。
3 转引自陈娴,《〈同类相食的星球〉:奥兹克作为犹太小说家的创作选择》,《外语研究》,2012年第2期,第93页。

作家并未放弃书写大屠杀。[1] 奥兹克的作品，也同样在反复书写着大屠杀这一犹太民族的沉重历史，如《信任》、《斯德哥尔摩的弥赛亚》（The Messiah of Stockholm，1987）、《食人星系》（The Cannibal Galaxy，1983）。

《披巾》于1980年刊登在《纽约客》杂志上，获得1981年欧·亨利短篇小说奖和美国最佳小说奖，在后大屠杀文学中具有重大的意义。小说讲述了波兰裔犹太女主人公罗莎·卢布林在纳粹集中营里的创伤经历。1983年其续篇《罗莎》出版，获1984年美国最佳小说奖，讲述了罗莎的创伤后遗症及复原的过程。1989年奥兹克将《披巾》和《罗莎》合为一部中篇小说出版，以《披巾》命名，成为犹太大屠杀书写的经典。

值得一提的是，我国对奥兹克的研究起步很早，也很重视。她最早被译介到我国是20世纪80年代，《披巾》作为其最重要的代表作之一，在国内受到格外的重视。早在1987年，冯亦代、郑之岱编译的《当代美国获奖短篇小说选》就收录了奥兹克的《披巾》，当时译为《大围巾》；1994年，陶洁再次翻译此文，她将题目译作《大披巾》，发表在当年《外国文学》第4期上；2004年，王祖友再次以《披肩》为名翻译了这部小说，发表在当年《外国文学》第5期上。我国20世纪80年代是"创伤文学风靡一时之际"，《披巾》的翻译，可以说既顺应了时代的潮流，又"契合了中国读者的心理需求"[2]，它的一再被翻译，证明了这部小说的地位和魅力。

《披巾》极为精炼短小，全文不足2000词，故事情节也不复杂，堪称奥兹克最优秀的作品之一。故事描写女主人公罗莎随身携带一条披巾，这条披巾在罗莎被德国纳粹押解途中和在集中营里一直包裹着她的孩子玛格达，维持了玛格达15个月的生命。但不幸的是，罗莎的侄女斯特拉因为怕冷把玛格达的神奇披巾拿走了。孩子失去了披巾，蹒跚着走出囚房寻找，来到了空旷的点名场，被德国兵发现并扔到了通电的铁丝网上。奥兹克创作这一故事的灵感来自她读到的威廉·夏伊勒的《第三帝国的兴亡》中记录的一个集中营弑婴的真实事件。沉重的民族灾难激发了她的创作灵感，而她的《披巾》也成了远比历史记录更震撼人心的揭露

---

[1] 转引自肖飚，《欧芝克小说的创伤书写》，《求索》，2013年第12期，第165页。
[2] 张晶晶，《辛西娅·奥兹克国内研究综述》，《西藏民族大学学报（哲学社会科学版）》，2016年第2期，第137页。

法西斯暴行的控诉书，成了整个犹太民族灾难的历史见证。

二、人物与主题

《披巾》以第二次世界大战为背景，但全文却并未出现任何与战争相关的字眼，也没有任何关于战争硝烟炮火的描写，而是以极为朴实的文字，以一种冷峻客观的风格，描写一位犹太母亲罗莎在纳粹集中营里千方百计用自己的披巾来保护襁褓中的女儿玛格达，却因侄女斯特拉拿走披巾御寒而让玛格达暴露，最终葬身纳粹电网之下的故事。第二次世界大战对整个人类来说都是一场浩劫，而对于遭受了种族大屠杀的犹太民族更是永远无法忘却的民族噩梦。纳粹在种族优越论的蛊惑下，疯狂屠杀犹太人，夺去了近600万犹太儿女的生命。据不完全统计，"'截止到1945年，波兰原有的350万犹太人只剩下7万余人，荷兰的14万犹太人只剩下3.5万人，而德国和奥地利的33万犹太人仅有4万人生还'，此外，希腊、乌克兰和俄罗斯等国的犹太人也几乎消灭殆尽。"[1]《披巾》的故事正发生在这样残暴的历史背景之下。小说的主要人物是三位女性：身心饱受摧残的犹太母亲罗莎、她那被纳粹军人强暴后生下的注定要死去的15个月大的女儿玛格达，和严重营养不良为了活下去而变得铁石心肠的侄女斯特拉。故事以冷静客观的文字，强烈控诉了纳粹德国对犹太人犯下的暴行，以及这些暴行对人性的扭曲。

罗莎是玛格达的母亲，也是斯特拉的姨妈。故事一开始以寥寥数语交代了犹太人被驱赶至集中营的死亡行军一事。15个月大的玛格达之所以还能活着，是因为罗莎有一条披巾，她用这条披巾紧紧地裹住怀中的婴儿，以逃过纳粹的搜查。虽然自己也身处险境、遭受各种非人的折磨，但在每一刻都生死攸关的集中营里，罗莎只有竭尽全力保守秘密，保护孩子，以尽可能推迟死亡的到来。人世间最珍贵、最美好的母女亲情，每时每刻都面临着死亡的威胁，这是何等惨烈的人间悲剧！罗莎爆发出惊人的母性力量来保护玛格达，身体越来越虚弱的她却把自己的食物都给了玛格达。她想尽一切方法隐藏玛格达，随时用披巾紧紧地包裹住她，就连睡觉时身体也紧紧地挨着玛格达。所幸玛格达是个出奇懂事的婴儿，她不哭也不闹，只是安静吸吮母亲干涸的乳头，在母亲的怀抱中得以生存。罗莎深

---

[1] 转引自孙鲁瑶，《电网下的哭泣——辛西娅·欧芝克的短篇小说〈大披巾〉》，《世界文化》，2015年第8期，第39页。

知,玛格达的暴露是迟早的事,她设想如果能在死亡行军途中把她塞给路人,或许是最好的结局,但她又怕路人不接受,或者当她走出队列时,纳粹士兵会开枪,不管出现哪种情况,她们都必死无疑。因此,她打消了这样的念头。当一切都变得不可能的时候,披巾就成了玛格达生存下去的唯一希望,它掩护着玛格达,同时又是母乳的替代物,玛格达在饥饿时会拼命地吮吸披巾的一角,安静地待在那里,不发出声音。因此,披巾既是玛格达生命的庇护所,也是罗莎的精神寄托:只要披巾在,玛格达就是安全的。不过,这样的安全实在太不可靠,玛格达能躲在披巾里存活15个月完全是个奇迹。罗莎自己也很清楚,玛格达必定会死,而且可能很快,她与孩子相伴的每一天都是在等候死亡的降临,这种无助的等待比死亡还要令人恐惧。有一天当充满妒意的斯特拉拖走了披巾用于御寒时,玛格达为了寻找披巾,蹒跚着来到了危机四伏的点名区。焦急万分的罗莎先去营房取披巾,接着跑去追回玛格达,试图用披巾来隐藏孩子。但是,在与死神赛跑的过程中,一切都为时已晚,罗莎只能眼睁睁看着自己殚精竭虑保护了15个月的女儿被纳粹士兵抛至带电的铁丝网上活活电死。可是,罗莎不动也不叫,因为"如果她跑的话,他们会开枪的,如果她去捡玛格达的柴火棍似的尸骨,他们会开枪的,如果让她沿着她骨架子升上来的狼般的痛苦的尖叫爆发出来的话,他们会开枪的"[1](She only stood, because if she ran they would shoot, and if she tried to pick up the sticks of Magda's body they would shoot, and if she let the wolf's screech ascending now through the ladder of her skeleton break out, they would shoot)。罗莎唯一能做的不过是"搂住玛格达的披巾,用它堵住自己的嘴,往嘴里塞进去,使劲地填进去,直到她咽下狼的尖叫,尝到玛格达口水里肉桂和杏仁的味道"(...so she took Magda's shawl and filled her own mouth with it, stuffed it in and stuffed it in, until she was swallowing up the wolf's screech and tasting the cinnamon and almond depth of Magda's saliva)。罗莎眼睁睁地看着玛格达惨死在自己面前,却无能为力,无法去认领她的尸体,甚至无法发出任何悲切的哭嚎。

从小说的字里行间,不难推测出玛格达是罗莎被强暴后所生的孩子,其父亲是集中营中看管犹太人的德国纳粹军人。在披巾的掩护下,玛格达似乎懂事

---

[1] 〔美〕辛西亚·奥齐克,《大披巾》,陶洁译,《外国文学》,1994年第4期,第57页。下文所引译文均出自该处,不再另行加注。

13. THE SHAWL

地形成了与母亲之间特殊的生存默契,她不哭也不闹,只会安静地蜷缩在披巾中,饿了就啃披巾的一角,罗莎甚至觉得她是个哑巴。她有一张化妆用的小圆镜般的脸,眼睛如蓝天般清澈。"不过,它跟罗莎那好像得了霍乱病似的黝黑憔悴的面色不一样。这完全是另一张脸,眼睛如蓝天般清澈,光滑柔软的毛发是浅黄色的,几乎跟缝在罗莎外衣里的星星一个颜色。你简直可以说她是他们的娃娃。"(...but it was not Rosa's bleak complexion, dark like cholera, it was another kind of face altogether, eyes blue as air, smooth feathers of hair nearly as yellow as the Star sewn in to Rosa's coat. You could think she was one of *their* babies.)玛格达蓝色的眼睛、金色头发都在向读者表明她混杂着德国血统,这一暗示得到了斯特拉的确证,斯特拉看着玛格达蓝色的眼睛时称她是雅利安人。纵使玛格达身上流淌着德国人的血,却是"血统不纯正"的私生子,注定会死在集中营里。在披巾的掩护下,她神奇地活到了15个月,直到斯特拉拿走披巾将她暴露在纳粹士兵的视线里。一个士兵抓起玛格达,"阳光照射在头盔上,头盔像个高脚酒杯闪烁光亮。头盔下面是个象(像)穿了连帽化装斗篷的黑身子,一双黑色皮靴大步迈向通电的铁丝网"(The light tapped the helmet and sparkled it into a goblet. Below the helmet a black body like a domino and a pair of black boots hurled themselves in the direction of the electrified fence)。这15个月大的婴孩对即将到来的危险并不知晓,她迈着小细腿,去寻找可以吸吮的披巾的一角。而这时,纳粹将她高高举起,扔到了嗞嗞作响的电网上。奥兹克将玛格达死亡的瞬间做了慢动作描绘:"玛格达的全身穿过高傲的长空。她像只蝴蝶在触摸银色的蔓藤。玛格达有柔软毛发的圆圆的脑袋,她铅笔似的细腰、气球似的肚子和弯曲的胳膊摔到铁丝网上,那些铁丝网里的声音发了疯地咆哮起来,催促罗莎快跑,赶快跑到玛格达从飞行中落到充电铁丝网的地方。"(The whole of Magda travelled through loftiness. She looked like a butterfly touching a silver vine. And the moment Magda's feathered round head and her pencil legs and balloonish belly and zigzag arms splashed against the fence, the steel voices went mad in their growling, urging Rosa to run and run to the spot where Magda had fallen from her flight against the electrified fence...)这一幕是故事的高潮,奥兹克用慢镜头特写将玛格达与罗莎的生死离别拉伸得十分漫长。罗莎眼睁睁看见玛格达触电网,撕心裂肺的痛苦却无处发泄,只有将披巾塞进嘴里,咽下喉咙里涌上来的哀嚎。

斯特拉是一位被集中营的迫害扭曲了人性的14岁少女,她身上处处透着冷漠。在集中营里,她唯一可以依靠的亲人是姨妈罗莎。然而玛格达诞生后,罗莎把全部的食物和关爱都给了玛格达,使正处于生理发育期的她充满嫉妒。她羡慕玛格达有披巾的保护,渴望能像她那样得到姨妈的关爱。她知道玛格达身上有德国人的血统,对她没有丝毫的怜爱之情。小说反复叙述斯特拉的冰冷,披巾是斯特拉渴望的温暖,她也想像玛格达一样躲在暖和的披巾里;然而披巾是玛格达的私有物品,没有罗莎的允许,她连碰都不能碰一下。但斯特拉无法忍受刺骨的寒冷,她想要披巾来取暖。她清楚地知道如果她拿走玛格达的披巾,玛格达就会暴露。但斯特拉还是这样做了,也许在她的心里,她希望玛格达被发现,只有这样,她才能将披巾占为己有,她才能得到罗莎的注意和关心。在集中营里,活下去都是奢望,因此,非人的环境扭曲了人性,罗莎、斯特拉和玛格达之间既是血浓于水的亲人,从某种意义上说也是生死存亡的对手。罗莎看到骨瘦如柴的斯特拉,却毫无恻隐之心,她不止一次地"相信斯特拉盼着玛格达快死,她可以啃她的大腿"。在食物极度匮乏的集中营里,死亡每天都在发生,玛格达的存在挤压了斯特拉极为有限的生存空间,她的嫉妒和生存欲望与日俱增,对玛格达的生命构成了直接威胁,这使罗莎十分忧虑。一日,斯特拉终于偷走了妹妹的披巾,玛格达瞬间暴露于纳粹的视线之下。从小说开始对斯特拉感到寒冷的不断强调,到她终于冷漠地揭开玛格达的披巾,我们仿佛也同斯特拉一样感受到寒冷与饥饿,感受到在那种特殊境遇下亲情的冷漠、人性的扭曲、死亡的威胁。小说反复强调的斯特拉的"冷",既是她真实的身体感受,也是她在极限生存环境里表现出来的人性的冷酷,更是对法西斯强盗摧残人性的无声控诉。

三、结构与技巧

奥兹克通过对罗莎、玛格达和斯特拉三位女性人物在集中营里的悲惨经历的描写,发出了对纳粹暴行的强烈控诉。这篇小说在创作技巧上也颇有独到之处,那就是奥兹克干脆利落的行文风格与结构安排,以及她在《披巾》中运用的撷取主要片段、处处留白的零度写作技巧。

《披巾》全文不到2000词,但传达的信息却十分丰富,塑造的人物也异常鲜明。奥兹克是怎样做到的呢？首先，小说在结构的安排上，线索非常清晰，情节极为紧凑。作者按照时间的线性序列，紧紧围绕披巾这一核心意象，串联起罗莎、玛格达、斯特拉之间的关系和冲突，讲述了玛格达从被披巾庇护、到失去披巾死亡的故事，没有过多的笔墨，文字极为精炼，安排非常巧妙。在小说中，作者主要采用全知的叙述视角，以一种冷峻的外部聚焦，客观地记录纳粹的暴行。同时又不时插入人物的有限视角，对人物的心理活动进行挖掘，深入人物的内心世界。例如，罗莎在死亡行军途中，在自己饿得几乎晕厥的情况下，一边麻木地跟随队伍前行，一边想着如何能保住玛格达。这一部分是罗莎的内心活动，她设想可以在某个村子把玛格达送给别人，但又想这是不可能实现的事。又如，当罗莎目睹玛格达被抛入电网烧死后，她呆呆站在原地时的心理活动。奥兹克巧妙地运用了第三人称的叙述视角，同时又辅以人物的有限视角，使她的叙述既可以居高临下，冷静地窥视全局，又可以深入人物内心，身临其境，体会在死亡面前的无助和绝望，收放自如，展现了高超的叙述技巧。

《披巾》的另一个突出的技巧是处处留白的零度写作方式。这一写作方式对我们而言并不陌生，读者十分熟悉的作品有海明威的《白象似的群山》。在这篇小说中，海明威就像一架摄像机，忠实地记录了发生的一切，没有掺入作家的情感与态度。《白象似的群山》虽是从生活中撷取的一个片段、一张快照，却真实还原了生活本身的戏剧性。热奈特在分析聚焦的类型时，曾把《白象似的群山》中的聚焦类型划分为叙述者知道的还不如人物多的外聚焦，其实意思也是一种无动于衷地展示而非讲述事实，它减少了作者对文本的介入，隐藏起作者的感情，也不发表任何议论，基本思路与我们在分析《献给爱米莉的玫瑰》时提到的福克纳的"作家的超脱"类似。虽然奥兹克在《披巾》中没有像海明威那样，全程如一部摄像机冷眼旁观，但《披巾》也表现出典型的零度写作的特点。正如王祖友指出的那样，"在短篇小说《披肩》中，欧芝克以置身事外的旁观者的身份，以单纯感知的方式，冷静地折射了法西斯的残忍，表现出一种零度写作"[1]。叙述者以超然物外的态度讲述了三位女性人物如何在地狱般的集中营里忍受饥饿，以及玛格达如何最终走向死亡的过程。作者既不做过多的评论，也不给出自己的价

---

[1] 王祖友，《后现代小说文本中的历史反思——评辛西娅·欧芝克的两篇短篇小说》，《外国文学》，2004年第5期，第15页。

值判断,而是让人物自己上场,来冷静地展示一个非人的世界。即使在描述玛格达惨死的景象时,作者也是细腻而冷静的。这种白描的客观风格,正如战争来临前的短暂和平,也如作家在叙述集中营里屎尿横流的污秽场景时还不忘描写电网外那"绿色草地上点缀的蒲公英和深色的紫罗兰"(green meadows speckled with dandelions and deep-colored violets)和夏日蝴蝶的飞舞,在宁静中蕴藏着泯灭人性的暴行,在美丽的外部世界和非人的集中营之间,形成了巨大的张力,这反而增强了叙述的力量,给读者的心灵带来更大的冲击和震撼。奥兹克没有选择对集中营里的虐待、毒打、残杀、惨死和惨无人道的活体实验进行现实主义的描写,也没有选择从历史的视角还原宏大叙事,而是选择了最震撼人心的纳粹弑婴一幕,对其进行不动声色,甚至显得冷漠的客观再现。或许只有这样的写作风格,才能更真实地还原纳粹集中营的冷酷无情,从而更深切地表达"对恐怖的深沉悲愤"和"对600万死难同胞无以言表的深切哀悼"。[1] 王祖友盛赞奥兹克的这一技巧,认为她"以零度写作和元小说的后现代写作技巧"来书写犹太民族的苦难史,从而"将历史语境转化为生命诗性的尺度,表现出后大屠杀时期犹太小说在反映犹太身份问题上的新范型,为犹太文学发展开辟了新的方向。"[2]

与此同时,作家在直陈的叙述中,还故意留白,让读者自行去填补空白之处,而把叙述的重心放在披巾和三位人物的命运上。这样做的好处一方面是重点突出,脉络清晰,通过将故事的时间、背景和人物淡化,将人物的悲惨命运前置,使悲剧显得更加惊心动魄;另一方面还留下悬念,增加了故事的丰富内涵。这就像作者有一些秘密,她越是刻意不告诉你,你就越想去揭穿它一样。例如,在小说中,除了时间和背景被刻意虚化以外,小说中的几个人物也只有朦胧的轮廓。玛格达看似"一只窝中松鼠"(a squirrel in a nest),被误作是"罗莎颤抖起伏的乳房"(the shivering mound of Rosa's breasts),斯特拉"膝盖如棍棒上的瘤,肘腕如雏鸡的骨"(Her knees were tumors on sticks, her elbows chicken bones...),"像个年轻的食人兽"(a young cannibal),罗莎则成了"走动的摇篮"(a walking cradle),像"飘浮的天使"(a floating angel)。这些形象模糊

---

[1] 王祖友,《后现代小说文本中的历史反思——评辛西娅·欧芝克的两篇短篇小说》,《外国文学》,2004年第5期,第17页。
[2] 同上,第19页。

的人物一出场就显出神秘、怪异的"非人"特色,这正好说明在集中营里她们只是模糊的、抽象化的符号,是可以被随意处置的物品。简洁的文字、干脆利落的结构、冷峻客观的风格、零度写作和故意留白,这些高超的叙述技巧,最终成就了奥兹克这篇名作。

Suggested Readings

1. Bloom, Harold. *Cynthia Ozick*. New York: Chelsea House Publishers, 1986.
2. Clendinnen, Inga. *Reading the Holocaust*. Cambridge: Cambridge University Press, 1999.
3. Friedman, Lawrence S. *Understanding Cynthia Ozick*. Columiba: Unierstiy of South Carolina Press, 1991.
4. Kauvar, Elaine M. *Cynthia Ozick's Fiction: Tradition and Invention*. Bloomington & Indianapolis: Indiana University Press, 1993.
5. Lang, Berel. *Writing and the Holocaust*. New York & London: Holmes & Meier, 1988.
6. Lowin, Joseph. *Cynthia Ozick*. Boston: Twayne, 1988.
7. Ozick, Cynthia. *A Cynthia Ozick Reader*. New York: Indiana University Press, 1996.
8. Ozick, Cynthia. *Trust*. New York: New American Library, 1966.
9. Ozick, Cynthia. *The Pagan Rabbi and Other Stories*. New York: Knopf, 1971.
10. Pinsker, Sanford. *The Uncompromising Fictions of Cynthia Ozick*. Columbia: University of Missouri Press, 1987.
11. Strandberg, Victor. *The Art of Cynthia Ozick*. New York: Chelsea, 1986.
12. 乔国强:《美国犹太文学》,北京:商务印书馆,2008年。

Questions for Reflection

1. What is the relationship between Rosa, Magda and Stella? How are these three people related in the story to the shawl?

2. Why does Cynthia Ozick employ the third-person omniscient point of view?

Would it be better if the author used the first-person point of view by filtering through the consciousness of one character in the story?

3. Why does Stella always feel cold? How has she treated Magda and Rosa? Is she an impassive, cold-hearted person?

4. When Magda is hurled unto the electrified fence, Rosa's reaction is to stuff the shawl deep into her mouth. Why?

5. What are the living conditions within the concentration camp? Why does the author mention the beautiful scenery outside?

Questions for Discussion

What is "Holocaust literature"? How are trauma and memory represented in literature? Why is "The Shawl" considered one of the representative works in this genre?

（王安　撰写）

14. MADE IN HEAVEN

By John Updike, 1985

Brad Schaeffer was attracted to Jeanette Henderson by her Christianity; at an office Christmas party, in Boston in the thirties, in one of those eddies of silence that occur amid gaiety like a swirl of backwater in a stream, he heard her crystal-clear voice saying, "Why, the salvation of my soul!"

He looked over. She was standing by the window, pinned between a hot radiator and Arthur Gleb, the office Romeo. Outside, behind the black window, it had begun to snow, and the lighted windows of the office building across Milk Street were blurring and fluttering. Jeanette had come to the brokerage house that fall, a tidy secretary in a pimento wool suit, with a prim ruffled blouse. For this evening's event she had dared open-toed shoes and a dress of lavender gabardine, with zigzag pleats marked at their points by flattened bows. The flush the party punch had put in her cheeks and throat helped him see for the first time the something highly polished about her compact figure, an impression of an object finely made, down to the toenails that peeked through the tips of her shoes. Her profile showed pert and firm as she strained to look up into Arthur's overbearing, beetle-browed, darkly suffused face. Brad stepped over to them, into the steamy warmth near the radiator. The snow was intensifying; across the street the golden windows were softening like pats of butter.

Jeanette's face turned to her rescuer. She was lightly sweating. The excited blush of her cheeks made the blue of her eyes look icy. "Arthur was saying," she appealed, "that only money matters!"

"Then I asked this crazy little gal what mattered to her," Arthur said, giving off heat through his black serge suit. A sprig of mistletoe, pale and withering, had been pinned to his lapel.

"And I told him the first thing I could think of," Jeanette said. Her hair, waved and close to her head, was a soft brown that tonight did not look mousy. "Of course a lot of things matter to me," she hurried on, "more than money."

"Are you Catholic?" Brad asked her.

This was a question of another order than Arthur's badinage. Her face composed itself; her voice became secretarial, factual. "Of course not. I'm a Methodist."

Brad felt relief. He was free to love her. In Boston, an aspiring man did not love Catholics, even if one came from Ohio with the name of Schaeffer.

"Did I sound so silly?" she asked, when Arthur had gone off in search of another cup of punch and another little gal.

"Unusual, but not silly." In his heart Brad did not expect capitalism to last another decade, and it would take with it what churches were left; he assumed religion was already as dead as Marx and Mencken had claimed. There was a gloom in the December streets, and in the statistics that came to the office, that made the cheer of Christmas carols sound obscene. From the deep doorways of Boston's business buildings, ornamented like little Gothic chapels, people actually starving peered out, too bitter and numb to beg. Each morning the Common was combed for frozen bodies.

"I do believe," Jeanette told him. The contrast between her blue eyes and rosy, glazed skin had become almost garish. "Ever since I can remember, even before anything was explained to me. It seems so natural, so necessary. Do you think that's strange?"

14. MADE IN HEAVEN

"I think that's lovely," he told her.

By Lententime they were going together to church. It was his idea, to accompany her; he loved seeing her in new settings, in the new light each placed her in. At work she was drab and brisk, a bit aloof from the other "girls," with a dry way of pursing her lips into crinkles that made her look older than she was. At her ancestral home in Framingham, with her parents and brothers, she became girlish and slightly drunk on family atmosphere, as she had been on punch; he greedily inhaled the air of this spicy old house, with its worn Orientals and sofas of leather and horsehair, knowing that this was the aroma of her childhood. On the streets and in restaurants Jeanette was perfectly the lady, like a figure etched on a city scene, making him, in their scenic anonymity, a gentleman, an escort, a gallant. Her smiling face, and the satin lapels of her blue wool coat, and the pointed tips of her shiny black boots. Involuntarily his arm encircled her waist at street crossings, and he could not let go even when they had safely crossed the street. Her bearing was so nicely honed in every move—the pulling off, for instance, finger by finger, of her kid gloves in Locke-Ober's—that Brad would sometimes clown or feign clumsiness just to crack her composed expression with a blush or a grimace. He was afraid that otherwise he might slip from her mind. It did not occur to him, when, during a rapt *pianissimo* moment in Symphony Hall, he nudged her and whispered a joke, that he was rending something precious to her, invading a fragile feminine space. In church he loved standing tall at her side and hearing her frail, crystalline voice lift up the words of the hymns. He basked in her gravity, which had something shy about it, and even uncertain, as if she feared that an excess of feeling might leap from the musty old forms and overwhelm her. He knew the forms; he had been raised as a Presbyterian, though only his mother attended services, and then only on those Sundays when she wasn't needed in the fields or at the barn. Jeanette had resisted, at first, his accompanying her. It would be, she murmured, distracting. And it was true; her shy, uncertain reverence made him, perversely, want to turn and hug her and lift her up with a shout of pride and animal gladness.

    He was twenty-eight, and she was twenty-five—old enough that marriage might have slipped her by. Her composure, the finished neatness of her figure, already seemed a touch old-maidenly. She shared rooms with another young woman on Marlborough Street; he lived on Joy, on the dark, Cambridge Street side of Beacon Hill. She had been going to church at the brick Copley Methodist over on Newbury Street, with its tall domed bell tower and Byzantine gold-leaf ceiling. Brad found within an easy walk of his own apartment—down Chamber Street as it curved, and then up a little court opposite the Mayhew School—a precious oddity, a Greek Revival clapboard church tucked among the brick tenements of the West End. Built by the Unitarians in the 1830s and taken over by the Wesleyans during their post-Civil War resurgence, the little building had box pews, small leaded panes of gray glass, and an oak pulpit shaped somewhat like a bass viol. Brad was to remember with special fondness coming here with Jeanette for the Wednesday-night Lenten services, on raw spring nights when the east wind brought the smell of brine in from the harbor. The narrow dim streets bent and resounded as they imagined old quarters in Europe did; the young couple walked through the babble and cooking odors of Jewish and Italian and Lithuanian families, and then came to this closet of Protestantism, this hushed vacant space—scarcely a dozen heads in the pews, and the church so chilly that overcoats were left on. There was no choir, and each shift of weight on a pew seat rang out like a cough. Perhaps Brad was still an unbeliever at that point, for he relished (as if he were whispering a joke to Jeanette) the emptiness, the chill, the pathos of the aged minister's trite and halting sermon as once again the old clergyman, set down to die in this dying parish, led his listeners along the worn path to the Crucifixion and the bafflement beyond. During these pathetic sermons Brad's mind would range wonderfully far, a falcon scouting his future, while Jeanette sat at his side, compact and still

14. MADE IN HEAVEN

and exquisite. She would lift him up, he felt. In the virtual vacancy of this old meetinghouse she seemed most intimately his.

Roosevelt was newly President then, and Curley was still mayor; their boasts came true, the country survived. The precious little hollow church, with its wooden Ionic columns and viol-shaped pulpit, was swept away in the fifties with the tenements of the West End. By this time Brad and Jeanette had moved with their children to Newton and become Episcopalians.

On their wedding night, hoping to please her, he held her body in his arms and prayed aloud. He thanked God for bringing them together, and asked that they be allowed to live fruitful and useful lives together. The prayer in time was answered, though on this occasion it did little to relax Jeanette. Always his love of her, when distinctly professed, made her a little reserved and tense, as if a certain threat was being masked, and a trap might be sprung.

Their four children were all born healthy, and Brad's four years as a naval officer passed with no more injury to him than the devastating impression the black firmament of spattered stars made when seen from the flight deck of an aircraft carrier, in the middle of the Pacific. How little, little to the point of nothingness, he was under those stars! Even the great ship, the *Enterprise*, that held him a tall building's height above the silvery-black swells, was reduced to the size of a pinpoint in such perspective. And yet, it was he who was witnessing the stars; they knew nothing of themselves, so in this dimension he was greater than they. As far as he could reason, religion begins with this strangeness, this standstill; faith tips the balance in favor of the pinpoint. So, though he had never had Jeanette's smiling intuitions or sensations of certainty, he became in his mind a believer.

Ten years later, in the mid-fifties, he suggested they become Episcopalians, because the church was handier to the Newton house—a shingled, many-dormered affair full of corridors for vanished servants and even a cupola.

Narrow stairs wound up to a small round room that became Jeanette's "retreat." She installed rugs and pillowed furniture, did crocheting and watercolors. From its curved windows one could see to the east the red warning light topping the spire of the John Hancock Building. Brad did not need to say that his associates and clients tended to be Episcopalians, and that this church held more of the sort of people they would like to get to know. Although he never quite grew accustomed to the droning wordiness of the service and the awkward and repetitive kneeling, he did love the look of the congregation—the ruddy men with their blue blazers and ever-fresh haircuts, the sleek Episcopalian women with their furs in winter and in summer their wide pastel garden hats that showed the backs of their necks when they bowed their heads. He loved Jeanette among them, in her black silk dress and the strand of real pearls, each costing as much as a refrigerator, with which he had paid tribute to their twentieth anniversary. Money gently glimmered on her fingers and ears. All capitalism had needed, it had turned out, was an infusion of war. The postwar stock market climbed; even plumbers and grocers needed a stockbroker now. Shares Brad had picked up for peanuts in the Depression doubled in value, and redoubled every few years.

Jeanette never took quite as active a role in the life of the church as he had expected. He himself taught Sunday school, passed the plate, sat on the vestry, read the lesson. It was like a playful extension of his business life; he felt at home in the committee room, in the linoleum-floored offices and robing rooms that mere worshippers never saw. There was always some practical reason for him to be at the church Sunday mornings, whereas in growing season Jeanette often stayed home to garden, much as Brad's mother had worked in the fields. Her body had added a sturdy plumpness to that polished, glossy quality that had first enchanted him. Her Christianity, as he imagined it, was, like water sealed into an underground cistern, unchangingly pure. Standing beside her in church, hearing her small true voice lifted in song, he still felt empowered by

14. MADE IN HEAVEN

her fineness, so that in the jostle after the service his arm involuntarily crept around her waist, and he would let go only to shake the minister's overworked hand.

"I wish you wouldn't paw me in church," she said one Sunday as they drove home. "We're too middle-aged."

"I wasn't so much pawing you as steering you through the mob," he offered, embarrassed.

"I don't need to be steered." Jeanette said. She tried to stamp her foot, but the gesture was ineffectual on the carpeted car floor.

Here we are, Brad thought, in our beige Mercedes coming home from church, having a quarrel; and he had no idea why. He saw them from afar, with the eyes of aspiration, like a handsome mature couple in a four-color ad, and there was no imperfection in the picture. "If I can't help touching you," he said, "it's because I still love you. Isn't that good?"

"It is," she said sulkily, then added, "Are you sure it's me you love or just some idea you have of me?"

This seemed to Brad a finicking distinction. She was positing a "real" her, a person apart from the one he was married to. But who would this be, unless it was the woman who took a cup of tea and went up the winding stairs to her cupola at odd hours? This woman disappeared. And no sooner did she disappear, when he was home, than two children began fighting, or the dry cleaner's delivery truck pulled into the driveway, and she had to be called down again.

"Did it ever occur to you," she asked now, "that you love me because it suits you? That for you it's an exercise in male power?"

"My God," he said indignantly, "who have you been reading? Would you rather I loved you because it *didn't* suit me?"

"That would be more romantic," she admitted, in her smallest, tidiest voice, and he knew this was a conciliatory joke, and their mysterious lapse of harmony would be smoothed away.

He became head of the vestry, and spent hours at the church, politicking, soothing ruffled feathers. After the last of the children had been confirmed and excused from faithful attendance, Jeanette began to go to the eight o'clock service, before Brad was fully awake. She would return, shiny-faced, just as he was settling, a bit foggy and hung over, into a second cup of coffee and the sheaves of the Sunday *Globe*. She loved the lack of a sermon, she said, and the absence of that oppressive choir with those Fred Waring-like arrangements. She did not say that she enjoyed being by herself in church, as she had been in Boston many years ago. At the ten o'clock service, he missed her, the thin sweet piping of her singing beside him. He felt naked, as when alone on the deck of the imperiled *Enterprise*. He explained to Jeanette that he would happily push himself out of bed and go with her to the eight o'clock, but the committee people he had to talk to expected him to be at the ten o'clock. She relented, gradually, and resumed her place at his side. But she complained at the length of the sermon, and winced when the choir came on too strong. Brad wondered if their sons, who had become more or less anti-establishment, and incidentally antichurch, had infected her with their rebellion.

Ike was President, and then JFK. Joseph Kennedy, when Brad was young, had been a man to gossip about in Boston financial circles—a cocky mick with the bad taste not only to make a pot of money but then to leave Boston and head up the SEC under Roosevelt and his raving liberals. The nuances of the regional Irish-Yankee feud escaped and amused Brad, since to his midwestern eyes the two hostile camps were very similar—thin-skinned, clubby men from damp green islands, fond of a nip and long, malicious stories. Though Brad eventually lived all his adult life in and around Boston, he never could catch the accent, never bring himself to force his *a*'s and to say "Cuber" and "idear" the way the young president did so ringingly on television.

With their own young, the Schaeffers were lucky—the boys were a bit too

14. MADE IN HEAVEN

old to fall into the heart of the drugs craze, and the girls were safely married before just living together became fashionable. One boy didn't finish college and became a carpenter in Vermont; the other did finish, at Amherst, but then moved to the West Coast to live. The two girls, however, stayed in the area, and provided new grandchildren at regular intervals. Brad's wedding-night prayer was, to all appearances, still being answered.

As the sixties wore into the seventies, some misfortunes befell the Schaeffers as well as the country. Both daughters went through messy divorces, involving countersuing husbands, scandalous depositions, and odd fits of nocturnal violence on the weedless lawns and in the neo-colonial bedrooms of Wellesley and Dover. Freddy, the son on the West Coast, never could seem to get what would be called a job; he was always "in" things—in real estate, in public relations, in investments—without ever drawing a salary or making, as far as Brad could figure, a profit. Like Brad, Freddy had turned gray early, and suddenly there he was, well over thirty, a gray-haired boy, sweet-natured and with gracious, expensive tastes, who had never found his way into the economy. It worried Jeanette that to keep him going out there they were robbing the other children, especially the carpenter son, who by now had become a condo contractor and part-owner of a ski resort. They were grieved but at some level not surprised when poor Freddy was found dead in Glendale, of what was called an accidental drug overdose. A cocaine habit had backed him, financially, to the wall. He was found neatly dressed in a blue blazer and linen slacks—to the end, a gentleman, something Brad, in his own mind, had never become.

The Newton house huge and empty around them, the couple talked of moving to an apartment, but it seemed easier to turn off the radiators in a few rooms and stay where they were. Amid the ramparts of familiar furniture were propped and hung photographs of the children at happy turning points—graduations, marriages, trips abroad. This grinning, tinted population extended now into the third generation, and was realer, more present, than the intermittent notes and phone calls from the children themselves. Brad knew in the abstract that he had changed diapers, driven boys to hockey and girls to ballet, supervised bedtime prayers, paternally stood by while tears were being shed and games were being played and the traumas of maturation endured; yet he could not muster much actual sensation of parenthood—those years were like a television sitcom during which he sat watching himself play the father. More vivid, returning in such unexpected detail that his eyes stung and the utter lostness of it all made him gasp, were moments of his and Jeanette's Boston days in the L-shaped apartment on St. Botolph Street and then in the fifth-floor Commonwealth Avenue place with its leaky skylight and birdcage elevator, and of old times at the firm, before it moved from the walnut-paneled offices on Milk Street to a flimsy, flashy new skyscraper on State. Certain business epiphanies—workday afternoons when an educated guess paid off in spades, or a carefully cultivated friendship produced a big commission—could still put the taste of triumph in his mouth. Fun like that had fled the business when the sixties bull market had collapsed. The people he had looked up to, the crusty Yankee money managers, had all retired. Brad himself retired at the age of sixty-eight, the same summer that Nixon resigned. In his loneliness those first months, in his guilty unease at being out of business uniform, he would visit Jeanette in her cupola.

  She did not say she minded, but everything seemed to halt when he climbed the last pie-slice-shaped steps, so the room had the burnished silence of a clock that has just stopped ticking. She sat surrounded by windows, lit from all sides, her soft brown hair scarcely touched by gray and the wrinkles of her face none of them deep, so that her head seemed her youthful head, softened by a webbed veil. The rug she had been hooking was set in its frame at the side of her armchair, and a magazine lay in her lap, but she did not appear to be doing anything—so deeply engaged in gazing out a window through

14. MADE IN HEAVEN

the tops of the beeches that she did not even move her head at his entrance. Her motionlessness slightly frightened him. He stood a second, getting his breath. Where just the tip of the old Hancock Building had once shown above the treetops, now a silvery cluster of tall glass boxes reflected the sun. He had always been nervous in high places, and as his eyes plunged down, parallel with her gaze, through the bare winter branches toward the dead lawn three stories below, his bowels tightened and he shuffled self-protectively toward the center of the room.

Since she said nothing, he asked, "Do you feel all right?"

"Of course," Jeanette answered, firmly. "Why wouldn't I?"

"I don't know, my dear. You seem so quiet."

"I like being quiet. I always have. You know that."

"Oh yes." He felt challenged and slightly dazed. "I know that."

"So let's think of something for you to do," she said, at last turning, with one of her usual neat motions, to give him her attention. And she would send him back down, down to the basement, say, to reglaze a storm window a neighbor child had broken with a golf ball. It was strange, Brad reflected, that in this room of her own Jeanette had hung no pictures of the children, or of him. But then, there was little wall space between the many windows, and the cushioned window seats, two-thirds of the way around the room, were littered with old paintings, crocheted cushions, and books whose cloth covers the circling sun had bleached. He thought of it as her meditation room, though he had no clear idea of what meditation was; in even the silent seconds inserted between rote petitions at church, his own brain skidded off into that exultant plotting that divine service stimulated in him.

Her illness came on imperceptibly at first, and then with cruel speed. They were watching television one night—the hostages had been taken in Iran, and every day it seemed something *had* to happen. Suddenly Jeanette put her hand on his wrist. They were sitting side by side on the red upholstered Hepplewhite-style settee, or love seat, that they had impulsively bought at Paine's in the late forties, during a blizzard, before the move to Newton. Because of the storm, the vast store had been nearly empty, and it seemed they must do something to justify their presence, and to celebrate the weather. His love for her always returned full force when it snowed. "What?" he asked now, startled by her unaccustomed gesture.

"Nothing." She smiled. "A tiny pain."

"Where?" he asked, monosyllabic as if just awakened. The news at that moment showed an interview with a young Iranian revolutionary who spoke fluent, midwestern-accented English, and Jeanette's exact answer escaped Brad. If in the course of their marriage there was one act for which he blamed himself, could identify as a sin for which he deserved to be punished, it was this moment of inattention, when Jeanette first, after weeks of hugging her discomforts to herself, began to confide, in her delicate voice, what she would rather have kept hidden.

The days that followed, full of doctors and their equipment, lifted all secrecy from the disease and its course. It was cancer, metastasizing from the liver, though she had never been a drinker. For Brad, these days were busy ones. After five years of retirement, of not knowing quite what to do with himself, he was suddenly housekeeper, cook, chauffeur, switchboard operator, nurse. Isolated in their big house, while their three children anxiously visited and then hurried back to their own problems, and their friends and neighbors tried to tread the thin line between kindness and interference, the couple that winter had a kind of honeymoon. An air of adventure, of the exotic, tinged their excursions to clinics and specialists tucked into sections of Boston they had never visited before. They spent all their hours together, and became more than ever one. His own scalp itched as her soft hair fell away under the barrage of chemotherapy; his own stomach ached when she would not eat. She would greet with a bright smile the warmth and aroma of the food he would bring to

14. MADE IN HEAVEN

the table or her bed, and she would take one forkful, so she could tell him how good it was; then, with a magical slowness meant to make the gesture invisible, Jeanette would let the fork slowly sink back to the plate, keeping her fingers on its silver handle as if at any moment she might decide to use it again. In this position she sometimes even dozed off, under the sway of medication. Brad learned to treat her not eating as a social lapse he must overlook. If he urged the food upon her, sternly or playfully, real anger, of the petulant sudden kind that a child harbors, would break through her stoical, drugged calm.

The other irritant, strangely, seemed to be the visits of the young Episcopalian clergyman. He had come to their church this year, after the long reign of a hearty facetious man no one had had to take seriously. The new man had a self-conscious, honey-smooth voice and curly blond hair already receding, young as he was, back from his temples. Brad, who of course knew of the infighting among the search-committee members that had preceded his selection, admired his melodious sermons and his conservative demeanor; ten years ago a clergyman his age would have been trying to radicalize everybody. But Jeanette complained that his visits to the house tired her, though they rarely extended for more than fifteen minutes. When she became too frail, too emaciated and constantly drowsy, to leave her bedroom, and the young man offered to bring Communion to her, she asked Brad to tell him, "Another time."

The room at Mass. General Hospital to which she was eventually moved overlooked, across a great air well, a brick wall of windows identical with hers. The wing was modern, built on the rubble of the old West End. It was late March, the first spring of a new decade. Though on sunny days a few giggling nurses and hardy patients took their lunches on cardboard trays out to the patio at the base of the air well, the sky was usually an agitated gray and the hospital heat was turned way up. During his visits Brad often removed his suit coat, it was so hot in Jeanette's room.

Dressed in a white hospital johnny and a pink quilted bed jacket with ribbons, she looked pretty against her pillows, though on a smaller scale than the woman he had known so long. Her cheeks still had some plumpness, and her fine straight nose and clear eyes and narrow arched brows—old-fashioned eyebrows that looked plucked, though they weren't—still made the compact, highly finished impression that had always excited him, her tidy face like a kindling within him. Her hair was growing back, a cap of soft brown bristle, since chemotherapy had been abandoned. Only her hands, laid inert and fleshless on the blanket, betrayed that something terrible was happening to her.

One day she told him, with a touch of mischief, "Our young parson was in from Newton this morning, and I told him not to bother anymore."

"You sent the priest away?" Brad's aged voice seemed to rumble and crackle in his ears, in contrast to Jeanette's, crystalline and distant as wind chimes.

"'Priest,' for heaven's sake," she said. "Why can't you just call him a minister?" It had been a joke of sorts between them, how High Church he had become. When on occasion they had visited the Church of the Advent on Brimmer Street, she had scorned the incense, the robed teams of acolytes. "He makes me tired," she said.

"But don't you want to keep up with Communion?" It was his favorite sacrament; he harbored an inner image, a kind of religious fantasy, of the wafer and wine turning, with a muffled explosion, to pure light in the digestive system.

"Like 'keeping up' an insurance policy," she sighed, and did sound tired, tired to death. "It seems so pointless."

"But you *must*," Brad said, panicked.

"I must? Why must I? Who says I must?" The blue of her challenging eyes and the fevered flush of her cheeks made a garish contrast.

"Why, because... you know why. Because of the salvation of your soul. That's what you used to talk about when I first met you."

14. MADE IN HEAVEN

She looked toward the window with a faint smile. "When I used to go alone to Copley Methodist. I loved that church; it was so bizarre, with its minaret. Dear old Doctor Stidger, on and on. Now it's just a parking lot. Salvation of the soul." Her gaunt chest twitched—a laugh that didn't reach her lips.

He lowered his eyes, feeling mocked. His own hands, an old man's gnarled spotted claws, were folded together between his knees. "You mean you don't believe?" In his inner ear he felt all the height of space concealed beneath the floor, down and down.

"Oh, darling," she said. "Doesn't it just seem an awful lot of bother?"

"Not a bit?" he persisted.

Jeanette sighed again and didn't answer.

"Since when?"

"I don't know. No," she said, "that's not being honest. We should start being honest. I do know. Since you took it from me. You moved right in. It didn't seem necessary, for the *two* of us to keep it up."

"But..." He couldn't say, so late, how fondly he had intended it, enlisting at her side.

She offered to console him, "It doesn't matter, does it?" When he remained silent, feeling blackness all about him, to every point on the horizon, as on those nights in the Pacific, she shifted to a teasing note: "Honey, why does it matter?"

She knew. Because his death was also close. He lifted his eyes and saw her as enviably serene, having wrought this vengeance. A nurse rustled at the door, her syringe tingling in its aluminum tray, and across the air well in the blue spring twilight, the lights had come on, rectangles of gold. It had begun, a few dry flakes, to spit snow.

Though she had asked that there be absolutely no religious service, Brad and the young minister arranged one, following the oldest-fashioned, impersonal rite. Jeanette would have been seventy-one in May, and he was three years older. He continued to go to the ten o'clock service, his erect figure carrying his white hair like a flag. But it was sheer inert motion, there were no falcon flights of his mind anymore, no small true voice at his side. There was nothing. He wished he could think otherwise, but he had believed in her all those years and could not stop now.

作品赏析

一、约翰·厄普代克与文学创作

厄普代克（John Updike，1932—2009），当代美国著名小说家、诗人，1932年3月18日生于美国宾夕法尼亚州瑞丁市。他的一生著述颇丰，涉及多种类别，有短篇小说、长篇小说、诗歌，还有音乐评论、艺术评论、社会时评等。

厄普代克是家里唯一的孩子，这在20世纪30年代的美国并不多见。父亲是当地高中的科学课老师，母亲是一位作家。父母都受过良好的教育，注重人文教化。母亲在幼年的厄普代克心里播下了文学和艺术的种子——厄普代克对写作和绘画尤其是文学产生了浓厚的兴趣。比较特别的是，他对幽默故事和神秘故事情有独钟，他大量阅读此类作品，甚至到了痴迷的程度，但这并没有影响他的学业。可以说，天赋和出类拔萃的学业都属于他。他十几岁时便在杂志上发表诗歌作品，而且诗歌创作没有停止过，与小说创作一起贯穿他的整个写作生涯。高中毕业时，厄普代克代表毕业生在毕业典礼上致辞，是两位获此殊荣的学生之一。同时，他收到哈佛大学的奖学金，前往哈佛大学主修英文。在校期间，他为哈佛大学《讽刺》杂志撰稿、设计插图。这是他早期的写作实践，以幽默作品为主。

大学期间，厄普代克续写他优等生的历史，并与当时在莱德克里夫求学的玛丽·佩灵顿恋爱。大学毕业前，两人步入婚姻的殿堂。1954年，他的一篇小说和一首诗在《纽约客》杂志上发表。这是他写作生涯的一个重要节点。此后，因为儿时的艺术梦，他携妻子去了英国，就读于罗斯金美术学院。再后来，厄普代克夫妇返回美国并在纽约市定居下来。厄普代克成为《纽约客》"城中话题"栏目的专栏作家。值得一提的是，厄普代克的创作生涯与《纽约客》有太多的交集，他在这本杂志上发表了大量的时文、诗歌、小说和评论文章。

14. MADE IN HEAVEN

他的第一部诗集《木匠母鸡和其他驯兽》(*The Carpentered Hen and Other Tame Creatures*)出版于1958年,颇受好评。终其一生,他诗歌创作的成就可比肩他的小说创作。主要诗歌作品有《面对大自然》(*Facing Nature: Poems*,1985)、《诗集1953—1993》(*Collected Poems: 1953–1993*)、《美利坚及其他诗集》(*Americana and Other Poems*,2001)。

他在第一部小说《贫民院集市》(*The Poorhouse Fair*,1959)中进一步展露了自己的才华,得到了评论界的肯定。接下来他的第二部长篇小说《兔子,跑吧》(*Rabbit, Run*,1960)大获成功,从此他开始了"兔子"系列小说持续三十余年的写作,并凭此系列小说两次获得普利策奖。小说《半人半马兽》(*The Centaur*,1963)获得了1964年的国家图书奖。1964年,33岁的厄普代克入选全国文学艺术协会,是协会成立以来获此荣誉的最年轻的作家。

20世纪70年代,他开始创作一个新的"贝克"系列小说,围绕主人公亨利·贝克置身于内在与外在、个人与他人、过去与现在的种种纷繁、错综变化的情形来展现其观察、体验、认知的过程,呈现个人选择与传统价值信念的冲突,以及内在的情感心理与外部现实的纠葛。

进入80年代,厄普代克仍然处于创作的活跃期,继续他的"兔子"系列(《兔子富了》,*Rabbit Is Rich*,1981,获普利策奖)和"贝克"系列(《贝克归来》,*Beck Is Back*,1982)。后来的作品有《东镇的女巫们》(*The Witches of Eastwick*,1984)、《兔子歇了》(*Rabbit at Rest*,1991,获普利策奖)、《葛特露和克劳狄斯》(*Gertrude and Claudius*,2000,故事取材于《哈姆雷特》)、《恐怖分子》(*Terrorist*,2006)。

厄普代克的短篇小说集有《同一扇门》(*The Same Door*,1959)、《鸽子的羽毛》(*Pigeon Feathers*,1962)、《博物馆和女人》(*Museums and Women*,1972)、《问题成堆》(*Problems*,1979)、《相信我》(*Trust Me*,1987)、《父亲的眼泪及其他故事》(*My Father's Tears and Other Stories*,2009)。厄普代克的短篇小说一如他的长篇小说,多涉及美国中产阶级的情感、婚姻、家庭、信仰等主题。

厄普代克的长篇小说中,"兔子"系列小说占有举足轻重的地位,总共四部,称为"兔子四部曲",依次为《兔子,跑吧》(1960)、《兔子归来》

(*Rabbit Redux*,1971)、《兔子富了》(1981)、《兔子歇了》(1991)。仅《兔子富了》就屡获大奖:普利策文学奖、国家图书奖、美国书评协会奖。从写作和出版的时期来看,这四部小说跨度有三十余年,既独立成篇,又相互关联。

一如厄普代克的其他作品,"兔子系列"也以美国中产阶级的生活为题材或描述对象,以绰号"兔子"的哈利从青年到老年的人生历程为主要线索,但是他所经历的婚恋、家庭、情爱、逃避、沮丧及其所折射出来的社会文化意涵远远超出个人的范畴,超越个体上升到了群体、时代的范畴,具有普遍性。

二、人物和故事情节

《天堂制造》讲述的故事时间跨度大约五十年。主要人物只有两位——布莱德·夏厄弗和珍妮特·汉得森。他们均是商务白领。他们的相识就是故事展开的起点。那是20世纪30年代在波士顿的一次公司圣诞聚会上。这是一次寻常却又不寻常的相遇。说寻常,因为圣诞年年有;说不寻常,因为这次圣诞聚会的背景是大萧条年代的肃杀氛围。彼时,布莱德是个思想激进的青年,"期望资本主义十年内就完蛋,连同教会一起消失"。尽管布莱德还有体面的工作,尚不至于流落街头挨饿,但糟糕的情形还是不停地把恐怖的一面呈现出来:"十二月的街道上有一种阴郁的气氛。传到办公室的统计数据使得圣诞颂歌的欢快显得不对味。波士顿的商务楼的正门入口一般都修得深,装饰得像哥特式教堂,饥肠辘辘的人向外张望,痛苦而又麻木,连乞讨都不想。每天早上在这样的公共地方总能找到冻僵的尸体。"(There was a gloom in the December streets, and in the statistics that came to the office, that made the cheer of Christmas carols sound obscene. From the deep doorways of Boston's business buildings, ornamented like little Gothic chapels with carvings and ironwork, people actually starving peered out, too bitter and numb to beg. Each morning the Common was combed for bodies.)大萧条所造成的社会惨剧由此可见一斑。回顾20世纪30年代,美国社会弥漫着绝望和怀疑的情绪,看似繁荣的经济形势急转直下,社会财富随着经济泡沫的破裂急剧减少,这些都加深了人们对资本主义和宗教信仰的怀疑。

但他钟情的女子珍妮特却有虔诚的宗教信仰。就这样,两个年轻人不是志同道合,而是带着怀疑和信仰的冲突相遇了。随后,两人相恋,结婚,生儿育女,

14. MADE IN HEAVEN

遭遇家庭矛盾、信仰冲突。他们见证了美国社会历史的变迁。他们的经历是一部社会编年史的微缩景观，既有作为背景一闪而过的重大历史事件，又不乏平淡琐碎的众生百态。

布莱德为了追求珍妮特，主动陪她一起去教堂。但在很长的一段时间里，布莱德人在教堂，心却在珍妮特身上。"在教堂里，他喜欢高大地站在她身边，听她用少女般水晶透明的声音高声朗诵赞美诗。布莱德沉浸在她庄重的气质中……"（In church he loved standing tall at her side and hearing her frail, crystalline voice lift up the words of the hymns. He basked in her gravity...）充盈他心里的是坠入情网的美妙体验，无论所处的场景是在大街上、音乐厅还是教堂，他想象自己"变成了一个绅士，一个护花使者，一个骑士"（a gentleman, an escort, a gallant）。但此时，他内心还不是一个信教者。即便后来布莱德求婚成功，两人步入婚姻的殿堂，这种情况也持续了很久。因此，可以说他去教堂不是因为信教，而只是为了享受与珍妮特在一起的感觉，或者是教堂的"空寂"更贴近珍妮特脱俗的气质，因为"他觉得她会让他升华"（She would lift him up, he felt）。

婚后的家庭生活丰衣足食，四个孩子相继出生。小说提到"罗斯福新近当选了总统。科利还当他的市长。他们的大话兑现了，国家劫后余生"（Roosevelt was newly President then, and Curley was still mayor; their boasts came true, the country survived）。罗斯福的新政让美国从大萧条的深渊里爬了出来的背景被作者一笔带过。

1941年，美国加入了第二次世界大战。布莱德参军入伍，成了海军军官，在航空母舰"企业号"上服役。伫立于航行在太平洋中部海域的航空母舰的甲板上，他受到了强烈的震撼：宇宙浩瀚无垠，人或人造之物（如巨兽般的航空母舰）也微不足道。感受到自身的"渺小"，他开始走近"信仰"。

战后的美国经济繁荣，财富增长，"现在即便是管道工和杂货商也需要股票经纪人。布莱德在大萧条时代购入了微不足道的股票，价格已翻了一番，而且每隔几年又翻一番"（...even plumbers and grocers needed a stockbroker now. Shares Brad had picked up for peanuts in the Depression doubled in value, and doubled again, and more）。但是，股票市场先走牛后崩盘，似乎熟悉的一幕在重演；城市也发生了巨大的变化。原来从家里的窗户望出去只有一座大厦的塔尖，后来摩天大楼越盖越多，占据了全部的视线，"现在可以看到许多高大的闪亮建筑——一个个反射着阳光的玻璃盒子"（now a silvery cluster of tall glass boxes reflected the sun）。富足和繁荣似乎是战后美国的标签，"在一件件熟悉的家具上立着或挂着孩子们在各个幸福的人生转折点拍下的照片——毕业照、结婚照、海外旅行照。咧着嘴笑、衣着花哨的这些人已生养出了第三代"（Throughout the rooms of familiar furniture were propped and hung photographs of the children at happy turning points—graduations, marriages, trips abroad. This grinning, tinted population extended now into the third generation...）。然而，物质繁荣的背后还有另一面，儿女们碰上一个毒品和性乱成为时髦的年代。一个儿子无所事事，死于吸毒，"弗雷迪因使用毒品过量，被发现死在克朗代尔。他们感到伤心，但并不太觉意外。吸食可卡因的习惯搞得他一贫如洗。尸体被发现时，他穿戴整齐——法兰绒的上衣，亚麻面料的裤子——终于在死的时候，他像一位绅士了"（...poor Freddy was found dead in Glendale, of what was called an accidental drug overdose. A cocaine habit had backed him, financially, to the wall. He was found neatly dressed in a blue blazer and linen slacks—to the end a gentleman...）。女儿们因频发的性丑闻先后离婚，声名狼藉。时代的变化与个人生活交织缠绕，布莱德夫妇精神上渐生疏离。

　　布莱德感受到了家庭的变化，儿女"已变得多少有些反体制，有时也反宗教"（more or less anti-establishment, and incidentally antichurch），而且珍妮特也变得有些"反叛"。她开始对教堂里的布道时间偏长、唱诗班的声音偏大有微词。不仅如此，在家里她更愿意一个人独处，在自己的房间里静静地沉思。但布莱德并不知道她在"默想"什么。"这样房间里就有一种闹钟停摆产生的平和静默⋯⋯她腿上放着一本杂志，但她现在什么也没有做——她望着窗外，目光穿过山毛榉的树梢，深深沉浸在注目凝望中。"（...so the room had the burnished silence of a clock that has just stopped ticking, ...and a magazine lay in her lap, but she did not appear to be doing anything—so deeply engaged in gazing out a window through the tops of the beeches...）布莱德感受到了周遭有一种氛围让他止步于房间。

　　他们的角色开始换位：布莱德变得越来越像虔诚的教徒了，他在教堂里读圣经,做杂务,礼拜天上午的时间都安排给了教堂事务,而珍妮特却不再积极参与教堂事务。后来,珍妮特被确诊患了肝癌。在生命行将终结的阴影下,珍妮特虽然没有明说,但在言语之中表露出她与曾经虔诚信奉的宗教信仰渐行渐远。她与布莱德的平静对话中暗含冲突。年轻的牧师提议把圣餐带到病房来,但她让布莱德转达她的婉拒,后来她干脆直接告诉牧师以后不用再来了。珍妮特给出的理由是"他让我厌烦"("He makes me tired")。但她的恼怒似乎不仅仅是针对牧师。

在死亡迫近时,珍妮特拒绝了领圣餐的仪式,她说,"就像'续购'保险……已经没有意义了"("Like keeping up an insurance policy, ...It seems so pointless")。她已不再信奉灵魂的救赎,要求布莱德在她离世后绝对不要举行宗教葬礼仪式。但布莱德还是在葬礼上安排了简单的宗教仪式。此后布莱德的生活延续着此前的惯性,但他似乎也与从前不一样了,至少他失去了珍妮特——他曾经的"信念"。

这对夫妇与美国一起经历了罗斯福、艾森豪威尔、肯尼迪、尼克松四个总统当政的时期,他们的经历对应着20世纪美国的社会历程,他们看上去幸福的婚姻却潜藏长达半个世纪的"五味杂陈",内中既有个人的冲突,也有社会冲突的反映。

三、写作技巧和主题

这篇小说凸显了厄普代克的写作特点或曰写作技巧,其中之一是化繁为简。针对短篇小说,亨利·詹姆斯(Henry James)认为,短篇小说在表现时间的进程和其对人物的复杂影响方面是受到限制的。[1] 厄普代克也承认:"让短篇小说去覆盖很长的时间跨度并把时间里最深刻的东西展露出来,这并不容易。"[2] 短篇小说的篇幅有限,但这并不意味着"容量有限"。《天堂制造》仅一万余词,却覆盖了长达半个世纪的时空。重大的社会历史事件与个人生活被同步展现出来,于交织互动中演绎。化繁为简主要指的是把大事件粗略化,

---

1 Henry James, qtd in "Introduction", *New American Short Stories: The Writers Select Their Own Favorites*, ed., Gloria Norris, New York: New American Library, 1986, pp. 1-8.
2 John Updike, qtd in "Introduction", *New American Short Stories: The Writers Select Their Own Favorites*, pp. 1-8.

或者说是化大为小。小说对历史背景的介绍像是一个极其简略的编年史，简略到用只言片语一笔带过。由于这些信息的碎片可能是一个人名、一个事件或一则新闻，读者需要在阅读的过程中重建小说的时间线，补足这些相关的信息才能更好地理解小说中的人物和发生在这些人物身上的事情，把时间线上的点连缀起来才可看清两者的互动。文学批评家弗莱（Northrop Frye）指出，文学是介于音乐和绘画之间的艺术，既有音乐的时间性，也有绘画的空间性。[1] 读者把握好这篇小说的时空结构，便能更好地理清人物与时间、人物与事件之间的脉络。如，小说中描写的12月"阴郁的气氛"、糟糕的统计数据、"痛苦而又麻木"的倒毙街头的饿殍，这些文字无疑指向美国历史上的经济崩溃引发的灾难——大萧条；罗斯福的"大话"指的是他为应对大萧条推行的新政；与"四年的海军军官生涯"关联的是第二次世界大战；"艾克做了总统，然后是JFK"关联的是战后五六十年代；"尼克松总统辞职""伊朗爆发了人质事件"关联到70年代，前者缘起"水门事件"丑闻，后者显示美国遇到的外部挑战，两者都让美国人感到深深的沮丧。

在把宏观背景粗略化的同时，厄普代克对微观层面的个体进行精心细致的刻画，从外在到心理，用第三人称叙述、人物对话呈现生活、情感之细微处。有研究者认为厄普代克的作品是现实主义的。这一点在厄普代克的小说中是可以找到佐证的。厄普代克在创作中没有运用太多实验性或先锋派的标新立异的手法，他把关注的普通人所经历的、在岁月的流淌中展现的生活用文字呈现出来。不过，这种呈现不是对现实的简单复制，而是带有他的思考和领悟。

此外，厄普代克运用对比的手法来展现差异。如，最主要的差异体现在布莱德夫妇与儿女在价值观念、生活方式上的冲突，通过对比展现两代人对婚姻、家庭、宗教、传统的态度以及时代的变迁。又如，老牧师和年轻牧师为两代人，他们的区别也多少体现了社会环境的变化。布莱德夫妇与老教士的相遇是在大萧条时期，老教士的布道也许更有受难和苍凉的意味，"老教士早已决心在这个奄奄一息的教区传教到死。他的布道充满悲悯，语句时断时续，又一次带着他的信众

---

1 Northrop Frye, "The Archetypes of Literature", *Criticism: Major Statements,* eds. Charles Kaplan and William Davis Anderson, Boston & New York: Bedford/St. Martins, 2000, p. 481.

沿荆棘之路走向受难和未知的痛苦"（...the old clergyman, set down to die in this dying parish, led his listeners along the worn path to the Crucifixion and the bafflement beyond）。而年轻牧师的出现已是20世纪70年代，他的声音自信、悦耳，布道富于韵律，注重领圣餐之类的仪式。

　　探究这篇小说的主题，应先从小说标题做一番思考。小说的英文标题是"Made in Heaven"，那么是否应该理解为"天作之合"或"天造地设"？这里其实大有考究。如果理解为"天作之合"或"天造地设"，那么表达出来的就是婚姻美满的意思。可是小说中布莱德夫妇的婚姻并不美满，他们逐渐产生隔阂、冲突，走向疏离。而且，小说似乎还想表达多重含义：许多事情的发生，其起因和结果都不是个人能控制的，个人和群体受制于某种"超然在上"的力量，由天命或某种冥冥之中的力量主宰，因而，把小说标题理解为"天堂制造"更能彰显小说的主题意涵。

　　虽然厄普代克的小说有现实主义的因素，但他关注的并不是外部的环境（尽管环境会对人施加影响），而是人的存在，探究的是人性和人的生存状况在内外因素交织作用下的变化。因而这篇小说不乏社会批判的表达。"资本主义最需要的东西就是战争的滋养。"这句话应被视为厄普代克借布莱德的体验和观察表达出的对资本主义的富有洞见的评判。第二次世界大战前，资本主义裹挟的种种异己力量给美国社会带来重大灾难——企业破产倒闭，雇员大量失业，财富灰飞烟灭。可是战争似乎给美国经济注入了强心剂，工商业的轮子又加速运转起来，并形成了发展的惯性。战后，股票市场成为投机的急先锋，又一次扮演了经济、财富增长的晴雨表。不过，繁荣过后是又一轮萧条。20世纪60年代，布莱德再次经历"牛市崩盘"，同时，生意场上"开心的事"也消失了。所以，资本的属性决定了资本主义通过战争获得的"滋养"并不能长久，也不能解决其固有的问题。

　　"资本主义与战争"的关系逻辑也指向对资本的拷问。资本主义与战争紧密关联，战争是暴力形式，因此支撑资本主义的资本不会是无辜的，肯定有其血腥、暴力的一面。故而，造成重大社会经济破坏的大萧条也可以说是一种杀人于无形的"暴力"，寥寥数语的描述让人震撼。曾有人问厄普代克为什么在作品中鲜有涉及暴力的描述和揭露，而把大部分篇幅放在日常生活的描写上。其实，这种说法也许忽略了厄普代克作品中的"隐蔽的暴力"。厄普代克的小说基本上没有以战乱为题材的,他以美国人的日常生活为题材,即便是在战争年代,美国本土普通人的生活也是远离战火的,因此厄普代克的聚焦点就难见显性的"暴力"。但这并不意味着厄普代克作品中没有对暴力的关注和反思。故而,"隐蔽的暴力"也是暴力,在一个混乱的、充满隐形"暴力"的时代,怀疑和焦虑的产生只能说是一个逻辑的结果。

由此可见,厄普代克的作品关注的主题与传统的现实主义小说不同。他的作品涉及自我和存在意义的主题。存在主义学说认为,应以人为出发点来理解存在,而不是以外部环境为出发点来理解人;重心不是影响人的环境,而是受环境影响的人。萨特(Jean-Paul Sartre)认为,"虚无"既内在于个体,也外在于个体,是一种"空"的状态,但"虚无"并非全然否定,正是因为"虚无"的存在,它促使个体思考、选择、行动,由此来填补"空"的"虚无"状态,让"无"中生出有意义的东西来。[1] 这样,个体便赋予了自我生命以意义。也即是说,面对困惑、怀疑和畏惧,只要不放弃对本真自我的把握和追寻,也可以面对否定生命的因素获得积极的意义。

布莱德夫妇之间的冲突也反映了双方性别立场的差异。珍妮特的"反叛"让布莱德有些茫然,不知所措。"你有没有想过,你爱我是因为爱适合你?对于你来说爱是体现男性权力的实践?"("Did it ever occur to you, ...that you love me because it suits you? That for you it's an exercise in male power?")珍妮特的发问已有一些问询女性的主体性意义的自觉,开始思考性别意识、"男性权力"这样的问题。显然,布莱德在思想层面缺少珍妮特这样的思考,缺乏对性别主体意义的理解。"天哪!你读了谁的书?"("My God, ... who have you been reading?...")当妻子提出"男性权力"这样的话题时,他的反应是惊讶和恼怒,表明他与社会思潮的脱节,以为仅仅是读了一本书的问题,而没有意识到女性性别意识的觉醒在第二次世界大战后已是普遍的社会思潮。

珍妮特通过怀疑去重新认知自己曾经笃信的宗教和熟悉的生活。她对熟悉的事务开始感到陌生。这反映了婚姻中并不鲜见的状况:夫妻转为互为熟悉的

---

1 Mary Warnock, "Jean-Paul Sartre (1)", *Existentialism*, Oxford: Oxford University Press, 1970, pp. 92-95.

陌生人。珍妮特和布莱德之间延续着对话，但心灵的沟通愈来愈少。也许，珍妮特选择了下面的方式与自己对话，做内省式的思考："一条狭窄的楼梯通向一间不大的圆形房间，这是珍妮特'独处'的地方。"（Narrow stairs wound up to a small round room that became Jeanette's "retreat."）有观点认为，生命唯有在觉察之际才存在。觉察需要通过观察、思考，获得对生活的批判性认知。看似平静的生活时不时有暗流的涌动。她对宗教仪式的微词显然是发自内心的疑虑：曾经给她以归属感的宗教信仰，现在还能给予灵魂以指引，还能担当救赎的重任吗？

珍妮特在生命最后阶段对那个年轻牧师、圣餐、宗教葬礼的表态无不透露出她内心的焦虑。平静表面下的迷茫和焦虑，彰显出求索归属感的主题，所谓的灵魂和救赎的问题，归根到底都关联到归属。

在西方文学中，灵魂的问题是几千来亘古不变的话题，无数的探究者试图一探究竟，但这是一个没有终极答案的问题，或注定永远是困惑大于认知，需要后来者对困扰古今的难题继续思考。正如福克纳在接受1949年诺贝文学奖时所言："我不想接受人类的末日的说法……我相信人类不但会历经劫难生存下去，而且还会发展兴盛。人是不朽的，并非因为是人在所有生物中拥有永不殆尽的声音，而是因为人有灵魂，有能够怜悯、牺牲和忍耐的精神。"[1] 故对应此义，厄普代克秉承了西方文学探究灵魂之归属的传统，也在现代意义上表现出对人之本体存在和生命意义的关怀。

Suggested Readings

1. Bloom, Harold, ed. *John Updike.* New York: Chelsea House, 1987.
2. Broer, Lawrence R., ed. *Rabbit Tales: Poetry and Politics in John Updike's Rabbit Novels.* Tuscaloosa: University of Alabama Press, 1998.
3. Detweiler, Robert. *John Updike.* New York: Twayne, 1972.
4. Frye, Northrop. "The Archetypes of Literature." *Criticism: Major Statements.* Charles Kaplan and William Davis Anderson, eds. Boston & New York: Bedford/

---

[1] William Faulkner, "Nobel Prize Acceptance Speech", August 15, 2020, http://www.nobel.se/laureates/literature-1949-press.html.

St. Martins, 2000.

5. Greiner, Donald J. *John Updike's Novels*. Athens: Ohio University Press, 1984.
6. James, Henry. *Selected Literary Criticism*. Norris Shapira, ed. New York: McGraw-Hill Book Company, 1965.
7. Luscher, Robert M. *John Updike: A Study of the Short Fiction*. New York: Twayne, 1993.
8. Norris, Gloria, ed. *New American Short Stories: The Writers Select Their Own Favorites*. New York: New American Library, 1986.
9. Plath, James. *Conversations with John Updike*. Jackson: University Press of Mississippi, 1994.
10. Updike, John. *Rabbit at Rest*. New York: Fawcett Crest, 1990.
11. Updike, John. *Rabbit Is Rich*. New York: Fawcett Crest, 1981.
12. Updike, John. *Rabbit Redux*. New York: Fawcett Crest, 1971.
13. Updike, John. *Rabbit, Run*. New York: Fawcett Crest, 1960.
14. Warnock, Mary. *Existentialism*. Oxford: Oxford University Press, 1970.
15. 约翰·厄普代克：《天堂制造》，查日新译，《译林》，2008年第2期，第119–126页。
16. 约翰·厄普代克：《厄普代克短篇小说集》，李康勤、王赟、杨向荣等译，上海：上海译文出版社，2019年。

Questions for Reflection

1. What is the relationship between the plotline and the timeline in Updike's short story "Made in Heaven"?

2. What is the difference between the man and woman protagonists regarding their spiritual worlds when they first meet with each other?

3. Why does the author make deliberate description of the disastrous situation caused by the Great Depression? What effect is shown by such description?

4. Why does the woman protagonist become skeptical of the traditional religious belief?

14. MADE IN HEAVEN

5. What are the typical features regarding the manner of presentation in this story?

Question for Discussion

What is the theme of the story "Made in Heaven"? How do you understand it?

（查日新　撰写）

15. RECITATIF

By Toni Morrison, 1983

My mother danced all night and Roberta's was sick. That's why we were taken to St. Bonny's. People want to put their arms around you when you tell them you were in a shelter, but it really wasn't bad. No big long room with one hundred beds like Bellevue. There were four to a room, and when Roberta and me came, there was a shortage of state kids, so we were the only ones assigned to 406 and could go from bed to bed if we wanted to. And we wanted to, too. We changed beds every night and for the whole four months we were there we never picked one out as our own permanent bed.

It didn't start out that way. The minute I walked in and the Big Bozo introduced us, I got sick to my stomach. It was one thing to be taken out of your own bed early in the morning—it was something else to be stuck in a strange place with a girl from a whole other race. And Mary, that's my mother, she was right. Every now and then she would stop dancing long enough to tell me something important and one of the things she said was that they never washed their hair and they smelled funny. Roberta sure did. Smell funny, I mean. So when the Big Bozo (nobody ever called her Mrs. Itkin, just like nobody ever said St. Bonaventure)—when she said, "Twyla, this is Roberta. Roberta, this is Twyla. Make each other welcome." I said, "My mother won't like you putting me in here."

15. RECITATIF

"Good," said Bozo. "Maybe then she'll come and take you home."

How's that for mean? If Roberta had laughed I would have killed her, but she didn't. She just walked over to the window and stood with her back to us."

"Turn around," said the Bozo. "Don't be rude. Now Twyla. Roberta. When you hear a loud buzzer, that's the call for dinner. Come down to the first floor. Any fights and no movie." And then, just to make sure we knew what we would be missing, "*The Wizard of Oz.*"

"Roberta must have thought I meant that my mother would be mad about my being put in the shelter. Not about rooming with her, because as soon as Bozo left she came over to me and said, "Is your mother sick too?"

"No," I said. "She just likes to dance all night."

"Oh," she nodded her head and I liked the way she understood things so fast. So for the moment it didn't matter that we looked like salt and pepper standing there and that's what the other kids called us sometimes. We were eight years old and got F's all the time. Me because I couldn't remember what I read or what the teacher said. And Roberta because she couldn't read at all and didn't even listen to the teacher. She wasn't good at anything except jacks, at which she was a killer: pow scoop pow scoop pow scoop.

We didn't like each other all that much at first, but nobody else wanted to play with us because we weren't real orphans with beautiful dead parents in the sky. We were dumped. Even the New York City Puerto Ricans and the upstate Indians ignored us. All kinds of kids were in there, black ones, white ones, even two Koreans. The food was good, though. At least I thought so. Roberta hated it and left whole pieces of things on her plate: Spam, Salisbury steak—even jello with fruit cocktail in it, and she didn't care if I ate what she wouldn't. Mary's idea of supper was popcorn and a can of Yoo-Hoo. Hot mashed potatoes and two weenies was like Thanksgiving for me.

It really wasn't bad, St. Bonny's. The big girls on the second floor pushed us around now and then. But that was all. They wore lipstick and eyebrow pencil and wobbled their knees while they watched TV. Fifteen, sixteen, even, some of them were. They were put-out girls, scared runaways most of them. Poor little girls who fought their uncles off but looked tough to us, and mean. God did they look mean. The staff tried to keep them separate from the younger children, but sometimes they caught us watching them in the orchard where they played radios and danced with each other. They'd light out after us and pull our hair or twist our arms. We were scared of them, Roberta and me, but neither of us wanted the other one to know it. So we got a good list of dirty names we could shout back when we ran from them through the orchard. I used to dream a lot and almost always the orchard was there. Two acres, four maybe, of these little apple trees. Hundreds of them. Empty and crooked like beggar women when I first came to St. Bonny's but fat with flowers when I left. I don't know why I dreamt about that orchard so much. Nothing really happened there. Nothing all that important, I mean. Just the big girls dancing and playing the radio. Roberta and me watching. Maggie fell down there once. The kitchen woman with legs like parentheses. And the big girls laughed at her. We should have helped her up, I know, but we were scared of those girls with lipstick and eyebrow pencil. Maggie couldn't talk. The kids said she had her tongue cut out, but I think she was just born that way: mute. She was old and sandy-colored and she worked in the kitchen. I don't know if she was nice or not. I just remember her legs like parentheses and how she rocked when she walked. She worked from early in the morning till two o'clock, and if she was late, if she had too much cleaning and didn't get out till two-fifteen or so, she'd cut through the orchard so she wouldn't miss her bus and have to wait another hour. She wore this really stupid little hat—a kid's hat with ear flaps—and she wasn't much taller than we were. A really awful little hat. Even for a mute, it was dumb—dressing like a kid and never saying anything at all.

"But what about if somebody tries to kill her?" I used to wonder about that. "Or what if she wants to cry? Can she cry?"

"Sure," Roberta said. "But just tears. No sounds come out."

"She can't scream?"

"Nope. Nothing."

"Can she hear?"

"I guess."

"Let's call her," I said. And we did.

"Dummy! Dummy!" She never turned her head

"Bow legs! Bow legs!" Nothing. She just rocked on, the chin straps of her baby-boy hat swaying from side to side. I think we were wrong. I think she could hear and didn't let on. And it shames me even now to think there was somebody in there after all who heard us call her those names and couldn't tell on us.

We got along all right, Roberta and me. Changed beds every night, got F's in civics and communication skills and gym. The Bozo was disappointed in us, she said. Out of 130 of us state cases, 90 were under twelve. Almost all were real orphans with beautiful dead parents in the sky. We were the only ones dumped and the only ones with F's in three classes including gym. So we got along—what with her leaving whole pieces of things on her plate and being nice about no tasking questions.

I think it was the day before Maggie fell down that we found out our mothers were coming to visit us on the same Sunday. We had been at the shelter twenty-eight days (Roberta twenty-eight and a half) and this was their first visit with us. Our mothers would come at ten o'clock in time for chapel, then lunch with us in the teachers' lounge. I thought if my dancing mother met her sick mother it might be good for her. And Roberta thought her sick mother would get a big bang out of a dancing one. We got excited about it and curled each other's hair. After breakfast we sat on the bed watching the road from the window. Roberta's socks were still wet. She washed them the night before and put them on the radiator to dry. They hadn't, but she put them on anyway because their tops were so pretty—scalloped in pink. Each of us had a purple construction-paper basket that we had made in craft class. Mine had a yellow crayon rabbit on it. Roberta's had eggs with wiggly lines of color. Inside were cellophane grass and just the jelly beans because I'd eaten the two marshmallow eggs they gave us. The Big Bozo came herself to get us. Smiling she told us we looked very nice and to come downstairs. We were so surprised by the smile we'd never seen before, neither of us moved.

"Don't you want to see your mommies?"

I stood up first and spilled the jelly beans all over the floor. Bozo's smile disappeared while we scrambled to get the candy up off the floor and put it back in the grass.

She escorted us downstairs to the first floor, where the other girls were lining up to file into the chapel. A bunch of grown-ups stood to one side. Viewers mostly. The old biddies who wanted servants and the fags who wanted company looking for children they might want to adopt. Once in a while a grandmother. Almost never anybody young or anybody whose face wouldn't scare you in the night. Because if any of the real orphans had young relatives they wouldn't be real orphans. I saw Mary right away. She had on those green slacks I hated and hated even more now because didn't she know we were going to chapel? And that fur jacket with the pocket linings so ripped she had to pull to get her hands out of them. But her face was pretty—like always, and she smiled and waved like she was the little girl looking for her mother—not me.

I walked slowly, trying not to drop the jelly beans and hoping the paper handle would hold. I had to use my last Chiclet because by the time I finished cutting everything out, all the Elmer's was gone. I am left-handed and the scissors never worked for me. It didn't matter, though; I might just as well have chewed the gum. Mary dropped to her knees and grabbed me, mashing the basket, the jelly beans, and the grass into her ratty fur jacket.

"Twyla, baby. Twyla, baby!"

15. RECITATIF

I could have killed her. Already I heard the big girls in the orchard the next time saying, "Twyyyyyla, baby!" But I couldn't stay mad at Mary while she was smiling and hugging me and smelling of Lady Esther dusting powder. I wanted to stay buried in her fur all day.

To tell the truth I forgot about Roberta. Mary and I got in line for the traipse into chapel and I was feeling proud because she looked so beautiful even in those ugly green slacks that made her behind stick out. A pretty mother on earth is better than a beautiful dead one in the sky even if she did leave you all alone to go dancing.

I felt a tap on my shoulder, turned, and saw Roberta smiling. I smiled back, but not too much lest somebody think this visit was the biggest thing that ever happened in my life. Then Roberta said, "Mother, I want you to meet my roommate, Twyla. And that's Twyla's mother."

I looked up it seemed for miles. She was big. Bigger than any man and on her chest was the biggest cross I'd ever seen. I swear it was six inches long each way. And in the crook of her arm was the biggest Bible ever made.

Mary, simple-minded as ever, grinned and tried to yank her hand out of the pocket with the raggedy lining—to shake hands, I guess. Roberta's mother looked down at me and then looked down at Mary too. She didn't say anything, just grabbed Roberta with her Bible-free hand and stepped tout of line, walking quickly to the rear of it. Mary was still grinning because she's not too swift when it comes to what's really going on. Then this light bulb goes off in her head and she says "That bitch!" really loud and us almost in the chapel now. Organ music whining; the Bonny Angels singing sweetly. Everybody in the world turned around to look. And Mary would have kept it up—kept calling names if I hadn't squeezed her hand as hard as I could. That helped a little, but she still twitched and crossed and uncrossed her legs all through service. Even groaned a couple of times. Why did I think she would come there and act right? Slacks. No hat like the grandmothers and viewers, and groaning all the while. When we stood for hymns she kept her mouth shut. Wouldn't even look at the words on the page. She actually reached in her purse for a mirror to check her lipstick. All I could think of was that she really needed to be killed. The sermon lasted a year, and I knew the real orphans were looking smug again.

We were supposed to have lunch in the teachers' lounge, but Mary didn't bring anything, so we picked fur and cellophane grass off the mashed jelly beans and ate them. I could have killed her. I sneaked a look at Roberta. Her mother had brought chicken legs and ham sandwiches and oranges and a whole box of chocolate-covered grahams. Roberta drank milk from a thermos while her mother read the Bible to her.

Things are not right. The wrong food is always with the wrong people. Maybe that's why I got into waitress work later—to match up the right people with the right food. Roberta just let those chicken legs sit there, but she did bring a stack of grahams up to me later when the visit was over. I think she was sorry that her mother would not shake my mother's hand. And I liked that and I liked the fact that she didn't say a word about Mary groaning all the way through the service and not bringing any lunch.

Roberta left in May when the apple trees were heavy and white. On her last day we went to the orchard to watch the big girls smoke and dance by the radio. It didn't matter that they said, "Twyyyyyla, baby." We sat on the ground and breathed. Lady Esther. Apple blossoms. I still go soft when I smell one or the other. Roberta was going home. The big cross and the big Bible was coming to get her and she seemed sort of glad and sort of not. I thought I would die in that room of four beds without her and I knew Bozo had plans to move some other dumped kid in there with me. Roberta promised to write every day, which was really sweet of her because she couldn't read a lick so how could she write anybody. I would have drawn pictures and sent them to her but she never gave me her address. Little by little she faded. Her wet socks with the pink scalloped tops and her big serious-looking eyes—that's all I could catch when I tried to

15. RECITATIF

bring her to mind.

I was working behind the counter at the Howard Johnson's on the Thruway just before the Kingston exit. Not a bad job. Kind of a long ride from Newburgh, but okay once I got there. Mine was the second night shift—eleven to seven. Very light until a Greyhound checked in for breakfast around six-thirty. At that hour the sun was all the way clear of the hills behind the restaurant. The place looked better at night—more like shelter—but I loved it when the sun broke in, even if it did show all the cracks in the vinyl and the speckled floor looked dirty no matter what the mop boy did.

It was August and a bus crowd was just unloading. They would stand around a long while: going to the john, and looking at gifts and junk-for-sale machines, reluctant to sit down so soon. Even to eat. I was trying to fill the coffee pots and get them all situated on the electric burners when I saw her. She was sitting in a booth smoking a cigarette with two guys smothered in head and facial hair. Her own hair was so big and wild I could hardly see her face. But the eyes. I would know them anywhere. She had on a powder-blue halter and shorts outfit and earrings the size of bracelets. Talk about lipstick and eyebrow pencil. She made the big girls look like nuns. I couldn't get off the counter until seven o'clock, but I kept watching the booth in case they got up to leave before that. My replacement was on time for a change, so I counted and stacked my receipts as fast as I could and signed off. I walked over to the booths, smiling and wondering if she would remember me. Or even if she wanted to remember me. Maybe she didn't want to be reminded of St. Bonny's or to have anybody know she was ever there. I know I never talked about it to anybody.

I put my hands in my apron pockets and leaned against the back of the booth facing them.

"Roberta? Roberta Fisk?"

She looked up. "Yeah?"

"Twyla."

She squinted for a second and then said, "Wow."

"Remember me?"

"Sure. Hey. Wow."

"It's been a while," I said, and gave a smile to the two hairy guys.

"Yeah. Wow. You work here?"

"Yeah," I said. "I live in Newburgh."

"Newburgh? No kidding?" She laughed then a private laugh that included the guys but only the guys, and they laughed with her. What could I do but laugh too and wonder why I was standing there with my knees showing out from under that uniform. Without looking I could see the blue and white triangle on my head, my hair shapeless in a net, my ankles thick in white oxfords. Nothing could have been less sheer than my stockings. There was this silence that came downright after I laughed. A silence it was her turn to fill up. With introductions, maybe, to her boyfriends or an invitation to sit down and have a Coke. Instead she lit a cigarette off the one she'd just finished and said, "We're on our way to the Coast. He's got an appointment with Hendrix." She gestured casually toward the boy next to her.

"Hendrix? Fantastic," I said. "Really fantastic. What's she doing now?"

Roberta coughed on her cigarette and the two guys rolled their eyes up at the ceiling.

"Hendrix. Jimi Hendrix, asshole. He's only the biggest—Oh, wow. Forget it."

I was dismissed without anyone saying goodbye, so I thought I would do it for her.

"How's your mother?" I asked. Her grin cracked her whole face. She swallowed. "Fine," she said. "How's yours?"

"Pretty as a picture," I said and turned away. The backs of my knees were damp. Howard Johnson's really was a dump in the sunlight.

15. RECITATIF

James is as comfortable as a house slipper. He liked my cooking and I liked his big loud family. They have lived in Newburgh all of their lives and talk about it the way people do who have always known a home. His grandmother is a porch swing older than his father and when they talk about streets and avenues and buildings they call them names they no longer have. They still call the A & P Rico's because it stands on property once a mom and pop store owned by Mr. Rico. And they call the new community college Town Hall because it once was. My mother-in-law puts up jelly and cucumbers and buys butter wrapped in cloth from a dairy. James and his father talk about fishing and baseball and I can see them all together on the Hudson in a raggedy skiff. Half the population of Newburgh is on welfare now, but to my husband's family it was still some upstate paradise of a time long past. A time of ice houses and vegetable wagons, coal furnaces and children weeding gardens. When our son was born my mother-in-law gave me the crib blanket that had been hers.

But the town they remembered had changed. Something quick was in the air. Magnificent old houses, so ruined they had become shelter for squatters and rent risks, were bought and renovated. Smart IBM people moved out of their suburbs back into the city and put shutters up and herb gardens in their backyards. A brochure came in the mail announcing the opening of a Food Emporium. Gourmet food it said—and listed items the rich IBM crowd would want. It was located in a new mall at the edge of town and I drove out to shop there one day—just to see. It was late in June. After the tulips were gone and the Queen Elizabeth roses were open everywhere. It railed my cart along the aisle tossing in smoked oysters and Robert's sauce and things I knew would sit in my cupboard for years. Only when I found some Klondike ice cream bars did I feel less guilty about spending James's fireman's salary so foolishly. My father-in-law ate them with the same gusto little Joseph did.

Waiting in the check-out line I heard a voice say, "Twyla!"

The classical music piped over the aisles had affected me and the woman leaning toward me was dressed to kill. Diamonds on her hand, a smart white summer dress. "I'm Mrs. Benson," I said.

"Ho. Ho. The Big Bozo," she sang.

For a split second I didn't know what she was talking about. She had a bunch of asparagus and two cartons of fancy water.

"Roberta!"

"Right."

"For heaven's sake. Roberta."

"You look great," she said.

"So do you. Where are you? Here? In Newburgh?"

"Yes. Over in Annandale."

I was opening my mouth to say more when the cashier called my attention to her empty counter.

"Meet you outside." Roberta pointed her finger and went into the express line.

I placed the groceries and kept myself from glancing around to check Roberta's progress. I remembered Howard Johnson's and looking for a chance to speak only to be greeted with a stingy "wow." But she was waiting for me and her huge hair was sleek now, smooth around a small, nicely shaped head. Shoes, dress, everything lovely and summery and rich. I was dying to know what happened to her, how she got from Jimi Hendrix to Annandale, a neighborhood full of doctors and IBM executives. Easy, I thought. Everything is so easy for them. They think they own the world.

"How long," I asked her. "How long have you been here?"

"A year. I got married to a man who lives here. And you, you're married too, right? Benson, you said."

"Yeah. James Benson."

"And is he nice?"

"Oh, is he nice?"

15. RECITATIF

"Well, is he?" Roberta's eyes were steady as though she really meant the question and wanted an answer.

"He's wonderful, Roberta. Wonderful."

"So you're happy."

"Very."

"That's good," she said and nodded her head. "I always hoped you'd be happy. Any kids? I know you have kids."

"One. A boy. How about you?"

"Four."

"Four?"

She laughed. "Step kids. He's a widower."

"Oh."

"Got a minute? Let's have a coffee."

I thought about the Klondikes melting and the inconvenience of going all the way to my car and putting the bags in the trunk. Served me right for buying all that stuff I didn't need. Roberta was ahead of me.

"Put them in my car. It's right here."

And then I saw the dark blue limousine.

"You married a Chinaman?"

"No," she laughed. "He's the driver."

"Oh, my. If the Big Bozo could see you now."

We both giggled. Really giggled. Suddenly, in just a pulse beat, twenty years disappeared and all of it came rushing back. The big girls (whom we called gar girls—Roberta's misheard word for the evil stone faces described in a civics class) there dancing in the orchard, the ploppy mashed potatoes, the double weenies, the Spam with pineapple. We went into the coffee shop holding on to one another and I tried to think why we were glad to see each other this time and not before. Once, twelve years ago, we passed like strangers. A black girl and a white girl meeting in a Howard Johnson's on the road and having nothing to say. One in a blue and white triangle waitress hat—the other on her way to see Hendrix. Now we were behaving like sisters separated for much too long. Those four short months were nothing in time. Maybe it was the thing itself. Just being there, together. Two little girls who knew what nobody else in the world knew—how not to ask questions. How to believe what had to be believed. There was politeness in that reluctance and generosity as well. Is your mother sick too? No, she dances all night. Oh—and an understanding nod.

We sat in a booth by the window and fell into recollection like veterans.

"Did you ever learn to read?"

"Watch." She picked up the menu. "Special of the day. Cream of corn soup. Entrees. Two dots and a wriggly line. Quiche. Chef salad, scallops..."

I was laughing and applauding when the waitress came up.

"Remember the Easter baskets?"

"And how we tried to *introduce* them?"

"Your mother with that cross like two telephone poles."

"And yours with those tight slacks."

We laughed so loudly heads turned and made the laughter harder to suppress.

"What happened to the Jimi Hendrix date?"

Roberta made a blow-out sound with her lips.

"When he died I thought about you."

"Oh, you heard about him finally?"

"Finally. Come on, I was a small-town country waitress."

"And I was a small-town country dropout. God, were we wild. I still don't know how I got out of there alive."

"But you did."

"I did. I really did. Now I'm Mrs. Kenneth Norton."

"Sounds like a mouthful."

"It is."

"Servants and all?"

Roberta held up two fingers.

"Ow! What does he do?"

"Computers and stuff. What do I know?"

"I don't remember a hell of a lot from those days, but Lord, St. Bonny's is as clear as daylight. Remember Maggie? The day she fell down and those gar girls laughed at her?"

Roberta looked up from her salad and stared at me. "Maggie didn't fall," she said.

"Yes, she did. You remember."

"No, Twyla. They knocked her down. Those girls pushed her down and tore her clothes. In the orchard."

"I don't—that's not what happened."

"Sure it is. In the orchard. Remember how scared we were?"

"Wait a minute. I don't remember any of that."

"And Bozo was fired."

"You're crazy. She was there when I left. You left before me."

"I went back. You weren't there when they fired Bozo."

"What?"

"Twice. Once for a year when I was about ten, another for two months when I was fourteen. That's when I ran away."

"You ran away from St. Bonny's?"

"I had to. What do you want? Me dancing in that orchard?"

"Are you sure about Maggie?"

"Of course I'm sure. You've blocked it, Twyla. It happened. Those girls had behavior problems, you know."

"Didn't they, though. But why can't I remember the Maggie thing?"

"Believe me. It happened. And we were there."

"Who did you room with when you went back?" I asked her as if I would know her. The Maggie thing was troubling me.

"Creeps. They tickled themselves in the night."

My ears were itching and I wanted to go home suddenly. This was all very well but she couldn't just comb her hair, wash her face and pretend everything was hunky-dory. After the Howard Johnson's snub. And no apology. Nothing.

"Were you on dope or what that time at Howard Johnson's?" I tried to make my voice sound friendlier than I felt.

"Maybe, a little. I never did drugs much. Why?"

"I don't know; you acted sort of like you didn't want to know me then."

"Oh, Twyla, you know how it was in those days: black—white. You know how everything was."

But I didn't know. I thought it was just the opposite. Busloads of blacks and whites came into Howard Johnson's together. They roamed together then: students, musicians, lovers, protesters. You got to see everything at Howard Johnson's and blacks were very friendly with whites in those days. But sitting there with nothing on my plate but two hard tomato wedges wondering about the melting Klondikes it seemed childish remembering the slight. We went to her car, and with the help of the driver, got my stuff into my station wagon.

"We'll keep in touch this time," she said.

"Sure," I said. "Sure. Give me a call."

"I will," she said, and then just as I was sliding behind the wheel, she leaned into the window. "By the way. Your mother. Did she ever stop dancing?"

I shook my head. "No. Never."

Roberta nodded.

"And yours? Did she ever get well?"

She smiled a tiny sad smile. "No. She never did. Look, call me, okay?"

"Okay," I said, but I knew I wouldn't. Roberta had messed up my past somehow with that business about Maggie. I wouldn't forget a thing like that. Would I?

15. RECITATIF

Strife came to us that fall. At least that's what the paper called it. Strife. Racial strife. The word made me think of a bird—a big shrieking bird out of 1,000,000,000 B.C. Flapping its wings and cawing. Its eye with no lid always bearing down on you. All day it screeched and at night it slept on the rooftops. It woke you in the morning and from the *Today* show to the eleven o'clock news it kept you an awful company. I couldn't figure it out from one day to the next. I knew I was supposed to feel something strong, but I didn't know what, and James wasn't any help. Joseph was on the list of kids to be transferred from the junior high school to another one at some far-out-of-the-way place and I thought it was a good thing until I heard it was a bad thing. I mean I didn't know. All the schools seemed dumps tome, and the fact that one was nicer looking didn't hold much weight. But the papers were full of it and then the kids began to get jumpy. In August, mind you. Schools weren't even open yet. I thought Joseph might be frightened to go over there, but he didn't seem scared so I forgot about it, until I found myself driving along Hudson Street out there by the school they were trying to integrate and saw a line of women marching. And who do you suppose was in line, big as life, holding a sign in front of her bigger than her mother's cross? MOTHERS HAVE RIGHTS TOO! it said.

I drove on, and then changed my mind. I circled the block, slowed down, and honked my horn.

Roberta looked over and when she saw me she waved. I didn't wave back, but I didn't move either. She handed her sign to another woman and came over to where I was parked.

"Hi."

"What are you doing?"

"Picketing. What's it look like?"

"What for?"

"What do you mean 'What for?' They want to take my kids and send them out of the neighborhood. They don't want to go."

"So what if they go to another school? My boy's being bussed too, and I don't mind. Why should you?"

"It's not about us, Twyla. Me and you. It's about our kids."

"What's more us than that?"

"Well, it is a free country."

"Not yet, but it will be."

"What the hell does that mean? I'm not doing anything to you."

"You really think that?"

"I know it."

"I wonder what made me think you were different."

"I wonder what made me think you were different."

"Look at them," I said. "Just look. Who do they think they are? Swarming all over the place like they own it. And now they think they can decide where my child goes to school. Look at them, Roberta. They're Bozos."

Roberta turned around and looked at the women. Almost all of them were standing still now, waiting. Some were even edging toward us. Roberta looked at me out of some refrigerator behind her eyes. "No, they're not. They're just mothers."

"And what am I? Swiss cheese?"

"I used to curl your hair."

"I hated your hands in my hair."

The women were moving. Our faces looked mean to them of course and they looked as though they could not wait to throw themselves in front of a police car, or better yet, into my car and drag me away by my ankles. Now they surrounded my car and gently, gently began to rock it. I swayed back and forth like a sideways yo-yo. Automatically I reached for Roberta, like the old days in the orchard when they saw us watching them and we had to get out of there, and if one of us fell the other pulled her up and if one of us was caught the other stayed to kick and scratch, and neither would leave the other behind. My arm shot out of the car window but no receiving hand was there. Roberta was looking at me sway from side to side in the car and her face was still. My purse slid from the car seat down under the dashboard. The four policemen who had been drinking Tab in their car finally got the message and strolled over, forcing their way through the women. Quietly, firmly they spoke. "Okay, ladies. Back in line or off the streets."

Some of them went away willingly; others had to be urged away from the car doors and the hood. Roberta didn't move. She was looking steadily at me. I was fumbling to turn on the ignition, which wouldn't catch because the gearshift was still in drive. The seats of the car were a mess because the swaying had thrown my grocery coupons all over it and my purse was sprawled on the floor.

"Maybe I am different now, Twyla. But you're not. You're the same little state kid who kicked a poor old black lady when she was down on the ground. You kicked a black lady and you have the nerve to call me a bigot."

The coupons were everywhere and the guts of my purse were bunched under the dashboard. What was she saying? Black? Maggie wasn't black.

"She wasn't black," I said.

"Like hell she wasn't, and you kicked her. We both did. You kicked a black lady who couldn't even scream."

"Liar!"

"You're the liar! Why don't you just go on home and leave us alone, huh?"

She turned away and I skidded away from the curb.

The next morning I went into the garage and cut the side out of the carton our portable TV had come in. It wasn't nearly big enough, but after a while I had a decent sign: red spray-painted letters on a white background—AND SO DO CHILDREN * * * *. I meant just to go down to the school and tack it up somewhere so those cows on the picket line across the street could see it, but when I got there, some ten or so others had already assembled—protesting the cows across the street. Police permits and everything. I got in line and we strutted in time on our side while Roberta's group strutted on theirs. That first day we were all dignified, pretending the other side didn't exist. The second day there was name calling and finger gestures. But that was about all. People changed signs from time to time, but Roberta never did and neither did I. Actually my sign didn't make sense without Roberta's. "And so do children what?" one of the women on my side asked me. Have rights, I said, as though it was obvious.

Roberta didn't acknowledge my presence in any way and I got to thinking maybe she didn't know I was there. I began to pace myself in the line, jostling people one minute and lagging behind the next, so Roberta and I could reach the end of our respective lines at the same time and there would be a moment in our turn when we would face each other. Still, I couldn't tell whether she saw me and knew my sign was for her. The next day I went early before we were scheduled to assemble. I waited until she got there before I exposed my new creation. As soon as she hoisted her MOTHERS HAVE RIGHTS TOO I began to wave my new one, which said, HOW WOULD YOU KNOW? I know she saw that one, but I had gotten addicted now. My signs got crazier each day, and the women on my side decided that I was a kook. They couldn't make heads or tails out of my brilliant screaming posters.

I brought a painted sign in queenly red with huge black letters that said, IS YOUR MOTHER WELL? Roberta took her lunch break and didn't come back for the rest of the day or any day after. Two days later I stopped going too and couldn't have been missed because nobody understood my signs anyway.

It was a nasty six weeks. Classes were suspended and Joseph didn't go to anybody's school until October. The children—everybody's children—soon got bored with that extended vacation they thought was going to be so great. They looked at TV until their eyes flattened. I spent a couple of mornings tutoring my son, as the other mothers said we should. Twice I opened a text from last year that he had never turned in. Twice he yawned in my face. Other mothers organized living room sessions so the kids would keep up. None of the kids could concentrate so they drifted back to *The Price Is Right* and *The Brady Bunch*. When the school finally opened there were fights once or twice and some sirens roared through the streets every once in a while. There were a lot of photographers from Albany. And just when ABC was about to send up a news crew, the kids settled down like nothing in the world had happened. Joseph hung my HOW WOULD YOU KNOW? sign in his bedroom. I don't know what became of AND SO DO CHILDREN * * * *. I think my father-in-law cleaned some fish on it. He was always puttering around in our garage. Each of his five children lived in Newburgh and he acted as though he had five extra homes.

I couldn't help looking for Roberta when Joseph graduated from high school, but I didn't see her. It didn't trouble me much what she had said to me in the car. I mean the kicking part. I know I didn't do that, I couldn't do that. But I was puzzled by her telling me Maggie was black. When I thought about it I actually couldn't be certain. She wasn't pitch-black, I knew, or I would have remembered that. What I remember was the kiddie hat, and the semicircle legs. I tried to reassure myself about the race thing for a long time until it dawned on me that the truth was already there, and Roberta knew it. I didn't kick her; I didn't join in with the gar girls and kick that lady, but I sure did want to. We watched and never tried to help her and never called for help. Maggie was my dancing mother. Deaf, I thought, and dumb. Nobody inside. Nobody who would hear you if you cried in the night. Nobody who could tell you anything important that you could use. Rocking, dancing, swaying as she walked. And when the gar girls pushed her down, and started roughhousing, I knew she wouldn't scream, couldn't—just like me—and I was glad about that.

We decided not to have a tree, because Christmas would be at my mother-in-law's house, so why have a tree at both places? Joseph was at SUNY New Paltz and we had to economize, we said. But at the last minute, I changed my mind. Nothing could be that bad. So I rushed around town looking for a tree, something small but wide. By the time I found a place, it was snowing and very late. I dawdled like it was the most important purchase in the world and the tree man was fed up with me. Finally I chose one and had it tied onto the trunk of the car. I drove away slowly because the sand trucks were not out yet and the streets could be murder at the beginning of a snowfall. Downtown the streets were wide and rather empty except for a cluster of people coming out of the Newburgh Hotel. The one hotel in town that wasn't built out of cardboard and Plexiglas. A party, probably. The men huddled in the snow were dressed in tails and the women had on furs. Shiny things glittered from underneath their coats. It made me tired to look at them. Tired, tired, tired. On the next corner was a small diner with loops and loops of paper bells in the window. I stopped the car and went in. Just for a cup of coffee and twenty minutes of peace before I went home and tried to finish everything before Christmas Eve.

"Twyla?"

There she was. In a silvery evening gown and dark fur coat. A man and another woman were with her, the man fumbling for change to put in the cigarette machine. The woman was humming and tapping on the counter with her fingernails. They all looked a little bit drunk.

"Well. It's you."

"How are you?"

I shrugged. "Pretty good. Frazzled. Christmas and all."

"Regular?" called the woman from the counter.

"Fine," Roberta called back and then, "Wait for me in the car."

She slipped into the booth beside me. "I have to tell you something, Twyla. I made up my mind if I ever saw you again, I'd tell you."

"I'd just as soon not hear anything, Roberta. It doesn't matter now,

15. RECITATIF

anyway."

"No," she said. "Not about that."

"Don't be long," said the woman. She carried two regulars to go and the man peeled his cigarette pack as they left.

"It's about St. Bonny's and Maggie."

"Oh, please."

"Listen to me. I really did think she was black. I didn't make that up. I really thought so. But now I can't be sure. I just remember her as old, so old. And because she couldn't talk—well, you know, I thought she was crazy. She'd been brought up in an institution like my mother was and like I thought I would be too. And you were right. We didn't kick her. It was the gar girls. Only them. But, well, I wanted to. I really wanted them to hurt her. I said we did it, too. You and me, but that's not true. And I don't want you to carry that around. It was just that I wanted to do it so bad that day—wanting to is doing it."

Her eyes were watery from the drinks she'd had, I guess. I know it's that way with me. One glass of wine and I start bawling over the littlest thing.

"We were kids, Roberta."

"Yeah. Yeah. I know, just kids."

"Eight."

"Eight."

"And lonely."

"Scared, too."

She wiped her cheeks with the heel of her hand and smiled. "Well that's all I wanted to say."

I nodded and couldn't think of any way to fill the silence that went from the diner past the paper bells on out into the snow. It was heavy now. I thought I'd better wait for the sand trucks before starting home.

"Thanks, Roberta."

"Sure."

"Did I tell you My mother, she never did stop dancing."

"Yes. You told me. And mine, she never got well." Roberta lifted her hands from the tabletop and covered her face with her palms. When she took them away she really was crying. "Oh shit, Twyla. Shit, shit, shit. What the hell happened to Maggie?"

作品赏析

一、作家及作品介绍

托尼·莫里森（Toni Morrison，1931—2019），美国著名的小说家、散文家、短篇小说家、教育家，编辑，诺贝尔文学奖获得者。从她的第一部小说《最蓝的眼睛》（*The Bluest Eye*，1970）到第六部小说《爵士乐》（*Jazz*，1992），托尼·莫里森作为一个作家、编辑和评论家，以其在非裔美国文学传统中的突出成就，改变了整个美国文学的格局。当她获得1993年诺贝尔文学奖时，瑞典学院称她"用充满想象力和诗意的文学作品，显示了美国现实生活的重要方面"[1]。通过作品中的文字，她为读者创造了新的空间，使他们将自己的想象和智慧带到我们这个时代复杂的文化、政治、社会和历史问题上。此外，通过自己编辑和小说家的工作，她让非裔美国作家和女性作家的文本有可能重塑所谓的美国文学的轮廓。莫里森的小说曾荣获多项文学奖，如《所罗门之歌》（*Song of Soloman*，1977）获得美国全国图书评论界奖，《宠儿》（*Beloved*，1987）获得普利策小说奖和美国国家图书奖。莫里森也是美国总统自由勋章的获得者。

莫里森1931年出生于俄亥俄州的洛兰市。她的父母是来自南方的移民，工人阶级，家庭生活充满了故事和音乐。1949年莫里森以优异的成绩从洛兰高中毕业，进入霍华德大学主修英语，辅修古典文学。1953年，她离开霍华德大学进入康奈尔大学。1955年获得英语文学硕士学位，她的论文是关于威廉·福克纳（William Faulkner）和弗吉尼亚·伍尔夫（Virginia Woolf）的小说研究。她在休

---

[1] William Andrews, Frances Smith Foster, and Trudier Harris, eds. *The Concise Oxford Companion to African American Literature,* New York: Oxford University Press, 2001, p. 295.

15. RECITATIF

斯敦德克萨斯南方大学任教两年，1957年至1964年在霍华德大学英文系任教。在霍华德大学教书一年后，她与牙买加建筑师哈罗德·莫里森（Harold Morrison）结婚，育有两子。莫里森认为，这段令人窒息的婚姻导致她在20世纪60年代初转向写作，以寻求慰藉。之后，她加入了一个作家工作室，开始创作一篇关于一个想要蓝眼睛的黑人女孩的短篇小说，这个短篇小说就是她第一部小说《最蓝的眼睛》的雏形。1964年，她辞去了在霍华德大学的教职，与丈夫离婚，带着两个儿子回到了她父母在洛兰的家中，在那里她待了18个月，后搬到纽约州找到了一份编辑的工作。虽然她承认，她在晚上儿子们熟睡之后才开始写作，以此来排解自己的孤独感，但很明显，这项活动已经开始重塑她的身份和整个生活。正如她所说的，她意识到："写作是……最特别的思考和感受方式。它成了我所做的唯一一件事，我绝对无意离开它而生活。"[1]

1970年到1992年间，莫里森一共出版了六部小说、一部戏剧、一本文学批评和一本社会批评选集。在本已繁重的编辑和写作工作之余，她又开始在东海岸的各个地方兼职教学，1971至1986年间分别在纽约州立大学普尔奇分校、耶鲁大学、纽约州立大学阿尔巴尼分校和巴德学院任职。自1988年以来，她一直是普林斯顿大学的人文科学教授，在那里教授非裔美国文化研究和创意写作课程。随着莫里森奖项和荣誉不断加身，评论家们开始关注她的作品，从多个角度审视她的作品，尤其是《所罗门之歌》和《宠儿》，并热情赞扬她的小说和她作为知识分子所发挥的作用。她经常在全国和世界各地举办自己的作品朗诵会和讲座。她还与凯瑟琳·巴特尔（Kathleen Battle）、杰西·诺曼（Jessye Norman）、安德烈·普雷文（Andre Previn）等著名音乐家合作进行各种创作，包括以《宠儿》中塞丝（Sethe）的历史原型玛格丽特·加纳（Magaret Garner）为原型的新歌剧。

然而，她在1970至1992年出版的六部小说比她的任何文学和文化批评作品更重要。这六部作品充满美学和政治力量，并且确立了她作为一个作家的文学声誉和地位。我们首先在《最蓝的眼睛》中见证了这种力量。这部小说讲述了一个黑人女孩对爱的渴望，而这种渴望体现在对蓝眼睛的渴望上，最终使她陷入疯狂。

---

[1] William Andrews, Frances Smith Foster, and Trudier Harris, eds. *The Concise Oxford Companion to African American Literature*, p. 296.

在她的第二部小说《秀拉》(*Sula*,1973)中,莫里森尝试接触女性友谊的话题。小说叙述了两位女性如何成为朋友的故事:当一个人选择传统的婚姻和家庭生活,另一个人选择挑战传统对女性的期望时,她们之间的裂痕及其所产生的影响。在她的第三部小说《所罗门之歌》(*Song of Solomonm*,1977)中,莫里森讲述了男主人公奶娃(Macon "Milkman" Dead Ⅲ)在家庭历史和种族政治的背景下寻求自我身份的故事。莫里森用她的第四部小说《焦油宝贝》(*Tar Baby*,1981)将对种族政治和非洲移民社群的兴趣与性别关系综合在一起。《宠儿》是莫里森最有名的一部作品,在作品中她将对历史的关注与对个人记忆、文化记忆在人际关系形成的探索联系起来。在《爵士乐》中,莫里森将哈莱姆文艺复兴时期的历史和音乐与对纽约市的迷恋结合起来,讲述了一段陈旧的婚姻和一段致命的爱情故事。1998年,莫里森出版了她的第七部小说《天堂》(*Paradise*,1997)。该书以美国西南部一个黑人小镇为背景,探讨了深色和浅色皮肤的黑人之间的关系,以及一个群体为建立一个免受歧视和偏见的避难所所做的努力。千禧年以来,莫里森又出版了四部小说,分别是《爱》(*Love*,2003)、《慈悲》(*A Mercy*,2008)、《家》(*Home*,2012)和《上帝救救孩子》(*God Help the Child*,2015)。

　　托尼·莫里森从塑造她自己的经历和非裔美国人及其生活的地域、语言、价值观、文化传统和政治观念中汲取灵感。她不提供任何解决问题的办法,也不会将过去或现在的复杂现实简单化。相反,出于对黑人群体为生活和生命带来的文化知识的尊重,她用想象的力量为同胞和任何对这些故事感兴趣的人讲述他们的故事。[1]

二、小说背景与人物分析

　　《宣叙》("Recitatif")是托尼·莫里森唯一的一篇短篇小说。为了更好地理解小说,我们首先来了解一下小说中故事的时代和社会背景。小说涉及20世纪美国发展的三个不同历史时期,每一个时期都见证了种族之间紧张局面的恶化

---

[1] 作家及作品介绍参考:William Andrews, Frances Smith Foster, and Trudier Harris, eds. *The Concise Oxford Companion to African American Literature*, pp. 295-297; Wilfred Samuels, ed., *Encyclopedia of African-American Literature*. New York: Facts On File, Inc., 2007, pp. 366-368.

或缓和。[1] 小说的第一部分发生在20世纪50年代，这时候小说的两位主角特怀拉和罗贝塔都只是八岁的小女孩。这一时期美国种族矛盾一天天激化，民权运动登上了历史舞台。1954年，最高法院对著名的布朗案（Brown v. Board of Education of Topeka）作出判决，宣布学校中的种族隔离制度是违法的。1957年发生了著名的小石城事件（Little Rock Nine），小石城学校委员会宣布逐步改变学校种族隔离的现象，在白人的中心中学首批录取了九名黑人学生。而这一事件直接导致了白人和黑人的正面冲突。小说的第二阶段发生在20世纪60年代，这时特怀拉和罗贝塔刚刚成年。1964年民权法案的颁布和1968年黑人民权运动领袖马丁·路德·金被刺杀事件推动黑人民权运动达到高潮。在同一时期，美国社会正经历一场文化变革，这场变革伴随新的嬉皮士文化崛起，一群充满反叛精神的年轻人蔑视社会传统规范，反对战争与武器，转而拥抱"性、毒品与摇滚乐"。嬉皮士文化中的一个代表人物就是吉米·亨德里克斯（Jimi Hendrix），一位摇滚电吉他演奏者。罗贝塔正是在去见亨德里克斯的路上路过霍华德·约翰逊饭店，并在那里碰到了特怀拉，这也是两人离开收容所之后的第一次见面。尽管种族矛盾在20世纪70年代稍有缓和，但是黑人社区仍然面临大量的贫困和高居不下的服刑率，这一情况在里根总统时期又进一步恶化。1974年，在地方法院法官就波士顿学校的种族不平等问题作出裁决后，法官决定对学校的儿童进行强制重新分组，以便使某个种族的学生超过50%的学校能够平衡其种族比例。实现这一比例的手段就是强制将不同种族的学生从不同社区转移到这些学校，以实现种族平衡。这一规定导致了学生家长的大规模抗议和更大的种族摩擦。这就是我们在小说中看到罗贝塔游行和罗贝塔与特怀拉爆发冲突的原因。

对小说发生背景的了解有助于我们更好地理解小说主题和情节发展，而小说主题和情节将在下一部分介绍，在这里我们先分析一下小说里面的主要人物和他们之间的关系。小说以女主角特怀拉对她在圣伯尼孤儿院度过的童年生活的叙述开篇，在那里她和罗贝塔——"一个来自不同种族的小女孩"——成了室友。这样的表述，再加上作者的黑人身份，很容易让读者开始关注两个小女孩的种族身份，而试图弄清两个小女孩种族身份的尝试则引领读者跟着情节的发展不断作出

---

1 Marie Knoflíčková, "Racial Identities Revisited: Toni Morrison's 'Recitatif'", *Litteraria Pragensia*, Vol. 21, No. 41 (June 2011), pp. 22-23.

各种猜测，但是作品从头至尾只给出了一些模棱两可的线索而没有给出确切的答案（作者故意将两人的种族身份隐去不谈和小说主题直接相关）。然而，"种族问题一直是贯穿小说的核心问题，尽管两位女主角的关系貌似完全不受肤色差异的影响，但两人离开孤儿院之后的冲突和矛盾却都与种族问题息息相关"[1]。在孤儿院时，特怀拉与罗贝塔"因为不是真正的孤儿，父母没有住在天堂"（...we weren't real orphans with beautiful dead parents in the sky...），而与其他孩子不同，这种不同使两人成了最好的朋友，有时甚至像一对亲姐妹。但是离开孤儿院，时隔12年后两位姐妹的第一次碰面却形同路人，而这次不友好的碰面一部分原因是当时紧张的种族关系和两人的种族差异。第二次见面两人关系的缓和和第三次两人之间爆发的冲突，都和当时社会的种族局面息息相关。在小说中我们可以看到，特怀拉和罗贝塔之间的关系，更多的是受到两人的共同经历、两人各自的生活经历（包括婚姻和阶级差异）和性格的影响，而不是种族差异。

除了两位女主角，麦吉是小说中备受关注的一个次要人物，虽然是次要人物，但是她的重要性却是不容忽视的。小说的最后一句"哦，该死！特怀拉。该死，该死，真该死！麦吉到底是怎么回事？"（Oh shit, Twyla. Shit, shit, shit. What the hell happened to Maggie?），再加上两位主角间最剧烈的冲突也是关于她们是否像其他大女孩一样踢了麦吉这件事情，自然而然地将读者和评论家的注意力引到了麦吉身上。麦吉是一个"两条腿活像一对括弧、不能说话、天生是个哑巴、年纪很大、皮肤泛黄，在厨房干活"（...with legs like parentheses... Maggie couldn't talk. The kids said she had her tongue cut out, but I think she was just born that way: mute. She was old and sandy-colored and she worked in the kitchen）的"蠢女人"。她总是打扮得像小孩，总是"戴着一顶笨拙的、带帽瓣的小孩帽子"（She wore this really stupid little hat—a kid's hat with ear flaps）。而更重要的是，像两位女主角一样，麦吉的肤色也是一件无法确定的事情，两人争论的焦点之一就是麦吉是不是黑人。围绕着麦吉的肤色和两人是否像其他大女孩一样踢了麦吉这两个问题，我们可以看到两位主角之间关系的变化和最后对自我良知的反思。

---

1 Susana M. Morris, "'Sisters Separated for Much Too Long': Women's Friendship and Power in Toni Morrison's 'Recitatif'", *Tulsa Studies in Women's Literature*, Vol. 32, No. 1 (2013), p. 165.

实际上，小说中所有人的肤色都是一个谜，比如特怀拉和罗贝塔两人的妈妈。在阅读小说的过程中，我们很容易通过一两个细节对小说中人物的种族身份作出判断，但是这些判断很快就被之后出现的细节给推翻。两位母亲形象在小说中也具有重要的意义，两位主角每次碰面都要问候对方的母亲。两位母亲的形象在小说中是截然相反的：特怀拉的妈妈总是整晚跳舞，而罗贝塔的妈妈身体不好；特怀拉的妈妈穿着一条令人讨厌的松垮而难看的绿裤子（green slacks）而罗贝塔的妈妈胸前挂着六英寸的十字架，臂里还夹着一本全世界最大的圣经（...on her chest was the biggest cross I'd ever seen. I swear it was six inches long each way. And in the crook of her arm was the biggest Bible ever made）去教堂参加礼拜。两位母亲拒绝握手更加深了两人的对立。这里面是否涉及种族差异读者是无从知晓的，不过两位母亲身上所表现出的特征在任何一个种族身上都能找得到。

三、小说主题与叙述策略

在《在黑暗中玩耍》（*Playing in the Dark*，1992）一书中，莫里森称《宣叙》"是一个实验，从一个关于两个不同种族的人物的叙事中去除所有种族代码，而对她们来说，种族身份是至关重要的"[1]。这部小说通过模糊主要人物的种族身份，挑战读者的认知和人们对种族的偏见。莫里森说服读者认识到种族刻板印象的谬误，并将通常被肤色分割的两个世界捆绑成一个整体。此外，她将种族身份从两个女主角友谊的核心位置上移开，向读者展示种族身份只是一个人一生中承担的众多身份之一，和其他身份相比也并没有什么特别之处。无论从其叙事策略还是处理种族关系和种族身份的方式来看，《宣叙》都是一部不寻常的作品。此外，它还总结了20世纪下半叶非裔美国人形成种族意识的关键时刻，并展示了这些时刻对美国白人和美国黑人这两个群体的共同影响。

小说解构了社会强加在个人身上的种族身份。主人公特怀拉和罗贝塔的友谊是一面镜子，反射出基于种族陈规的刻板观念的种族身份之间并没有明确的界限，因此不能也不会作为一个人人格的构成要素。通过证明它们的不足和模糊性，莫里森解构了固化的种族身份，并将其从女孩人格的核心部分剔除。"对个

---

[1] İnci Bilgin Tekin, "The Turkish Reader's Reception of Toni Morrison's 'Rrecitatif'", *Journal of American Studies of Turkey* (*JAST*), No. 37 (Spring 2013), p. 55.

人来说，日常生活具有重要意义的不是肤色或任何其他身体属性，而是社会赋予这些身体特征的观念和假设。莫里森的小说对种族刻板印象的解构直接导致了种族身份的解构。"[1]虽然特怀拉首先注意到的是她和罗贝塔之间的种族差异，但她们之间因肤色而产生的等级差异却沿着不同的路线进行。此外，莫里森特别注重细节，她以一个孩子视角来观察世界，那些从一个经历过社会化和文化熏陶的成年人的角度来看重要的东西对孩子来讲并不重要，并不影响她们的日常生活。因此，她们可以随便换床，罗贝塔懂事更早，让特怀拉吃饭，和特怀拉一样学习成绩不好，这些日常小事似乎比她们的种族差异更重要。当特怀拉回忆孤儿院时期的罗贝塔时，她只记得"她湿漉漉的袜子，粉红色的扇形上衣，还有一双看起来很严肃的大眼睛"（her wet socks with the pink scalloped tops and her big serious-looking eyes），而根本没有提到任何有关肤色的事情。

一开始，女孩们的种族就与对种族的刻板观念直接相关。因为作者本人是非裔美国作家，读者一开始会认为叙述者也是非裔美国人。然而，当特怀拉用人们在描述非裔美国人时惯用的语言来描述罗贝塔时，读者的确定性就动摇了，这是传统上白人显示自身优越性的语言。特怀拉震惊于她要和一个"来自另一个种族"的女孩在一起，并记得她母亲说过"他们从不洗头，而且气味怪异"（they never washed their hair and they smelled funny）。这种显示自身优越性的修辞，使读者重新考虑他们的第一个假设，即特怀拉作为非裔美国作家小说的叙述者，她本人一定是同一出身，因为通常情况下是这样的。同样的情况也会发生在罗贝塔、特怀拉和罗贝塔两人的母亲、女仆人麦吉和两位主角的家人身上，对他们的种族身份读者不断提出各种假设又不断推翻自己的假设，直到把肤色问题抛诸脑后。

莫里森巧妙借用了关于两个对立群体的刻板观念来揭露种族刻板观念的谬误。这也证明了不能以肤色来评判种族成员的身份：同样的特征可以被应用于对立双方的任何一方，而且都可以说得通。两位主人公对种族身份的解构，在圣诞节最后一次见面时完成。她们又回到了对麦吉的记忆中。罗贝塔承认，她也不确定麦吉的种族身份。她这样说显然是为了安慰特怀拉，证明她并没有伤害一个非裔美国女人。但更重要的是，她们到底有没有把老麦吉踢下楼梯，麦吉身上到底发生了什么事情。莫里森在让读者放弃对两位主人公种族身份的追问之后，把重

---

1 Marie Knoflíčková, "Racial Identities Revisited: Toni Morrison's 'Recitatif'", pp. 23-24.

15. RECITATIF

点放在了她们的道德和良知上，而这些才是决定一个人的人格的核心要素。特怀拉和罗贝塔的友谊既不取决于她们的种族身份，也不取决于麦吉的种族身份，而取决于她们的良知。这说明种族身份与一个人的生活无关，因为种族身份只是一个人人格的众多要素之一。此外，她们的友谊是基于她们在收容所的共同经历，基于她们"被抛弃"的命运。莫里森指出了种族身份的表面性，将其从一个人的人格决定性因素中移除掉。

Suggested Readings

1. Baker, Houston A., Jr. *Afro-American Poetics: Revisions of Harmem and the Black Aesthetic.* Madison: University of Wisconsin Press, 1988.
2. Beaulieu, Elizabeth Ann, ed. *The Toni Morrison Encyclopedia.* Westport, CT: Greenwood Press, 2003.
3. Bloom, Harold, ed. *Toni Morrison.* Philadelphia: Chelsea Publishers, 2005.
4. David, Ron. *Toni Morrison Explained: A Reader's Road Map to the Novels.* New York: Random House, 2000.
5. Gates, Henry Louis, Jr. *The Signifying Monkey: A Theory of Afro-American Literary Criticism.* New York: Oxford University Press, 1988.
6. Gates, Henry Louis, Jr. & K. A. Appiah, eds. *Toni Morrison: Critical Perspectives Past and Present.* New York: Amistad Press, Inc., 1993.
7. Gillespie, Carmen. *Critical Companion to Toni Morrison.* New York: Facts on File, Inc., 2008.
8. Graham, Maryemma, ed. *Cambridge Companion to The African Amrican Novel.* Cambridge: Cambridge University Press, 2004.
9. Harris, Trudier. *Fiction and Folklore: The Novels of Toni Morrison.* Knoxville: University of Tenneessee Press, 1991.
10. Li, Stephanie. *Toni Morrison: A Biography.* Santa Barbara, CA: Greenwood Press, 2010.
11. McKay, Nellie Y., ed. *Critical Essays on Toni Morrison.* Boston: G. K. Hall, 1988.
12. Middleton, David L. *Toni Morrison's Fiction: Contemporary Criticism.* New

York: Garland, 1997.

13. Morrison, Toni. *Beloved*. New York: Knopf, 1987.
14. Morrison, Toni. *Playing in the Dark: Whiteness and the Literary Imagination*. New York: Vintage Books, 1992.
15. Morrison, Toni. *Song of Solomon*. New York: Vintage Books, 2004.
16. O'reilly, Andrea. *Toni Morrison and Motherhood: A Politics of the Heart*. New York: State University of New York Press, 2004.
17. Rigney, Barbara Hill. *The Voices of Toni Morrison*. Columbus: Ohio State University Press, 1991.
18. Tally, Justine, ed. *The Cambridge Companion to Toni Morrison*. Cambridge: Cambridge University Press, 2007.

Questions for Reflection

1. What happens to the two heroines when they first meet after they leave the orphanage?

2. Where do the two heroines meet for the second time and what is the biggest difference between them at this time?

3. The climax of the story is the third meeting of the two heroines, and why is there such a fierce conflict between them?

4. What is the racial identity of the old Maggie? Why do the two heroines always hold on to this point?

5. How do you see the influence of the two mothers on the two heroines and their relationship with each other?

Questions for Discussion

Can we be certain of the racial identity of the two heroines in the novel? If we can, what evidence is available? If not, what is the author's purpose in doing so? Is it relevant to the theme of the novel?

（方小莉　撰写）

16. A GUIDE TO BERLIN

By Vladimir Nabokov, 1925

In the morning I visited the zoo and now I am entering a pub with my friend and usual pot companion. Its sky-blue sign bears a white inscription, "LÖWENBRÄU," accompanied by the portrait of a lion with a winking eye and mug of beer. We sit down and I start telling my friend about utility pipes, streetcars, and other important matters.

1 THE PIPES

In front of the house where I live a gigantic black pipe lies along the outer edge of the sidewalk. A couple of feet away, in the same file, lies another, then a third and a fourth—the street's iron entrails, still idle, not yet lowered into the ground, deep under the asphalt. For the first few days after they were unloaded, with a hollow clanging, from trucks, little boys would run on them up and down and crawl on all fours through those round tunnels, but a week later nobody was playing any more and thick snow was falling instead; and now, when, cautiously probing the treacherous glaze of the sidewalk with my thick rubberheeled stick, I go out in the flat gray light of early morning, an even stripe of fresh snow stretches along the upper side of each black pipe while up the interior slope at the very mouth of the pipe which is nearest to the turn of the tracks, the reflection of a still illumined tram sweeps up like bright-orange heat lightning. Today someone wrote "Otto" with his finger on the strip of virgin snow and I thought how beautifully that name, with its two soft o's flanking the pair of gentle consonants, suited the silent layer of snow upon that pipe with its two orifices and its tacit tunnel.

2 THE STREETCAR

The streetcar will vanish in twenty years or so, just as the horse-drawn tram has vanished. Already I feel it has an air of antiquity, a kind of old-fashioned charm. Everything about it is a little clumsy and rickety, and if a curve is taken a little too fast, and the trolley pole jumps the wire, and the conductor, or even one of the passengers, leans out over the car's stern, looks up, and jiggles the cord until the pole is back in place, I always think that the coach driver of old must sometimes have dropped his whip, reined in his four-horse team, sent after it the lad in long-skirted livery who sat beside him on the box and gave piercing blasts on his horn while, clattering over the cobblestones, the coach swung through a village.

The conductor who gives out tickets has very unusual hands. They work as nimbly as those of a pianist, but instead of being limp, sweaty, and soft-nailed, the ticketman's hands are so coarse that when you are pouring change into his palm and happen to touch that palm, which seems to have developed a harsh chitinous crust, you feel a kind of moral discomfort. They are extraordinarily agile and efficient hands, despite their roughness and the thickness of the fingers. I watch him with curiosity as he clamps the ticket with his broad black fingernail and punches it in two places, rummages in his leather purse, scoops up coins to make change, immediately slaps the purse shut, and yanks the bell cord, or, with a shove of his thumb, throws open the special little window in the forward door to hand tickets to people on the front platform. And all the time the car sways, passengers standing in the aisle grab at the overhead straps, and surge back and forth—but he will not drop a single coin or a single ticket

16. A GUIDE TO BERLIN

torn from his roll. In these winter days the bottom half of the forward door is curtained with green cloth, the windows are clouded with frost, Christmas trees for sale throng the edge of the sidewalk at each stop, the passengers' feet are numb with cold, and sometimes a gray worsted mitten clothes the conductor's hand. At the end of the line the front car uncouples, enters a siding, runs around the remaining one, and approaches it from behind. There is something reminiscent of a submissive female in the way the second car waits as the first, male, trolley, sending up a small crackling flame, rolls up and couples on. And (minus the biological metaphor) I am reminded of how, some eighteen years ago in Petersburg, the horses used to be unhitched and led around the potbellied blue tram.

The horse-drawn tram has vanished, and so will the trolley, and some eccentric Berlin writer in the twenties of the twenty-first century, wishing to portray our time, will go to a museum of technological history and locate a hundred-year-old streetcar, yellow, uncouth, with old-fashioned curved seats, and in a museum of old costumes dig up a black, shiny-buttoned conductor's uniform. Then he will go home and compile a description of Berlin streets in bygone days. Everything, every trifle, will be valuable and meaningful: the conductor's purse, the advertisement over the window, that peculiar jolting motion which our great-grandchildren will perhaps imagine—everything will be ennobled and justified by its age.

I think that here lies the sense of literary creation: to portray ordinary objects as they will be reflected in the kindly mirrors of future times; to find in the objects around us the fragrant tenderness that only posterity will discern and appreciate in the far-off times when every trifle of our plain everyday life will become exquisite and festive in its own right: the times when a man who might put on the most ordinary jacket of today will be dressed up for an elegant masquerade.

3 WORK

Here are examples of various kinds of work that I observe from the crammed tram, in which a compassionate woman can always be relied upon to cede me her window seat—while trying not to look too closely at me.

At an intersection the pavement has been torn up next to the track; by turns, four workmen are pounding an iron stake with mallets; the first one strikes, and the second is already lowering his mallet with a sweeping, accurate swing; the second mallet crashes down and is rising skyward as the third and then the fourth bang down in rhythmical succession. I listen to their unhurried clanging, like four repeated notes of an iron carillon.

A young white-capped baker flashes by on his tricycle; there is something angelic about a lad dusted with flour. A van jingles past with cases on its roof containing rows of emerald-glittering empty bottles, collected from taverns. A long, black larch tree mysteriously travels by in a cart. The tree lies flat; its tip quivers gently, while the earth covered roots, enveloped in sturdy burlap, form an enormous beige bomblike sphere at its base. A postman, who has placed the mouth of a sack under a cobalt-colored mailbox, fastens it on from below, and secretly, invisibly, with a hurried rustling, the box empties and the postman claps shut the square jaws of the bag, now grown full and heavy. But perhaps fairest of all are the carcasses, chrome yellow, with pink blotches, and arabesques, piled on a truck, and the man in apron and leather hood with a long neck flap who heaves each carcass onto his back and, hunched over, carries it across the sidewalk into the butcher's red shop.

4 EDEN

Every large city has its own, man-made Eden on earth.

If churches speak to us of the Gospel, zoos remind us of the solemn, and tender, beginning of the Old Testament. The only sad part is that this artificial Eden is all behind bars, although it is also true that if there were no enclosures the very first dingo would savage me. It is Eden nonetheless, insofar as man is able to reproduce it, and it is with good reason that the large hotel across from the Berlin Zoo is named after that garden.

In the wintertime, when the tropical animals have been hidden away, I recommend visiting the amphibian, insect, and fish houses. Rows of illuminated displays behind glass in the dimly lit hall resemble the portholes through which Captain Nemo gazed out of his submarine at the sea creatures undulating among the ruins of Atlantis. Behind the glass, in bright recesses, transparent fishes glide with flashing fins, marine flowers breathe, and, on a patch of sand, lies a live, crimson five-pointed star. This, then, is where the notorious emblem originated—at the very bottom of the ocean, in the murk of sunken Atlantica, which long ago lived through various upheavals while pottering about topical Utopias and other inanities that cripple us today.

Oh, do not omit to watch the giant tortoises being fed. These ponderous, ancient corneous cupolas were brought from the Galápagos Islands. With a decrepit kind of circumspection, a wrinkly flat head and two totally useless paws emerge in slow motion from under the two-hundred-pound dome. And with its thick, spongy tongue, suggesting somehow that of a cacological idiot slackly vomiting his monstrous speech, the turtle sticks its head into a heap of wet vegetables and messily munches their leaves.

But that dome above it—ah, that dome, that ageless, well-rubbed, dull bronze, that splendid burden of time...

5 THE PUB

"That's a very poor guide," my usual pot companion says glumly. "Who cares about how you took a streetcar and went to the Berlin Aquarium?"

The pub in which he and I are sitting is divided into two parts, one large, the other somewhat smaller. A billiard table occupies the center of the former; there are a few tables in the corners; a bar faces the entrance, and bottles stand on shelves behind the bar. On the wall, between the windows, newspapers and magazines mounted on shot staffs hang like paper banners. At the far end there is a wide passageway, through which one sees a cramped little room with a green couch under a mirror, out of which an oval table with a checked oilcloth topples and takes up its solid position in front of the couch. That room is part of the publican's humble little apartment. There his wife, with faded looks and big breasts, is feeding soup to a blond child.

"It's of no interest," my friend affirms with a mournful yawn. "What do trams and tortoises matter? And anyway the whole thing is limply a bore. A boring, foreign city, and expensive to live in, too..."

From our place near the bar one can make out very distinctly the couch, the mirror, and the table in the background beyond the passage. The woman is clearing the table. Propped on his elbows, the child attentively examines an illustrated magazine on its useless handle.

"What do you see down there?" asks my companion and turns slowly, with a sigh, and the chair creaks heavily under him.

There, under the mirror, the child still sits alone. But he is now looking our way. From there he can see the inside of the tavern—the green island of the billiard table, the ivory ball he is forbidden to touch, the metallic gloss of the bar, a pair of fat truckers at one table and the two of us at another. He has long since grown used to this scene and is not dismayed by its proximity. Yet there is one thing I know. Whatever happens to him in life, he will always remember the picture he saw every day of his childhood from the little room where he was fed his soup. He will remember the billiard table and the coatless evening visitor who used to draw back his sharp white elbow and hit the ball with his cue, and the blue-gray cigar smoke, and the din of voices, and my empty right sleeve and scarred face, and his father behind the bar, filling a mug for me from the tap.

"I can't understand what you see down there," says my friend, turning back toward me.

What indeed! How can I demonstrate to him that I have glimpsed somebody's future recollection?

作品赏析

一、作家与情节

弗拉基米尔·弗拉基米洛维奇·纳博科夫（Vladimir Vladimirovich Nabokov，1899—1977）是举世闻名的、天才般的俄裔美国作家，号称"当代小说之王"。他出生于沙俄贵族家庭，俄国二月革命后随家人逃亡欧洲，1919年来到柏林，1919年至1923年在英国剑桥大学学习。在流亡柏林（1923—1937）和巴黎的十多年里，他以弗拉基米尔·西林（Vladimir Sirin）为笔名进行文学创作，逐渐在俄罗斯流亡文学界声名鹊起。1940年移居美国，先在威尔斯利学院（Wellesley College）任教，同时兼任哈佛大学比较昆虫学博物馆研究员，后受聘为康奈尔大学英文系教授（1948—1958）。在美国他开始用英语创作，1955年发表的小说《洛丽塔》（Lolita）获得了巨大成功，此后放弃大学教职专事写作和蝶类研究。1961年移居瑞士，1977年去世。纳博科夫不仅是一位多才多艺的天才作家，还是一位蝶类研究专家。在文学创作领域，他15岁便出版个人诗集，能熟练运用英语、俄语和法语写作，并且都取得了令世人瞩目的成就。他创作了18部长篇、约70篇短篇，还出版有自传、诗歌、散文、戏剧等大量作品。他还是一位翻译家和文学评论家，翻译了自己的大部分作品，由其翻译并详尽注释的《叶甫盖尼·奥涅金》（Eugene Onegin，1964）迄今仍是权威英文译本，而《文学讲稿》（Lectures on Literature，1950）等专著则毋庸置疑地让他跻身大批评家和大学者的行列。作为科学家，他著有20余篇有关蝴蝶研究的学术论文。此外，他还精通绘画、国际象棋、网球等。因此，美国学者夏皮洛对他评价极高，认为他是20世纪最伟大的作家之一和人类文明已知的最后一位最多才多艺的人。[1]

在小说创作方面，纳博科夫取得的成就是巨大的，影响极为深远，数不清

1　Gavriel Shapiro, *The Sublime Artist's Studio: Nabokov and Painting*. Evanston, Illinois: Northwestern University Press, 2009, p. 27.

的现当代作家都毫不讳言对纳博科夫的崇拜,并称受到的他的影响,其中包括厄普代克(John Updike)、品钦(Thomas Pynchon)、巴斯(John Barth)、阿尔比(Edward Albee)、德里罗(Don DeLillo)、拉什迪(Salman Rushide)、马丁·埃米斯(Martin Amis)、扎迪·史密斯(Zadie Smith)、约翰·班维尔(John Banville)、埃德蒙·怀特(Edmund White)、安东尼·伯吉斯(Anthony Burgess)等。在1998年美国现代图书馆编委会遴选的20世纪100部最伟大的英语小说榜单中,《洛丽塔》(1955)列第4位,《微暗的火》(*Pale Fire*,1962)列第53位,自传《说吧,记忆》(*Speak, Memory*,1951)位列最好的100部非小说作品的第8位。[1] 除上述作品外,他用俄语创作的《防守》(«Защита Лужина»,1930)、《天赋》(«Дар»,1937)、《斩首之邀》(«Приглашение на казнь»,1938),用英语创作的《普宁》(*Pnin*,1957)、《阿达》(*Ada or Ardor: A Family Chronicle*,1969)以及访谈录《固执己见》(*Strong Opinions*,1973)等都深受读者喜爱和评论界的好评。在小说技巧方面,纳博科夫是世人公认的"文体大师"。他以其令人眼花缭乱的文字技巧打动了无数的读者和批评家,他对英语表达潜力的挖掘达到了一个无人能企及的高度,以至于后现代小说家们将其尊奉为他们的鼻祖。约翰·巴斯和约翰·斯塔克(John O. Stark)分别在同样名为"枯竭的文学"("The Literature of Exhaustion")的文章和专著中,指出类似《微暗的火》的小说已经穷尽了英语表达的可能,标志着文学已经走向了枯竭。不过,尽管世人往往视纳博科夫为后现代主义作家,他本人却拒绝被归入某个文学流派。他小说中散文诗般优美的文字、精心设计的结构、无处不在的文字游戏、情节简单但又引人入胜的故事、高超娴熟的音韵技巧、令人哑然失笑的诙谐、大量的互文指涉和用典、突破体裁边界的文类杂糅等,构成了一个个语言的迷宫。而在主题方面,更是包罗万象,记忆、时间、艺术、想象、流亡、蝴蝶、绘画、象棋、网球、电影、汽车文化、爱情、谋杀、畸恋、乱伦、镜像、死亡、幽灵、彼岸世界、流行时尚等,在他的很多小说中都有表现。单单是《洛丽塔》这部小说,借用于晓丹发表在《外国文学》1995年第1期上的文章标题,就可以说"你说什么就是什么"。由此可见,纳博科夫

---

1 "100 Best Nonfiction," 25 June 2020, 〈http://www.randomhouse.com/modernlibrary/100bestnonfiction.html〉。100部最伟大英语小说榜单见同一网站。

的小说，不管是在技巧层面还是主题层面，都是极为深邃复杂的，对普通读者而言着实是不小的挑战。

《柏林导游》是纳博科夫公开发表的第14篇短篇小说。1917年俄国二月革命后，作为沙俄贵族的纳博科夫一家流亡欧洲。1922年他在剑桥大学获得学士学位，读书期间曾担任流亡报纸《船舵》（*The Rudder*）的主编，同年其父被误刺身亡，此后他前往柏林，以翻译、写作，教人英语、俄语和网球为生。他在柏林待了15年，其间开始尝试新的文学创作方法。小说正是以作家在柏林时期的生活为背景。在柏林期间，1924年1月，纳博科夫发表了自己的第一部短篇小说《振翅一击》（"Wingstroke"），此后陆续发表了22篇短篇。到1930年时，加上他已发表的长篇小说《玛丽》（*Mary*，1926）、《王，后，杰克》（*King, Queen, Knave*，1928）、《防守》（«Защита Лужина»，1930），纳博科夫已在俄罗斯流亡文学圈崭露头角，奠定了自己的文学地位。他将早年发表的15篇短篇和24首诗歌集结为《乔伯归来：故事和诗歌》（*The Return of Chorb: Stories and Poems*，1930）一书，署名"V. 西林"（V. Sirin，纳博科夫以此名享誉流亡文学圈）。在这部短篇小说集中，有评论家认为《乔伯归来》是最好的一篇，约翰逊（D. Barton Johnson）则认为其中的《柏林导游》最优秀。纳博科夫本人也在写给朋友的信中认为该集子里最好的一篇是《柏林导游》，他的这一偏爱一直没有改变。在1976年该小说的英译版序言里，他指出，"虽然看上去简单，《柏林导游》却是我最微妙的篇目之一，翻译该小说让我和我的儿子颇费周章"[1]。

故事由第一人称的匿名叙述者讲述，从全文来看，他的身份是一位俄裔流亡作家。故事开篇，叙述者与一位朋友来到柏林的一家酒吧，他向朋友讲述了当天上午他去柏林动物园，以及途中观察"下水管、电车和其他重要事件"（utility pipes, streetcars, and other important matters）的见闻。小说由叙述者观察到的五幕小场景组成。

第一幕场景是"下水管"。在前往柏林动物园的路上，叙述者看到了家门口的人行道上倒放着一排尚未安放到沟渠里的下水管，他描述了工人们怎样将下水管运来、孩子们怎样在水管旁玩耍，以及头天夜里一场雪后水管的模样。这一幕

---

[1] D. Barton Johnson, "A Guide to Nabokov's 'A Guide to Berlin'", *The Slavic and East European Journal*, Vol. 23, No. 3 (Autumn, 1979), pp. 353-354.

结尾处,他注意到有人在雪后的水管上写下了自己的名字Otto,感慨这一名字如此完美地映射了水管本身的形状。

第二幕场景是"电车"。叙述者登上了前往柏林动物园的电车,电车的样子让他联想到圣彼得堡街头如今早已消失了的马拉车。叙述者描写了车上的售票员像钢琴家那样,用一双粗糙却灵活的手为乘客找零钱、撕车票。电车抵达线路尽头后,叙述者描写了前后车厢如何脱锁、换位、对调,他认为在20年后电车将从街头消失,进入博物馆。在他快到柏林动物园时,他想象一位21世纪的作家在未来的博物馆里可以通过观察作为藏品的电车来再现20世纪20年代的柏林生活,而这辆"黄色斑驳的"(yellow, uncouth)电车那时将成为见证历史的文物。

第三幕是"工作"。叙述者"我"透过电车的车窗,观察柏林街头人们日常的生产与生活场景。在一个十字路口,四位工人在修补被车辆压毁的路面,他们的工作像是配合默契的合奏。一位浑身沾满面粉的面包师骑着三轮车快速驶过,紧接着驶过的是一辆从酒馆回收了旧瓶子的垃圾车,有养护工用推车拉着根部包裹着泥土和麻袋的落叶松经过,一位邮差将街头邮筒里的信件倒进邮包里。叙述者尤为欣赏的是工人们正从卡车上将肉卸下扛进肉店里。

第四幕是"伊甸园"。叙述者来到柏林动物园,他将其描述为人间的伊甸园,认为它是地球上最接近天堂的人类乌托邦。动物园对面的"伊甸园酒店"恰好诠释了叙述者对它的描述。时值冬季,无法观赏热带动物,"我"来到了爬行动物、昆虫和鱼类馆。"我"将灯光下的水族馆与《海底两万里》中的潜艇舷窗联系起来,把红色海星喻为红色苏联。"我"最后像旅行手册中建议的那样,不忘去喂食巨龟,虽然它进食的场面并不让人愉悦,它的壳却让"我"联想到"时间那辉煌的重负"(that splendid burden of time)。

第五幕回到了开篇的"酒吧"。在这两部分里作者使用了现在时,与其他部分不同。叙述者的朋友对他的讲述并不满意,他抱怨道"谁在乎你如何搭乘电车去了柏林水族馆"("Who cares about how you took a streetcar and went to the Berlin Aquarium?"),还称他"真是十分糟糕的导游"(a very poor guide)。叙述者没有回答,而是将视线转向了酒吧的后厅。酒吧前厅是一间大屋子,正对入口的是吧台和酒架,中间摆放着台球桌和一些吧桌,与前厅的过道相连的是一间杂乱的小屋，从墙上的镜子里可以看到一张椭圆形的桌子偏斜立在一只绿色沙发前。这间小屋是酒吧主人的住所，他的妻子正在给儿子喂汤。这时叙述者的同伴再次抱怨他的讲述枯燥乏味，而"我"依然没有回答，而是看向后屋的小男孩，他此时正在望向"我们"。叙述者描述了小男孩眼中看到的景象，这颇有些"你在桥上看风景，看风景的人在楼上看你"的味道。叙述者认为不管小男孩将来会过什么样的生活，他将永远记得此时此刻的所见。同伴再次抱怨"我"不可理喻，"我"则在心里默默回应，"我怎么向他展示我已窥见了某人未来的记忆"（How can I demonstrate to him that I have glimpsed somebody's future recollection?）？

二、人物与主题

小说有两位主要人物。第一人称的匿名叙述者"我"是故事的主人公，他对搭乘电车去柏林动物园的半日游描述是读者了解故事来龙去脉的唯一来源。通过"我"的讲述，读者了解到20世纪20年代魏玛共和国时期（1918—1933）德国柏林市井生活的点点滴滴，这些记录忠实地再现了柏林的城市布局与人民生活，无疑具有写实和历史见证的作用。就此而言，纳博科夫的高明之处在于，小说标题起名为《柏林导游》，从形式和内容上来说的确符合一篇货真价实的旅行指南的标准，还真称得上是对柏林的导游。

故事发生在1925年12月圣诞前夕柏林的一天早晨。那时第一次世界大战后的柏林正经历重大的变迁，经济凋敝，社会动荡，重建工作正如火如荼展开。小说为读者呈现的是信手拈来的碎片化、近景聚焦式的五幕小场景，再现了当时柏林的真实面貌。彼时纳博科夫和与他一样流亡德国的俄裔作家群体主要居住在位于柏林市中心的柏林动物园以南的舍讷贝格区（Schöneberg）。小说描写了重建中的柏林。它是一个繁忙的现代工业城市，既有老旧的电车，也有忙碌的建筑工地和劳动者，叙述者在电车上还两度回忆起比现代气息浓郁的柏林更为古老的圣彼得堡。

由于小说采用受限的第一人称视角，读者无法了解叙述者"我"的具体生平，但从故事细节中可以看出，他与作家纳博科夫一样，应该是曾在圣彼得堡生活过的流亡柏林的俄国作家，这是因为故事里不仅两次提到了圣彼得堡，还明确表达了叙述者对苏联的厌恶，将其比作"空想的乌托邦与其他空虚之物"（topical Utopias and other inanities），表明他是在俄国革命后流亡到柏林的。读者甚至可以断定，叙述者应该像纳博科夫一样，是生活在柏林动物园以南的舍讷贝格区的流亡作家，因为他的导游就是围绕目的地柏林动物园展开的。不过，与现实中的纳博科夫不同的是，叙述者很可能在战争或事故中受过伤，这在小说里有多处交代。例如，故事中交代他拄着一根"橡胶头的拐杖"（rubberheeled stick）；他搭上电车时，临窗的女性同情地让座给他，还刻意避免与他直视以免他察觉；第五幕里酒吧小男孩从后厅看到了他"空荡荡的右边衣袖和刀疤脸"（empty right sleeve and scarred face）。在这部小说中，叙述者以平静的口吻讲述自己在柏林街头半天的见闻，可以看出他长于观察，善于思考，专注于细节，对柏林街头的一事一物一人一景都充满了艺术家的同情与热爱，他的观察与思考中纠缠着对时间流逝的痴迷与不舍，使故事弥漫着一股怀旧的情愫。

小说中的另一位主要人物是叙述者的同伴兼酒友，他的姓名、外貌、生平等信息读者也无从知晓。他是叙述者的听众、朋友和酒伴，后者在酒吧里向他讲述了去柏林动物园半日游的经历。不过，作为受述者的他，却是小说中唯一开口说话的人，故事里的直接引语都来自这位匿名的酒友。在小说第五幕里他多次抱怨"那真是糟糕透顶的导游"，"这毫无意义，讲电车和乌龟有什么用？说白了这一切纯粹就是无聊。一座无聊的外国城市，而且生活昂贵……"（"What do trams and tortoises matter? And anyway the whole thing is limply a bore. A boring, foreign city, and expensive to live in, too..."），"我无法理解你在后厅那里看到了什么"（"I can't understand what you see down there"）。叙述者兴致盎然地讲述着，得到的却是同伴完全无法理解的回应，可以看出讲述者对柏林的风物充满同情与好感，而受述者却持相反的看法。如果说讲述者体现了艺术家对生活敏锐的洞察与深刻体悟，这位听众则像是对生活反应迟钝、缺乏想象的尘世俗人。

对纳博科夫有所了解的读者都知道，纳博科夫的小说往往看似情节简单，实则有着丰富的主题。这篇故事也是如此，编者在此不可能穷尽其全部主题，而是主要讨论艺术、时间、记忆这几个比较明显的主题。

16. A GUIDE TO BERLIN

乍看上去，《柏林导游》是一幅实实在在的城市导游图，再现的是20世纪20年代魏玛共和国时期柏林的真实街景，其中的下水管、酒吧、电车、动物园等景物，乘客、工人、面包师、屠夫等人物，都是基于作家对柏林的真实观察，但如果将小说简单地理解为真实的旅游指南，显然太肤浅了。事实上，这篇小说更像是纳博科夫写给读者的创作指南，其核心主题是艺术本身，或者更具体地说，是一位作家如何通过自己美妙的文字对生活的细节进行艺术加工，从而为后世留下永恒的记忆。众所周知，纳博科夫对细节有着近乎变态的痴迷，在他看来艺术家的职责在于一丝不苟地精确记录日常生活的细节，这倒颇有俄罗斯形式主义的韵味，即以细节的精确让经过艺术陌生化还原的生活经验在时间长河里留驻为永恒，从而对抗时间的流逝与对死亡的恐惧。这篇小说正是撷取了柏林日常生活中的五幕小景，通过细致入微的观察将其中的细节记录下来，将其升华为艺术。在叙述者眼里，每一件平凡的事物仿佛都有艺术的魔力，堆放在人行道上的下水管道，与有人写在上面的名字"OTTO"相映成趣，电车售票员粗糙黝黑的双手像钢琴师的双手一般灵巧，建筑工人劳动时发出的嘈杂的声音被比作钢铁质地般的合奏，从电车旁一闪而过的浑身落满面粉的面包师仿佛天使一般，水族馆的窗玻璃让"我"想到了凡尔纳《海底两万里》中潜艇的舷窗，正在吃草的丑陋的巨龟则是"时间那辉煌的重负"，卡车停在肉店外卸肉的场景在叙述者眼里成了街上最美的风景，动物园则被他比作伊甸园。柏林街头平凡的景物，被叙述者以优美的文字进行了加工，赋予其艺术的美感，同时也表明了他对柏林的同情与好感。所有这些来源于他对生活的细致观察与深切体悟，他与对他的讲述颇为不满的麻木无感的同伴形成了强烈的反差。作家意在表明，好的艺术应关注细节、深入生活，他的这篇导游仿佛在手把手地教读者如何去抓细节，去细致入微地观察和体悟生活，而这正是艺术创作的精髓。正如纳博科夫传记学者菲尔德评论的那样，《柏林导游》与其说是一篇旅行指南，不如说是一篇"艺术家的指南"。[1]

艺术家通过主观意识的加工让普通的场景成为时间长河里的永恒一刻是纳博科夫作品中另一个常见的主题，这一观念与西方艺术史中的"意孕时刻"（pregnant moment）或人们在观看一幅照片时感受到的"时间的静止"有些类

---

[1] Andrew Field, *Nabokov: His Life in Art*, Boston: Little, Brown, 1967, p.152.

似，也与东西方文学中常见的以艺术对抗时间与死亡的观念类似。纳博科夫深受伯格森（Henri Bergson）时间观的影响，在他看来，过去是永恒的，现在转瞬即逝又变为过去，而将来则不可企及。因此，时间与记忆成为他几乎所有作品的重要主题。单从形式上看，这篇小说在第一段里以过去时开始讲述，其余的部分则是现在时，在小说结尾部分又影射到将来时：当叙述者的同伴对他的讲述表达不满的时候，叙述者声称："我该如何向他展示我已窥见了某人未来的记忆？"我们都知道，通常来说故事都是已发生的，因此是过去时，读完一篇故事与人们在观看一幅照片的效果是类似的，即读者与观众与它保持距离，在现实中回溯过去，让过去复现在眼前，因此带有追忆往昔、感叹世事不再的怀旧与共情。纳博科夫在《说吧，记忆》中有一句名言："宇宙何其之小（袋鼠的袋子就可以装下它），它与人类意识、某个个体的回忆以及文字的记录相比是多么的微不足道、不值一提。"[1] 因此，故事第一段里使用的过去时，似乎印证了作家一贯的做法，即这篇小说是艺术家记录下来的生活片段的永恒记忆。然而，导游文字是给不分时间的所有旅游者参考使用的，因此小说接下来的段落都使用现在时。而且使用现在时还具有现场展演的效果，即所发生的一切正在进行，这与照片的比喻仍然相似：照片虽拍摄于过去，但照片里的事仿佛正在发生。纳博科夫在小说里对时间的这种微妙的艺术处理收到了如下效果：柏林街头的景物已镌刻在记忆里成为永恒，而它将如鲜活的现在，在时刻发生着。最后一句话，叙述者其实是透过墙上的镜子，看到了小男孩眼中看到的景象，于是他设想"无论他（小男孩）的生活中发生了什么"，"他将永远记得母亲喂他喝汤时从小屋里见到的童年的日常景象"（Whatever happens to him in life, he will always remember the picture he saw every day of his childhood from the little room where he was fed his soup）。正如1925年12月的这个冬天的上午会成为某位21世纪作家笔下的艺术作品，叙述者确信，他也将在小男孩"友善的回忆里"长存。小说从过去开始，以现在接续，以未来结尾，又与未来的过去勾连，形成了过去—现在—未来交织的复杂局面。不仅如此，对时间和记忆的痴迷，也表现在叙述者的思考与回忆中。例如，在"电车"一幕里，叙述者回忆了18年前圣彼得堡街头的马拉车，在"伊甸园"一幕里，他将柏林

---

1 Vladimir Nabokov, *Speak, Memory*, New York: Pyramid Books, 1966, p. 17.

动物园比作失落的亚特兰蒂斯，而加拉帕戈斯海龟古老的壳，则像古建筑铜色的穹顶，海龟作为"辉煌时间的重负"本身就是时间的象征。总体来看，整篇小说可谓是纳博科夫的主动怀旧，对当时日常生活细节的记录，供未来的读者与艺术家追忆和加工。

三、结构与技巧

上文的分析可以充分诠释纳博科夫本人对《柏林导游》的评价："虽然看上去简单，《柏林导游》却是我最微妙的篇目之一。"小说看上去情节简单，讲"我"冬日上午去柏林动物园的所见所闻，然而它不仅内容与主题十分丰富，在结构与技巧等方面的探索也非常全面和深刻，因此被评论界认为是他最优秀的短篇小说之一。

从体裁的形式来看，作家突破了传统短篇小说的限制，戏仿了旅游手册的写法，模糊了真实（旅游指南）与虚构（小说）的界限。考虑到这是纳博科夫早期的作品，这一尝试无疑是十分大胆的，是其后期诸多作品中跨越体裁界限的形式创新的预演，如《洛丽塔》中的日记、广告与班级花名册，《阿达》中的长篇学术论文，《天赋》中的作家传记，《微暗的火》对学术专著的戏仿（小说由序言、长诗、注释和索引构成）等。如果说仅有体裁边界的突破，并不能证明纳博科夫的高明与伟大。纳博科夫最了不起的地方，就在于通过精心的设计，将文本的形式与内容完美地结合在一起。在这篇小说中，正如前文分析的那样，旅游指南的形式不仅实实在在像一部旅游指南，更不动声色地在叙述者与同伴的故事讲述中，融合了艺术、时间、记忆等深刻的主题（当然如果进一步挖掘，还可以发现纳博科夫其他作品中常见的自我与他者、艺术与现实、镜像复制等主题）。

如果把小说当作一本旅行指南来看，它在结构上的安排也是十分合理而巧妙的。全文以首尾两部分叙述者向同伴讲述柏林半日游为总体框架，一开始就完美符合旅游指南和小说两种体裁的要求：既像是导游在引导自己的听众去了解一个不熟悉的城市，又像是他在向同伴讲述自己的故事。叙述者的讲述中嵌入了五个日常生活场景，以动物园为目的地，以电车为轴心，巧妙地将看似各自独立、互不相关的部分连接为一个整体，各部分过渡自然而不留痕迹。从第一幕到第四幕场景，作家均以简单的陈述句开始，渐渐引出一系列长句，这与每部分讨论的对象类似，都是由简入繁，从四根倒放在人行道上的下水管开始，延伸到电车中看到的景象，再到街头众人的劳动场景和动物园里的各种动物。每个部分虽然相对独立，但在逻辑上又是密切相关的。叙述者先是出门看到了下水管，然后在电车灯光的照射下注意到下水管上有人写下了自己的名字"OTTO"，于是自然过渡到第二幕的电车。叙述者在行驶的电车上看到了窗外劳动的场景，于是有了第三幕"工作"。酒馆招牌上眨眼的狮子、叙述者回忆的马拉车、卡车上运的肉，似乎又为第四部分的目的地动物园埋下了伏笔。电车部分作为轴心，自然衔接了前后部分的内容，动物园则是当天上午叙述者旅行的终点。第五幕回到了开始的酒吧，整个故事由此实现了完美的闭环。

如果把小说看作一本艺术创作指南，它的结构安排则更为巧妙。叙述者向同伴讲述的其实是他对艺术创作的认识，他以充满哲思和艺术美感的文字向同伴描述观察到的柏林市井生活的诸多细节。如果同伴是对艺术敏感的人，他或许能从中有所体会和收获，然而遗憾的是，他似乎缺乏把日常生活艺术化的能力，多次对叙述者表达了不满。这恰好说明，艺术创作的奥秘似乎并不难懂，然而真正实践它的人常常曲高和寡，难以为常人所理解。这正是为什么叙述者在"电车"一幕的最后一段用大段的篇幅主动说明自己的动机："我想这就是文学创作的意义：描写普通的事物，就像它们会在将来友善的镜子中折射出来的那样；从我们身边的事物中去发现只有久远的后世才能赏识的芳香的柔情，到那时我们平庸日常的每一个细微之处都将展现出自身的精致与喜悦：到那时，今天穿着最普通夹克的男子将盛装出席典雅的假面舞会。"（I think that here lies the sense of literary creation: to portray ordinary objects as they will be reflected in the kindly mirrors of future times; to find in the objects around us the fragrant tenderness that only posterity will discern and appreciate in the far-off times when every trifle of our plain everyday life will become exquisite and festive in its own right: the times when a man who might put on the most ordinary jacket of today will be dressed up for an elegant masquerade.）这段话清晰地表明，叙述者意图通过如实记录当下日常生活的微小细节，让普通的事物留驻在文字的芳香与典雅中，成为未来人们追忆中的艺术品，从而享有不朽的生命。由此可见，艺术、时

16. A GUIDE TO BERLIN

间、记忆便是文学创作的核心主题,而对生活细节的专注则是文学创作的现实基础。作者在小说中对时态的精心安排无疑服务于这一脉络:开篇的过去时,中间的现在时,结尾处"我"从现在窥见将来某人的回忆,这一时间的螺旋再次回到了开篇处的过去,仿佛小说变成了"我"预见中的将来某人的记忆。于是,小说实现了叙述者所追求的"文学创作的意义":记录当下,成为将来美好的追忆。显然,《柏林导游》这篇艺术创作指南的点睛之笔,正是"电车"一幕最后一段叙述者的深邃思考。

在对细节的处理上,纳博科夫无疑也是深思熟虑的,这符合他一直以来的创作习惯:他总是精心布局每一个段落、每一句话、每一个单词,直到它们构成一个完美的整体。小说五个部分的场景描写,颇有些像电影的特写镜头。纳博科夫夫妇对电影的钟爱是世人皆知的,他们经常去看电影。20世纪20年代德国电影出现了可与美国媲美的空前繁荣的局面,各种先锋派技法纷纷运用于电影制作,电影的流派异彩纷呈。《柏林导游》正好创作于德国电影鼎盛时期,纳博科夫深受德国电影的影响,受到其影响是可以预料的事。据称,德国表现主义电影中的哥特式主题、浮士德式人物、先锋派技法、人的堕落与毁灭、现代都市中个体的疏离、人物视角与镜头的运用等对其俄语小说的创作影响尤为深刻。他熟悉朗(Fritz Lang)、维恩(Robert Wiene)、斯坦伯格(Josef von Sternberg)、茂瑙(Friedrich Wilhelm)、爱森斯坦(Sergei Eisenstein)等著名导演的作品,喜欢茂瑙的《最卑贱的人》(*Der letzte Mann*,1924)、维恩的《奥拉克之手》(*Orlacs Hände*,1924)、斯坦伯格的《上海快车》(*Shanghai Express*,1932)等影片。[1]

五幕场景均没有全景式的宏大场面,而是通过叙述者的视角与意识过滤,攫取了随时间和空间运动的几个画面,将其拼接在一起构成了一个整体。鉴于爱森斯坦1923年就提出了蒙太奇的手法,纳博科夫的这部短篇是否受到其影响倒是一个有趣的话题,不过从效果来看,《柏林导游》的五幕场景的选择与电影蒙太奇的技法倒是十分契合的。从色彩的运用来看,纳博科夫所有的小说中都大量使用了各种各样的颜色词,这部小说也不例外。小说在描述下水管和

---

1 Alfred Appel, Jr. *Nabokov's Dark Cinema*, New York: Oxford University Press, 1974, p. 58.

酒吧小男孩眼中的景象时，以黑白色调为主："一条平坦的新雪沿着每根黑色的管道上方延伸"（an even stripe of fresh snow stretches along the upper side of each black pipe）；从酒吧过道往后厅望去，叙述者眼里出现了"逼仄的屋子，镜子下方绿色的沙发，镜子里一张倾斜的椭圆桌子，硬生生倒在沙发前"（...a cramped little room with a green couch under a mirror, out of which an oval table with a checked oilcloth topples and takes up its solid position in front of the couch），仿佛是一幅幅静物写生。小说里大量的色彩词汇，又似乎构成了一幅印象派的绘画：天蓝色的酒馆招牌、白色的LOWENBRAU店名，雪地中折射的暖橙色的电车汽灯、猩红色的海星、黄铜色的海龟……很多类似的例子在文中，构成了一幅色彩斑斓的画卷。整篇小说符合纳博科夫这位文体大师的一贯风格，用词考究，语言犀利凝练，音韵优美，颇有散文诗的味道；其散漫而不拘一格的行文又颇有屠格涅夫《猎人日记》（«Записки охотника»）的风格。

Suggested Readings

1. Alexandrov, Vladimir E., ed. *The Garland Companion to Vladimir Nabokov.* New York & London: Garland Publishing, Inc., 1995.

2. Bader, Julia. *Crystal Land: Artifice in Nabokov's English Novels.* Berkeley, Los Angeles, London: University of California Press, 1972.

3. Boyd, Brian. *Vladimir Nabokov: The American Years.* Princeton: Princeton University Press, 1991.

4. Boyd, Brian. *Vladimir Nabokov: The Russian Years.* Princeton: Princeton University Press, 1990.

5. Connolly, Julian W., ed. *Nabokov and His Fiction: New Perspectives.* Cambridge: Cambridge University Press, 1999.

6. Connolly, Julian W., ed. *The Cambridge Companion to Nabokov.* Cambridge: Cambridge University Press, 2005.

7. Field, Andrew. *VN: The Life and Art of Vladimir Nabokov.* New York: Crown Publishers, Inc., 1977.

8. Navokov, Vladimir. *Lectures on Literature.* Fredson Bowers, ed. Introduced by

John Updike. New York: Harcourt Brace Janovich, 1980.
8. Nabokov, Vladimir. *Pale Fire*. New York: Vintage, 1989.
9. Nabokov, Vladimir. *Speak, Memory*. New York: Pyramid Books, 1966.
10. Nabokov, Vladimir. *Strong Opinions*. New York, St. Louis, San Francisco, Toronto: McGraw-Hill Book Company, 1973.
11. Nabokov, Vladimir. *The Annotated Lolita*. Alfred Appel, Jr., ed. New York: Vintage, 1991.
12. Nabokov, Vladimir. *The Stories of Vladimir Nabokov*. Dmitri Nabokov, ed. New York: Vintage, 1997.
13. Parker, Stephen Jan. *Understanding Vladimir Nabokov*. Columbia, SC: University of South Carolina Press, 1987.
14. Stegner, Page. *Escape Into Aesthetics: The Art of Vladimir Nabokov*. New York: Dial Press, 1966.
15. Tammi, Pekka. *Problems of Nabokov's Poetics: A Narratological Analysis*. Helsinki: Suomalainen Tiedeakatemia, 1985.

Questions for Reflection

1. Under what social context did the story take place? Why is it important in the story?

2. Who is the narrator? How much do we know about him? Why is he in sharp contrast with his companion?

3. In the last paragraph of the "Streetcar" section, the narrator mentions the value of literary creation. How do you understand it?

4. Why do we say "time" and "memory" are two of the many themes in the story?

5. Can the story be taken as a tourist guide? Why does the author take the form of a tourist guide in the story?

Questions for Discussion

Although Nabokov has repeatedly denied any alliance of himself with certain literary school or genre, this does not stop critics from regarding him as a precursor in postmodern fiction, why? As a short story written in the early years of his career, in what aspects has it demonstrated the characteristics of Nabokov in his later literary creation?

（王安　撰写）

参考文献

艾尔雅维茨，2003. 图像时代[M]. 胡菊兰，张云鹏，译. 长春：吉林人民出版社.

奥齐克，1994. 大披巾[J]. 陶洁，译. 外国文学（4）：55-57.

欧芝克，2004. 披肩[J]. 王祖友，译. 外国文学（5）：12-14.

波特，1984. 波特中短篇小说集[M]. 鹿金，等译. 上海：上海译文出版社.

陈娴，2012.《同类相食的星球》：奥兹克作为犹太小说家的创作选择[J]. 外语研究（2）：93-96，102.

程锡麟，王晓路，2001. 当代美国小说理论[M]. 北京：外语教学与研究出版社.

程锡麟，2005. 献给爱米莉的玫瑰在哪里——《献给爱米莉的玫瑰》叙事策略分析[J]. 外国文学评论（3）：67-73.

程锡麟，王安，黄邦福，等，2014. 菲茨杰拉德学术史研究[M]. 南京：译林出版社.

厄普代克，2019. 厄普代克短篇小说集[M]. 李康勤，王赟，杨向荣，等译. 上海：上海译文出版社，2019.

厄普代克，2008. 天堂制造[J]. 查日新，译. 译林（2）：119-126.

菲茨杰拉德，1990. 冰宫[J]. 苏珊，译. 当代外国文学（3）：96-111.

冯亦代，郑之岱，1987. 当代美国获奖短篇小说选[M]. 北京：中国文联出版公司.

顾悦，2017. 鲍勃·迪伦、离家出走与60年代的"决裂"问题：欧茨《何去何来》中的家庭系统[J]. 外国文学（5）：60-68.

金莉，2012. 20世纪末期（1980—2000）的美国小说：回顾与展望[J]. 外国文学研究（4）：87-97.

李慧明，2006. 爱伦·坡人性主题创作的问题意识探讨[J].《学术论坛》（5）：

152-155.

李宜燮，常耀信，2011. 美国文学选读（上册）[M]. 天津：南开大学出版社.

李宜燮，常耀信，1991. 美国文学选读（下册）[M]. 2版. 天津：南开大学出版社.

刘海平，王守仁，2002. 新编美国文学史（第四卷）[M]. 上海：上海外语教育出版社.

孙鲁瑶，2015. 电网下的哭泣——辛西娅·欧芝克的短篇小说《大披巾》[J]. 世界文化（8）：39-40.

孙鲁瑶，2015. 击碎偶像，终得涅槃——从《陌生的身体》看辛西娅·欧芝克的反偶像崇拜思想[J]. 名作欣赏（17）：89-92.

吐温，2005. 哈克贝利·费恩历险记[M]. 张友松，等译. 北京：中国戏剧出版社.

吐温，2005. 马克·吐温短篇小说选[M]. 董衡巽，等译. 北京：中国戏剧出版社.

王中强，2013. 翻译文本的选取：论美国短篇小说的翻译[J]. 名作欣赏（8）：114-115.

王祖友，2004. 后现代小说文本中的历史反思——评辛西娅·欧芝克的两篇短篇小说[J]. 外国文学（5）：15-19.

王佐良，2020. 我们能认识美国文学吗？——关于美国短篇小说选[OL]. 〈http://www.china.com.cn/chinese/RS/12166.htm〉，2020-08-15.

王佐良，1986. 美国短篇小说选[M]. 北京：中国青年出版社.

肖飚，2013. 欧芝克小说的创伤书写[J]. 求索（12）：165-166，24.

肖旭，2013. 国外乔伊斯·卡罗尔·欧茨研究评析[M]. 李维屏. 英美文学研究论丛. 22辑. 上海：上海外语教育出版社：313-321.

肖旭，2017. 乔伊斯·卡罗尔·欧茨在中国的译介与接收研究[J]. 外国文学动态研究（3）：28-38.

亚里士多德，1996. 诗学[M]. 陈中梅，译注. 北京：商务印书馆.

袁平，李爱庆，2011.《泄密之心》到底泄了什么密[J]. 学周刊（5）：191.

张晶晶，2016. 辛西娅·奥兹克国内研究综述[J]. 西藏民族大学学报（哲学社会科学版）（2）：136-141.

朱振武，2007. 爱伦·坡的效果美学论略[J]. 外国文学评论（3）：128-137.

参考文献

ANDREWS, FOSTER, HARRIS, 2001. The concise Oxford companion to African American literature [M]. New York: Oxford University Press.

APPEL, 1974. Nabokov's dark cinema [M]. New York: Oxford University Press.

BERMAN, 2005. Modernity and progress: Fitzgerald, Hemingway, Orwell [M]. Tuscaloosa: The University of Alabama Press.

BLOOM, 1994. The western canon: the books and school of the ages [M]. New York, San Diego, London: Harcourt Brace & Company.

BOWEN, VANDERBBEETS, 1970. American short fiction: readings & criticism [M]. New York: The Bobbs-Merill Company, Inc.

BROWN, 2019. Both boy and man; neither boy nor man: liminality in Richard Wright's "the man who was almost a man" [J]. Midwest quarterly, 60 (4): 435-450.

BRUCCOLI, et al., 1996. F. Scott Fitzgerald on authorship [M]. Columbia, SC: University of South Carolina Press.

BRUCCOLI, 1981. Some sort of epic grandeur: the life of F. Scott Fitzgerald [M]. New York: Harcourt Brace Jovanovich.

BRYER, 1978. F. Scott Fitzgerald: the critical reception [M]. New York: Burt Franklin.

BRYER, 1996. New essays on F. Scott Fitzgerald's neglected stories [M]. Columbia, London: University of Missouri Press.

CARVER, 2009. Raymond Carver: collected stories [M]. New York: Literary Classics of the United States, Inc.

CHEEVER, 2009. John Cheever: collected stories and other writings [M]. New York: Library of America.

CHEEVER, 2000. The stories of John Cheever [M]. New York: Vintage International.

CHILTON, 2015. John Cheever: "the Chekhov of the suburbs" [OL]. The daily telegraph, UK. October 15, 2015. 〈https://www.telegraph.co.uk/books/authors/john-cheever-master-of-the-short-story/〉.

CLARIDGE, 1991. F. Scott Fitzgerald: critical assessments [M]. 4 Vols. Near Robertsbridge, UK: Helm Information.

COCHRANE, 1969. The penguin book of American short stories [M]. Beijing: Foreign

Languages Press.

CRANE, 2005. 50 great short stories [M]. New York: Bantam Classic.

FAULKNER, 1930. Selected short stories of William Faulkner [M]. New York: The Modern Library.

FIELD, 1967. Nabokov: his life in art [M]. Boston: Little, Brown and Company.

FITZGERALD, 1920. Flappers and philosophers [M]. New York, London, Toronto, Sydney: Pocket Books.

FRYE, 2000. The Archetypes of Literature [M] // Criticism: major statements. Charles Kaplan, William Davis Anderson, eds. Boston, New York: Bedford/St. Martins: 475-486.

HEMINGWAY, 1955. Men without women [M]. London: Penguin Books.

HEMINGWAY, 1932. Death in the afternoon [M]. New York: Charles Scribner's Sons.

HEMMINGSON, 2008. The dirty realism duo: Charles Bukowski & Raymond Carver [M]. San Bernardino, California: The Borgo Press.

JOHNSON, 1979. A guide to Nabokov's "A Guide to Berlin" [J]. The Slavic and East European journal, 23 (3): 353-361.

KAZIN, 1962. F. Scott Fitzgerald: the man and his work [M]. New York: Collier Books.

KLINKOWITZ, WALLACE, 2007. The Norton anthology of American literature: literature since 1945 [M]. 7th ed. Vol. E. New York & London: W. W. Norton & Company.

KNOFLÍČKOVÁ, 2011. Racial identities revisited: Toni Morrison's "Recitatif" [J]. Litteraria pragensia, 21 (41): 22-33.

KUEHL, BRYER, 1971. Dear Scott / Dear Max: the Fitzgerald-Perkins correspondence [M]. New York: Charles Scribner's Sons.

LOEFFELHOLZ, 2007. The Norton anthology of American literature [M]. 7th ed. Vol. D. New York & London: W.W. Norton & Company, 2007.

LOFTIS, 1986. Domestic prey: Richard Wright's parody of the hunt tradition in "the man who was almost a man" [J]. Studies in short fiction, 23 (4): 437-442.

MORRIS, 2013. "Sisters separated for much too long": women's friendship and power in Toni Morrison's "Recitatif" [J]. Tulsa studies in women's literature, 32 (1): 159-180.

NABOKOV, 1966. Speak, memory [M]. New York: Pyramid Books.

NABOKOV, 1997. The stories of Vladimir Nabokov [M]. Dmitri Nabokov, ed. New York: Vintage Books.

NORRIS, 1986. New American short stories: the writers select their own favorites [M]. New York: New American Library.

PICKERING, 1974. Fiction 100: an anthology of short stories [M]. New York: MacMillan Publishing Co., Inc.

PIPER, 1970. Fitzgerald's "The Great Gatsby": the novel, the critics, the background [M]. New York: Charles Scribner's Sons.

POE, 2006. The portable Edgar Allan Poe [M]. Gerald Kennedy, ed. London: Penguin Books.

ROSS, 2004. Manning the race: reforming black men in the Jim Crow Era [M]. New York: New York University Press.

SAMUELS, 2007. Encyclopedia of African-American literature [M]. New York: Facts On File, Inc.

SECREAST, 2012/2013. Using scene structure to explore character complexity in Richard Wright's "The Man Who Was Almost a Man" [J]. The Virginia English journal, 62 (2): 42-62.

SHAPIRO, 2009. The sublime artist's studio: Nabokov and painting [M]. Evanston, Illinois: Northwestern University Press.

SKLENICKA, 2009. Raymond Carver: a writer's life [M]. New York: Charles Scribner's Sons.

TEKIN, 2013. The Turkish reader's reception of Toni Morrison's "Recitatif" [J]. Journal of American studies of Turkey (JAST), 37: 53-62.

TWAIN, 2005. The complete short stories of Mark Twain [M]. Charles Neider, ed. New York: Bantam Classics.

UPDIKE, KENISON, 1999. The best American short stories of the century [M]. Boston & New York: Houghton Mifflin Company.

WARNOCK, 1970. Existentialism [M]. Oxford: Oxford University Press.

WILSON, 1993. F. Scott Fitzgerald: the crack-up [M]. New York: New Directions Books.

WILSON, 1977. Letters on literature and politics: 1912-1972 [M]. Farrar, Straus, Giroux.